V

VICTORIAN WOMEN POETS

LONGMAN ANNOTATED TEXTS

GENERAL EDITORS
Charlotte Brewer, Hertford College, Oxford
H. R. Woudhuysen, University College London
Daniel Karlin, University of Sheffield

PUBLISHED TITLES
Chaucer's Dream Poetry Helen Phillips and Nick Havely
Women's Writing in Middle English Alexandra Barratt
Women Writers in Renaissance England Randall Martin
King Lear: A Parallel Text Edition René Weis
Alexander Pope: The Dunciad in Four Books Valerie Rumbold
William Blake: Selected Poetry and Prose David Fuller
Thomas Hardy: Selected Poems Tim Armstrong

VICTORIAN WOMEN POEMS

A New Annotated Anthology

Edited by

VIRGINIA BLAIN

PEARSON
Longman

Harlow, England • London • New York • Boston • San Francisco • Toronto
Sydney • Tokyo • Singapore • Hong Kong • Seoul • Taipei • New Delhi
Cape Town • Madrid • Mexico City • Amsterdam • Munich • Paris • Milan

Pearson Education Limited

Edinburgh Gate
Harlow CM20 2JE
United Kingdom
Tel: +44 (0)1279 623623
Fax: +44 (0)1279 431059
Website: www.pearsoned.co.uk

Published in the United States of America
By Pearson Education Inc:, New York

First edition published in Great Britain in 2001
Revised edition published 2009

© Pearson Education Limited 2001, 2009

ISBN: 978-1-4082-0498-6

British Library Cataloguing in Publication Data
A CIP catalogue record for this book can be obtained from the British Library

Library of Congress Cataloging in Publication Data
A CIP catalog record for this book can be obtained from the Library of Congress

10 9 8 7 6 5 4 3 2 1
13 12 11 10 09

Set by 35 in 9/12pt Stone Serif
Printed and bound in Malaysia (CTP-KHL)

The Publisher's policy is to use paper manufactured from sustainable forests.

CONTENTS

AUTHOR'S ACKNOWLEDGEMENTS

First and foremost I would like to thank Daniel Karlin, a General Editor of the series, for his unfailingly generous and knowledgeable help in the preparation of this volume. I would also like to thank the two research assistants who, at different times, have worked with me in the often laborious task of preparing the typescript for printing and searching out obscure footnote material. These are Lee O'Brien (in the early stages of the project) and, over a longer period, Kelly Stephens, whose dedication to the task often helped me when my spirits were flagging, and whose assistance in the final stages was particularly welcome. The Australian Research Council funded a Small Grant which enabled their employment on the project, and for this I am most grateful. I am also grateful to Macquarie University for allowing me a period of study leave during 1998 which greatly helped in bringing the project nearer completion.

A number of other people have helped in various indispensable ways, providing references and suggestions, including in particular Linda Hughes, Yopie Prins, Sharon Bickle and Paula Feldman. Lalla Reeves has, as always, been helpful and supportive, and has also assisted from time to time with parts of the typing work. I would also like to thank the staff of Macquarie University Library, Fisher Library at Sydney University, the British Library, and in particular the Bodleian Library, Oxford, for their always courteous and helpful responses to queries.

PUBLISHER'S ACKNOWLEDGEMENTS

We are grateful to Louisiana State University Press for permission to reproduce extracts from *The Complete Poems of Christina Rossetti: A Variorium Edition* edited by R. W. Crump.

INTRODUCTION

THE CURRENT STATUS OF VICTORIAN WOMEN POETS

Victorian poetry has been held until recently to have been largely a male preserve, with exceptions being made, on occasion, for Elizabeth Barrett Browning, Christina Rossetti and possibly Emily Brontë. This view has been consistently reflected in texts set for study in university courses, where Victorian poetry has been most often represented by the Big Four: Tennyson, Browning, Arnold and Hopkins, plus one or two of Hardy, Swinburne and the Pre-Raphaelites. Over the last five or ten years, however, increasing numbers of women poets have been rediscovered,[1] and it is now being recognised that Victorian readers and critics paid much more attention to the work of these women than was previously thought. Here is an immensely rich new field of study to be explored by today's reader, much of which has not been available in print since it was first published in the nineteenth century. The problem which faces the modern anthologist, therefore, is not one of exclusion so much as of inclusion. We now know that there are so many remarkable women poets of the Victorian era, each of whom is well worthy of study on her own, that the necessary process of selection becomes increasingly difficult.

The most significant anthologies from this new field to have been published so far are those edited respectively by Leighton and Reynolds (1995) and Armstrong and Bristow (1996). Each has aimed at as wide a range as possible. I believe this was the right – and, in a sense, inevitable – choice at the time for these pioneers in the field. Their value resides largely in their ability to be inclusive, to spread out for a new reader as much of the buried treasure brought back from the archives as physically possible within prescribed volume limits. Yet even an anthology which aims to be the most representative in its selections will always encounter the paradox inherent in the notion that selection *can* ever represent fullness. Anthologies, by their very nature, always simultaneously invoke and revoke the idea of a 'full' representation.[2] This is well understood to be both the limitation and the appeal of an anthology, and it is for this reason that it will always reflect the cultural assumptions of the time of its own making as strongly as those of the time from which it draws material.

---

[1] The pioneer work of reference in the field was *The Feminist Companion to Literature in English: Women's Writing from the Middle Ages to the Present* (1990), eds V. Blain, P. Clements, I. Grundy. Since its publication, other scholars have followed up its leads and rediscovered a surprising number of forgotten women poets from the Victorian period.

[2] I am grateful to Dr Yopie Prins for this useful formulation.

THE BASIS OF THE PRESENT SELECTION

The policy of this series is to provide the reader with full annotations for each poem as required. Naturally this cannot be done without some cost in terms of the space available. The question then becomes: how best to allocate that space. The choice I have made here is to offer a representative selection from thirteen poets rather than a much briefer sampling from a larger number. Brief selections are useful in providing a kind of aerial survey of a new terrain; but their drawback is that they skim over the work and flatten out variety. Scholarship in the field has now reached a point from which firmer choices can be made. The thirteen poets included here provide a varied and wide-ranging coverage of the kinds of subjects and poetic treatments most often employed by Victorian women poets, while also giving a close-up view of each individual chosen. I have aimed to include a teachable range of poems for each poet, rather than a choice of my personal favourites, or what I see as the 'best' poems. While it would have been perfectly possible to have made a different selection of poets and still to have fulfilled the general aim of this volume (my original long list contained 64 names), these are the poets who have seemed to me to be among the most likely to be appealing in what they have to offer us today. Of course, there are many others I would like to have been able to include: Anne Evans, for example, with her understated wit and wonderful musical sense; Louisa S. Bevington with her radical political stance; Harriet Hamilton King with her fascination for the Italian struggle for independence; the sharp-minded Bohemian Edith Nesbit (more generally known as a children's writer); the intellectually distinguished and influential Alice Meynell; the remarkable and tormented Charlotte Mew (post-Victorian in her publication, but not in her upbringing); even the immensely popular Jean Ingelow, whose largely sentimental output can yet offer the occasional sharp surprise. In my view it is quite premature to suggest anything like the formation of a new canon: the longer the field remains open to new contenders the more firmly it will continue to establish (rather than entrench) itself. The ongoing struggle for position among champions of different poets is an important part of what brings life to the subject.

I have made a deliberate choice not to include a 'token' working-class poet in the present selection. This may provoke a knee-jerk reaction among the so-called 'politically correct', but my policy is certainly not meant to imply the non-significance of such different voices; rather the opposite. Ellen Johnson ('the factory girl') and Janet Hamilton are the usual choices for working-class 'representation'. Their work is certainly of much interest, yet as Florence Boos and others have shown,[3] these two are only the tip of the iceberg. There is a vast treasure trove of these lost voices awaiting rediscovery, often in the dingy pages of regional newspapers, or between the paper covers of cheap pamphlets.[4] Furthermore, it is important to remember

---

[3] See the ground-breaking work by Julia Swindells (1985) and, more recently, by Florence Boos (1995, 1996, 1998).

[4] For example, the pamphlet published as *A Bitter Cry from the Ploughfield* by 'E.H.' in 1885 or 1886, who identifies herself further only as 'a ploughman's daughter', contains some extraordinary poems; it has not been possible to discover anything further about their author. See Blain, 1999, pp. 135–63.

that the tradition of working-class women's verse-making belongs primarily within an oral rather than a written culture, and can seem ill-at-ease in its often palpable struggle for literacy when placed cheek-by-jowl with the more self-consciously literary world underwritten by middle-class privilege. In my view, it is almost impossible to avoid patronising writers like Glasgow, Hamilton and others by placing them in a context which fits them so ill. I prefer to let them await their time to appear in the more congenial climate of other working-class voices who faced similar constraints and hardships in their struggle to be heard.

Similarly, I have chosen not to include any of the many and varied 'colonial voices': middle-class Englishwomen who emigrated – often not through their own choice – to live in India, Canada, Australia, and who preserved a special relationship with the mother country while simultaneously offering a unique perspective on the notion of Empire as it manifested itself in the minds of the colonists. Again, these writers seem to me to be crying out for their own anthology which can throw their own particular context into relief.

FELICIA HEMANS AS THE FIRST 'VICTORIAN' POET

Felicia Hemans, a poet quintessentially both English and bourgeois, has been chosen to open this anthology. There will no doubt be literal-minded readers who notice immediately that she is not a Victorian. Strictly speaking, this is true, in that she died in 1835, two years before Victoria succeeded to the throne. Her claim to a place in this anthology comes from her significance as an emblematic Victorian. Her poetry was taken so much to heart by Victorian readers and chimed so closely with their needs and desires that it became part of the Victorian psyche, continuing to command large sales throughout the period. Hemans is a good example, too, of the essential fallacy of periodising literature according to external events, or even according to what might seem to be the prevailing fashion. For although according to traditional chronology she should be classified as a Romantic poet, her verse has little in common with that of Wordsworth (whom she nevertheless revered), Coleridge, Shelley or Keats, and it does her a disservice to look for their concerns and aspirations in her work.[5]

In fact, so identified did she become, over time, with the high Victorian period, that her fame, which remained considerable throughout the nineteenth century, was virtually extinguished with the rapid devaluing of Victorianism by the subsequent generation of modernist writers and critics of the early twentieth century. In a sense, she became a sort of scapegoat for the traits we most strongly repudiate in our ancestors: moral priggishness, prudery, jingoistic patriotism, glorification of war, meek acceptance of women's secondary role in public affairs. When the inevitable reversal of taste occurred and the 'great' Victorians were recuperated from their over-zealous detractors, Hemans was not among them. She was discarded, virtually disowned, although (or perhaps because) she had been so powerful in her influence

---

[5] See, for example, Anne K. Mellor (1993), who writes that 'Hemans' poetry locates ultimate human value within the domestic sphere' (p. 124).

on the formation of Victorian tastes. Recent critics have argued, however, that not only does Hemans not deserve such obloquy, but that it is based on too simplistic a reading of her work, which obscures the self-reflexive irony that throws into question previous assumptions about her conservative beliefs.[6] Her contemporaries regarded her as something of a saint: she had been left to bring up their five children alone by her husband, who had gone to live in Italy 'for the sake of his health' – though really, because the marriage had failed – and she never once complained of him in public, instead choosing to write poem after poem extolling the 'domestic affections'. With hindsight, we can see more clearly just how shrewdly she manipulated the publicity machine of her time, so that no whiff of an indiscretion ever came near her to injure her chance of supporting herself and her family by her writing. In this she was unusually successful, managing to raise and educate her five sons on the proceeds of her poetry.[7] It should not surprise a modern reader, perhaps, to find that among all her poems praising domestic virtues, very few focus on male virtue; characteristically, it is female courage and power of self-sacrifice, often in the face of male pusillanimity, that receives the accolade. Even in her most famous poem, 'Casabianca', it is the pre-pubescent child who is venerated for his outstanding loyalty to the impossible demand of an absent father in the face of almost certain death.

The poet most often associated with Hemans in critical discussion, Letitia Elizabeth Landon (1802–1838), or 'L.E.L.' as she signed herself, is in fact in almost every respect entirely her opposite. Their only true similarity lay in their ability to market themselves to the public: L.E.L. as idealised female victim was adored by a generation of readers. Many of these were young males (the future novelist Edward Bulwer Lytton among them) who happily swallowed the projected image of a mournful poetess who had turned to her lyre for consolation only after her heart had been broken, and who, like the Greek poet Sappho on whom she modelled herself, could look forward only to death to bring her release from the anguish of her abandonment.[8] Landon rode the coat-tails of Romanticism, manipulating its expressive machinery without believing in it. Yet she, too, like Hemans, needed to support herself (as well as her mother and younger brother) by her writing, and she tapped a rich vein in her contributions to the popular albums and annuals that were *de rigueur* for the middle-class drawing-room table display in the 1820s and 1830s. Had she been less pressed for money, she might have developed into a much more interesting poet, for some of her later work gives evidence of a sharp critical intellect, while her facility for writing verse at speed and under pressure was always remarkable. Her reputation was enhanced by the mystery of her premature death, soon after her marriage to George Maclean, Governor of Cape Coast Castle in West Africa. All kinds of gothic rumours were spread (was it suicide? or even – murder?), and sales of her work multiplied. But in the long run, her brand of poetry – which

---

[6] Tricia Lootens (1994) was among the first to problematise simplistic readings of Hemans.

[7] Paula Feldman (1999) examines Hemans's earnings in some detail.

[8] For a richly nuanced discussion of the influence of Victorian notions of Sappho on women poets, see Yopie Prins (1999).

characteristically featured heroine-as-victim – had far less influence on the succeeding generation of Victorians than did that of Hemans. If anything, she served as a negative model, a warning: it is interesting that both Rossetti and Barrett Browning were moved to write poems rebuking her narcissism.[9]

THE PROFESSIONALISATION OF THE WOMAN POET

One theme, however, picked up by both Hemans and Landon, which was to remain of central concern to the poets who followed them, was that of the dilemma of professionalism for the woman poet. Professionalism, not in the modern sense – for many women would have deplored any suggestion that they were more than inspired amateurs[10] – but in the sense of making a serious attempt to reconcile the demands of ambition with the demands of romance, a woman's traditional role in life being to play second fiddle to the male on whom she was generally financially dependent, whether he be husband, father or brother. Placed in the unpleasantly ambiguous personal situation of being separated from her husband, rather than bewail her own distressing circumstance in her verse, Hemans chose instead to deflect it into a series of hints that, for women, the gift of poetic genius was bound to be a source of sorrow rather than joy, as it would inevitably alienate men's affections, thereby standing in the way of any achievement of lasting happiness. The remedy offered, however, is not death but moral courage and religious resignation, thus, in a sense, allowing the poet (or 'poetess' as she was then called) to have her cake and eat it. In other words, she could have her fame, as long as she acknowledged (as Hemans did) that she would assuredly have to pay the price in her life (but not in her poetry). This theme of the peculiar dilemma faced by any female artist in a patriarchal culture who longs both to develop her difference from other women, but also to keep her commonality with them, by achieving fulfilment through romantic love, has a number of variations, and it can be traced in one form or other through the work of many of the poets in this volume.[11]

Those poets who come to terms more readily with this problem are those who appear to be less oriented (in their poetry, at any rate) towards the fulfilment of heterosexual desires: Webster, Blind, Naden, Levy, Coleridge, Kendall and Field. The prime example here, of course, is Michael Field, the pen-name adopted by two women poets who actually lived together as lovers, and who jointly produced a large number of volumes. These were Katharine Bradley and Edith Cooper, an aunt and niece, who vowed early to dedicate themselves to poetry and to each other (see their poem titled 'Prologue') and who were enabled to do so for the rest of

---

[9] EBB's poem 'L.E.L.'s Last Question' (1844) quotes from one of Landon's last poems as epigraph: 'Do you think of me as I think of you?', while Rossetti's poem, titled simply 'L.E.L.' (1866), in turn quotes from EBB's poem as its epigraph: 'Whose heart was breaking for a little love'.

[10] See, for example, my discussion of the link between notions of amateurism and those of ladylike (or gentlemanly) behaviour (Blain, 1998).

[11] For a full discussion of these and related issues, see Dorothy Mermin (1993).

their lives thanks to their possession of inherited wealth. Such a privileged social position enabled them to hold themselves aloof from the marketplace (much of their work was privately printed), thus avoiding many of the pressures placed on their less fortunate fellows to negotiate with a reading public. Although their main aspiration centred on the writing of (very unfashionable) verse tragedies in the Shakespearean tradition, as time went on they also produced eight volumes of lyric poetry, the best of which is often the love poetry (where the 'voice' adopted is generally that of a male lover). Michael Field's initial reception by reviewers was excellent – 'he' was hailed by critics (including Robert Browning) as a major new voice: 'a poet of distinguished powers', 'something almost of Shakespearean penetration', 'a fresh gift of song' (reviews cited in Sturgeon, 1922, pp. 27–8). Once their secret was out, however, and people knew that Michael Field was a woman – worse, two women – their work was no longer taken seriously, except by a few who saw in it something noble and who admired the writers' dedication to their love of beauty and each other. So their work, too, sank without much trace somewhere between the two world wars, once those who championed them had died.

Not only was Michael Field relatively untrammelled by the more usual constraints imposed upon women under patriarchy, this pair also managed, until late in their lives at any rate, to avoid the penitential meshes of conventional Christianity that so troubled many women poets. Bradley and Cooper, indeed, took great pride in their avowed paganism, declaring themselves to be like maenads in their rebellion against the cultural stereotypes of femininity. Again, unlike less privileged women, they had both studied Greek, and knew that the Meinades, or Bacchantes – priestesses of Bacchus – renowned for their seeming madness or frenzy in their worship, could keep *hoi polloi* at bay and find new freedom by embracing such an outrageous identity. Sadly, however, they appear to have functioned in a cultural vacuum with regard to other women writers, being both so male-identified that they felt little affinity with their female contemporaries, who equally seem to have entirely disregarded them. Dorothy Wordsworth was the only other woman regarded by Bradley, at least, as a true poet.[12]

Their own lasting strength, though, owes much to their unswerving sense of vocation, a sense shared by some, if not all, of the poets included here. Again, such a sense is largely underwritten by privilege: access to education and contact with a supportive literary milieu. Certainly Barrett Browning had it, and so did Rossetti, though she never had the private income which in EBB's case enabled her to support her husband and fellow-poet Robert Browning as well as herself. Neither woman had to work for a living, though if Rossetti had been stronger, she might well have been obliged to teach. Although these two each published some prose works, they certainly regarded themselves first and foremost as poets, and they received enough acclaim for their work during their lifetimes to maintain such a belief in themselves.

---

[12] See Bradley's letter to Cooper held in the Bodleian Library, Oxford, quoted by permission: 'Dorothy Wordsworth . . . is the only English woman I rank as a poet – a divine creature for whom William could not have altogether sufficed. What other woman has ever had her heart right toward nature, has ever felt of one blood with the forests, the little hills, & the mountain breezes . . .' (MS Eng.poet d.56 fols. 135–6, n.d.)

However, compared with women novelists, who usually wrote for money, often with great success, poets were placed in a very different position. During the 1830s, particularly with the popularity of the annuals and gift books, verse was a highly prized commodity, but from the late 1840s prose fiction began to dominate the market. While Felicia Hemans and Letitia Landon were each able to support an extended family by their writing during the 1830s, the pressure of this financial expectation could often compromise their poetry as art (Landon also wrote fiction for money). Later poets like Augusta Webster and Mathilde Blind, on the other hand, developed quite a different professional attitude, producing journalism for money and poetry, at the very least, as a non-profit-making exercise. The seriousness with which they took their poetry was likely to be different in kind, if not in degree, from that of the earlier writers.

CHANGING POETIC TASTES AND STYLES

The Victorian period itself covered such a generous time span (1837–1901) that poetic tastes and styles changed immensely throughout those 60-odd years. The richness of variety in this volume is a testament to these changes. The romantic glorification of abandonment in love, for example, dropped quickly out of fashion in favour of a burgeoning Victorian interest in the psychology of couples.[13] The motif of abandonment did not disappear entirely, but was given a different slant, most notably in Christina Rossetti's verse, both secular and devotional. In the twentieth century, Virginia Woolf wrote of Rossetti that when God was finally called to account, Rossetti would be one of the chief witnesses for the prosecution.[14] By this she meant that in her view, Rossetti's poetic gift had been grossly compromised by her religious belief. But Woolf was part of the generation that was determined to throw off the shackles (including religion) of the Victorians who were its immediate ancestors, and we can now recognise other ways of looking at this issue. For example, it can be argued that, for the truly devout, the realm of religion was a space marked out separately from the everyday, and that, since souls – unlike bodies – are unsexed, gender hierarchies could be kept at bay in this private space. This might help to account for at least part of the strong attraction towards religion shown by many women poets of the period. EBB, for example, always retained her firm belief in a Christian God, which runs like a silk thread through the fabric of her writing: not always visible, but always there. Dora Greenwell (not included here), a friend and admirer of Rossetti's and author of a number of theological essays as well as devotional and other poems, once wrote that mixing Christianity with poetry was 'like eating honey off the tip of a sword'[15] – a telling image of the powerful sway still occupied by Christian thinking at the time.

---

[13] See P. M. Ball (1976) for a development of this notion.

[14] See Anne Olivier Bell, ed., *The Diary of Virginia Woolf* (1977), I, pp. 178–9.

[15] See Dora Greenwell's essay 'An Inquiry as to How Far the Spirit of Poetry is Alien, and How Far Friendly, to Christianity' in her *Liber Humanitatis* (1875). The essay ends: '[though the Christian] may sometimes taste of song's sweet, intoxicating wild honey, it will be as did the mighty men in the scriptural story, but "sparingly, and on the tip of his spear"'.

Others, however, especially those of more radical tendencies, like Mathilde Blind, stepdaughter of a German revolutionary, were influenced by scientific and evolutionary thinkers to abandon Christianity altogether. Constance Naden and May Kendall were also followers of the new sciences rather than the old belief systems, while Amy Levy grew up in and later rebelled against the orthodox Anglo-Jewish community of north London. It is now widely believed that she too was what we would today call lesbian, though unlike the two women behind Michael Field, she was not destined to find the happiness of a reciprocated love. While her work never confronts the theme of same-sex desire directly, certainly it can lend itself to this interpretation by modern readers accustomed to looking for coded hints of even heterosexual desire in Victorian writing.[16] Another social outsider, Adah Isaacs Menken took a Jew as one of her numerous husbands (it is not known whether there were four or five) and to some extent at least, also took upon herself the role of Jewish champion. Like Levy, though, and with as much cause (for Menken was an actress – then a marker of social undesirability – as well as an alien, being American born and bred), she felt isolated and deeply unhappy in the London society of her time. Tragically, while Levy committed suicide at the early age of 28, despite her burgeoning career as published novelist and poet, Menken also died young, though of tuberculosis (known then as consumption) rather than by her own hand. Clearly, to be an outsider because of one's extreme Christian devotion (or even one's atheism) was one thing in Victorian society, but to be an outsider because of one's sexuality was quite another, and even more irredeemable.

ANXIETY OF GENRE

Rossetti, of course, along with Barrett Browning, is one of the very few women poets of the period to have been accorded recognition by postwar literary critics. In fact, she is the only one of these poets never entirely to have slipped out of view. Emily Brontë has also received respectful attention, though it is generally agreed that her masterpiece remains her one published novel, *Wuthering Heights* (1847), rather than her poetry, unique and thrilling as that can be. To my mind, Brontë is in some important respects removed from the Victorian ethos inhabited by her fellow-poets. Her poetry, lifted as much of it is from her own private dreamland of the Gondal saga, has an air of other-worldliness that, however powerful in its own right, does not sit well in the context of her contemporaries. It ignores most of the issues that were important to them, such as the dilemma of fame, the psychology of individuals, the place of the church, the domestic affections, the role of patriotism, the importance of marriage. Nor does Brontë share in what might be called 'the anxiety of genre', whereby many poets of the period – partly, at least, in response to the increasing popularity of the novel – were busily searching for new expressive means in their verse, often reaching out towards narrative or epic forms, as Barrett Browning did, with her extraordinary 'verse-novel', *Aurora Leigh* (1856), as Emily Pfeiffer did, with her experimental mixed-genre *Rhyme of the Lady of the*

---

[16] See my essay mentioned in note 4 above.

Rock; and how it grew (1884) (which embeds a folk ballad on a historical subject into a contemporary prose commentary), or as Mathilde Blind did, with her powerful, politically engaged verse narratives on the entrenched misogyny of the Christian church (*The Prophecy of Saint Oran*, 1881) and the scandal of the Highland clearances in Scotland (*The Heather on Fire*, 1886). Other poets explored the possibilities of dramatic monologue or even verse drama, a form which attracted a surprising number of women poets. The influence of Robert Browning was a potent one in this regard: his willingness to explore, through dramatisation, viewpoints other than that of the conventional bourgeois male endeared him to women writers. Augusta Webster, for example, a strong admirer, produced some fine dramas, which tackle a number of contentious contemporary issues under cover of a historical setting; verse drama was also written (copiously) by Michael Field and by Emily Pfeiffer. Sadly, this is a genre impossible to represent in an anthology, but it is important to realise that it was so popular with many women poets. Drama thrives on conflict, and direct expression of conflict was something convention denied to young women. Dramatic forms offered the opportunity to inhabit less socially acceptable positions without taking direct responsibility for them: with the lyric forms, by contrast, poets were too often assumed to *be* the speaking 'I' of their poem, and in the case of women poets, this assumption was a powerful agent for self-censorship.

In the nineteenth century, the more 'classical' forms like verse tragedy and epic were supposedly unavailable to women, owing to their exclusion from the universities and, in many cases, from any form of serious schooling. However, a surprisingly large number of future poets did manage to scrounge an education for themselves: vicars' daughters (like Frances Havergal) listened in on their fathers' tutoring sessions; younger sisters (like Emily Brontë and Eliza Hamilton) persuaded their more fortunate brothers to teach them; wives of enlightened husbands (like Mary Howitt[17]) went on educating themselves after marriage; clever daughters of rich men (like Elizabeth Barrett and Constance Naden) were allowed tutors of their own; women who lived with female partners (notably Katharine Bradley and Edith Cooper) supported each other's efforts to overcome deficiencies in formal education. Amy Levy was the only one to attend university (Newnham College at Cambridge). The thirst for knowledge remained intense. Knowledge of the classics was particularly prized for its association with the idea of true learning at Oxford and Cambridge, and for its relative inaccessibility to females. In fact, classical translations as well as – to a lesser extent – translations from the modern romance languages became something of a status symbol among nineteenth-century women poets. Elizabeth Barrett and Augusta Webster each produced scholarly translations from the Greek; both had benefited from a classical education, at least in the sense that they had been enabled to study Greek in a serious manner and reach a level of proficiency high enough for them to produce original translations (see Webster's 1866 verse translation of

---

[17] Mary Howitt (1799–1888), wife of William Howitt, was a lively-minded Quaker who wrote for a living: novels and translations as well as poems. Eliza Mary Hamilton (1807–1851) was an extraordinarily brilliant Anglo-Irish poet who published only one volume: *Poems* (1838). Frances Havergal (1836–1879) was a poet and hymnist, devoting herself to study of languages and to the spiritual life.

Aeschylus's *Prometheus Bound*, and her 1868 *Medea*; EBB also translated *Prometheus Bound* [first attempted 1833, revised in 1845 for publication in 1850]).

'FEMININITY' AND SEXUAL DIFFERENCE

In a sense, of course, this kind of work was always undertaken by women in order to prove a point: to illustrate their own ability in what too often went unchallenged as male intellectual territory. But though creative (much more so than is often credited) it was not original work, and we need to move on to ask the hard question about the scope and nature of women's creative contribution to Victorian poetry. To a large extent, post-Romantic women poets were obliged to find a way to utilise or to abandon an inherited stockpile of expressive machinery that increasingly appeared to be stiff, creaky and cumbersome, and in which the allotted role of 'woman' did not at all chime with their own desire. Different poets rose to this challenge in different ways. Some, most notably the American poet Menken, who came to live in London and published her poetry there (cheekily dedicating her volume to Charles Dickens), responded to the challenge by ditching 'feminine' expressive forms altogether. Instead, by adapting Walt Whitman's chanting speech-rhythms, throwing in a dash of Swinburne's highly coloured rhetoric and imbuing the whole with a fair dose of feminist rage, Menken created a new and quite shocking voice. With it, her poetry enacts the strident uncertainties of self-appointed power, anointing its speaker, the poet-figure, as 'genius' in the full bardic tradition of Romanticism, at the same time as it strips away the complacency of patriarchal superiority by insisting on female supremacy. In her poem 'Judith', Menken enacts an Old Testament-style revenge with full melodramatic props of blood and gore, but this indulgence in an erotics of violence should not be allowed to obscure from the modern reader the courage with which she openly denounces the hypocrisy of the double standard.

Not surpringly, perhaps, Menken found no immediate followers among her fellow-poets in England; her voice was the voice of the actress, and too strident by far to find approval in Victorian England. Her sister poets may have shared many of her views, but they would not have dreamed of expressing them so forcefully. Even when dealing with the same subject, the hypocrisy of the double standard in connection with permissible sexual behaviour for men and for women, the preferred mode was indirection. Rosemary Marriott Watson is the only other poet who comes near to expressing Menken's unbridled rage, but even she chooses to mask her women as were-wolves and witches. This was not necessarily owing to any difference in courage, rather to a different strategy. Menken is very useful as a point of contrast and as a kind of boundary marker (standing, as she does, well beyond the pale). At the same time, it should be noted that a number of these poets do deal with one of the most notorious social evils of the time, that of prostitution – or, more widely inclusive as a category, the 'Fallen Woman' – and they deal with it in a manner which recognises their own unique and yet implicated position as middle-class women. It is instructive to compare the poems on this subject by Augusta Webster ('The Castaway'), Amy Levy ('Magdalen'), and – less well known – 'The Message', by Mathilde Blind.

If we go back from these to a poem like Dante Gabriel Rossetti's 'Jenny' (1870), often acclaimed for its anti-moralistic sympathy with the prostitute of its title, it is interesting what uneasy gaps and cover-ups suddenly appear, and how much more patronising its narrator becomes in this context. To treat the same subject from the opposite gender position makes a surprising difference. Certainly, women wrote about traditional lyric subject-matter – love poetry, devotional poetry, poems of elegy and meditation, poems about nature – but very often these are poems which adopt quite a different perspective from the one most readers of Victorian poetry will expect. Women poets were traditionally expected to produce a prettified kind of 'nature' poetry – regarded as a fitting and safe subject – but very few of these women fall into that role. A number of them are in fact more interested in cityscapes than landscapes, Blind and Levy in particular. To take another example of a difference in gender affect: Augusta Webster's fine, though sadly unfinished, sequence of sonnets written to her daughter, 'Mother and Daughter', published posthumously in an edition by W. M. Rossetti, attests to this power of a different viewpoint in a manner more striking even than *Sonnets from the Portuguese* or 'Monna Innominata'. It is unique in its celebration of maternal same-sex love within the classical format of traditional heterosexual romantic love. This claims affinity with Felicia Hemans's poetry, which laid such an emphasis on what she called 'the domestic affections', particularly maternal love, yet it goes a step further in its appropriation of the category of traditional love poetry. That Webster knew she was mortally ill when she was writing the sequence no doubt accounts for some of the intensity with which her speaker's voice is imbued as she dwells on the beloved with such evident longing somehow to 'fix' her love, to give her daughter some tangible evidence of value (hers for her mother, her mother's for her) that would last beyond the grave.

THE 'POETESS' AND THE WOMAN POET

Webster's sonnet sequence is one of the works which is most vividly illustrative of the difference in women's poetry. Yet not all of the poets themselves wished to be thought of as 'different' from male poets, and none was in any way trying to be what we now call 'separatist', that is, writing consciously in an exclusively female tradition. It seems fair to say that while almost all of them held strong views on issues such as the education of girls and women, most would have seen their own writing as contributing, in whatever way, to a poetic mainstream rather than to a realm of women poets. This is an attitude that showed marked changes over the period we are dealing with. While Felicia Hemans, for example, had no objection to being labelled a 'poetess', the feminised title with its connotations of 'prettiness' and 'lightness' became less popular as the century went on.[18] While Elizabeth Barrett Browning once famously lamented the absence of literary grandmothers,[19] this has

---

[18] See Ross (1989), Leighton (1992b), Curran (1993), Mellor (1993), Blain (1995) and Linley (1999) for further discussion of the usage of the term 'poetess'.

[19] 'England has many learned women . . . and yet where are the poetesses? . . . I look everywhere for grandmothers and see none.' *The Letters of EBB*, ed. F. Kenyon (London, 1898), I, p. 231.

since been shown to be evidence only of the general suppression and 'forgetting' of earlier work by women, not of their non-existence. Perhaps also, like Michael Field and Mathilde Blind and possibly Mary Coleridge, EBB cared more to find acceptance with male readers than with female. Mary Coleridge was especially alert to the difficulties of her position as woman poet bearing the name of a famous male poet (who happened to be her great-great-uncle). In her decision to publish anonymously, she appears to have been torn between not wishing to hang on the coat-tails of a famous name, and a fear of being dismissed by readers and critics as a mere 'she', a 'poetess':

> Indeed I don't want to be thought a her – how could I? – I only don't want to be thought me – which is bad grammar, & as feminine as all the rest of it, I'm afraid![20]

Even more strongly, she wrote to her friend Edith Sichel:

> Woman with a big W bores me supremely. How Λ would have puzzled the beautiful and concrete Greeks. It is a mere abstraction born of monks and the mists of the North. A woman I know, but what on earth is Woman? She has done her best to spoil history, poetry, novels, essays, and Sir Thomas Browne and Thoreau are the only things safe from her; that's why I love them.[21]

Yet, contrariwise, she will not be driven into denial of sexual difference, writing to Sichel elsewhere:

> When you spoke about sex the other night, I didn't think much about it, but to-day I did, and I know now that I didn't feel with you, and that it does seem to me to be an eternal distinction. I don't think we are separate only in body and in mind, I think we are separate in soul too, and that a woman's prayer is as different from a man's as a woman's thought or a woman's hand. I cannot think of souls that are not masculine or feminine . . . but just as the negation of sex is inconceivable to me, so is its unification; I cannot think that we shall be men as well as women, and men women as well as men. If we do not retain sex I don't see how we can retain identity. Male and female we were created; it is of the very essence of our nature.[22]

Certainly it would be a mistake to assume that the work of these women can be read as part of an isolated female tradition. Although such a tradition can be mapped onto the poetry by way of allusions and cross-references, many of which will appear in the annotations – for these women did read each other (and some knew each other personally[23]) – the work also contains numerous traces of influence by male poets, including many examples of what can best be described as a dialogue,

---

[20] Quoted with permission, from an unpublished letter to Robert Bridges dated 27 May [1896], held in the Bodleian Library, Oxford, dep. Bridges 108 f.5.

[21] See Coleridge, ed. Sichel, 1910, p. 234.

[22] Ibid., pp. 233–4.

[23] For example, Christina Rossetti knew Dora Greenwell, Adelaide Procter, Jean Ingelow, Katherine Tynan and Augusta Webster; but she rather drew back from much contact with other women poets, who had a habit of sending her their volumes for approbation (see Marsh, 1994a, p. 537). Michael Field and Dora Greenwell published sonnets to her, Amy Levy wrote an essay on her work, and she herself always revered Elizabeth Barrett Browning.

either with a particular male poet or poem, or with certain assumptions underlying male-authored poetry. This dialogue is most noticeable in the love poetry written by women. Here, many of them are concerned to point the difference of their own gendered subjectivity, in terms of a poetic tradition predicated on a male viewpoint and speaking position. This kind of challenge to male authority had of course been initiated in similar ways by women poets in earlier periods – Aphra Behn (1640–1689) is a prime example. But Victorian women poets seem to have their own characteristic ways of continuing the discussion: EBB's 'A Man's Requirements', Pfeiffer's 'Any Husband to Many a Wife', Naden's 'Scientific Wooing', Kendall's 'The Sandblast Girl and the Acid Man' are but some examples of the lighter side of this subject. More serious explorations occur in Hemans's 'Wife of Asdrubal', which scorns the husband's self-serving sacrifice of his family; EBB's deceptively gentle 'Bertha in the Lane', which quietly subverts the ideal of female self-sacrifice; Rossetti's 'In an Artist's Studio', where the gazed-upon model returns the scrutiny; Menken's violent anti-patriarchal protest poem 'Judith'; Webster's sympathetic portrayal of Medea, whose infanticide one might conventionally have expected to call up nothing but outrage from a Victorian mother; Rosamund Marriott Watson's chilling 'Ballad of the Were-wolf', another tale deeply at odds with the myth of domestic bliss in the patriarchal household; and Amy Levy's sardonic little poem 'A Ballad of Religion and Marriage', which further exposes this myth for the fantasy it is.

Interestingly, it is the well-known male poets of the period – Tennyson and Browning in particular – who most forcefully uphold the idea of domestic harmony as a sure-fire route to heaven, not the women writers. An ideal of domesticity centring on a good and patient wife sitting by the hearth ready to minister to his needs may have been immensely reassuring for the Victorian male, but it seems to have been summarily rejected by most of the women poets. When the husband in Watson's 'Ballad' struggles with the were-wolf who has destroyed his children, he finds on arriving home with his trophy, a severed paw, that his 'gudewife' is indeed sitting next to the hearth and waiting for him, but instead of her right hand she unwraps for his horrified gaze a bleeding stump. The implications – of his wife's infanticide, of her 'double life' – are not spelt out, but rather left to be savoured at leisure by Watson's reader.

Again, however, it would be wrong to convey the idea that the overriding impulse of Victorian women's poetry was to denigrate the opposite sex, whether poets or not. EBB's famous *Sonnets from the Portuguese* have long served as eloquent testimony to the contrary. But it is true that when one searches for further evidence of the central importance loving a man might have held in these poet's lives, one is more often than not disappointed. The ideal of masculinity seems less important to women poets than its converse, the ideal of femininity, is to men poets. Yet in a curious manner, the ideal of femininity was so much an ingrained motif in the poetic tradition, so bound up with the time-honoured belief that poems ought to be 'beautiful', or at least pretty, that some women poets seem almost reluctant to abandon it, fearing, perhaps, that they will lose something essential if they do. Ideas of the aesthetic needed to change along with ideas of the feminine. So instead, these poets often refashion femininity to suit another agenda. Felicia Hemans, for example, rather than reject the inclusion of charm, beauty and gentleness as desirable feminine qualities (for poetry as well as for women), takes care to add a strong infusion of moral courage along with a superior capacity for true love, thus endowing her female figures (particularly those featured in her celebratory volume *Records of Woman*) with an exalted position in the moral hierarchy. In a more radical move, Christina Rossetti in her 'sonnet of sonnets', 'Monna Innominata', takes the traditional trope of a male lover celebrating his desire for an unattainable female and re-positions the female figure to be both poet and subject, rather than doubly an object.

Although Rossetti does pick up the theme of lamenting the loss of love, she does it in a far less sentimental, self-pitying way than had earlier been so popular in Landon's work. As suggested earlier, after Landon's death, dying for love seems to have gone out of fashion among women as the century progressed, with the Victorians developing instead a growing interest in the psychology of the couple. EBB's 'Bertha in the Lane' marks a move toward this mode, while Pfeiffer's poem 'Nathaniel to Ruth' is another example: here, the husband reveals his own anxieties while justifying his choice of a wife. Where Alfred Tennyson was the male poet largely responsible for the development of the stereotypical view of Woman as poised eternally between the twin impulses of purity and passion (the lily and the rose), it was Robert Browning's exploration of the vagaries of individual psychology in *Men and Women* (as he significantly titled his 1855 volume of dramatic monologues) that really chimed with many of the women poets. And of course, as is now more readily acknowledged, he had himself been strongly influenced by Elizabeth Barrett's poetry. In her lifetime she was always held to be the superior poet, and certainly her fame was secure long before he even began to make his name. There was even a chance, after the death of Wordsworth in 1850, that she might be chosen to replace him as Poet Laureate: though in the event, of course, the laurel went to Tennyson.

THE CHALLENGE OF THE NEW SCIENCES TO RELIGIOUS ORTHODOXY

Tennyson was famously fascinated by pre-Darwinian evolutionary theory – 'Nature red in tooth and claw'[24] – but how did women poets react to the controversies between the new science and established religion? Mathilde Blind published in 1889 an entire volume of poems devoted to evolutionary themes, called *The Ascent of Man*. Unlike Tennyson's more gloomy view, her poetry appears unequivocally to welcome and celebrate progressivist theories foretelling the continued improvement of the human race. Not for her any hankering after established religion: she sets her face against such worn-out creeds and places her faith in the innate capacity of human beings to change and adapt. Her ambitious long poem 'Chaunts of Life' from this volume offers a schematic history of the planet from its beginnings 'Struck out of dim fluctuant forces and shock of electrical vapour', through the initiation of life to the birth of Man and his discovery of fire. It then moves on to

---

[24] Tennyson, *In Memoriam* (1850), LVI, l. 15.

cover topics like the human need for religion causing man to invent a god, the growth of Christianity, the Inquisition, the French revolution, finally ending up with a celebration of liberty of the soul, which seems somehow to be derived from an aesthetic appreciation of nature: 'Yea, all rhythms of air and ocean / Married to the heart's emotion . . .'. Noticeable here is the deep reliance on a mystical union between Man and Nature: her progressive vision remains locked in a world of idealism (it is not surprising that Shelley was her favourite poet). The rhetoric she chooses for this hugely ambitious project (a Miltonic alternative) is largely unsuccessful, being far too wordy, vague, bombastic: the poem, an experiment in the visionary mode, fails. Yet elsewhere, Blind shows an acute awareness of material social conditions affecting the underprivileged classes, in poems like 'Manchester by Night' and 'Haunted Streets'; while her poem 'Motherhood' is possibly unique in Victorian literature on this subject in its focus on the physical agony of childbearing.

Other women poets who were particularly concerned with the new scientific discoveries and the changing world-view these brought into focus were Constance Naden and May Kendall. These two poets were both very different from Blind, being much more intellectually astringent, and inclined to tackle esoteric subjects with a disruptive wit rather than a cloudy idealism. Naden, extremely intelligent and exceptionally well educated, is more inclined to metaphysical speculation than Kendall, and less class-conscious; that is, she is not self-reflexive about her own social position of privilege in the way Kendall can be. Her sense of humour comes out particularly in the series titled 'Evolutionary Erotics', in poems like 'Scientific Wooing' and 'Natural Selection'. Kendall goes further, however, deftly driving her sly critique of science and scientists to the edge of farce, with wickedly comic, almost absurdist, poems like 'The Lay of the Trilobite' and 'The Philanthropist and the Jelly-fish'. But 'Church Echoes', which contrasts the viewpoints of the vicar's daughters with that of the poor charity children and also of the tramp, setting them quizzically against an orthodox Christian frame, is soberingly pessimistic in its conclusions; it is certainly very far from the meliorism offered by Blind's 'Chaunts of Life'.

HUMOUR AND DREAMS IN WOMEN'S POETRY

An even more startling difference occurs in women's humorous poetry, where instead of being (however subtly) the butt of the jokes, as happens rather often in traditional comic verse, Woman becomes their maker. It is understandable that male foibles are often the object of her wit, be it gentle or sharp. Verse somehow provided a safer territory for turning the tables, a kind of sanctuary against immediate censure through the medium of its aesthetic concern. The fact that there is a body of excellent comic verse by women at this period goes some way to showing up the limitations of the common belief that most female poets of the Victorian age devoted themselves singlemindedly to God. Even when they do write religious or devotional lyrics, we can now recognise, as mentioned earlier, that the space afforded to a woman by this mode of discourse, fashioning itself out of a communion between an individual soul and its Maker, could in itself offer an escape from the power of the domestic patriarch. Again, poetry dealing with the stuff of fairy tales, often popular with women writers, has been belittled in the past in a way which utterly obscures the often subversive intent behind it. Christina Rossetti's 'Goblin Market' has of course long been recuperated for serious attention, but less well-known women poets have had their work dismissed without a fair hearing. The discourse of the fairy tale can often disguise a subversive allegiance to paganism. One of the intriguing aspects of 'Goblin Market' is that it somehow works the other way, appropriating the imagery of fairy tale into a Christian framework.

Rossetti combines symbolism and dream imagery with hypnotic skill, not just in her most famous poem, but elsewhere as well. For example, her enigmatic poem entitled simply 'My Dream' relies on nightmarish images of cannibalistic crocodiles to convey its suggestion of a subversive vision of patriarchal attitudes. Other women poets followed her example, venturing across the border from narrative realism into a strange country of fantasy drawn from the preconscious. Mary Coleridge and Rosamund Marriott Watson were both extremely gifted at surreal symbolism, hinting at realms of darkness in the human spirit which are anything but congruent with any ideal of happy domesticity as the natural goal of female desires. Even the age-old 'language of flowers', traditionally associated with women, whereby feelings could be expressed in a kind of code well understood by readers familiar from childhood with the meanings attributed to different species, lends itself to some unexpected manipulation in the verse of Rossetti and others.

A restless undercurrent of energy inhabits Victorian women's poetry – it pulses through the narcissistic rage and excess of Manken, runs underground in Levy and Pfeiffer, finds comic relief in Naden and Kendall, dramatises itself in Barrett Browning and Webster, broods in Coleridge and Watson, seeks transcendence in Blind and Rossetti, finds a momentary balance in Hemans and Field. But however we as readers interpret this power, and judge its results, I think we can sense its emanation from the daily struggle these women felt in their desire to rise above their status as second-class citizens and produce a first-rate memorial to themselves, their times and their lived experience.

NOTE ON THE TEXT OF THIS ANTHOLOGY

Each of the thirteen poets selected for this anthology has her work introduced by a headnote giving biographical and critical information. Wherever possible, copy-texts have been taken from a lifetime collected edition, or from a lifetime volume publication. The poets have been arranged in chronological order of birth date. Each poem has been comprehensively annotated with explanatory notes intended to help students new to the study of nineteenth-century poetry. Placed at the end of the volume is a Bibliography of secondary sources of relevance to the further study of Victorian women's poetry both in general, and in relation to individual poets.

THE POETS

FELICIA HEMANS (1793–1835)

Felicia Dorothea Hemans (*pronounced Hemmans*) was born in Liverpool, where her Irish father, George Browne, was a merchant. Her mother, Felicity Dorothea, *née* Wagner, was of German origin. In 1800, after her father suffered business reverses, the family moved to North Wales, a country Hemans came to love, and here the unusually gifted child (with a phenomenal memory) learned Latin, drawing and modern languages. Although she never travelled abroad, she later wrote many poems about other European countries, based mainly on her reading. She grew up to be one of the most widely read and influential poets of the nineteenth century, both at home in Britain, and in America (where she was especially well loved).

At 14 she published her first collection of verse, called simply *Poems*; notwithstanding its 17-page list of subscribers, it was treated harshly by reviewers. In the same year, she also published a poem inspired by the exploits of her two brothers who were engaged in fighting in the Peninsular Wars; this was called *England and Spain, or Valour and Patriotism*. Her attraction to such topics must have helped draw her into an early engagement and then marriage in 1812 to Captain Alfred Hemans, a charming Irish ex-soldier. At this time, she published another volume of poems, *The Domestic Affections*. This title denoted a theme which was to become, in a sense, her trademark. But by 1818, after she had produced two more volumes of poems and four sons (and was pregnant with a fifth), her husband left her to live abroad 'for the sake of his health' – or so they put it about. Thereafter, she remained in her mother's house (until her mother's death in 1827) with her sons and brought them up herself. Although she maintained a sporadic correspondence with her husband, and sent him a copy of each of her volumes as it was published, he never returned to the family. Yet she was never heard to complain publicly about his apparently cavalier treatment of her and the boys, preferring instead to avoid any scandal and devote herself to home life and her poetry. This was, in fact, how she made a living and educated her sons, for her poetry became a very marketable commodity and Hemans herself grew extremely skilled at selling it. In modern terminology, she exploited her 'image' as a blameless and submissive (*never* rebellious) victim of sad circumstances, selflessly doing her best for her five sons, to arouse a paternalistic generosity in her publishers (John Murray and, later, William Blackwood) and an eagerly sympathetic mood in her readers.

Hemans's first poem to be taken seriously by reviewers was *The Restoration of the Works of Art to Italy* (1816), a poem concerned with issues about Europe's recovery from the war, particularly Napoleon's theft of Italian masterpieces. Byron – who was an early hero of Hemans – himself admired this poem, though he scorned her next, *Modern Greece* (1817), as the work of one who had never travelled there. But the poem aims not to describe Greece so much as to argue for its importance in the (British) liberal imagination and, hence, the importance of its national freedom. Like the work of many people who are made to feel anxious about the adequacy of their education, the poem is burdened by copious learned footnotes. Yet Hemans was in fact very widely read and very skilled in languages, and her next volume, published in 1818, consisted of translations from Portuguese, Spanish and Italian, as well as some poems of her own. By this time, she had succeeded in making herself known to a wide readership and most of her subsequent publications proceeded quickly to a second edition. Her poems were admired by Shelley, Wordsworth, Arnold, and by Elizabeth Barrett, George Eliot and William Michael Rossetti. Her work was particularly praised for its moral purity as well as for the beauty and aptness of its form. The impression of purity comes from the fact that Hemans was never drawn to write anything resembling passionate love poetry, the 'domestic affections' remaining for her the safe ground in terms of subject matter, just as traditional verse forms satisfied a certain need for regularity. Hemans was never an experimental poet.

Hemans really found her *métier* in 1828 with the publication of *Records of Woman*. This volume contained a series of dramatic lyrics each dedicated to celebrating the achievements of a number of widely assorted women, some of whom are famous figures like Joan of Arc, but others far less widely known and operating entirely within a domestic sphere (like 'Pauline', for example, a mother who died trying to save her daughter from a fire), yet nonetheless demonstrating remarkable powers of fortitude under extreme conditions. It is probably significant that Hemans's own much-loved mother had died the previous year, in 1827, and that her other major female support, her sister Harriet (who was later to write her memoir), was preparing to leave home for marriage. Fire is a recurring motif in these poems – not only Pauline dies in the flames, but also the 'Wife of Asdrubal', a Medea-like figure who refuses to condone her husband's cowardly behaviour during the siege of Carthage and chooses instead to kill her two young sons and then consign her own living body with their dead ones to the conflagration (see p. 23 below). Joan of Arc is of course another famous example of female heroism, and it is notable that the traits Hemans chooses to emphasise in her Joan (or Joanne, as she spells it) are those of the domestic affections once again (see p. 31). It is her father and brothers, suddenly glimpsed in the throng, that she yearns towards during her hour of crisis. Calling for her father's blessing, she suddenly longs to revisit her peasant home, with its serenity and natural beauty. But it is of course too late for that: Fate has caught her up on a quite different path, and the poem turns at its end to point a moral dear to Hemans's own heart:

> Oh! never did thine eye
> Through the green haunts of happy infancy
> Wander again, Joanne! – too much of fame
> Had shed its radiance on thy peasant name;
> And bought alone by gifts beyond all price –
> The trusting heart's repose, the paradise
> Of home, with all its loves – doth fate allow
> The crown of glory unto woman's brow.

('Joan of Arc in Rheims', ll. 87–94)

The key dramatic moment for Hemans appears always to be the moment of recognition that domestic happiness is shattered beyond recall. She replayed the theme of woman and fame almost compulsively, turning it over and over in her verse, always to arrive at the same conclusion: they do not mix. Or, if they do, they cannot remain compatible with the woman's happiness. Her poem 'Properzia Rossi' (see p. 26), about a female sculptor who dies from unrequited love, reiterates the point, when its gifted heroine declares her longing to weep on her beloved's breast: 'But that were happiness, and unto me / Earth's gift is *fame*.' It is rather like some ceremony based on superstition, whereby the poet (or 'poetess' as she would have called herself) could only keep the feared evil consequences of her own increasing fame at bay by constantly forswearing any desire for it. Yet we have to remember that it was her fame that brought her the much-needed income to raise her growing family.

With a poet like Hemans, it is never wise to underestimate the intelligence at work behind the seemingly conservative façade. Recent criticism by Tricia Lootens, Paula Feldman and others has shown that the conservative values of her poetry were not unmixed with a certain power of criticism. Her famous set-piece, so often recited at school gatherings, 'Casabianca' – 'The boy stood on the burning deck . . .' – is the most well-known case in point, as it is quite possible to move away from a traditional reading of the poem as a celebration of warfare and patriotism towards an appreciation of its subtle critique of pig-headed patriarchal values that sacrifice young lives for vainglorious causes (see pp. 37–9). The penchant for the dramatic moment evidenced in this poem had been exploited more fully in 1823 with the publication of *The Siege of Valencia. A Dramatic Poem*, and *The Vespers of Palermo*, her one full-length drama written to be acted, which was staged successfully in Edinburgh after a failure in London.

Hemans's poetry demonstrates a more subtle use of language than is often appreciated, despite her liberal use of poeticisms and archaisms. She had a very good ear, and operates in a variety of verse forms from blank verse to comic couplets to rhyming quatrains. Although she does not baulk at the sentimental set-piece (e.g. 'The Homes of England', p. 34) and glorifies national virtues, she reveres courage – especially female courage – above all other virtues, and domestic affection (as against romantic love) over all other values. Nor was she devoid of a sense of humour, as is shown in the first poem reproduced below, 'Epitaph on Mr W—' (p. 22). This poem, as well as being amusing in its light-hearted teasing of scientific earnestness, is interesting as a precursor to verse by later women poets such as Kendall and Naden, who also enjoyed making fun of (male) scientific pretension. But whereas their poems ranged themselves on the side of the new spirit of scientific enquiry and debate, and against old-style Christianity, Hemans makes no such move. Instead, she treats geology and the evidence of fossils as a quaintness, an idiosyncracy, and certainly gives no sense that she feels pressed by them to question the existence of God.

Text: The poems chosen are from *Tales and Historic Scenes, in Verse* (1819), *Records of Woman with Other Poems* (1828), *The Forest Sanctuary, and Other Poems* (1825; 2nd edn 1829), Henry Fothergill Chorley, *Memorials of Mrs. Hemans, with Illustrations of her Literary Character from her Private Correspondence* (1836; 2nd edn 1837), and *Works* (1839). The date of first publication in volume form is given in square brackets at the foot of each poem. The copy-text used is *The Works of Mrs. Hemans; with a Memoir of her Life, by her Sister*, 7 vols, Edinburgh: William Blackwood & Sons; London:

Thomas Cadell (1839), with the exception of 'Epitaph on Mr W—', which is taken from Chorley, *Memorials of Mrs. Hemans, with Illustrations of her Literary Character from her Private Correspondence*, 2nd edn, 2 vols, London: Saunders and Otley (1837).

Epitaph on Mr W—.

A Celebrated Mineralogist

STOP, passenger! a wondrous tale to list –
Here lies a famous mineralogist!
Famous, indeed, – such traces of his power,
He's left from Penmanbach to Penmanmawr, –
5   Such caves, and chasms, and fissures in the rocks,
His works resemble those of earthquake shocks;
And future ages very much may wonder
What mighty giant rent the hills asunder;
Or whether Lucifer himself had ne'er
10   Gone with his crew to play at foot-ball there.

His fossils, flints, and spars, of every hue,
With him, good reader, here lie buried too!
Sweet specimens, which, toiling to obtain,
He split huge cliffs, like so much wood, in twain:
15   We knew, so great the fuss he made about them,
Alive or dead, he ne'er would rest without them;
So, to secure soft slumber to his bones,
We paved his grave with all his favourite stones.

Epitaph on Mr W—, A Celebrated Mineralogist] Great strides were made in the science of studying minerals during the eighteenth and nineteenth centuries, and the search for evidence of earlier life forms embedded in rock strata gained wide popularity. 'Mr W—' was C. Pleydell N. Wilton, a Cambridge mathematics student who spent the summer of 1816 (when the poem was written) with other students in the Welsh countryside; later he emigrated to New South Wales. Hemans presented him with a copy of this and another poem (addressed to his hammer), but did not publish it. It was first published in Chorley (1836); it is also included in Hemans, ed. Hughes (1839).

1. list] listen (to).

4. Penmanbach, Penmanmawr] Welsh place names.

9. Lucifer] Prince of devils.

11. spars] a general term for a number of crystalline minerals.

17–22.] The poem jokes here with the idea that this very modern scientist is buried in the Anglo-Saxon (and, of course, pagan) ritual manner of enclosing with him in his grave precious relics symbolising aspects of his life.

His much-loved hammer's resting by his side,
20   Each hand contains a shell-fish petrified;
His mouth a piece of pudding-stone incloses,
And at his feet a lump of coal reposes:
Sure he was born beneath some lucky planet,
His very coffin-plate is made of granite!

25   Weep not, good reader! he is truly blest
Amidst chalcedony and quartz to rest –
Weep not for him! but envied be his doom,
Whose tomb, though small, for all he loved had room: –
And, O ye rocks! schist, gneiss, whate'er ye be,
30   Ye varied strata, names too hard for me,
Sing, 'Oh, be joyful!' for your direst foe,
By death's fell hammer is at length laid low.
Ne'er on your spoils again shall — riot,
Shut up your cloudy brows and rest in quiet!
35   He sleeps – no longer planning hostile actions, –
As cold as any of his petrifactions;
Enshrined in specimens of every hue,
Too tranquil e'en to dream, ye rocks! of you.

[1836: written 1816]

The Wife of Asdrubal

['This governor, who had braved death when it was at a distance, and protested that the sun should never see him survive Carthage – this fierce Asdrubal was so mean-spirited as to come alone, and privately throw himself at the conqueror's feet.

---

20. petrified] changed into stone.

21. pudding-stone] properly called 'conglomerate': a composite rock of smooth fragments cemented together.

24. coffin-plate] name-plate on a coffin.

26. chalcedony] a term that covers a number of quartz-like precious stones, e.g. agate, onyx. *quartz*] a crystalline mineral.

29. schist] a species of crystalline rock with parallel internal structures.   *gneiss*] a rock with a laminated structure.

The Wife of Asdrubal] *Asdrubal* (or Hasdrubal) was governor of Carthage and leader of its army at the time of the third Punic War, when Carthage was sacked by Rome. The war lasted three years, and this famous ancient city finally fell to the Roman general Scipio Aemilianus in 146 BC. Byrsa was the main citadel or fortress guarding Carthage.

The general, pleased to see his proud rival humbled, granted his life, and kept him to grace his triumph. The Carthaginians in the citadel no sooner understood that their commander had abandoned the place, than they threw open the gates, and put the proconsul in possession of Byrsa. The Romans had now no enemy to contend with but the nine hundred deserters, who, being reduced to despair, retired into the temple of Esculapius, which was a second citadel within the first: there the proconsul attacked them; and these unhappy wretches, finding there was no way to escape, set fire to the temple. As the flames spread, they retreated from one part to another, till they got to the roof of the building: there Asdrubal's wife appeared in her best apparel, as if the day of her death had been a day of triumph; and after having uttered the most bitter imprecations against her husband, whom she saw standing below with Emilianus, – "Base coward!" said she, "the mean things thou hast done to save thy life shall not avail thee; thou shalt die this instant, at least in thy two children." Having thus spoken, she drew out a dagger, stabbed them both, and while they were yet struggling for life, threw them from the top of the temple, and leaped down after them into the flames.' – *Ancient Universal History*. Author's note.]

THE sun sets brightly – but a ruddier glow
O'er Afric's heaven the flames of Carthage throw;
Her walls have sunk, and pyramids of fire
In lurid splendour from her domes aspire;
5   Sway'd by the wind, they wave – while glares the sky
As when the desert's red simoom is nigh;
The sculptured altar, and the pillar'd hall,
Shine out in dreadful brightness ere they fall;
Far o'er the seas the light of ruin streams,
10   Rock, wave, and isle are crimson'd by its beams;
While captive thousands, bound in Roman chains,
Gaze in mute horror on their burning fanes;
And shouts of triumph, echoing far around,
Swell from the victors' tents with ivy crown'd.
15   But mark! from yon fair temple's loftiest height
What towering form bursts wildly on the sight,
All regal in magnificent attire,
And sternly beauteous in terrific ire?
She might be deem'd a Pythia in the hour
20   Of dread communion and delirious power;

---

6. *simoom*] a hot, suffocating sand wind.

12. *fanes*] temples.

14.] It was a Roman custom to adorn the tents of victors with ivy [Author's note].

19.] Pythia, a priestess of Apollo, the sun-god, delivered spectacular oracles at Delphi while enthroned amidst swirling sulphurous vapours which provided her inspiration.

A being more than earthly, in whose eye
There dwells a strange and fierce ascendancy.
The flames are gathering round – intensely bright,
Full on her features glares their meteor-light;
25   But a wild courage sits triumphant there,
The stormy grandeur of a proud despair;
A daring spirit, in its woes elate,
Mightier than death, untameable by fate.
The dark profusion of her locks unbound,
30   Waves like a warrior's floating plumage round;
Flush'd is her cheek, inspired her haughty mien,
She seems th' avenging goddess of the scene.
Are those *her* infants, that with suppliant cry
Cling round her, shrinking as the flame draws nigh,
35   Clasp with their feeble hands her gorgeous vest,
And fain would rush for shelter to her breast?
Is that a mother's glance, where stern disdain,
And passion, awfully vindictive, reign?

Fix'd is her eye on Asdrubal, who stands
40   Ignobly safe amidst the conquering bands;
On him who left her to that burning tomb,
Alone to share her children's martyrdom;
Who, when his country perish'd, fled the strife,
And knelt to win the worthless boon of life.
45   'Live, traitor, live!' she cries, 'since dear to thee
E'en in thy fetters, can existence be!
Scorn'd and dishonour'd live! – with blasted name,
The Roman's triumph not to grace, but shame.
O slave in spirit! bitter be thy chain
50   With tenfold anguish to avenge my pain!
Still may the manes of thy children rise
To chase calm slumber from thy wearied eyes;
Still may their voices on the haunted air

---

24. *meteor-light*] with a light like that of a shooting star, luminous from its own heat.

27. *elate*] proud or lofty in spirit.

31. *mien*] bearing or expression.

33. *suppliant*] entreating.

48.] i.e. Asdrubal's personal surrender to Rome will only add to the sum of Rome's shame, not to its glory, in its victory over Carthage.

51. *manes*] the ghost of a dead person demanding propitiation. Pronounced in two syllables.

In fearful whispers tell thee to despair,
55   Till vain remorse thy wither'd heart consume,
Scourged by relentless shadows of the tomb!
E'en now my sons shall die – and thou, their sire,
In bondage safe, shalt yet in them expire.
Think'st thou I love them not? – 'Twas thine to fly –
60   'Tis mine with these to suffer and to die.
Behold their fate! – the arms that cannot save
Have been their cradle, and shall be their grave.'

Bright in her hand the lifted dagger gleams,
Swift from her children's hearts the life-blood streams;
65   With frantic laugh she clasps them to the breast
Whose woes and passions soon shall be at rest;
Lifts one appealing, frenzied glance on high,
Then deep 'midst rolling flames is lost to mortal eye.

[1819]

Properzia Rossi

[Properzia Rossi, a celebrated female sculptor of Bologna, possessed also of talents
for poetry and music, died in conseqence of an unrequited attachment. A paint-
ing, by Ducis, represents her showing her last work, a basso-relievo of Ariadne, to
a Roman knight, the object of her affection, who regards it with indifference.
Author's note.]

---

65. *frantic*] Used here in the archaic sense of ragingly mad: or, as Johnson's *Dictionary* gives it:
'transported by violence of passion'.

Properzia Rossi. *Note.*] *Properzia Rossi* (c.1490–1530) reputedly began her career as a carver of
peach-stones, later becoming a leading sculptor in marble for churches in *Bologna*, an
Italian city located north of Florence. Her story is told by Georgio Vasari in his *Lives of the
Painters* (rev. edn, 1568), who recounts her manifold talents. (Jean)-Louis *Ducis* (1775–1847)
was a French artist known for his technically brilliant 'story' paintings taken from history
and a kind of sentimental mythology. *Basso-relievo* or bas-relief is a sculpture or carving in
which the figures project less than half their true proportions from the background. *Ariadne*
was the daughter of King Minos who saved Theseus from being devoured by the Minotaur by
giving him a thread by which he found his way out of the labyrinth. Although Theseus then
married Ariadne, who loved him tenderly, he subsequently abandoned her. The volume from
which this poem is taken, *Records of Woman, with Other Poems* (1828), was dedicated to Joanna
Baillie (1762–1851), a Scottish poet and dramatist, 'as a slight token of grateful respect and
admiration'.

Tell me no more, no more
Of my soul's lofty gifts! Are they not vain
To quench its haunting thirst for happiness?
Have I not loved, and striven, and fail'd to bind
One true heart unto me, whereon my own
Might find a resting-place, a home for all
Its burden of affections? I depart,
Unknown, though Fame goes with me; I must leave
The earth unknown. Yet it may be that death
Shall give my name a power to win such tears
As would have made life precious.

I

ONE dream of passion and of beauty more!
And in its bright fulfilment let me pour
My soul away! Let earth retain a trace
Of that which lit my being, though its race
5   Might have been loftier far. Yet one more dream!
From my deep spirit one victorious gleam
Ere I depart! For thee alone, for thee!
May this last work, this farewell triumph be –
Thou, loved so vainly! I would leave enshrined
10   Something immortal of my heart and mind,
That yet may speak to thee when I am gone,
Shaking thine inmost bosom with a tone
Of lost affection; – something that may prove
What she hath been, whose melancholy love
15   On thee was lavish'd; silent pang and tear,
And fervent song, that gush'd when none were near,
And dream by night, and weary thought by day,
Stealing the brightness from her life away –
While thou – Awake! not yet within me die!
20   Under the burden and the agony
Of this vain tenderness – my spirit, wake!
Even for thy sorrowful affection's sake,
Live! in thy work breathe out! – that he may yet,
Feeling sad mastery there, perchance regret
25   Thine unrequited gift.

Epigraph.] Untraced: Hemans herself may have invented it for the occasion. Andrew Ashfield believes that the epigraph is 'probably by Hemans herself': Ashfield, 1995, p. 313.

II

It comes – the power
Within me born flows back – my fruitless dower
That could not win me love. Yet once again
I greet it proudly, with its rushing train
30   Of glorious images: – they throng – they press –
A sudden joy lights up my loneliness –
I shall not perish all!
         The bright work grows
Beneath my hand, unfolding, as a rose,
Leaf after leaf, to beauty; line by line,
35   I fix my thought, heart, soul, to burn, to shine,
Through the pale marble's veins. It grows! – and now
I give my own life's history to thy brow,
Forsaken Ariadne! thou shalt wear
My form, my lineaments; but oh! more fair,
40   Touch'd into lovelier being by the glow
     Which in me dwells, as by the summer light
All things are glorified. From thee my woe
     Shall yet look beautiful to meet his sight,
When I am pass'd away. Thou art the mould,
45   Wherein I pour the fervent thoughts, th' untold,
The self-consuming! Speak to him of me,
Thou, the deserted by the lonely sea,
With the soft sadness of thine earnest eye –
Speak to him, lorn one! deeply, mournfully,
50   Of all my love and grief! Oh! could I throw
Into thy frame a voice, a sweet, and low,
And thrilling voice of song! when he came nigh,
To send the passion of its melody
Through his pierced bosom – on its tones to bear
55   My life's deep feeling, as the southern air
Wafts the faint myrtle's breath – to rise, to swell,
To sink away in accents of farewell,

32.] Cf. Horace: 'Non omnis moriar', I shall not wholly die (*Odes* III.xxx.6). This famous ode addresses the question of posthumous fame, and asserts the poet's confidence that his works will form a monument 'more lasting than brass, and more sublime than the . . . pyramids' (Christopher Smart's translation, rev. T. A. Buckley, *The Works of Horace*, London: G. Bell & Sons, 1888, p. 93).

56. *the faint myrtle's breath*] The myrtle was held sacred to Venus and is used as an emblem of love.

Winning but one, *one* gush of tears, whose flow
Surely my parted spirit yet might know,
60   If love be strong as death!

III

Now fair thou art,
Thou form, whose life is of my burning heart
Yet all the vision that within me wrought,
 I cannot make thee! Oh! I might have given
65   Birth to creations of far nobler thought;
 I might have kindled, with the fire of heaven,
Things not of such as die! But I have been
Too much alone; – a heart whereon to lean,
With all these deep affections that o'erflow
70   My aching soul and find no shore below;
An eye to be my star; a voice to bring
Hope o'er my path like sounds that breathe of spring:
These are denied me – dreamt of still in vain –
Therefore my brief aspirings from the chain,
75   Are ever but as some wild fitful song,
Rising triumphantly, to die erelong
In dirge-like echoes.

IV

Yet the world will see
Little of this, my parting work, in thee –
80   Thou shalt have fame! – Oh, mockery! give the reed
From storms a shelter – give the drooping vine
Something round which its tendrils may entwine –
 Give the parch'd flower a rain-drop, and the meed
Of love's kind words to woman! Worthless fame!
85   That in *his* bosom wins not for my name
Th' abiding place it ask'd! Yet how my heart,
In its own fairy world of song and art,
Once beat for praise! Are those high longings o'er?
That which I have been can I be no more?
90   Never! oh, never more! though still thy sky

60.] Cf. Song of Solomon 8: 6: 'Set me as a seal upon thy heart, as a seal upon thine arm: for love is strong as death.'

77. dirge-like] like a funeral song.

83. meed] reward.

Be blue as then, my glorious Italy!
And though the music, whose rich breathings fill
Thine air with soul, be wandering past me still;
And though the mantle of thy sunlight streams,
95   Unchanged on forms, instinct with poet-dreams:
Never! oh, never more! Where'er I move,
The shadow of this broken-hearted love
Is on me and around! Too well *they* know,
    Whose life is all within, too soon and well,
100   When there the blight hath settled! – but I go
      Under the silent wings of peace to dwell;
From the slow wasting, from the lonely pain,
The inward burning of those words – '*in vain,*'
    Sear'd on the heart – I go. 'Twill soon be past,
105   Sunshine, and song, and bright Italian heaven,
     And thou, Oh! thou, on whom my spirit cast
Unvalued wealth – who know'st not what was given
In that devotedness – the sad, and deep,
And unrepaid – farewell! If I could weep
110   Once, only once, beloved one! on thy breast,
Pouring my heart forth ere I sink to rest!
But that were happiness, and unto me
Earth's gift is *fame*. Yet I was form'd to be
So richly bless'd! With thee to watch the sky,
115   Speaking not, feeling but that thou wert nigh:
With thee to listen, while the tones of song
Swept even as part of our sweet air along –
To listen silently: with thee to gaze
On forms, the deified of olden days –
120   This had been joy enough; and hour by hour,
From its glad well-springs drinking life and power,
How had my spirit soar'd, and made its fame
    A glory for thy brow! Dreams, dreams! – the fire
Burns faint within me. Yet I leave my name –
125   As a deep thrill may linger on the lyre
When its full chords are hush'd – awhile to live,
And one day haply in thy heart revive
Sad thoughts of me: – I leave it, with a sound,
A spell o'er memory, mournfully profound –

---

119. forms, the deified of olden days] classical statues of the gods.

121. well-springs] sources of never-ending supply.

130   I leave it, on my country's air to dwell –
        Say proudly yet – ' *'Twas hers who loved me well!'*

[1828]

Joan of Arc in Rheims

['Jeanne d'Arc avait eu la joie de voir à Chalons quelques amis de son enfance. Une joie plus ineffable encore l'attendait à Rheims, au sein de son triomphe: Jacques d'Arc, son père, y se trouva, aussitôt que de troupes de Charles VII. y furent entrées; et comme les deux frères de notre heroine l'avaient accompagnés, elle se vit, pour un instant au milieu de sa famille, dans les bras d'un père vertueux.' – *Vie de Jeanne d'Arc.*]

       Thou hast a charmed cup, O Fame!
        A draught that mantles high,
       And seems to lift this earthborn frame
        Above mortality:
       Away! to me – a woman – bring
       Sweet waters from affection's spring.

     THAT was a joyous day in Rheims of old,
     When peal on peal of mighty music roll'd
     Forth from her throng'd cathedral; while around,
     A multitude, whose billows made no sound,
5   Chain'd to a hush of wonder, though elate
     With victory, listen'd at their temple's gate.
     And what was done within? – within, the light

Joan of Arc in Rheims. *Title.*] *Rheims*, or Reims, a cathedral city north-east of Paris, was the goal of Joan's mission to place the dauphin on the throne of France as Charles VII, and she saw him crowned in the cathedral there on 17 July 1429. Hemans may have been partly inspired by the famous epic poem *Joan of Arc* produced in 1796 (revised 1798) by the young Robert Southey (1774–1843). No one reads Southey now, but many did then, and Southey's sympathetic treatment of *Joan* ensured his popularity with a generation of women poets. However, the episode treated here by Hemans does not figure in Southey's poem.

Note.] Duncan Wu gives the following translation: 'Joan of Arc had had the pleasure of seeing some childhood friends at Châlons. A yet more sublime joy awaited her at Rheims, at the peak of her triumph. Jacques d'Arc, her father, had arrived there as soon as the troops of Charles VII had entered the city, and as our heroine's two brothers had accompanied him, she found herself momentarily amidst her family, and in the arms of a virtuous father.' He also notes that 'There were many lives of Joan of Arc in French; Hemans is probably using Jean Baptiste Prosper Jollois, *Histoire abrégée de la vie et des exploits de Jeanne d'Arc* (Paris, 1821)'. See Wu, 1997, p. 554.

Epigraph.] From one of her own poems, 'Woman and Fame' (see p. 39 below). Hemans had the habit of lifting chunks from her own works for her epigraphs.

Through the rich gloom of pictured windows flowing,
Tinged with soft awfulness a stately sight,
10   The chivalry of France their proud heads bowing
In martial vassalage! – While 'midst that ring,
And shadow'd by ancestral tombs, a king
Received his birthright's crown. For this, the hymn
Swell'd out like rushing waters, and the day
15   With the sweet censer's misty breath grew dim,
As through long aisles it floated o'er th' array
Of arms and sweeping stoles. But who, alone
And unapproach'd, beside the altar stone,
With the white banner forth like sunshine streaming,
20   And the gold helm thro' clouds of fragrance gleaming,
Silent and radiant stood? – the helm was raised,
And the fair face reveal'd, that upward gazed,
Intensely worshipping: – a still, clear face,
Youthful, but brightly solemn! – Woman's cheek
25   And brow were there, in deep devotion meek,
Yet glorified, with inspiration's trace
On its pure paleness; while, enthroned above,
The pictured Virgin, with her smile of love,
Seem'd bending o'er her votaress. That slight form!
30   Was that the leader through the battle storm?
Had the soft light in that adoring eye
Guided the warrior where the swords flash'd high?
'Twas so, even so! – and thou, the shepherd's child,
Joanne, the lowly dreamer of the wild!
35   Never before, and never since that hour,
Hath woman, mantled with victorious power,
Stood forth as *thou* beside the shrine didst stand,
Holy amidst the knighthood of the land;
And beautiful with joy and with renown,
40   Lift thy white banner o'er the olden crown,
Ransom'd for France by thee!

---

10. chivalry] noblemen.

11. martial vassalage] 'Vassals' are servants of a feudal lord; here the meaning suggests a war-like subjection or homage.

15. censer's misty breath] vessel containing smoking incense used as part of church rites.

17. stoles] ceremonial robes.

20. helm] archaic poetic word for helmet.

29. votaress] a female bound to the religious life.

The rites are done.

Now let the dome with trumpet notes be shaken,
And bid the echoes of the tomb awaken,
   And come thou forth, that Heaven's rejoicing sun
45   May give thee welcome from thine own blue skies,
      Daughter of victory! – A triumphant strain,
A proud rich stream of warlike melodies,
      Gush'd through the portals of the antique fane,
And forth she came. Then rose a nation's sound –
50   Oh! what a power to bid the quick heart bound,
The wind bears onward with the stormy cheer
Man gives to glory on her high career!
Is there indeed such power? – far deeper dwells
In one kind household voice, to reach the cells
55   Whence happiness flows forth! The shouts that fill'd
The hollow heaven tempestuously, were still'd
One moment; and in that brief pause, the tone,
As of a breeze that o'er her home had blown,
Sank on the bright maid's heart. – 'Joanne!' – Who spoke
60   Like those whose childhood with *her* childhood grew
Under one roof? – 'Joanne!' – *that* murmur broke
      With sounds of weeping forth! – She turn'd – she knew
Beside her, mark'd from all the thousands there,
In the calm beauty of his silver hair,
65   The stately shepherd; and the youth, whose joy
From his dark eye flash'd proudly; and the boy,
The youngest born, that ever loved her best: –
'Father! and ye, my brothers!' – On the breast
Of that grey sire she sank – and swiftly back,
70   Even in an instant, to their native track
Her free thoughts flow'd. – She saw the pomp no more
The plumes, the banners: – to her cabin-door,
And to the Fairy's fountain in the glade,
Where her young sisters by her side had play'd,
75   And to her hamlet's chapel, where it rose
Hallowing the forest unto deep repose,
Her spirit turn'd. The very wood-note, sung
      In early spring-time by the bird, which dwelt

---

48. *portals . . . fane*] doors . . . temple.

73. *Fairy's fountain*] a beautiful fountain near Domremi, believed to be haunted by fairies, and a favourite resort of Jeanne d'Arc in her childhood [Author's note]. Wu notes: 'Domremy La Pucelle, a village in the department of Meuse, was Joan's birthplace': Wu, 1997, p. 556.

Where o'er her father's roof the beech leaves hung,
80   Was in her heart; a music heard and felt,
Winning her back to nature. She unbound
    The helm of many battles from her head,
And, with her bright locks bow'd to sweep the ground,
    Lifting her voice up, wept for joy and said –
85 'Bless me, my father, bless me! and with thee,
To the still cabin and the beechen-tree,
Let me return!'
                              Oh! never did thine eye
Through the green haunts of happy infancy
Wander again, Joanne! – too much of fame
90 Had shed its radiance on thy peasant name;
And bought alone by gifts beyond all price –
The trusting heart's repose, the paradise
Of home, with all its loves – doth fate allow
The crown of glory unto woman's brow.

[1828]

The Homes of England

'Where's the coward that would not dare
To fight for such a land?'

Marmion

THE stately Homes of England,
    How beautiful they stand!
Amidst their tall ancestral trees,
    O'er all the pleasant land.
5   The deer across their greensward bound,
    Through shade and sunny gleam,
And the swan glides past them with the sound
    Of some rejoicing stream.

The Homes of England. *Epigraph.*] *Marmion. A Tale of Flodden Field* (1808), a poem in six can-
tos by Sir Walter Scott. Widely popular in its day, it encompasses tales of true love and perfidy
set amidst scenes of martial heroics in the defeat of the Scots by the English. This quotation
occurs at IV.xxx.34–5. The lines are spoken by Fitz-Eustace, an English squire, although he is
describing the city of Edinburgh and its surrounds. When this poem was first printed in
Blackwood's Edinburgh Magazine XXIV (Nov 1828), the epigraph was taken from a play by the
Scottish writer Joanna Baillie (*Ethwald: a tragedy*), to whom *Records of Woman* is dedicated. See
Ashfield, 1995, p. 312.

5. *greensward.*] turf. See the usage in *Marmion* IV.iv.1: 'The green-sward way was smooth and
good' cited in the *OED*.

The merry Homes of England!
10   Around their hearths by night,
What gladsome looks of household love
        Meet in the ruddy light!
There woman's voice flows forth in song,
        Or childhood's tale is told,
15 Or lips move tunefully along
        Some glorious page of old.

The blessed Homes of England!
        How softly on their bowers
Is laid the holy quietness
20   That breathes from Sabbath hours!
Solemn, yet sweet, the church-bell's chime
        Floats through their woods at morn;
All other sounds, in that still time,
        Of breeze and leaf are born.

25 The Cottage Homes of England!
        By thousands on her plains,
They are smiling o'er the silvery brooks,
        And round the hamlet fanes.
Through glowing orchards forth they peep,
30   Each from its nook of leaves,
And fearless there the lowly sleep,
        As the bird beneath their eaves.

The free, fair Homes of England!
        Long, long, in hut and hall,
35 May hearts of native proof be rear'd
        To guard each hallow'd wall!
And green for ever be the groves,
        And bright the flowery sod,
Where first the child's glad spirit loves
40   Its country and its God!

[1828]

23–4.] i.e. the only other sounds to be heard at this quiet time are those made by ('born of')
breeze and leaf.

28. hamlet fanes] village churches.

35. of native proof] i.e. of the tried strength and quality of the native-born English person.

The Palm-tree

IT waved not through an eastern sky,
Beside a fount of Araby;
It was not fann'd by southern breeze
In some green isle of Indian seas;
5   Nor did its graceful shadow sleep
O'er stream of Afric, lone and deep.

But fair the exiled palm-tree grew
'Midst foliage of no kindred hue;
Through the laburnum's dropping gold
10   Rose the light shaft of orient mould,
And Europe's violets, faintly sweet,
Purpled the moss-beds at its feet.

Strange look'd it there! – the willow stream'd
Where silvery waters near it gleam'd;
15   The lime bough lured the honey-bee
To murmur by the desert's tree,
And showers of snowy roses made
A lustre in its fan-like shade.

There came an eve of festal hours –
20   Rich music fill'd that garden's bowers:
Lamps, that from flowering branches hung,
On sparks of dew soft colour flung,
And bright forms glanced – a fairy show –
Under the blossoms to and fro.

25   But one, a lone one, 'midst the throng,
Seem'd reckless all of dance or song:
He was a youth of dusky mien,
Whereon the Indian sun had been,
Of crested brow and long black hair –
30   A stranger, like the palm-tree, there.

The Palm-tree] This incident is, I think, recorded by De Lille, in his poem of *Les Jardins* [Author's note]. There is indeed an account of a smiliar incident in Canto 2 involving a tree of an exotic species, although the palm tree is not specifically named in the translation. See *The Gardens, A Poem*, translated from the French of the Abbé De Lille by Mrs Montolieu, 1798; 2nd edn, London: T. Bensley, 1805, pp. 63–4. Jacques, Abbé Delille (1738–1813) published *Les Jardins* in 1782.

27. mien] appearance.

And slowly, sadly, moved his plumes,
Glittering athwart the leafy glooms:
He pass'd the pale green olives by,
Nor won the chestnut flowers his eye;
35   But when to that sole palm he came,
Then shot a rapture through his frame!

To him, to him its rustling spoke,
The silence of his soul it broke!
It whisper'd of his own bright isle,
40   That lit the ocean with a smile;
Ay, to his ear that native tone
Had something of the sea wave's moan!

His mother's cabin home, that lay
Where feathery cocoas fringed the bay;
45   The dashing of his brethren's oar –
The conch-note heard along the shore;
All through his wakening bosom swept –
He clasp'd his country's tree and wept!

Oh, scorn him not! – the strength whereby
50   The patriot girds himself to die,
Th' unconquerable power which fills
The freeman battling on his hills –
These have one fountain deep and clear –
The same whence gush'd that childlike tear!

[1828]

Casabianca

THE boy stood on the burning deck
    Whence all but he had fled;
The flame that lit the battle's wreck,
    Shone round him o'er the dead.

---

32. *athwart*] across, in the sense of impeding forward progress.

46. *conch-note*] A conch is a kind of seashell that can be used to make a trumpet-like call.

Casabianca. *Title.*] Young Casabianca, a boy about 13 years old, son to the Admiral of the Orient, remained at his post (in the Battle of the Nile) after the ship had taken fire, and all the guns had been abandoned; and perished in the explosion of the vessel, when the flames had

5   Yet beautiful and bright he stood,
    As born to rule the storm;
  A creature of heroic blood,
    A proud, though child-like form.

  The flames roll'd on – he would not go
10   Without his Father's word;
  That Father, faint in death below,
    His voice no longer heard.

  He call'd aloud: – 'Say, Father, say
    If yet my task is done?'
15   He knew not that the chieftain lay
    Unconscious of his son.

  'Speak, Father!' once again he cried,
    'If I may yet be gone!'
  And but the booming shots replied,
20   And fast the flames roll'd on.

  Upon his brow he felt their breath,
    And in his waving hair,
  And look'd from that lone post of death,
    In still, yet brave despair.

25   And shouted but once more aloud,
    'My Father! must I stay?'
  While o'er him fast, through sail and shroud,
    The wreathing fires made way.

  They wrapt the ship in splendour wild,
30   They caught the flag on high,
  And stream'd above the gallant child,
    Like banners in the sky.

---

reached the powder [Author's note]. This note is mistaken in claiming the boy was son to the Admiral: his father, Louis de Casabianca (1762–1798), Corsican naval officer, was captain of the *Orient* under Admiral Brueys. The Battle of the Nile was a great victory for Lord Nelson against Napoleon's navy in which all but two of the French ships were destroyed. Young *Casabianca*, whose name was Giacomo Jacante, refused to leave his father's ship when it caught fire and is reputed to have died trying to save his father.

19. but] only.

27. shroud] set of ropes attached to the mast and forming part of a ship's rigging; can also suggest another meaning, of a winding sheet in which a corpse is laid out for burial.

There came a burst of thunder sound –
The boy – oh! where was he?
35   Ask of the winds that far around
With fragments strew'd the sea! –

With mast, and helm, and pennon fair,
That well had borne their part –
But the noblest thing which perish'd there
40   Was that young faithful heart!

[1829]

Woman and Fame

THOU hast a charmed cup, O Fame!
A draught that mantles high,
And seems to lift this earthly frame
Above mortality.
5   Away! to me – a woman – bring
Sweet waters from affection's spring.

Thou hast green laurel leaves, that twine
Into so proud a wreath;
For that resplendent gift of thine,

---

37. *pennon*] long, pointed streamer.

Date.] 'Casabianca' first appeared in volume form in America, in *The League of the Alps; The Siege of Valencia; The Vespers of Palermo; and Other Poems* (1826–8), 2 vols, ed. A. Norton, Boston, MA. 1829 is the date of first volume publication in England.

Woman and Fame] In some editions, 'Woman and Fame' had an epigraph taken from Hemans's poem 'Corinne at the Capitol': 'Happy – happier far than thou, / With the laurel on thy brow; / She that makes the humblest hearth / Lovely but to one on earth.' Susan J. Wolfson notes that 'Woman and Fame' is the title of Book II of de Staël's novel *Corinne, ou l'Italie* (1807) Wilson and Haefner, 1994, p. 159. For the importance of de Staël's novel to nineteenth-century women writers, see Moers, 1963, pp. 173–210.

1. *charmed*] Pronounced in two syllables: charmèd.

2. *A draught that mantles high*] a drink that foams up; or, possibly, that causes a high colour or blush: i.e. an intoxicating drink.

7–8.] A laurel wreath (made from the bay-tree or bay-laurel) was the traditional reward for heroic victory, and also for distinction in poetry.

10   Heroes have smiled in death:
             Give *me* from some kind hand a flower,
             The record of one happy hour!

             Thou hast a voice, whose thrilling tone
                Can bid each life-pulse beat
15   As when a trumpet's note hath blown,
                Calling the brave to meet:
             But mine, let mine – a woman's breast,
             By words of home-born love be bless'd.

             A hollow sound is in thy song,
20   A mockery in thine eye,
             To the sick heart that doth but long
                For aid, for sympathy –
             For kindly looks to cheer it on,
             For tender accents that are gone.

25   Fame, Fame! thou canst not be the stay
                Unto the drooping reed,
             The cool fresh fountain in the day
                Of the soul's feverish need:
             Where must the lone one turn or flee? –
30   Not unto thee – oh! not to thee!

             [1839]

To a Wandering Female Singer

             THOU hast loved and thou hast suffer'd!
                Unto feeling deep and strong,
             Thou hast trembled like a harp's frail string –
                I know it by thy song!

To a Wandering Female Singer] This poem might possibly be addressed to Letitia Elizabeth
Landon, or 'L.E.L.' (1802–1838), a well-known contemporary of Hemans whose major
poetic subject was the abandoned woman, dying for love, who is often also a poet (see, for
example, her 'Legacy of the Lute'). For a later echo, see Elizabeth Barrett Browning's *Sonnets
from the Portuguese*: 'A poor, tired, wandering singer, singing through / The dark, and leaning
up a cypress tree' (Sonnet III). Wordsworth's 'Solitary Reaper' also makes for an interesting
comparison.

5   Thou hast loved – it may be vainly –
       But well – oh! but too well –
     Thou hast suffer'd all that woman's breast
       May bear – but must not tell.

     Thou hast wept and thou hast parted,
10   Thou hast been forsaken long,
     Thou hast watch'd for steps that came not back –
       I know it by thy song!

     By the low clear silvery gushing
       Of its music from thy breast,
15   By the quivering of its flute-like swell –
       A sound of the heart's unrest.

     By its fond and plaintive lingering,
       On each word of grief so long,
     Oh! thou hast loved and suffer'd much –
20   I know it by thy song!

     [1839]

ELIZABETH BARRETT BROWNING (1806–1861)

Elizabeth Barrett Browning (EBB), poet, essayist, letter-writer, born in 1806, was the eldest of 12 children of Edward Moulton-Barrett, English gentleman and Jamaican landowner, and his wife, Mary, who died when Elizabeth was 22. Most of her childhood was spent at Hope End, the luxurious family home (from 1809) in idyllic rural surroundings in Herefordshire. Intellectually precocious, she began writing verse at an early age, encouraged and helped to publication by her parents. She devoted herself also to classical studies, learning Latin and Greek from her brother's tutor, and later taught herself Hebrew. By 13 she had written an imitative epic, 'The Battle of Marathon' (priv. pr. 1820). Her reading was prodigious, while her writing continued to develop as her main focus. Not unusually for a young woman poet, Byron was a strong early influence, along with the other Romantics. Yet she also enjoyed the outdoors, riding her beloved pony and exploring the family estate.

This carefree physical existence came to an end in her mid-teens, when she suffered a debilitating illness that marked the beginning of a lifelong invalidism, accompanied by an increasing addiction to opium, at that time commonly prescribed as medicine in the form of laudanum. In 1828 her mother died, and in 1832, upon the collapse of the family fortune, the household was suddenly forced to quit Hope End for London. EBB certainly knew of and later abhorred the slave-owning tradition of her family, though recent claims that the Barretts had African blood (see, for example, Markus, 1995) remain controversial. In 1836 EBB first met Mary Russell Mitford (1786–1855), an established writer who became her literary 'aunt' of sorts (Blain, 1990), and one of her most important literary correspondents. The 1830s also saw the beginning of her real poetic career with the publication of *The Seraphim* in 1838. In 1840 she suffered a tragic blow with the death by drowning of her favourite brother, during his visit to her at the seaside. In 1841 Mitford presented her with the spaniel Flush, who famously became her close companion in her room at Wimpole Street, but it took her several years to come to terms with the loss of her brother. Occupying her bedroom as a sort of literary sanctum, and protected by her invalid status from the usual duties of an eldest daughter to a widowed father, she applied herself with great intensity to her writing at this time.

In 1844 she published a book, titled simply *Poems*, which brought her general popularity, particularly for its ballads; it also contained 'A Drama of Exile', a narrative poem revising Milton's view of Eve, which gave the volume its title for the American market. It was *Poems* which first drew Robert Browning's attention to her, resulting in their correspondence, subsequent meeting in 1845, and elopement in 1846.

> Poetry has been so serious a thing to me as life itself; and life has been a very serious thing: there has been no playing at skittles for me in either. I never mistook pleasure for the final cause of poetry; nor leisure, for the hour of the poet.
> (*Poems*, 1844; repr. in Browning, ed. Porter and Clarke, 1990, Preface, vol. 2, p. 148)

EBB was unusually well educated for a woman of her time, and her fine intelligence makes excellent use of her classical reading in poems like 'A Musical Instrument' (see p. 79 below). EBB understood death and mortality, and her poetry often explores new ways of assimilating this knowledge: 'A Thought for a Lonely Death-bed' (see p. 45), for example, though less well known than 'Grief', indicates her recognition that each human being must finally make his or her spiritual journey alone as one individual soul. And like one who has truly faced up to mortality, she has a boundless relish for life and the living, and a deep appreciation of the supreme importance of love as the key positive value in human existence. Loving, for her, is always an active virtue, in contradistinction to the stereotyped view of Victorian females as gentle, passive, affectionate creatures who exist to receive strong passionate love, but not to offer it. Constancy and loyalty become in her hands the mainstay of truth to self as well as of romantic love for another, both being founded on the idea of a strong Christian love of God (see 'Loved Once', p. 61 for example, where the idea of a fickle or transient love having any value is roundly dismissed). A congregational Christian, EBB believed in the direct relation of the soul to God, with suffering and sorrow as part of God's purpose. Religion was not separate from daily life, but religion and poetry were both felt to be higher orders of existence.

Her deep belief in the truth of Christianity prompted her horror at the treatment of young children in the factories, such exploitation being sanctioned by the law in a supposedly Christian country. The hypocrisy of the capitalists appalled her, as it did many others, and EBB makes skilful use of the traditional role of women as mediators, as pleaders for mercy, even while she oversteps it by accusing the aptly named 'Fatherland' – a tacit recognition that political power indeed rests in the hands of the fathers – over the extent of the cruelties inflicted on very young and defenceless children by a society driven by greed. Later in her career, after her first-hand experience of marriage and motherhood, she was able to write equally feelingly (in 'Mother and Poet', p. 81) of the sense of outrage, grief and loss experienced by an Italian woman patriot, also a poet, whose own patriotic songs both inspired her sons to fight for their country's liberation from tyranny and, at the same time, sent them to their deaths, leaving her without a purpose in living. There are interesting connections to be made between these themes and some of those of Felicia Hemans, for example.

Yet, on the lighter side, EBB also has a sharp sense of humour, not above poking a little fun at the vanities of the opposite sex. Or, indeed, at her own, as the subtle interplay of the two sisters reveals in the ironies of 'Bertha in the Lane' (see p. 53), a dramatic monologue designed to expose the self-deceptions of the apparently righteous; the dying elder sister does her best to imbue the younger with a crippling load of guilt before she goes. But nevertheless, the genuine poignancy of loss of a mother pervades this poem too, alongside the ironised false feeling.

Perhaps partly because she felt herself to be implicated through her family's connection to slave-ownership, her protest poetry against slavery is especially heartfelt: as she wrote to John Ruskin in 1855, 'I belong to a family of West Indian slaveholders, and if I believed in curses, I should be afraid' (Browning, ed. Kenyon, 1897, vol. 2, p. 220; cited in Mermin, 1993, p. 157). 'The Runaway Slave', 'Hiram Powers' Greek Slave', and 'A Curse for a Nation' (see pp. 63, 72 and 75) are all powerful polemics utilising a range of rhetorical effect (repetitions with variations, sometimes in the form of a chorus or refrain, remain a favourite device) to maximise their impact on the reader. But EBB's best-known poem remains the sonnet beginning 'How do I love thee? Let me count the ways', from her sequence of love poems written privately for Robert and later published as *Sonnets from the Portuguese* (1850). 'How do I love thee?' has probably achieved by now the dubious distinction of citation in more advertising copy than any other poem in the language. However, all these sonnets retain their appeal not only for their tender and subtle expressions of love, but for their intriguing reversal of the standard poetic convention of a male poet addressing his female lover.

EBB's most impressive major work is surely her long verse-novel *Aurora Leigh* (1856; now available in a scholarly modern edition edited by Margaret Reynolds, 1992), which tells the story of a gifted young woman's determination to live an independent life as an artist, and her struggles to come to terms with an alien and unloving English culture (by this time, EBB had become a thorough Italophile). Aurora's resistance of the implied patronage of her arrogant cousin Romney's love for her, her enlightenment, through her friend Marian's experience, as to the unjust consequences of rape for women, her growing sympathy with the underclass, and her final realisation that no woman is an island, all chart the growth of a (woman) poet's mind. *Aurora Leigh* had a profound effect on her contemporaries, and echoes from it can be heard down the rest of the century through different forms of women's writing. For the present volume, it was felt that it would not do this fine long poem (or the reader) any service to reproduce a short extract, which is all that could have been included here. Instead, it is hoped that those interested will have the chance to discover the poem whole for themselves.

Elizabeth and Robert's marriage years spent in Italy have been exhaustively documented. Although not perhaps as untroubled a paradise as it has sometimes been represented, the opportunities it gave to both poets to refine their talents were real. Elizabeth at that time was by far the more popular of the two in England, and it was even rumoured that she might be invited to succeed Wordsworth as Poet Laureate in 1850. (Alfred Tennyson was chosen: there still has been no woman Laureate.) A major happiness for Elizabeth was the birth of her son Pen, safely delivered in 1849 after a series of debilitating miscarriages. A major sorrow, however, was the continuing adamant refusal of her furiously stubborn father ever to forgive her marriage against his wishes, or to allow any communication between them. EBB became very involved emotionally with the political struggle for Italian national freedom, as evidenced particularly in her 1860 volume *Poems Before Congress*, to an extent that even Robert found increasingly difficult to sympathise with. He was still less inclined to tolerate her growing reliance on spiritualist beliefs, to which she turned as her health grew weaker, with increasing bouts of serious illness. But he did remain devotedly by her side until her lungs finally gave way and she died in his arms.

At her death her poetic reputation was very high, but it subsequently slipped behind Robert's, and it is only in comparatively recent times that her work has undergone a strong revival of interest and revaluation. Her gift, unlike Rossetti's, is not a major lyric genius, but instead a complex, probing, deeply thoughtful and socially responsible sensibility committed to her craft as a means to an end rather than an end in itself.

Text: Poems chosen are from *Poems* (1844), *Poems* (1850), *Poems Before Congress* (1860) and *Last Poems* (1862). The date of first publication in volume form is given in square brackets at the foot of each poem. The copy-text used is *The Complete Works of Elizabeth Barrett Browning*, 6 vols, eds Charlotte Porter and Helen A. Clarke, New York: Thomas Y. Crowell & Co., 1900; repr. AMS, New York, 1973.

A Thought for a Lonely Death-bed

Inscribed to my friend E. C.

IF God compel thee to this destiny,
To die alone, with none beside thy bed
To ruffle round with sobs thy last word said
And mark with tears the pulses ebb from thee, –
5   Pray then alone, 'O Christ, come tenderly!
By Thy forsaken Sonship in the red
Drear wine-press, – by the wilderness outspread, –
And the lone garden where Thine agony
Fell bloody from Thy brow, – by all of those
10   Permitted desolations, comfort mine!
No earthly friend being near me, interpose
No deathly angel 'twixt my face and Thine,
But stoop Thyself to gather my life's rose,
And smile away my mortal to Divine!'

[1844]

A Thought for a Lonely Death-bed, Inscribed to my friend E. C.] It has not been possible to identify 'E. C.' One negative identification exists, however. With respect to the word 'friend', EBB wrote in her diary: 'I never applied it to any person but one; & that person is not Eliza Cliffe.' Entry for Tuesday 4 Oct 1831, *Diary*, p. 149.

3.] 'Ruffle' has a number of meanings which could be relevant in this context: to spoil the smoothness of something; to roughen it; to draw it together in a ruffle; to disorder, stir up, annoy, irritate; to trouble, disturb.

7–9.] See Revelation 14: 18–20: 'the great wine-press of the wrath of God'; 'blood came out of the wine-press, even unto the horse's bridles'. The fullest accounts of Christ's temptation in the wilderness are in Matthew 4: 1–11 and Luke 4: 1–13. After the Last Supper with his disciples, Jesus retired to the garden at Gethsemane to prepare himself for the crucifixion. There he experienced what has become known as the Agony of Christ, sweating great drops of blood as he prayed. Cf. also Isaiah 63: 3: 'I have trodden the winepress alone; and of the people there was none with me: for I will tread them in mine anger, and trample them in my fury; and their blood shall be sprinkled upon my garments, and I will stain all my raiment.'

The Lady's 'Yes'

I

'Yes,' I answered you last night;
  'No,' this morning, sir, I say:
Colours seen by candle-light
  Will not look the same by day.

II

When the viols played their best,
  Lamps above and laughs below,
Love me sounded like a jest,
  Fit for *yes* or fit for *no*.

III

Call me false or call me free,
  Vow, whatever light may shine, –
No man on your face shall see
  Any grief for change on mine.

IV

Yet the sin is on us both;
  Time to dance is not to woo;
Wooing light makes fickle troth,
  Scorn of *me* recoils on *you*.

V

Learn to win a lady's faith
  Nobly, as the thing is high,
Bravely, as for life and death,
  With a loyal gravity.

VI

Lead her from the festive boards,
  Point her to the starry skies;
Guard her, by your truthful words,
  Pure from courtship's flatteries.

The Lady's 'Yes'. *5. viols*] an archaic term for violas (or, possibly, violins).
15. troth] promise.

VII

25   By your truth she shall be true,
             Ever true, as wives of yore;
          And her *yes*, once said to you,
             SHALL be Yes for evermore.

[1844]

The Cry of the Children

'Φεῦ, φεῦ, τί προσδέρκεσθέ μ ' ὄμμασιν, τέκνα;'

– Medea.

I

Do ye hear the children weeping, O my brothers,
      Ere the sorrow comes with years?
They are leaning their young heads against their mothers,
      And *that* cannot stop their tears.
5   The young lambs are bleating in the meadows,
      The young birds are chirping in the nest,
The young fawns are playing with the shadows,
      The young flowers are blowing toward the west –
But the young, young children, O my brothers,
10   They are weeping bitterly!
They are weeping in the playtime of the others,
      In the country of the free.

II

Do you question the young children in the sorrow
      Why their tears are falling so?
15   The old man may weep for his to-morrow
      Which is lost in Long Ago;

The Cry of the Children] EBB was not the first woman poet to draw attention to the exploitation of factory children. Caroline Bowles (later Southey) (1786–1854) published *Tales of the Factories* in 1831 and the Hon. Caroline Norton (1808–1877) published *A Voice from the Factories* in 1836. See also EBB's other protest poems, 'The Runaway Slave' and 'A Curse for a Nation'.

Epigraph.] 'Alas, alas, why do you look upon me with your eyes, my children?' Euripides, *Medea*.

1. O my brothers] An allusion to a slogan used extensively by those engaged in the movement to abolish the slave trade, viz. 'Am I not a man and a brother?'

The old tree is leafless in the forest,
    The old year is ending in the frost,
The old wound, if stricken, is the sorest,
20   The old hope is hardest to be lost:
But the young, young children, O my brothers,
      Do you ask them why they stand
Weeping sore before the bosoms of their mothers,
      In our happy Fatherland?

III

25   They look up with their pale and sunken faces,
      And their looks are sad to see,
For the man's hoary anguish draws and presses
      Down the cheeks of infancy;
'Your old earth,' they say, 'is very dreary,
30   Our young feet,' they say, 'are very weak;
Few paces have we taken, yet are weary –
      Our grave-rest is very far to seek:
Ask the aged why they weep, and not the children,
      For the outside earth is cold,
35   And we young ones stand without, in our bewildering,
      And the graves are for the old.

IV

'True,' say the children, 'it may happen
      That we die before our time:
Little Alice died last year, her grave is shapen
40   Like a snowball, in the rime.
We looked into the pit prepared to take her:
      Was no room for any work in the close clay!
From the sleep wherein she lieth none will wake her,
      Crying, "Get up, little Alice! it is day."
45   If you listen by that grave, in sun and shower,
      With your ear down, little Alice never cries;
Could we see her face, be sure we should not know her,
      For the smile has time for growing in her eyes:

---

24. Fatherland] The choice of this term over motherland or mother country emphasises the patriarchal character of the laws governing manufacture.

35. bewildering] The usual noun form is 'bewilderment'. 'Bewildering' suggests not just mental confusion, but also, by association with the older form 'wildering', a going (or being led) astray.

40. rime] white frost.

And merry go her moments, lulled and stilled in
50   The shroud by the kirk-chime.
It is good when it happens,' say the children,
    'That we die before our time.'

V

Alas, alas, the children! they are seeking
    Death in life, as best to have:
55   They are binding up their hearts away from breaking,
    With a cerement from the grave.
Go out, children, from the mine and from the city,
    Sing out, children, as the little thrushes do;
Pluck your handfuls of the meadow-cowslips pretty,
60   Laugh aloud, to feel your fingers let them through!
But they answer, 'Are your cowslips of the meadows
    Like our weeds anear the mine?
Leave us quiet in the dark of the coal-shadows,
    From your pleasures fair and fine!

VI

65   'For oh,' say the children, 'we are weary,
    And we cannot run or leap;
If we cared for any meadows, it were merely
    To drop down in them and sleep.
Our knees tremble sorely in the stooping,
70   We fall upon our faces, trying to go;
And, underneath our heavy eyelids drooping
    The reddest flower would look as pale as snow.
For, all day, we drag our burden tiring
    Through the coal-dark, underground;
75   Or, all day, we drive the wheels of iron
    In the factories, round and round.

VII

'For all day the wheels are droning, turning;
    Their wind comes in our faces,
Till our hearts turn, our heads with pulses burning,
80   And the walls turn in their places:

---

50. *kirk-chime*] church bell tolling for the funeral.

56. *cerement*] waxed wrapping for the dead.

Turns the sky in the high window, blank and reeling,
    Turns the long light that drops adown the wall,
Turn the black flies that crawl along the ceiling:
    All are turning, all the day, and we with all.
85   And all day the iron wheels are droning,
        And sometimes we could pray,
"O ye wheels" (breaking out in a mad moaning),
        "Stop! be silent for to-day!"'

VIII

Ay, be silent! Let them hear each other breathing
90   For a moment, mouth to mouth!
Let them touch each other's hands, in a fresh wreathing
    Of their tender human youth!
Let them feel that this cold metallic motion
    Is not all the life God fashions or reveals:
95   Let them prove their living souls against the notion
    That they live in you, or under you, O wheels!
Still, all day, the iron wheels go onward,
        Grinding life down from its mark;
And the children's souls, which God is calling sunward,
100   Spin on blindly in the dark.

IX

Now tell the poor young children, O my brothers,
    To look up to Him and pray;
So the blessed One who blesseth all the others,
    Will bless them another day.
105   They answer, 'Who is God that He should hear us,
    While the rushing of the iron wheels is stirred?
When we sob aloud, the human creatures near us
    Pass by, hearing not, or answer not a word.
And *we* hear not (for the wheels in their resounding)
110   Strangers speaking at the door:
Is it likely God, with angels singing round Him,
        Hears our weeping any more?

105.] The Bible, and especially the Psalms, are full of exhortations to God to hear; as well as alluding to such passages, this ironically transposes another well-known biblical phrase: 'What is man, that thou art mindful of him? and the son of man, that thou visitest him?' (Psalm 8: 4).

X

'Two words, indeed, of praying we remember,
　　And at midnight's hour of harm,
115　"Our Father," looking upward in the chamber,
　　We say softly for a charm.
We know no other words except "Our Father,"
　　And we think that, in some pause of angels' song,
God may pluck them with the silence sweet to gather,
120　　And hold both within His right hand which is strong.
"Our Father!" If He heard us, He would surely
　　(For they call Him good and mild)
Answer, smiling down the steep world very purely,
　　"Come and rest with me, my child."

XI

125　'But, no!' say the children, weeping faster,
　　'He is speechless as a stone:
And they tell us, of His image is the master
　　Who commands us to work on.
Go to!' say the children, – 'up in Heaven,
130　　Dark, wheel-like, turning clouds are all we find.
Do not mock us; grief has made us unbelieving:
　　We look up for God, but tears have made us blind.'
Do you hear the children weeping and disproving,
　　O my brothers, what ye preach?
135　For God's possible is taught by His world's loving,
　　And the children doubt of each.

---

115. 'Our Father'] The first words of the Lord's Prayer, the words in which Jesus taught his disciples to pray (Matthew 6: 9–13). Cf. Charles Dickens's usage of the prayer – especially this phrase – at the death scene of Jo the crossing-sweeper in *Bleak House* (1853).

116.] 'A fact rendered pathetically historical by Mr. Horne's report of his Commission. The name of the poet of "Orion" and "Cosmo de' Medici" has, however, a change of associations, and comes in time to remind me that we have some noble poetic heat of literature still, – however open to the reproach of being somewhat gelid in our humanity. – 1844' [Author's note]. Richard Henry (or Hengist) Horne (1803–1884) published *Cosmo* in 1837 and his epic *Orion* in 1843. He had much correspondence with EBB, who collaborated (anonymously) with him in his *A New Spirit of the Age* (1844). He was a member of the 1841 Royal Commission on Labour of Young Persons in Mines and Manufactures. 'Gelid' means frigid or frosty.

120. *His right hand which is strong*] Cf. Psalm 20: 6: 'Now I know that the Lord saveth his anointed; he will hear him from his holy heaven with the saving strength of his right hand.'

129. *Go to!*] an exclamation of impatient disbelief.

XII

And well may the children weep before you!
    They are weary ere they run;
They have never seen the sunshine, nor the glory
140   Which is brighter than the sun.
They know the grief of man, without its wisdom;
    They sink in man's despair, without its calm;
Are slaves, without the liberty in Christdom,
    Are martyrs, by the pang without the palm:
145   Are worn as if with age, yet unretrievingly
        The harvest of its memories cannot reap, –
Are orphans of the earthly love and heavenly.
        Let them weep! let them weep!

XIII

They look up with their pale and sunken faces,
150   And their look is dread to see,
For they mind you of their angels in high places,
    With eyes turned on Deity.
'How long,' they say, 'how long, O cruel nation,
    Will you stand, to move the world, on a child's heart, –
155   Stifle down with a mailed heel its palpitation,
    And tread onward to your throne amid the mart?
Our blood splashes upward, O gold-heaper,
    And your purple shows your path!
But the child's sob in the silence curses deeper
160   Than the strong man in his wrath.'

[1844]

---

139. the glory] a circle or ring of light shown surrounding the head or whole figure of Christ.

143. Christdom] Christendom (the *OED* gives this poem as the only source of the shortened form).

144. the palm] symbol of victory or triumph.

150. dread] dreadful, in the dual sense of: greatly to be feared or revered.

151. they mind you] remind you; put you in mind of; also carrying the connotation: they make you mind, or care.

153. How long] 'How long' recalls the book of Job in which the question emphasises both the length of his divinely ordained suffering and his struggle against it. See Job 7: 19 and 8: 2. EBB's usage also strongly reflects Revelation 6: 10: 'And they cried with a loud voice, saying, How long, O Lord, holy and true, dost thou not judge and avenge our blood on them that dwell on the earth?'

155. mailed] iron-clad, as with armour.

156. mart] marketplace.

158. purple] Suggests either the privilege of royalty or the colour of blood (or both).

Bertha in the Lane

I

PUT the broidery-frame away,
    For my sewing is all done:
The last thread is used to-day,
    And I need not join it on.
5 Though the clock stands at the noon
    I am weary. I have sewn,
    Sweet, for thee, a wedding-gown.

II

Sister, help me to the bed,
    And stand near me, Dearest-sweet.
10 Do not shrink nor be afraid,
    Blushing with a sudden heat!
No one standeth in the street? –
By God's love I go to meet,
Love I thee with love complete.

III

15 Lean thy face down; drop it in
    These two hands, that I may hold
'Twixt their palms thy cheek and chin,
    Stroking back the curls of gold:
'Tis a fair, fair face, in sooth –
20 Larger eyes and redder mouth
    Than mine were in my first youth.

IV

Thou art younger by seven years –
    Ah! – so bashful at my gaze,
    That the lashes, hung with tears,

Bertha in the Lane] This poem can be compared with others on the theme of sisterly rivalry or self-sacrifice, such as 'Noble Sisters' and 'Goblin Market' by Christina Rossetti. See p. 114 below.

1. broidery-frame] Archaic term for embroidery frame, viz. a frame on which the cloth to be embroidered is stretched in order to facilitate the stitching process; young ladies were expected to spend their leisure time at such occupations.

4. join it on] Each thread was spliced onto the next as it was used up, rather than finished with a knot, to cause least disruption of the smooth surface.

15–18.] Robert Browning borrowed this image for his poem 'Andrea del Sarto': 'Let my hands frame your face in your hair's gold' (l. 174).

19. in sooth] in truth.

25   Grow too heavy to upraise?
        I would wound thee by no touch
        Which thy shyness feels as such.
        Dost thou mind me, Dear, so much?

V

        Have I not been nigh a mother
30   To thy sweetness – tell me, Dear?
        Have we not loved one another
          Tenderly, from year to year,
        Since our dying mother mild
        Said with accents undefiled,
35   'Child, be mother to this child!'

VI

        Mother, mother, up in heaven,
          Stand up on the jasper sea,
        And be witness I have given
          All the gifts required of me, –
40   Hope that blessed me, bliss that crowned,
        Love that left me with a wound,
        Life itself that turneth round!

VII

        Mother, mother, thou art kind,
          Thou art standing in the room,
45   In a molten glory shrined
          That rays off into the gloom!
        But thy smile is bright and bleak
        Like cold waves – I cannot speak,
        I sob in it, and grow weak.

VIII

50   Ghostly mother, keep aloof
          One hour longer from my soul,
        For I still am thinking of
          Earth's warm-beating joy and dole!

34.] Spoke in a pure tone.

37. *jasper*] A precious stone, green being its most prized colour. It occurs in the description of the New Jerusalem in the book of Revelation, and is one of the stones mentioned at the end of *Aurora Leigh*: '. . . And when / I saw his soul saw, – "Jasper first," I said' (Book IX, ll. 961–2).

53. *dole*] grief.

On my finger is a ring
55   Which I still see glittering
When the night hides everything.

IX

Little sister, thou art pale!
   Ah, I have a wandering brain –
But I lose that fever-bale,
60   And my thoughts grow calm again.
Lean down closer – closer still!
I have words thine ear to fill,
And would kiss thee at my will.

X

Dear, I heard thee in the spring,
65   Thee and Robert – through the trees, –
When we all went gathering
   Boughs of May-bloom for the bees.
Do not start so! think instead
How the sunshine overhead
70   Seemed to trickle through the shade.

XI

What a day it was, that day!
   Hills and vales did openly
Seem to heave and throb away
   At the sight of the great sky:
75   And the silence, as it stood
In the glory's golden flood,
Audibly did bud, and bud.

XII

Through the winding hedgerows green,
   How we wandered, I and you,
80   With the bowery tops shut in,
   And the gates that showed the view!
How we talked there; thrushes soft

59.] 'Bale' can mean either an active evil or a pain or torment suffered. Here the words seem to suggest the fantastic diseased visions or thoughts that the fevered state engenders.

67. *May-bloom*] hawthorn blossom: an ancient symbol of springtime, hope and marriage.

80. *bowery*] like a bower or leafy grove.

Sang our praises out, or oft
Bleatings took them from the croft:

XIII

85 Till the pleasure grown too strong
   Left me muter evermore,
And, the winding road being long,
   I walked out of sight, before,
And so, wrapt in musings fond,
90 Issued (past the wayside pond)
On the meadow-lands beyond.

XIV

I sate down beneath the beech
   Which leans over to the lane,
And the far sound of your speech
95   Did not promise any pain;
And I blessed you full and free,
With a smile stooped tenderly
O'er the May-flowers on my knee.

XV

But the sound grew into word
100   As the speakers drew more near –
Sweet, forgive me that I heard
   What you wished me not to hear.
Do not weep so, do not shake,
Oh, – I heard thee, Bertha, make
105 Good true answers for my sake.

XVI

Yes, and HE too! let him stand
   In thy thoughts, untouched by blame.
Could he help it, if my hand
   He had claimed with hasty claim?
110 That was wrong perhaps – but then
Such things be – and will, again.
Women cannot judge for men.

---

84. croft] small enclosed field next to a cottage.
90. Issued] Emerged.

XVII

Had he seen thee when he swore
   He would love but me alone?
115   Thou wast absent, sent before
   To our kin in Sidmouth town.
When he saw thee who art best
Past compare, and loveliest,
He but judged thee as the rest.

XVIII

120   Could we blame him with grave words,
   Thou and I, Dear, if we might?
Thy brown eyes have looks like birds
   Flying straightway to the light:
Mine are older. – Hush! – look out –
125   Up the street! Is none without?
How the poplar swings about!

XIX

And that hour – beneath the beech,
   When I listened in a dream,
And he said in his deep speech
130   That he owed me all *esteem* –
Each word swam in on my brain
With a dim, dilating pain,
Till it burst with that last strain.

XX

I fell flooded with a dark,
135   In the silence of a swoon.
When I rose, still cold and stark,
   There was night; I saw the moon
And the stars, each in its place,
And the May-blooms on the grass,
140   Seemed to wonder what I was.

---

116. Sidmouth town] A market town and seaside resort on the south coast of Devon. EBB stayed here with her family during the years 1832–5 after leaving Hope End, the family estate in Herefordshire, and before moving to London.

130. all esteem] Robert Browning (who was fascinated by this poem, which coincidentally used his first name) reminded EBB of this phrase when he cited it to her in a letter of 6 Jan 1846: '. . . as I told you once, what most characterizes my feeling for you is the perfect *respect* in it, the full *belief* . . . (I shall get presently to poor Robert's very avowal of "owing you all esteem"!)'. See Browning, ed. Karlin, 1989, p. 185.

57

XXI

And I walked as if apart
   From myself, when I could stand,
And I pitied my own heart,
   As if I held it in my hand –
145   Somewhat coldly, with a sense
Of fulfilled benevolence,
And a 'Poor thing' negligence.

XXII

And I answered coldly too,
   When you met me at the door;
150   And I only *heard* the dew
   Dripping from me to the floor:
And the flowers, I bade you see,
Were too withered for the bee, –
As my life, henceforth, for me.

XXIII

155   Do not weep so – Dear, – heart-warm!
   All was best as it befell.
If I say he did me harm,
   I speak wild, – I am not well.
All his words were kind and good –
160   *He esteemed me.* Only, blood
Runs so faint in womanhood!

XXIV

Then I always was too grave, –
   Like the saddest ballad sung, –
With that look, besides, we have
165   In our faces, who die young.
I had died, Dear, all the same;
Life's long, joyous, jostling game
Is too loud for my meek shame.

XXV

We are so unlike each other,
170   Thou and I, that none could guess
We were children of one mother,
   But for mutual tenderness.
Thou art rose-lined from the cold,
And meant verily to hold
175   Life's pure pleasures manifold.

XXVI

I am pale as crocus grows
　　Close beside a rose-tree's root;
Whosoe'er would reach the rose,
　　Treads the crocus underfoot.
180　*I*, like May-bloom on thorn-tree,
Thou, like merry summer-bee, –
Fit that I be plucked for thee!

XXVII

Yet who plucks me? – no one mourns,
　　I have lived my season out,
185　And now die of my own thorns
　　Which I could not live without.
Sweet, be merry! How the light
Comes and goes! If it be night,
Keep the candles in my sight.

XXVIII

190　Are there footsteps at the door?
　　Look out quickly. Yea, or nay?
Some one might be waiting for
　　Some last word that I might say.
Nay? So best! – so angels would
195　Stand off clear from deathly road,
Not to cross the sight of God.

XXIX

Colder grow my hands and feet.
　　When I wear the shroud I made,
Let the folds lie straight and neat,
200　　And the rosemary be spread,
That if any friend should come,
(To see *thee*, Sweet!) all the room
May be lifted out of gloom.

XXX

And, dear Bertha, let me keep
205　　On my hand this little ring,
Which at nights, when others sleep,
　　I can still see glittering!
Let me wear it out of sight,
In the grave, – where it will light
210　All the dark up, day and night.

XXXI

On that grave drop not a tear!
  Else, though fathom-deep the place,
Through the woollen shroud I wear
  I shall feel it on my face.
215 Rather smile there, blessèd one,
Thinking of me in the sun,
Or forget me – smiling on!

XXXII

Art thou near me? nearer! so –
  Kiss me close upon the eyes,
220 That the earthly light may go
  Sweetly, as it used to rise
When I watched the morning-grey
Strike, betwixt the hills, the way
He was sure to come that day.

XXXIII

225 So, – no more vain words be said!
  The hosannas nearer roll.
Mother, smile now on thy Dead,
  I am death-strong in my soul.
Mystic Dove alit on cross,
230 Guide the poor bird of the snows
Through the snow-wind above loss!

XXXIV

Jesus, Victim, comprehending
  Love's divine self-abnegation,
Cleanse my love in its self-spending,
235   And absorb the poor libation!
Wind my thread of life up higher,

---

212. *fathom-deep*] six feet deep; a fathom is normally used as a measure of sea-depth.

226. *hosannas*] shouts of praise to God.

229.] The *Dove* symbolises the Holy Spirit, envisioned here as having landed on the cross, the Christian symbol of redemption.

234. *self-spending*] self-consuming.

235. *libation*] pouring out of liquid; usually, of wine in honour of a god.

Up, through angels' hands of fire!
I aspire while I expire.

[1844]

Loved Once

I

I CLASSED, appraising once,
Earth's lamentable sounds, – the welladay,
    The jarring yea and nay,
The fall of kisses on unanswering clay,
5   The sobbed farewell, the welcome mournfuller, –
    But all did leaven the air
With a less bitter leaven of sure despair
Than these words – 'I loved ONCE.'

II

And who saith 'I loved ONCE'?
10 Not angels, – whose clear eyes, love, love foresee,
    Love, through eternity,
And by To Love do apprehend To Be.
Not God, called LOVED, His noble crown-name casting,
    A light too broad for blasting:
15 The great God, changing not from everlasting,
    Saith never 'I loved ONCE.'

III

Oh, never is 'Loved ONCE'
Thy word, Thou Victim-Christ, misprizèd friend!

---

237. angels' hands of fire] EBB often introduces angels in her poetry: see, for instance, *The Seraphim, A Drama of Exile*, 'A Vision of Poets' and *Sonnets from the Portuguese*.

Loved Once] This poem consciously reverses the refrain from Barry Cornwall's 'Last Song' (*English Songs*, 1832). Barry Cornwall was the pseudonym for Bryan Waller Procter, father of the poet Adelaide Procter.

2. the welladay] the sound of lamentation: 'Alas!'

4. clay] the mortal body, either dead, or as if dead.

7. leaven] most usually, a rising agent for bread; but in the broader sense, as here, leaven (noun) is a modifying element; in the previous line, used as a verb, it means to introduce a modifying element.

14. blasting] blighting or cursing.

18. misprizèd] despised, scorned.

Thy cross and curse may rend,
20   But having loved Thou lovest to the end.
This is man's saying – man's: too weak to move
    One spherèd star above,
Man desecrates the eternal God-word Love
    By his No More, and Once.

IV

25   How say ye 'We loved once,'
Blasphemers? Is your earth not cold enow,
    Mourners, without that snow?
Ah friends, and would ye wrong each other so?
And could ye say of some whose love is known,
30   Whose prayers have met your own,
Whose tears have fallen for you, whose smiles have shown
    So long, – 'We loved them ONCE'?

V

Could ye 'We loved her once'
Say calm of me, sweet friends, when out of sight?
35   When hearts of better right
Stand in between me and your happy light?
Or when, as flowers kept too long in the shade,
    Ye find my colours fade,
And all that is not love in me decayed?
40   Such words – Ye loved me ONCE!

VI

Could ye 'We loved her once'
Say cold of me when further put away
    In earth's sepulchral clay,
When mute the lips which deprecate today?
45   Not so! not then – least then! When life is shriven
    And death's full joy is given, –

---

19. *rend*] burst or break.

22. *One spherèd star above*] Man is too feeble to rise above even one of the heavenly stars. In the Ptolemaic system of astronomy, the heavens revolved around the earth in a series of spheres, one of which was the sphere of the fixed stars.

26. *enow*] enough (archaism).

41–3.] Transposed syntax: Could you say coldly of me, when I am put into my grave, 'We loved her once'?

44. *deprecate*] plead against (some evil outcome).

45. *shriven*] absolved through confession.

Of those who sit and love you up in heaven
    Say not 'We loved them once.'

VII

    Say never ye loved ONCE:
50   God is too near above, the grave beneath,
      And all our moments breathe
Too quick in mysteries of life and death,
For such a word. The eternities avenge
    Affections light of range.
55   There comes no chance to justify that change,
    Whatever comes – Loved ONCE!

VIII

And yet that same word ONCE
Is humanly acceptive. Kings have said,
    Shaking a discrowned head,
60   'We ruled once,' – dotards, 'We once taught and led,'
Cripples once danced i' the vines, and bards approved,
    Were once by scornings moved:
But love strikes one hour – LOVE! Those *never* loved
    Who dream that they loved ONCE.

[1844]

The Runaway Slave at Pilgrim's Point

I

I STAND on the mark beside the shore
    Of the first white pilgrim's bended knee,
Where exile turned to ancestor,
    And God was thanked for liberty.
5   I have run through the night, my skin is as dark,

---

54. *light of range*] of small extent.

58. *humanly acceptive*] fit for acceptance.

60. *dotards*] people in their dotage: in senile decay.

62.] Poets who have now won recognition were previously vulnerable to criticism.

The Runaway Slave at Pilgrim's Point] Pilgrim's Point refers to the spot in Plymouth, Massachusetts, on the North American eastern seaboard where the Pilgrim Fathers were supposed to have landed from their voyage in the *Mayflower*, in quest of religious liberty in a new land. EBB wrote this poem in support of the movement to abolish slavery, and it was first published

I bend my knee down on this mark:
I look on the sky and the sea.

II

O pilgrim-souls, I speak to you!
I see you come proud and slow
10 From the land of the spirits pale as dew
And round me and round me ye go.
O pilgrims, I have gasped and run
All night long from the whips of one
Who in your names works sin and woe!

III

15 And thus I thought that I would come
And kneel here where ye knelt before,
And feel your souls around me hum
In undertone to the ocean's roar;
And lift my black face, my black hand,
20 Here, in your names, to curse this land
Ye blessed in freedom's, evermore.

IV

I am black, I am black,
And yet God made me, they say:
But if He did so, smiling back
25 He must have cast His work away
Under the feet of His white creatures,
With a look of scorn, that the dusky features
Might be trodden again to clay.

V

And yet He has made dark things
30 To be glad and merry as light:
There's a little dark bird sits and sings,
There's a dark stream ripples out of sight,
And the dark frogs chant in the safe morass,
And the sweetest stars are made to pass
35 O'er the face of the darkest night.

---

in the abolitionist paper *Liberty Bell* (Boston, 1848). She wanted this poem to appear next to 'The Cry of the Children' when it was published in volume form. When she wrote it (before Feb 1847) she had only recently escaped from her father's despotism by eloping to Italy with Robert Browning. According to Bolton and Holloway (Browning, 1995), EBB based the poem on a story told her by a part-black Jamaican Barrett cousin.

VI

But *we* who are dark, we are dark!
   Ah God, we have no stars!
About our souls in care and cark
   Our blackness shuts like prison-bars:
40   The poor souls crouch so far behind
That never a comfort can they find
   By reaching through the prison-bars.

VII

Indeed we live beneath the sky,
   That great smooth Hand of God stretched out
45   On all His children fatherly,
   To save them from the dread and doubt
Which would be if, from this low place,
All opened straight up to His face
   Into the grand eternity.

VIII

50   And still God's sunshine and His frost,
   They make us hot, they make us cold,
As if we were not black and lost;
   And the beasts and birds, in wood and fold,
Do fear and take us for very men:
55   Could the whip-poor-will or the cat of the glen
   Look into my eyes and be bold?

IX

I am black, I am black!
   But, once, I laughed in girlish glee,
For one of my colour stood in the track
60   Where the drivers drove, and looked at me,
And tender and full was the look he gave –
Could a slave look *so* at another slave? –
   I look at the sky and the sea.

---

38. cark] burden of anxiety.

53. fold] sheep-pen, or other enclosure for animals.

55. whip-poor-will] popular name (based on its call) for a common species of American bird.
cat of the glen] American wildcat.

60. the drivers] slave-drivers: overseers armed with whips.

X

And from that hour our spirits grew
65   As free as if unsold, unbought:
Oh, strong enough, since we were two,
      To conquer the world, we thought.
The drivers drove us day by day;
We did not mind, we went one way,
70   And no better a freedom sought.

XI

In the sunny ground between the canes,
      He said 'I love you' as he passed;
When the shingle-roof rang sharp with the rains,
      I heard how he vowed it fast:
75   While others shook he smiled in the hut,
As he carved me a bowl of the cocoa-nut
      Through the roar of the hurricanes.

XII

I sang his name instead of a song,
      Over and over I sang his name,
80   Upward and downward I drew it along
      My various notes, – the same, the same!
I sang it low, that the slave-girls near
Might never guess, from aught they could hear,
      It was only a name – a name.

XIII

85   I look on the sky and the sea.
      We were two to love, and two to pray:
Yes, two, O God, who cried to Thee,
      Though nothing didst Thou say!
Coldly Thou sat'st behind the sun:
90   And now I cry who am but one,
      Thou wilt not speak to-day.

---

71. canes] sugar canes.

73. shingle-roof] roof of wooden tiles.

76. cocoa-nut] coconut. The spelling used here originated (apparently by error) in Samuel Johnson's *Dictionary*.

83. aught] anything whatever.

XIV

We were black, we were black,
  We had no claim to love and bliss,
What marvel if each went to wrack?
95   They wrung my cold hands out of his,
They dragged him – where? I crawled to touch
His blood's mark in the dust . . . not much,
  Ye pilgrim-souls, though plain as *this*!

XV

Wrong, followed by a deeper wrong!
100   Mere grief's too good for such as I:
So the white men brought the shame ere long
  To strangle the sob of my agony.
They would not leave me for my dull
Wet eyes! – it was too merciful
105   To let me weep pure tears and die.

XVI

I am black, I am black!
  I wore a child upon my breast,
An amulet that hung too slack,
  And, in my unrest, could not rest:
110 Thus we went moaning, child and mother,
One to another, one to another,
  Until all ended for the best.

XVII

For hark! I will tell you low, low,
  I am black, you see, –
115 And the babe who lay on my bosom so,
  Was far too white, too white for me;
As white as the ladies who scorned to pray
Beside me at church but yesterday,
  Though my tears had washed a place for my knee.

---

94. wrack] ruin, disaster.

101–2.] i.e. they raped her.

108. amulet] lucky charm against evil.

XVIII

120   My own, own child! I could not bear
          To look in his face, it was so white;
      I covered him up with a kerchief there,
          I covered his face in close and tight:
      And he moaned and struggled, as well might be,
125   For the white child wanted his liberty –
          Ha, ha! he wanted the master-right.

XIX

      He moaned and beat with his head and feet,
          His little feet that never grew;
      He struck them out, as it was meet,
130   Against my heart to break it through:
      I might have sung and made him mild,
      But I dared not sing to the white-faced child
          The only song I knew.

XX

      I pulled the kerchief very close:
135   He could not see the sun, I swear,
      More, then, alive, than now he does
          From between the roots of the mango . . . where?
      I know where. Close! A child and mother
      Do wrong to look at one another
140   When one is black and one is fair.

XXI

      Why, in that single glance I had
          Of my child's face, . . . I tell you all,
      I saw a look that made me mad!
          The *master's* look, that used to fall
145   On my soul like his lash . . . or worse!
      And so, to save it from my curse,
          I twisted it round in my shawl.

---

122. *kerchief*] a woman's headdress, or cloth used to cover the head.

126. *master-right*] the right to be a white master, like his father.

129. *meet*] fitting: to be expected.

XXII

And he moaned and trembled from foot to head,
    He shivered from head to foot;
150 Till after a time, he lay instead
    Too suddenly still and mute.
I felt, beside, a stiffening cold:
I dared to lift up just a fold,
    As in lifting a leaf of the mango-fruit.

XXIII

155 But *my* fruit . . . ha, ha! – there, had been
    (I laugh to think on't at this hour!)
Your fine white angels (who have seen
    Nearest the secret of God's power)
And plucked my fruit to make them wine,
160 And sucked the soul of that child of mine
    As the humming-bird sucks the soul of the flower.

XXIV

Ha, ha, the trick of the angels white!
    They freed the white child's spirit so.
I said not a word, but day and night
165   I carried the body to and fro,
And it lay on my heart like a stone, as chill.
– The sun may shine out as much as he will:
    I am cold, though it happened a month ago.

XXV

From the white man's house, and the black man's hut,
170   I carried the little body on;
The forest's arms did round us shut,
    And silence through the trees did run:
They asked no question as I went,
They stood too high for astonishment,
175   They could see God sit on His throne.

XXVI

My little body, kerchiefed fast,
    I bore it on through the forest, on;
And when I felt it was tired at last,

---

157. angels] See note to 'Bertha in the Lane', l. 237.

I scooped a hole beneath the moon:
180   Through the forest-tops the angels far,
With a white sharp finger from every star,
    Did point and mock at what was done.

XXVII

Yet when it was all done aright, –
    Earth, 'twixt me and my baby, strewed, –
185   All, changed to black earth, – nothing white, –
    A dark child in the dark! – ensued
Some comfort, and my heart grew young;
I sate down smiling there and sung
    The song I learnt in my maidenhood.

XXVIII

190   And thus we two were reconciled,
    The white child and black mother, thus;
For as I sang it soft and wild,
    The same song, more melodious,
Rose from the grave whereon I sate:
195   It was the dead child singing that,
    To join the souls of both of us.

XXIX

I look on the sea and the sky.
    Where the pilgrims' ships first anchored lay
The free sun rideth gloriously,
200   But the pilgrim-ghosts have slid away
Through the earliest streaks of the morn:
My face is black, but it glares with a scorn
    Which they dare not meet by day.

XXX

Ha! – in their stead, their hunter sons!
205   Ha, ha! they are on me – they hunt in a ring!
Keep off! I brave you all at once,
    I throw off your eyes like snakes that sting!
You have killed the black eagle at nest, I think:
Did you ever stand still in your triumph, and shrink
210   From the stroke of her wounded wing?

---

208. *the black eagle*] By contrast, the white-headed eagle is the emblem of the USA.

XXXI

(Man, drop that stone you dared to lift! –)
    I wish you who stand there five abreast,
Each, for his own wife's joy and gift,
    A little corpse as safely at rest
215   As mine in the mangoes! Yes, but *she*
    May keep live babies on her knee,
      And sing the song she likes the best.

XXXII

I am not mad: I am black.
    I see you staring in my face –
220   I know you staring, shrinking back,
    Ye are born of the Washington-race,
And this land is the free America,
And this mark on my wrist – (I prove what I say)
    Ropes tied me up here to the flogging-place.

XXXIII

225   You think I shrieked then? Not a sound!
    I hung, as a gourd hangs in the sun;
I only cursed them all around
    As softly as I might have done
My very own child: from these sands
230   Up to the mountains, lift your hands,
    O slaves, and end what I begun!

XXXIV

Whips, curses; these must answer those!
    For in this UNION you have set
Two kinds of men in adverse rows,
235   Each loathing each; and all forget
The seven wounds in Christ's body fair,
    While HE sees gaping everywhere
      Our countless wounds that pay no debt.

211.] Cf. John 8: 7, the woman taken in adultery: 'He that is without sin among you, let him first cast a stone at her.'

221. the Washington-race] George Washington (1732–1799), first President of the United States, was noted for his moral courage, lofty ideals, and wisdom; he was also a slave-holder.

233. UNION] i.e. the United States of America.

236. seven wounds] Christ received five, not seven, wounds from the cross, seen as redemptive for sinners; the reference to seven wounds here is mysterious. EBB could be confusing the

XXXV

Our wounds are different. Your white men
240   Are, after all, not gods indeed,
Nor able to make Christs again
    Do good with bleeding. *We* who bleed
(Stand off!) we help not in our loss!
We are too heavy for our cross,
245   And fall and crush you and your seed.

XXXVI

I fall, I swoon! I look at the sky.
    The clouds are breaking on my brain;
I am floated along, as if I should die
    Of liberty's exquisite pain.
250 In the name of the white child waiting for me
In the death-dark where we may kiss and agree,
White men, I leave you all curse-free
    In my broken heart's disdain!

[1850]

Hiram Powers' 'Greek Slave'

THEY say Ideal beauty cannot enter
The house of anguish. On the threshold stands
An alien Image with enshackled hands,
Called the Greek Slave! as if the artist meant her
5 (That passionless perfection which he lent her,
Shadowed not darkened where the sill expands)
To so confront man's crimes in different lands
With man's ideal sense. Pierce to the centre,

---

seven sorrows of the Virgin Mary, often represented as wounds. Jane Francesca Elgee, later Lady Wilde (1823?–1896), who published poetry as 'Speranza', uses the same reference in her poem 'Foreshadowings': 'I see the pale forms from the seven wounds bleeding.'

Hiram Powers' 'Greek Slave'. *Title*.] *Hiram Powers* (1805–1873) was an American sculptor who lived in Florence from 1837, where he later met and became a friend of the Brownings. EBB believed he was part American Indian. His statue of the *Greek Slave*, made in 1843, made him famous: in 1851 it was shown in the Great Exhibition in London, where it achieved huge popularity, and was later exhibited in America. The figure was of a Greek Christian virgin, sold as a slave by the Turks.

Art's fiery finger, and break up ere long
10 The serfdom of this world. Appeal, fair stone,
From God's pure heights of beauty against man's wrong!
Catch up in thy divine face, not alone
East griefs but west, and strike and shame the strong,
By thunders of white silence, overthrown.

[1850]

A Man's Requirements

I

Love me, Sweet, with all thou art,
    Feeling, thinking, seeing;
Love me in the lightest part,
    Love me in full being.

II

5   Love me with thine open youth
        In its frank surrender;
With the vowing of thy mouth,
        With its silence tender.

III

Love me with thine azure eyes,
10   Made for earnest granting;
Taking colour from the skies,
        Can Heaven's truth be wanting?

IV

Love me with their lids, that fall
        Snow-like at first meeting;
15 Love me with thine heart, that all
        Neighbours then see beating.

V

Love me with thine hand stretched out
        Freely – open-minded:
Love me with thy loitering foot, –
20   Hearing one behind it.

VI

Love me with thy voice, that turns
　　Sudden faint above me;
Love me with thy blush that burns
　　When I murmur *Love me*!

VII

25　　Love me with thy thinking soul,
　　Break it to love-sighing;
Love me with thy thoughts that roll
　　On through living – dying.

VIII

Love me in thy gorgeous airs,
30　　When the world has crowned thee;
Love me, kneeling at thy prayers,
　　With the angels round thee.

IX

Love me pure, as musers do,
　　Up the woodlands shady:
35　Love me gaily, fast and true,
　　As a winsome lady.

X

Through all hopes that keep us brave,
　　Farther off or nigher,
Love me for the house and grave,
40　　And for something higher.

XI

Thus, if thou wilt prove me, Dear,
　　Woman's love no fable,
I will love *thee* – half a year –
　　As a man is able.

[1850]

A Curse for a Nation

Prologue

I HEARD an angel speak last night,
    And he said 'Write!
Write a Nation's curse for me,
And send it over the Western Sea.'

5   I faltered, taking up the word:
    'Not so, my lord!
If curses must be, choose another
To send thy curse against my brother.

    'For I am bound by gratitude,
10   By love and blood,
To brothers mine across the sea,
Who stretch out kindly hands to me.'

    'Therefore,' the voice said, 'shalt thou write
    My curse to-night.
15   From the summits of love a curse is driven,
As lightning is from the tops of heaven.'

    'Not so,' I answered. 'Evermore
    My heart is sore
For my own land's sins: for little feet
20   Of children bleeding along the street:

A Curse for a Nation] This poem was written as an indictment of slavery in America, underlining the crippling hypocrisy of any declaration of freedom while such abomination was allowed to continue. However, on its first publication the whole poem (rather than the first half of the Prologue, which *is* clearly aimed at England) was read as being directed against EBB's own country, and she was accused by English reviewers of being unpatriotic. She was not unduly displeased by the misreading, feeling that if the shoe fitted, it should be worn: although she did point out that the 'curse' was intended entirely to be the action of slave-holding.

12.] The American reviewers and reading public were fervent admirers of EBB.

15–16.] i.e. the greater the love felt, the more potent the curse.

20.] A reference to the exploitation of child labour (see 'The Cry of the Children').

'For parked-up honours that gainsay
      The right of way:
For almsgiving through a door that is
Not open enough for two friends to kiss:

25   'For love of freedom which abates
      Beyond the Straits:
For patriot virtue starved to vice on
Self-praise, self-interest, and suspicion:

'For an oligarchic parliament,
30   And bribes well-meant.
What curse to another land assign,
When heavy-souled for the sins of mine?'

'Therefore,' the voice said, 'shalt thou write
      My curse to-night.
35   Because thou hast strength to see and hate
A foul thing done *within* thy gate.'

'Not so,' I answered once again.
      'To curse, choose men.
For I, a woman, have only known
40   How the heart melts and the tears run down.'

'Therefore,' the voice said, 'shalt thou write
      My curse to-night.
Some women weep and curse, I say
(And no one marvels), night and day.

45   'And thou shalt take their part to-night,
      Weep and write.
A curse from the depths of womanhood
Is very salt, and bitter, and good.'

So thus I wrote, and mourned indeed,
50   What all may read.
And thus, as was enjoined on me,
I send it over the Western Sea.

---

21. *parked-up*] stored-up.   *gainsay*] contradict.

29. *an oligarchic parliament*] a parliament in which power is confined to a very few individuals or families: government by the few.

The Curse

I

BECAUSE ye have broken your own chain
    With the strain
55   Of brave men climbing a Nation's height,
Yet thence bear down with brand and thong
On souls of others, – for this wrong
    This is the curse. Write.

Because yourselves are standing straight
60   In the state
Of Freedom's foremost acolyte,
Yet keep calm footing all the time
On writhing bond-slaves, – for this crime
    This is the curse. Write.

65   Because ye prosper in God's name,
    With a claim
To honour in the old world's sight,
Yet do the fiend's work perfectly
In strangling martyrs, – for this lie
70   This is the curse. Write.

II

Ye shall watch while kings conspire
Round the people's smouldering fire,
    And, warm for your part,
Shall never dare – O shame!
75   To utter the thought into flame
    Which burns at your heart.
    This is the curse. Write.

Ye shall watch while nations strive
With the bloodhounds, die or survive,
80   Drop faint from their jaws,

---

56. *brand and thong*] Slaves were literally branded with their master's symbol of ownership and were whipped for disobedience.

61. *acolyte*] devoted follower.

63. *bond-slaves*] slaves to be bought and sold.

Or throttle them backward to death;
And only under your breath
  Shall favour the cause.
        This is the curse. Write.

85 Ye shall watch while strong men draw
  The nets of feudal law
    To strangle the weak;
  And, counting the sin for a sin,
  Your soul shall be sadder within
90   Than the word ye shall speak.
        This is the curse. Write.

  When good men are praying erect
  That Christ may avenge His elect
    And deliver the earth,
95 The prayer in your ears, said low,
  Shall sound like the tramp of a foe
    That's driving you forth.
        This is the curse. Write.

  When wise men give you their praise,
100 They shall praise in the heat of the phrase,
    As if carried too far.
  When ye boast your own charters kept true,
  Ye shall blush; for the thing which ye do
    Derides what ye are.
105   This is the curse. Write.

  When fools cast taunts at your gate,
  Your scorn ye shall somewhat abate
    As ye look o'er the wall;
  For your conscience, tradition, and name
110 Explode with a deadlier blame
    Than the worst of them all.
        This is the curse. Write.

---

86. *nets of feudal law*] Under the old feudal law, landholders had hereditary rights of owner-
ship and their workers were serfs entirely beholden to their masters.

102. *your own charters*] The American Declaration of Independence (1776) took the form of a
charter, or contract, purporting to protect the right to freedom of every individual citizen,
in the belief 'that all men are created equal . . . [and have the right to] Life, Liberty and the
pursuit of Happiness'.

Go, wherever ill deeds shall be done,
Go, plant your flag in the sun
115   Beside the ill-doers!
And recoil from clenching the curse
Of God's witnessing Universe
     With a curse of yours.
          THIS is the curse. Write.

[1860]

A Musical Instrument

I

WHAT was he doing, the great god Pan,
     Down in the reeds by the river?
Spreading ruin and scattering ban,
Splashing and paddling with hoofs of a goat,
5   And breaking the golden lilies afloat
     With the dragon-fly on the river.

II

He tore out a reed, the great god Pan,
     From the deep cool bed of the river:
The limpid water turbidly ran,
10   And the broken lilies a-dying lay,
And the dragon-fly had fled away,
     Ere he brought it out of the river.

A Musical Instrument. *1.*] Half-man, half-goat, *Pan* was the god of shepherds and flocks, frequenter of streams and woodlands and sexually voracious lover of nymphs and boys. He played a musical instrument of reeds, the pan-pipes or syrinx. This poem takes the Greek myth of the nymph Syrinx (interestingly, not named here) who, when pursued by the lusty Pan, was changed into reeds by the water-nymphs, whereupon Pan cut the reeds (whose plaintive wind-music charmed him) to fashion into pipes, for his own musical instrument. Ovid gives a version of the myth in his *Metamorphoses*, and it had appealed to other poets before EBB, such as Andrew Marvell (1621–1678), who refers to it in 'The Garden': 'And Pan did after Syrinx speed, / Not as a Nymph, but as a reed'.

3. ban] anathema, curses.

9.] The clear water ran cloudy or muddy.

III

High on the shore sat the great god Pan
  While turbidly flowed the river;
15   And hacked and hewed as a great god can,
With his hard bleak steel at the patient reed,
Till there was not a sign of the leaf indeed
  To prove it fresh from the river.

IV

He cut it short, did the great god Pan,
20   (How tall it stood in the river!)
Then drew the pith, like the heart of a man,
Steadily from the outside ring,
And notched the poor dry empty thing
  In holes, as he sat by the river.

V

25   'This is the way,' laughed the great god Pan
    (Laughed while he sat by the river),
'The only way, since gods began
To make sweet music, they could succeed.'
Then, dropping his mouth to a hole in the reed,
30   He blew in power by the river.

VI

Sweet, sweet, sweet, O Pan!
  Piercing sweet by the river!
Blinding sweet, O great god Pan!
The sun on the hill forgot to die,
35   And the lilies revived, and the dragon-fly
  Came back to dream on the river.

VII

Yet half a beast is the great god Pan,
  To laugh as he sits by the river,
Making a poet out of a man:
40   The true gods sigh for the cost and pain, –
For the reed which grows nevermore again
  As a reed with the reeds in the river.

[1862]

Mother and Poet

(Turin, after news from Gaeta, 1861)

I

DEAD! One of them shot by the sea in the east,
   And one of them shot in the west by the sea.
Dead! both my boys! When you sit at the feast
   And are wanting a great song for Italy free,
5   Let none look at *me!*

II

Yet I was a poetess only last year,
   And good at my art, for a woman, men said;
But *this* woman, *this*, who is agonised here,
   – The east sea and west sea rhyme on in her head
10   For ever instead.

III

What art can a woman be good at? Oh, vain!
   What art *is* she good at, but hurting her breast
With the milk-teeth of babes, and a smile at the pain?
   Ah boy, how you hurt! you were strong as you pressed,
15   And I proud, by that test.

IV

What art's for a woman? To hold on her knees
   Both darlings! to feel all their arms round her throat,
Cling, strangle a little! to sew by degrees
   And 'broider the long-clothes and neat little coat;
20   To dream and to doat.

V

To teach them . . . It stings there! *I* made them indeed
   Speak plain the word *country*. I taught them, no doubt,
That a country's a thing men should die for at need.
   I prated of liberty, rights, and about
25   The tyrant cast out.

Mother and Poet. *19. long-clothes*] clothes worn by a babe-in-arms.
24. prated] chattered.

VI

And when their eyes flashed . . . O my beautiful eyes!
   I exulted; nay, let them go forth at the wheels
Of the guns, and denied not. But then the surprise
   When one sits quite alone! Then one weeps, then one kneels!
30   God, how the house feels!

VII

At first, happy news came, in gay letters moiled
   With my kisses, – of camp-life and glory, and how
They both loved me; and soon coming home to be spoiled
   In return would fan off every fly from my brow
35   With their green laurel-bough.

VIII

Then was triumph at Turin: 'Ancona was free!'
   And some one came out of the cheers in the street,
With a face pale as stone, to say something to me.
   My Guido was dead! I fell down at his feet,
40   While they cheered in the street.

IX

I bore it; friends soothed me; my grief looked sublime
   As the ramsom of Italy. One boy remained
To be leant on and walked with, recalling the time
   When the first grew immortal, while both of us strained
45   To the height he had gained.

X

And letters still came, shorter, sadder, more strong,
   Writ now but in one hand, 'I was not to faint, –
One loved me for two – would be with me ere long:
   And *Viva l'Italia!* – *he* died for, our saint,
50   Who forbids our complaint.'

---

31. moiled] moistened.

35. laurel-bough] an emblem of victory.

36. Ancona was free] Ancona was a strategic seaport and fortress.

49. Viva l'Italia!] Long live Italy!

XI

My Nanni would add, 'he was safe, and aware
  Of a presence that turned off the balls, – was imprest
It was Guido himself, who knew what I could bear,
  And how 'twas impossible, quite dispossessed
55   To live on for the rest.'

XII

Of which, without pause, up the telegraph line
  Swept smoothly the next news from Gaeta: – *Shot*.
Tell his mother. Ah, ah, 'his,' 'their' mother, – not 'mine,'
  No voice says '*My* mother' again to me. What!
60   You think Guido forgot?

XIII

Are souls straight so happy that, dizzy with Heaven
  They drop earth's affections, conceive not of woe?
I think not. Themselves were too lately forgiven
  Through THAT Love and Sorrow which reconciled so
65   The Above and Below.

XIV

O Christ of the five wounds, who look'dst through the dark
  To the face of Thy mother! consider, I pray,
How we common mothers stand desolate, mark,
  Whose sons, not being Christs, die with eyes turned away,
70   And no last word to say!

XV

Both boys dead? but that's out of nature. We all
  Have been patriots, yet each house must always keep one.
'Twere imbecile, hewing out roads to a wall;
  And, when Italy's made, for what end is it done
75   If we have not a son?

---

52. *that turned off the balls*] i.e. that deflected the musket shots.

66. *Christ of the five wounds*] the five wounds received on the cross. Cf. note to 'The Runaway Slave', l. 236.

XVI

Ah, ah, ah! when Gaeta's taken, what then?
    When the fair wicked queen sits no more at her sport
Of the fire-balls of death crashing souls out of men?
    When the guns of Cavalli with final retort
80   Have cut the game short?

XVII

When Venice and Rome keep their new jubilee,
    When your flag takes all heaven for its white, green, and red,
When *you* have your country from mountain to sea,
    When King Victor has Italy's crown on his head,
85   (And *I* have my Dead) –

XVIII

What then? Do not mock me. Ah, ring your bells low,
    And burn your lights faintly! *My* country is *there*,
Above the star pricked by the last peak of snow:
    My Italy's THERE, with my brave civic Pair,
90   To disfranchise despair!

XIX

Forgive me. Some women bear children in strength,
    And bite back the cry of the pain in self-scorn;
But the birth-pangs of nations will wring us at length
    Into wail such as this – and we sit on forlorn
95   When the man-child is born.

XX

Dead! One of them shot by the sea in the east,
    And one of them shot in the west by the sea.
Both! both my boys! If in keeping the feast
    You want a great song for your Italy free,
100   Let none look at *me!*

[1862]

---

77. the fair wicked queen] Francis II's policy of no surrender at Gaeta caused great suffering and resulted in many casualties. His young wife reportedly influenced his costly resolution and 'was frequently seen on the ramparts encouraging the artillery-men at their guns' (Casaresco, 1912, p. 328).

81–4.] i.e. when the battle for Italy's unification is won (which was not to be until 1870). King Victor was Victor Emmanuel II of Sardinia and Piedmont, later declared King of Italy.

90. disfranchise] disempower.

EMILY PFEIFFER (1827–1890)

Emily Pfeiffer grew up in Wales (as Emily Davis) and retained a strong patriotic feeling for her native country all her life. Regarded as 'delicate' and fondly indulged by her parents, she was encouraged to write from an early age, and her father paid for the publication of her first work when she was 15. This was a miscellany of her own stories, verses and illustrations, entitled *The Holly Branch: An Album for 1843*. Soon afterwards, her father lost his money in a bank failure and the family was thrown on hard times. It was not until after her marriage in 1850 to a wealthy German merchant living in London that Emily, now Mrs Jurgen Pfeiffer, took up writing for publication again, this time with the full support of her husband, who seems to have been unusually generous in his unstinting enthusiasm for his wife's pursuit of literary, artistic and political activities. Emily Pfeiffer, who remained childless, became a great supporter of women's causes. Not only did she produce feminist poems (like her two sonnets 'Peace to the odalisque', of which one is included here, p. 91), but she also wrote articles in favour of women's suffrage and the need for higher education for women (a cause to which she was to leave a large sum when she died as a widow), and a book entitled *Women and Work* (1888).

As a poet, she earned respect from reviewers particularly with the publication of her 1876 volume titled simply *Poems*, and she was widely praised for her sophisticated use of the sonnet form. She liked to 'pair' her sonnets (see 'The Moth That Drinketh' and 'Kassandra' (pp. 93, 96), both of which consist of two linked sonnets) but did not go in for elaborate sequences like other Victorian poets, including Rossetti and Webster. She was also drawn to more dramatic forms, even attempting a stage play (*The Wynns of Wynhavod: A Drama of Modern Life*, 1881) which, however – and quite typically for women playwrights – she could not get put on. More successful was her experimental long poem, *The Rhyme of the Lady of the Rock and How it Grew* (1884). Unlike *The Wynns*, which is a fairly conventional melodrama, this is a unique work in its self-reflexive use of a prose narrative to frame a poem which, while appearing to treat a traditional legend, actually subverts its material for a feminist purpose. The work was inspired by a trip to the Western Isles of Scotland that she took with her husband (she loved the wildness of the Scottish landcape: see 'Among the Hebrides', p. 91 below). While staying on the Isle of Mull, she first heard the legend of the rebellious wife in a forced marriage who was abandoned by her chieftain husband to a death by drowning on a lonely rock because she refused to submit to his unwelcome embraces, defending herself with a dagger. The poem Pfeiffer wrote based upon this legend emerges in sections framed by a prose narrative recounting the reactions of a diverse group of holiday-makers and locals to whom the poem is read by the poet during its composition. This narrative is lively and amusing, and it builds an ironic awareness of common views of the productions of female poets: as one listener remarks, 'The ladies . . . their sphere is *here*, and *now*; let them try to emancipate themselves from us others as they will . . . they will never follow us into the clouds' (Pfeiffer, 1884, p. 147). Because of its length and its mixture of genres, this work is not suitable for anthologising, but it is well worth further study.

Dramatic irony is a technique which informs some of Pfeiffer's short poems also, as for instance the unusual 'love' poem 'Nathaniel to Ruth' (see p. 88 below). Here the narrator reveals himself to be torn between his sexual desire for Ruth and his narrow puritanical religious beliefs which urge him to condemn the woman as some-how responsible for male lust. As in all good dramatic monologues, the narrator reveals a great deal more about his own unconscious drives than he thinks he does. The influence of both Brownings is evident in these aspects of Pfeiffer's work, with Elizabeth predominating (as contemporary reviewers noted). However, it is Robert Browning's 'Any Wife to Any Husband' which once again draws a response from a female poet in Pfeiffer's 'Any Husband to Many a Wife' (see p. 109). In this poem, Pfeiffer anticipates Virginia Woolf's famous dictum that a man's view of himself depends on having his image reflected back from a woman, at twice its normal size (Woolf, 1929, p. 35). Pfeiffer's approach, however, is comparatively gentle, as the poem teases out of its male speaker a plea to his wife that she not deflate him by ceasing to admire him. Another of her teasing poems is 'The Sonsy Milkmaid' (p. 110), on the one hand a humorous treatment of the age-old theme of seduction across class barriers, but on the other, a kind of celebration of the triumph of natural dignity and commonsense as a way of debunking hypocrisy. Pfeiffer elsewhere makes a plea for the recognition of the rightness and naturalness of the expression of female sexuality, not in any polemical format, but simply in the way she weaves a subtle erotic thread through many of her poems.

For example, the first of the pair of linked sonnets titled 'To a Moth . . .' can be read as a kind of hymn of praise to the sensual and the erotic, however short-lived those feelings might be: 'Not vainly, sprite, thou drawest careless breath, / Strikest ambrosia from the cool-cupped flowers'. The poem's careful language keeps it within the bounds of Victorian propriety, but nevertheless, through its manipulation of natural imagery, it still serves as a clear signal of a celebration of the expression of human sexuality. It also signals a certain liberation achieved by women at this period (the 1870s), in contrast to the cultural conventions which had constrained earlier poets like Felicia Hemans.

Pfeiffer is a poet who (unlike Levy, for example, or Menken) feels in touch wih the natural world, and often gives expression to a sense of man's (or woman's) deep bonds with Nature. There are interesting shifts in perspective, however, from poems which celebrate the power and mystery of Nature ('Among the Hebrides') to those which contemplate with some dismay the new scientific ideas of its mindless force and alienation from man. This attitude is conveyed in the rather sombre sonnet sequence 'To Nature' (see p. 92), with its subtitle reminiscent of some of Thomas Hardy's more pessimistic views: '(*In her ascribed character of unmeaning and all-performing force*)'. Other poems again – like 'A Chrysalis' (p. 95) – seem to sub-scribe to a belief in the notion of a meliorist evolutionary progress. No doubt all of these ideas formed part of the debate internalised by many intelligent Victorians as they struggled to come to terms with the implications of post-Darwinian scientific discoveries. Pfeiffer is also capable of turning her back on this debate and immersing herself in a pastoral elegy mourning a lost childhood innocence, like 'The Bower among the Beans' (p. 102), or a wild fantasy of female subversive power dominating Nature, as in 'The Witch's Last Ride' (p. 105). This last poem mingles with its rollicking enjoyment of a good story a certain compassion for the figure of the witch at the crisis-point in her decline from power, a compassion which seems to include, by suggestion, all of society's outsiders.

Despite this compassion, however – which also enters her treatment of other much-maligned women from legend, such as Kassandra and Klytemnestra – Pfeiffer suffered from her own particular blind spots too. The decision to include her poem 'The Fight at Rorke's Drift' (p. 98), which is a jingoistic celebration of British (and particularly Welsh) valour in an imperialistic war (the Zulu wars in Africa), was not taken lightly. To modern readers, educated to abhor the kind of racist imperialism so taken for granted here, the poem introduces a jarring note. Yet Pfeiffer was by no means alone in her support of imperialism: it was a majority support, and shared by poets far more powerful than she – Alfred Lord Tennyson, for example. I believe it has an educative value for us to try to understand how such a comparatively intelligent, civilised and enlightened woman as Pfeiffer could have conceived of her country's righteousness in such a war. Yet she appears to have been quite convinced of British racial superiority against the Zulu 'savage', and to have equated it unquestioningly with moral right. If nothing else, this poem stands as testament to the power of cultural propaganda and, further, points the way to the infamous 'white feather' brigade (of women who sent white feathers, signifying cowardice, to men who failed to volunteer for active service in World War I). However alert Pfeiffer might have been to the social and cultural restraints imposed on women by patriarchal codes of conduct, she evidently remained blind to the equally insidious constraints on men imposed by rigid masculine codes of militaristic 'honour' under an imperialist regime. In addition, it is perhaps not unlikely that for a woman in her social position, denied access to a life of physical adventure or heroism, a certain vicarious pleasure could be obtained by revelling in bloodthirsty scenes of battle set in exotic locations. So this poem also, in one sense at least, deals with the larger topic dear to Pfeiffer's heart, of woman's power and its circumscription. In 'Rorke's Drift', the tell-tale pronoun 'we' creeps in and takes over the poet's speaking position as the action grows stronger. In Pfeiffer's more considered verse – as, for example, 'Peace to the odalisque', which points out that modern women no longer need be slaves, but can work for their living rather than sell their souls to 'sated masters' – she preserves a detachment absent from 'Rorke's Drift'. Yet her overall view of the poet's role, like Menken's, seems to be essentially romantic and idealistic, and is probably encapsulated in the short poem 'Aspiration' (see p. 95 below; Menken had written a similar poem with the identical title), which likens the poetic soul to a 'callow eagle', driven to defy death, despite its puny unreadiness, by soaring to a great height 'upon an unknown quest'.

Text: Poems chosen are from *Gerard's Monument and Other Poems* (1873; 2nd edn, rev. and enl., 1878), *Poems* (1876), *Quarterman's Grace and Other Poems* (1879), *Under the Aspens* (1882), *Sonnets* (1886) and *Flowers of the Night* (1889). In each case, the copy-text is the first edition, with the exception of *Gerard's Monument and Other Poems*, for which the second edition has been used. Dates of first publication in volume form are shown in square brackets at the foot of each poem.

Nathaniel to Ruth

I KNOW not how, dear heart, I came to love you as I do, –
    Too much, I fear, for one who feels the value of his soul;
And mother's choice, you know, was set on Hannah, not on you, –
    And mother had a calm, wise way of judging, on the whole.

5   Tho' Hannah is by some few years my elder, that they say
    Gives promise of a prudent home; and Hannah is no doubt
A rare God-fearing woman, one who treads the narrow way,
    And cares not what the heathen world are striving for without.

You have a great example in your sister, and indeed,
10   I give you justice, you have tried to profit by that light,
But then you love, and where you love, you cling like any weed, –
    I fear it is to pleasure me you chiefly do the right.

You've tried to keep in check the wayward nature of your hair,
    Which fain would wanton into curl for other eyes than mine;
15   But, smoothing it away, have laid the blue-veined temples bare,
    Whereon some naughty golden rings still break away and shine.

Nathaniel to Ruth] Nathanael (note different spelling) is the exemplar of the guileless soul (see John 1: 47), while Ruth represents true spiritual virtue as well as female beauty and modesty (see the book of Ruth). The biblical Ruth is celebrated for unselfish devotion (first to her mother-in-law, Naomi, then to her second husband, Boaz). Both names were popular among evangelical Christians in the nineteenth century. Pfeiffer's poem offers a sly satire on the kind of loveless repressed piety represented by her sister Hannah as opposed to the 'religion of the heart' represented by Ruth. Christina Rossetti has a number of poems on the theme of contrasted sisters, while the characters here could have walked out of EBB's 'Bertha in the Lane'.

7. the narrow way] Cf. Matthew 7: 14: 'Because strait is the gate, and narrow is the way, which leadeth unto life, and few there be that find it.'

14.] i.e. which would gladly stray playfully and heedlessly into curls regardless of who was looking.

13–16.] Cf. Robert Herrick's 1648 poem 'Delight in Disorder', which begins: 'A sweet disorder in the dress / Kindles in clothes a wantonness'. Cf. also the description of Eve in Milton's *Paradise Lost* (1667; Bk iv, l. 306), which gives 'wanton' ambivalent connotations.

And so the master's son must stop to tell you as you pass,
 You put it back to show your ear of rosy-tinted pearl;
I told him that his weapon was the jaw-bone of an ass –
20   Not used upon the Philistines, but turned against a girl!

The kerchief that on Hannah's neck sets down without a fold,
 Takes quite another curve on yours, but you are not to blame
If beauty in its nature has a something almost bold; –
 I would you were more homely, while I loved you still the same!

25 And now I'm on the subject, Ruth, I'll speak out all my mind:
 Two months ago, when Janet Byrne lay dying on her bed,
And Hannah (such a gift of prayer as hers where shall you find?)
 Improved on the occasion till the dying child was dead.

Then in the midst, – when Hannah urged that each one should put up
30   A cry that in this death his soul should hear a special call, –
I saw you rise and steal towards Jane (not dead yet) with a cup,
 Her feeble call for water you had heard above it all.

My spirit was so lifted up with Hannah's fervent prayer,
 I thought you were an angel come to take the child away;
35 You sat there, with your tender eyes and glory of bright hair,
 Which fell upon your shoulders, – as an angel's haply may.

Jane's head upon your bosom, and her little hands in yours,
 Your living sigh gone forth to meet the infant's dying breath, –
A trance of bliss came over me, – such blessedness ensures
40   The narrow way we walk in, – that I envied her her death!

But you, my Ruth, what thoughts were yours as low you laid her head?
 Your eyes were dry, but in your smile a watery radiance shone:
I fear that in that moment – by that orphan child's death-bed –
 It was her crown you thought of, all too heedless of your own.

19–20.] Cf. Judges 15: 14–16. Samson 'found a new jawbone of an ass, and put forth his hand, and took it, and slew a thousand men therewith' (Judges 15: 15).

21. kerchief] here short for neckerchief, a cloth used to cover the neck and breast.

24. homely] plain or unattractive.

28. Improved on] Made it better; took the opportunity for imparting moral instruction.

36. haply] by chance or accident.

39–40. ensures . . . we walk in] i.e. guarantees that our chosen path of righteousness will lead to heaven.

44. crown] heavenly reward.

45 I would not blame a loving heart nor yet an angel face,
      I only say that one like you 'tis hard to judge aright;
    The work I take for nature's is too like the work of grace; –
      The darker ground of Hannah's mind throws up a clearer light.

    Her words so gracious when in prayer, are only gracious then,
50   And faith in her is strong enough without a prop to stand;
    She owns no carnal bonds, and only loves the souls of men; –
      Such shining lights as Hannah are the saving of the land!

    It is not safe for Christian folk to be too good or fair;
      A spirit like a blood-stained sword, just hidden by a sheath –
55 A sheath like that you wot of – is less like to be a snare;
      The thoughts must still be humbled by the filthiness beneath.

    My own awakening, too, I own was never of the best;
      The roots of this vile will of mine were set so deep in love;
    I loved the stars, the creeping things, and God with all the rest,
60   And long before I turned within, I dared to look above.

    So much the more it did behove the sharer of my life
      To show a clearer calling. Were it better we should part?
    No! there's a feeling here with which to call another wife
      Were breaking of a law – far worse than breaking of a heart.

65 Well, well, some needs must walk in light, some follow in the shade;
      Some hold their course triumphant, others totter to the goal;
    I humbly sue for guidance, but, dear Ruth, I am afraid
      I could not break your tender heart, – no, not to save my soul.

    [1873]

---

47. grace] i.e. heavenly grace, the free and unmerited love of God.

51. owns no carnal bonds] acknowledges no fleshly or sexual ties.

55. A sheath like that you wot of] The 'sheath' here is possibly a sly allusion to Hannah's ugliness, i.e. her outward appearance. 'Wot' is an archaic word for 'know'.

57. awakening] The term 'awakening' has a quasi-technical sense in this kind of religious culture, as one of the necessary stages followed by the 'elect' – the 'awakening' of conscience precedes the inner conflict which leads eventually to 'assurance' of God's grace and the conviction that one is saved.

61–2.] i.e. So much the more ought my wife (the sharer of my life) to show a clearer sense of spiritual prompting.

'Peace to the odalisque, whose morning glory'

PEACE to the odalisque, whose morning glory
Is vanishing, to live alone in story;
Firm in her place, a dull-robed figure stands,
With wistful eyes, and earnest, grappling hands:
5   The working-woman, she whose soul and brain –
Her tardy right – are bought with honest pain.
Oh woman! sacrifice may still be thine –
More fruitful than the souls ye did resign
To sated masters; from your lives, so real,
10   Will shape itself a pure and high ideal,
That ye will seek with sad, wide-open eyes,
Till, finding nowhere, baffled love shall rise
To higher planes, where passion may look pale,
But charity's white light shall never fail.

[1873]

Among the Hebrides

FROM blue Loch Carron rise white and sheer
   Its bare rock faces and island cones,
   And they glitter as frost and wind-bleached bones;
Coral and sapphire far and near,
5   Pearl-white coral and sapphire clear,
   Finely-chiselled as cameo stones,

'Peace to the odalisque'. *1–2.*] By wishing peace to the odalisque (female slave or concubine in a harem), whose early flowering in civilisation ('morning glory') is now disappearing, only to figure in stories of the past, the poet indicates her non-judgemental position. This sonnet is one of a pair written on the same subject, the gradual transition of women from the position of 'kept' women to working women, with both losses and gains.

6. Her tardy right] i.e. her right (of ownership of her own soul and brain) which has only tardily been granted her by so-called civilised society.

7–8.] Sacrifice with a more positive outcome for a woman than surrender of her soul to a master who is already satiated.

14. charity's white light] Charity, or loving-kindness, held to be a never-failing source of strength, is here opposed to erotic love, too often a source of sorrow for women.

Among the Hebrides] The Hebrides, or Western Isles, are a large group of islands off the west coast of Scotland.

1. Loch Carron] a large sea loch or inlet on the coast of Scotland directly opposite the Isle of Skye.

No blurred edges or soft mixed tones:
Blue as the bottomless, white as fear.

Do I sleep, do I dream, in the hard clear day,
10   On the windy deck, in the afternoon,
With the sough of the wave, and the spume of the spray,
     And my hair like the dank sea-tangle blown
On the landward breeze? Is it Portree bay
     That we make, or some cove in the long dead moon?

[1876]

To Nature

(In her ascribed character of unmeaning and all-performing force.)

I

O NATURE! thou whom I have thought to love,
     Seeing in thine the reflex of God's face,
     A loathed abstraction would usurp thy place, –
While Him they not dethrone, they but disprove.
5   Weird Nature! can it be that joy is fled,
     And bald unmeaning lurks beneath thy smile?
     That beauty haunts the dust but to beguile,
And that with Order, Love and Hope are dead?

Pitiless Force, all-moving, all-unmoved,
10   Dread mother of unfathered worlds, assuage
Thy wrath on us, – be this wild life reproved,

---

11. sough] sighing or murmuring sound.   *spume*] foam or froth.

13. Portree bay] Portree is a seaport on the east coast of the Isle of Skye.

14. cove] small bay or inlet.

To Nature] A sequence of four sonnets registering the poet's reaction to the scientific demystification of the Romantic view of Nature as a spirit.

3.] i.e. new scientific thought sought to replace sentimental, anthropomorphic ideas of Nature as a spiritual force with logical, rationalist notions based on empirical evidence.

7.] i.e. that beauty appears to add a spirit to what is only earthly just to divert our attention in some charming way. 'Dust' here has a biblical reference; cf. 'And the Lord God formed man of the dust of the ground, and breathed into his nostrils the breath of life; and man became a living soul' (Genesis 2: 7); 'dust thou art, and unto dust shalt thou return' (Genesis 3: 19).

10–11.] i.e. Nature, the feared mother of worlds which have no father (since God is 'disproved' by science), should reprove humankind by venting her rage on it for daring to assume she has no will of her own.

And trampled into nothing in thy rage!
Vain prayer, although the last of human kind, –
Force is not wrath, – but only deaf and blind.

. . .

IV

If we be fools of chance, indeed, and tend
   No whither, then the blinder fools in this:
   That, loving good, we live, in scorn of bliss,
Its wageless servants to the evil end.
5   If, at the last, man's thirst for higher things
   Be quenched in dust, the giver of his life,
   Why press with growing zeal a hopeless strife, –
Why – born for creeping – should he dream of wings?

O Mother Dust! thou hast one law so mild
10   We call it sacred – all thy creatures own it –
The tie which binds the parent and the child, –
   Why has man's loving heart alone outgrown it?
Why hast thou travailed so to be denied,
So trampled by a would-be matricide?

[1876]

To a Moth that Drinketh of the Ripe October

I

A MOTH belated, – sun and zephyr-kist –
   Trembling about a pale arbutus bell,

13.] Such a *prayer*, although it is the last one available to humankind, is in vain because force like that invoked from Nature signifies not Nature's anger, but her deafness and blindness.

IV.1–4.] If humans are the products of chance rather than of any godly design, and so have no particular aim in living, no heaven to look forward to, then they are all the more foolish to continue to love what is good and scorn their own happiness, since good has no benefit to offer, and death is the evil end regardless.

13. travailed] laboured (in both senses: physical toil, and giving birth).

14. a would-be matricide] one who would kill his mother, i.e. one of the new scientists.

To a Moth that Drinketh of the Ripe October] October is traditionally the time of the vintage in the northern hemisphere.

I.1. zephyr-kist] A zephyr is a very light breeze.

2. arbutus bell] the flower of the ornamental strawberry tree.

Probing to wildering depths its honeyed cell, –
A noonday thief, a downy sensualist!
5 Not vainly, sprite, thou drawest careless breath,
    Strikest ambrosia from the cool-cupped flowers,
    And flutterest through the soft, uncounted hours,
To drop at last in unawaited death; –
'Tis something to be glad! and those fine thrills
10   Which move thee, to my lip have drawn the smile
Wherewith we look on joy. Drink! drown thine ills,
    If ill have any part in thee; erewhile
May the pent force – thy bounded life – set free,
Fill larger sphere with equal ecstasy!

II

With what fine organs art thou dowered, frail elf!
    Thy harp is pitched too high for dull annoy,
    Thy life a love-feast, and a silent joy,
As mute and rapt as Passion's silent self.
5 I turn from thee, and see the swallow sweep
    Like a winged will, and the keen-scented hound
    That snuffs with rapture at the tainted ground, –
All things that freely course, that swim or leap, –
Then, hearing glad-voiced creatures men call dumb,
10   I feel my heart – oft sinking 'neath the weight
Of Nature's sorrow – lighten at the sum
    Of Nature's joy; its half-unfolded fate
Breathes hope – for all but those beneath the ban
Of the inquisitor and tyrant, man.

[1876]

---

3. *wildering*] perplexing (to both the moth and its beholder).

4. *downy*] having a fine, soft, fluffy surface.

6. *ambrosia*] food of the gods.

12. *erewhile*] before long.

13. *thy bounded life*] i.e. the moth's life is constrained by the laws of nature and the limits of its instinct.

II.1. *dowered*] endowed, given at birth.

2.] i.e. the insect produces sounds too high for human hearing.

8. *course*] run, hunt.

13. *ban*] curse.

14. *inquisitor*] Probably an allusion to man as scientific investigator.

Aspiration

('*As an eagle stirreth up her nest, fluttereth over her young, spreadeth abroad her wings, taketh them, beareth them on her wings . . . He made him ride on the high places.*' – DEUT. xxxii.11–13.)

I

THE callow eagle in its downy nest,
　　Betwixt the blue above and blue beneath,
　　Or wrapped in swirling cloud or misty wreath,
　Drops its weak wings and folds itself to rest.
5　But hardly is it settled ere its breast
　　Is pierced with anguish, which, in face of death,
　　Drives it to mount on the unquiet breath
　Of viewless winds, upon an unknown quest.

　Thou art a callow eagle, O my soul!
10　　Forth driven from the home of thy content
　And made to stretch t'wards some far distant goal
　　Of Glory, on thine upward journey sent
　By warning of the Spirit, ere the whole
　　Frame of thy trust from under thee be rent.

[1876]

A Chrysalis

WHEN gathering shells cast upwards by the waves
　　Of progress, they who note its ebb and flow,
　　Its flux and re-flux, surely come to know
　That the sea-level rises; that dark caves
5　Of ignorance are flooded, and foul graves

Aspiration] See the note to the title of Menken's poem on a similar theme, published in 1868, p. 180 below. Pfeiffer follows a more regular sonnet format than Menken.

1. *callow*] Strictly speaking this means the bird is unfledged, or without feathers; here, however, it appears to refer more generally to a young bird.

8. *viewless*] invisible. Cf. John Keats, 'Ode to a Nightingale' (1820): 'Away! away! for I will fly to thee, / Not charioted by Bacchus and his pards, / But on the viewless wings of Poesy' (ll. 31–3).

14. *rent*] torn.

A Chrysalis. *Title.*] The larvae of most insects pass through a state where they are wrapped in a hard sheath or chrysalis while their wings develop.

Of sin are cleansed; albeit the work is slow;
Till, seeing great from less for ever grow,
Law comes to mean for them the Love that saves.

And leaning down the ages, my dull ear,
10   Catching their slow-ascending harmonies,
I am uplift of them, and borne more near,
    I feel within my flesh – laid pupa-wise –
A soul of worship, tho' of vision dim,
    Which links me with wing-folded cherubim.

[1876]

Studies from the Antique

Kassandra

I

Virgin of Troy, the days were well with thee
    When wandering singing by the singing streams
    Of Ilion, thou beheldest the golden gleams
Of the bold sun that might not facèd be
5   Come murmuring to thy feet caressingly;
    But best that day when, steeped in noontide dreams,
    The young Apollo wrapped thee in his beams,
And quenched his love in thine as in a sea!

---

8. *Law*] i.e. the natural law of evolution.

12. *pupa-wise*] like an insect in the stage of metamorphosis where it lies passively in a chrysalis.

14. *cherubim*] one of the second order of angels: often represented in art in the form of a winged child.

Studies from the Antique. Kassandra. *Title.*] In Greek legend, Kassandra, or Cassandra, daughter of Priam and Hecuba, was passionately loved by Apollo, the sun god, who granted her wish to see into the future. But when she slighted him, he punished her by ensuring her prophecies would never be believed, and she was subsequently regarded as insane and even imprisoned. After the fall of Troy, she was alloted as a slave to Agamemnon: she foresaw their joint murder by Clytemnestra but to no avail.

I.1–3. Troy . . . Ilion] Troy, or Troja, is sometimes taken to be a city, capital of Troas, sometimes a region, of which Ilium or Ilion is the capital. Homer's *Iliad* is based on the Trojan wars.

And later, in thy tower 'twas sweet to teach
10   The loveless night the joys high day had known;
To dream, to wake – and find thy love impeach
    Late sleep with kisses, and thy spirit flown
To his, and at the ivory gates of speech
    Breaking in words as burning as his own.

II

How far from Ilion, and how far from joy,
    Captive Kassandra, wert thou, when in sight
    Of conquering Greece thou satest on thy height
Of shame – a waif from out the wreck of Troy!
5 Thine still the burning word, but slave's employ
    Had from thy trembling lip effacèd quite
    The kisses of the god, and heaven's light
Now shone upon thee only to destroy.

For thee, sun-stricken one, th' abysmal sties
10   Of sin lay open as the secret grave –
Things of which speech seemed madness while thy cries
    On wronged Apollo lost the way to save;
Till at the last, the faith of upturned eyes
    Brought him to right, as death to free the slave.

Klytemnestra

I

DAUGHTER of gods and men, great ruling will,
    Seething in oily rage within the sphere
    Which gods and men assign the woman here,

---

9. *thy tower*] Cassandra was imprisoned in a tower.

11. *impeach*] hinder.

13. *ivory gates*] teeth.

14. *in*] into.

II.13–14.] Apollo was deaf to Cassandra's 'cries' while she was alive (because she had 'wronged' him), but in the end he rewarded her faith in him by granting her death as a release from slavery.

Klytemnestra] In Greek legend, Klytemnestra, or Clytæmnestra, daughter of Zeus and Leda, wife of Agamemnon, formed a liaison with her husband's cousin, Ægisthus, when Agamemnon left to fight the Trojan wars after sacrificing their daughter, Iphigenia, in order to get a fair wind for his ship. In revenge, she had Ægisthus kill him on his return.

2. *oily rage*] The allusion may be to oil boiling in a cauldron.

Till, stricken where the wound approved thee still
5   Mother and mortal, all the tide of ill
      Rushed through the gap, and nothing more seemed dear
      But power to wreak high ruin, nothing clear
But the long dream you waited to fulfil.

Mother and spouse – queen of the king of men –
10   What fury brought Ægysthus to thy side –
That bearded semblant, man to outward ken,
      But else mere mawworm, made to fret man's pride?
Woman, thy foot was on thy tyrant then –
      Mother, thou wert avenged for love defied!

[1879]

The Fight at Rorke's Drift

January 23rd, 1879.

It was over at Isândula, the bloody work was done,
And the yet unburied dead looked up unblinking at the sun;
Eight hundred men of Britain's best had signed with blood the story
Which England leaves to time, and lay there scanted e'en of glory.

---

4. *wound*] the murder of her daughter.   *approved*] a poeticism for proved.

8. *long dream*] i.e. the dream of revenge against Agamemnon, which she nurtured for the ten years of his absence in Troy.

9. *king of men*] Agamemnon's tag in Homer.

10. *fury . . . Ægysthus*] There were three Furies in Greek legend: Tisiphone (the avenger of blood), Alecto (the implacable) and Magæra (the jealous one). For Ægisthus, see note on Title, above.

11.] i.e. that seemingly grown-up man.

12. *mawworm*] any intestinal worm; a pious humbug (from the character of this name in Isaac Bickerstaffe's play *The Hypocrite* [1769]).

The Fight at Rorke's Drift] During the Zulu wars in South Africa, the British army was initially defeated by a surprise attack at Isândhlwana (spelled Isândula in this poem) on 22 Jan 1879. Next to be attacked was the garrison stationed at Rorke's Drift, which held 80 men, plus 30 or 40 in the hospital quarters. Late in the afternoon of the 22nd, about 4000 Zulu attacked, and were repulsed about six times. At dawn they withdrew, leaving 350 dead. The British loss: 17 killed and 10 wounded. It was naturally a victory much celebrated by British patriots, and the unquestioning assumption of British racial superiority – however repellent to a modern reader – is very much in tune with public sentiment of the time.

4. *scanted*] stinted.

5   Steuart Smith lay smiling by the gun he spiked before he died;
     But gallant Gardner lived to write a warning and to ride
     A race for England's honour and to cross the Buffalo,
     To bid them at Rorke's Drift expect the coming of the foe.

     That band of lusty British lads camped in the hostile land
10   Rose up upon the word with Chard and Bromhead to command;
     An hour upon the foe that hardy race had barely won,
     But in it all that men could do those British lads had done.

     And when the Zulus on the hill appeared, a dusky host,
     They found our gallant English boys' 'pale faces' at their post;
15   But paler faces were behind, within the barricade –
     The faces of the sick who rose to give their watchers aid.

     Five men to one the first dark wave of battle brought, it bore
     Down swiftly, while our youngsters waited steadfast as the shore;
     Behind the slender barricade, half hidden, on their knees,
20   They marked the stealthy current glide beneath the orchard-trees.

     Then forth the volley blazed, then rose the deadly reek of war;
     The dusky ranks were thinned; the chieftain, slain by young Dunbar,
     Rolled headlong, and their phalanx broke, but formed as soon as
        broke,
     And with a yell the Furies that avenge man's blood awoke.

25   The swarthy wave sped on and on, pressed forward by the tide,
     Which rose above the bleak hill-top, and swept the bleak hill-side;
     It rose upon the hill, and, surging out about its base,
     Closed house and barricade within its murderous embrace.

---

5. *spiked*] rendered unserviceable, by 'spiking' the touch-hole.

5–7. *Steuart Smith . . . Gardner . . . Buffalo*] Major Stuart Smith died at Isândhlwana; his fellow-officer, Captain Alan Gardner, escaped across the River Buffalo to take the warning to Rorke's Drift. Neither David Clammer in *The Zulu War*, Melbourne, 1973, nor Donald R. Morris in *The Washing of the Spears*, London, 1966, mentions that Smith spiked his gun; in fact, Clammer claims he was killed while trying to haul it away (p. 91).

10. *Chard and Bromhead*] lieutenants at Rorke's Drift. They were among those who survived, and were each promoted to major and awarded the Victoria Cross. (Nine others were also awarded, more than in any other single action: until 1907 a VC could not be awarded posthumously.)

13. *host*] army.

23. *phalanx*] Originally a Greek term for a body of infantry closely lined up with shields overlapping.

24. *the Furies*] In Greek legend, three goddesses of vengeance (see note to l.10 'Klytemnestra').

With savage faces girt, the lads' frail fortress seemed to be
30 An island all abloom within a black and howling sea;
And only that the savages shot wide, and held the noise
As deadly as the bullets, they had overwhelmed the boys.

Then in the dusk of day the dusky Kaffirs crept about
The bushes and the prairie-grass, to rise up with a shout,
35 To step, as in a war-dance, all together, and to fling
Their weight against the sick-house till they made its timbers spring.

When beaten back, they struck their shields, and thought to strike
    with fear
Those British hearts, – their answer came, a ringing British cheer!
And the volley we sent after showed the Kaffirs to their cost
40 The coolness of our temper, – scarce an ounce of shot was lost.

And the sick men from their vantage at the windows singled out
From among the valiant savages the bravest of the rout;
A pile of fourteen warriors lay dead upon the ground
By the hand of Joseph Williams, and there led up to the mound

45 A path of Zulu bodies on the Welshman's line of fire,
Ere he perished, dragged out, assegaied, and trampled in their ire;
But the body takes its honour or dishonour from the soul,
And his name is writ in fire upon our nation's long bead-roll.

Yet, let no name of any name be set above the rest,
50 Where all were braver than the brave, each better than the best,
Where the sick rose up as heroes, and the sound had hearts for those
Who, in madness of their fever, were contending as with foes.

---

29. With savage faces girt] Surrounded by savage faces (i.e. both cruel, and belonging to barbarians).

31–2.] Had 'the savages' (the Zulus) not shot wide of the mark, believing their own noise to be as deadly as their bullets, they would have overpowered 'the boys' (the British).

33. Kaffirs] Not an ethnological term, rather a name applied loosely by Europeans to all East African blacks.

42. rout] riotous crowd (archaic).

44–6.] Private Joseph Williams showed immense courage in defending the hospital almost single-handed. He was eventually dragged out and quartered alive.   *the Welshman's*] Pfeiffer herself was Welsh.   *assegaied*] speared. The Zulu assegai or assagai was a light 6-foot throwing spear made of wood and pointed with iron.

48. bead-roll] roll of honour (originally: list of persons to be especially prayed for).

For the hospital was blazing, roof and wall, and in its light
The Kaffirs showed like devils, till so deadly grew the fight
55   That they cowered into cover, and one moment all was still,
When a Kaffir chieftain bellowed forth new orders from the hill.

Then the Zulu warriors rallied, formed again, and hand to hand
We fought above the barricade; determined was the stand;
Our fellows backed each other up, – no wavering and no haste,
60   But loading in the Kaffir's teeth, and not a shot to waste.

We had held on through the dusk, and we had held on in the light
Of the burning house, and later, in the dimness of the night;
They could see our fairer faces; we could find them by their cries,
By the flash of savage weapons and the glare of savage eyes.

65   With the midnight came a change – that angry sea at length was
         cowed,
Its waves still broke upon us, but fell fainter and less loud;
When the 'pale face' of the dawn rose glimmering from his bed
The last black sullen wave swept off and bore away the dead.

That island all abloom with English youth, and fortified
70   With English valour, stood above the wild, retreating tide;
Those lads contemned Canute, and shamed the lesson that he
         read, –
For them the hungry waves withdrew, the howling ocean fled.

Britannia, rule Britannia! while thy sons resemble thee,
And are islanders, true islanders, wherever they may be;
75   Islands fortified like this, manned with islanders like these,
Will keep thee Lady of thy Land, and Sovereign of all Seas.

[1882]

---

71. *Canute*] Refers to the story in which Canute the Great, tenth-century King of England and Denmark, is supposed to have attempted unsuccessfully to turn back the waves from the seashore, thus exposing the limits of divine kingship on purpose to his courtiers, by way of a moral lesson.

73. *Britannia*] England, Wales and Scotland were collectively called 'Britannia' by the Romans. 'Rule Britannia' is the title and chorus of a song written by James Thomson (1700–1748).

EMILY PFEIFFER

The Bower among the Beans

WE had a bower among the beans,
My little love and I,
Where by his side as kings set queens
He throned me graciously;
5   The branching stalks made honied screens
For two who were but half as high;
We had a bower among the beans,
My little love and I.

We sate and toyed there hour by hour,
10   My little love and I,
Above our heads the beans in flower,
Above the beans the sky.
How softly fell the summer shower,
How softly rose the sea-wind's sigh,
15   As there we dallied hour by hour,
My little love and I.

And up that flowery avenue
At whiles my love and I
Would see, enlarging on our view
20   A subject train draw nigh.
Each brought for tribute something new,
A cowrie-shell, a butterfly,
Or starfish, which we took as due,
My little love and I.

25   The bean-flowers velvet-black, and white,
My little love and I
Found sweet to scent, and fair to sight
Beneath the morning's eye;

The Bower among the Beans. *1.*] A possible influence on this poem is Andrew Lang's (1844–1912) 'Ballade of Autumn', which begins: 'We built a castle in the air, / In summer weather, you and I' and which has as refrain, 'My love returns no more again!' (from *Ballades in Blue China*, 1880, p. 41). Lang was popular with a number of women poets, including Levy, Kendall (who collaborated with him) and Naden.

5. honied] honeyed; presumably, laden with flowers for the bees (see l. 11).

15. dallied] spent time idly; possibly with the suggestion of indulging in some amorous caresses.

18. At whiles] From time to time.

20.] A band of subjects (to the 'king' and 'queen') approach.

21. for tribute] as an offering (due to the monarch).

But oft with fallen blossoms dight
30   At eve, my love and I
Would pine, as sick with long delight,
And weep, we knew not why.

And later, in the golden gloom,
My little love and I
35   Would hear the sea-waves sadly boom,
And, gazing up on high,
Would see that parti-coloured bloom
Grow dusk upon the molten sky,
And feel it charactered with doom,
40   My little love and I.

The sea has made our realm his own
Since then; my love and I
Have seen the barren sands, our throne
And kingdom, overlie.
45   For me alone the waves long moan,
For me the sea-winds idle sigh;
My love is only dead and gone:
I live – and I am I!

[1882]

The Cruse of Tears. A Russian Legend

THERE went a widow woman from the outskirts of the city,
Whose lonely sorrow might have moved the stones she trod to pity.

She wandered, weeping through the fields, by God and man forsaken,
Still calling on a little child, the reaper Death had taken.

5   When, lo! upon a day she met a white-robed train advancing,
And brightly on their golden heads their golden crowns were glancing;

---

29. *dight*] arrayed, decked out.

41–4.] In some parts of England (e.g. Norfolk) the sea regularly encroaches on the land.

The Cruse of Tears. A Russian Legend. *Title.*] A cruse is an earthenware vessel for holding liquids. Cf. the widow's cruse in 2 Kings 4.

4. *the reaper*] Death, like Time, is often depicted with a scythe.

6. *glancing*] gleaming or flashing in the light.

Child Jesus led a happy band of little ones a-maying,
With flowers of spring, and gems of dew, all innocently playing.

Far from the rest the widow sees, and flies to clasp, her treasure;
10   'What ails thee, darling, that thou must not take with these thy
          pleasure?'

'Oh, mother, little mother mine, behind the rest I tarry,
For see, how heavy with your tears the pitcher I must carry;

'If you had ceased to weep for me, when Jesus went a-maying,
I should have been among the blest, with little Jesus playing.'

[1882]

Mid-ocean

(On board the 'Bothnia' for New York.)

WILD fields of Ocean, piling heap on heap
    Thy mountainous wealth of water, but to fling
    Abroad in spendthrift haste, still gathering
And scattering to the winds what none would keep;
5   Thou canst not know so sweet a thing as sleep
    For all thy toil, nor hope whereto to cling, –
    Ploughed by the winds in one unending spring –
What harvest of the storm hast thou to reap?

My spirit owns, but will not bend before
10   This dull brute might and purposeless, of thine;
The sea-bird resting on thy wave is more
    Than thou, by all its faculty divine
To suffer; pang is none in this thy roar,
    And all the joy that lifts thy wave, is mine!

[1886]

---

7. *a-maying*] celebrating May-day, the first day of spring, by a ceremonial gathering of flowers.

Mid-ocean. *Subtitle*.] In 1884 Pfeiffer and her husband undertook a trip through eastern Europe, Asia and North America. Her travel writings were published as *Flying Leaves from East and West* (1885). The *Bothnia* is presumably the name of the ocean liner in which the couple crossed the Atlantic. The poem is dated September 11, 1884.

3. *Abroad*] Widely.

9. *owns*] acknowledges.

The Witch's Last Ride

The earth smells dank, the weeds grow rank,
   The cold rain drowns the moon,
The old barn-owl has called me thrice,
   And I must ride eftsoon.

5   The brindled cat has spared the rat,
   And circles round my seat,
He winds me with his tail as he
   Would lift me off my feet.

My every bone is stiff, ohone!
10   I scarce can grip the broom;
But hist! – the hour has warned, and I
   Must mount and meet my doom.

If I should fail upon the gale
   To ride o'er tower and town,
15   And falling headlong through the rift,
   Go down, and down, and down!

It was not so awhile ago,
   When every turn of spite, –
The fools that fret me dealt by day,
20   I paid them back at night.

When I aloft o'er roof and croft
   Went sailing at my ease,
And sowed my curses on their sleep
   As thick as mites in cheese.

The Witch's Last Ride] Other Victorian witch poems, besides those represented here by Coleridge and Watson, include William Bell Scott's 'The Witch's Ballad' (1875) and Walter Thornbury's 'The Witches' Ride' (1876). Thornbury's poem begins: 'Come, come, gossips, now mount, now mount – / Mount, mount, gossips, and spur away. / Brown bog-rushes, or brooms, or crutch. / We've far to ride ere the break of day.'

4. eftsoon] again (archaic).

5. brindled] marked with streaks, tabby.

9. ohone!] Oh, alas! (Scottish or Irish, from the Gaelic).

11. hist!] Hark! Listen!

21. croft] small patch of enclosed ground.

25   Oh, it was rare, high up in air,
            To shoot from out the drift,
        Or with a gossip cheek by jowl
            To spin across the lift;

        With but one word to turn to curd
30   The nursing-mother's milk,
        And make a weanling's bones to wind
            About your thumbs like silk;

        To know that lambs beside their dams
            Would sicken as you pass;
35   To poison all the earing wheat
            And blight the meadow-grass!

        We mustered from the right and left,
            We came from field and alley,
        We steered our brooms and dodged the wind
40   That whistled down the valley;

        We saw the gibbet on the height,
            We heard the rattling bones,
        We lighted on a barren moor
            Beside a ring of stones;

45   We struck live sparks from out the flint,
            We lit our brimstone matches,
        We blew the embers into flame,
            We sung and curst by snatches.

        Each brought a sample of her work,
50   Exchanging gift for gift; –
        An adder's fang, a viscous herb
            For slow death or for swift.

        It gave your curses strength, it warmed
            Your bones the coldest night,
55   To feel you were not all alone
            Again the world to fight.

---

27. *gossip*] female chum.

28. *lift*] sky (Scottish).

46. *brimstone matches*] matches dipped in sulphur. Brimstone is also associated with hell and the devil.

51. *viscous*] glutinous, sticky.

This darkening room smells like a tomb,
    Come, Brindle, cease to scold,
We'll make the wind our hobby-horse
60   As in the nights of old.

It sings so loud of wreckage proud
    These pitiless Novembers,
And down the chimney spits the sleet
    To sting the dying embers.

65   Well, let it drive, we'll look alive,
    And would though we were dying;
Come, once more o'er the world we'll ride,
    And pay off scores outlying.

My broomstick here will help me steer
70   To where the mist lies pale,
And wraps the village-green and pond,
    And whitens all the vale.

Young Daisy there, with yellow hair,
    Lies on the cheek so red
75   I stroked one day till it grew white,
    And Daisy turned and fled.

Then to the mill which crowns the hill; –
    Ugh! mother's arms are warm,
But can they shut out evil spells
80   As they can cold and storm?

A mort of pains, of scabs and blains,
    Be on their beauties poured,
Or ere their soft young skins like mine
    The teeth of Time has scored!

85   Again aloft o'er roof and croft,
    Na – keep your curses ready
To go with mine, you foul-mouthed mate, –
    No claws, my deary, steady!

---

59. *hobby-horse*] toy horse; originally, a term used to describe the wicker horse frame used in traditional morris dances.

81.] i.e. a great deal of pains, of scabs and boils.

83. *Or ere*] Before (archaic).

84. *scored*] marked with cuts.

Now one, two, three, we're off, I see
90   The savage rain and scud,
It beats the smoke into your maw, –
It freezes all your blood.

The rough winds rieve your skirts, and leave
Your legs as clem as stones;
95   Your arms are weak, your head is faint,
A curse upon old bones!

Awhile ago the wind might blow, –
My veins would prick delighted;
Now, now I grab at weather-cocks, –
100   So dizzy and affrighted.

They shake, they shake, they bend, they break!
I slide from off the steeple,
I light 'mid new-made graves, I see
The ghosts of long-dead people;

105   Their hollow eyes in kind surprise
Look hard at me, and tears,
Or something like 'em, dims my sight,
As in the buried years.

My senses reel; what is't I feel
110   The bed where I lie shaking
Is in the old dark nook, and this
Is just the old dull waking.

Nay, Brindle, nay, stand off, away!
Your eyeballs on me glaring,
115   Your breath that draws my breath, your purr
Is worse than all your swearing.

Off, off, damned cat! The rat, the rat;
He dares you with his shriek;
Avaunt, or I shall strike; ohone!
120   Too weak, my arm, too weak!

---

90. *scud*] gust of wind.

91. *maw*] mouth or throat.

93. *rieve*] pull to splitting (usually spelt 'rive').

94. *clem*] pinched, starved.

119.] Be off! or I shall strike (you), oh alas!

My limbs are stark, – all dark, so dark; –
  The very hell-fire's wink
From out those eyes; beneath some soft
  Warm weight I sink, sink, sink.

125 Can this be sleep? You creep, still creep,
  Your mouth to mine so near, –
Your head upon my breast, where once
  There lay a head – so dear –

So dear to me! How could that be?
130   I dream again, – good-night!
No, little one – this starveling breast –
  Light! Light is it? What light?

[1889]

Any Husband to Many a Wife

I scarcely know my worthless picture,
As seen in those soft eyes and clear;
But oh, dear heart, I fear the stricture
You pass on it when none are near.

5 Deep eyes that smiling give denial
To tears that you have shed in vain;
Fond heart that summoned on my trial,
Upbraids the witness of its pain.

Eyes, tender eyes, betray me never!
10 Still hold the flattered image fast
Whereby I shape the fond endeavour
To justify your faith at last.

[1889]

---

121. stark] rigid, incapable of movement.

131. starveling] emaciated.

Any Husband to Many a Wife] Cf. Robert Browning's poem 'Any Wife to any Husband' (*Men and Women*, 1855). A number of women poets rose to the challenge of responding to this poem.

3. stricture] adverse criticism.

8. Upbraids] Reproaches.

The Sonsy Milkmaid

Now gie me back my milkin' stool,
An' leave me to my work,
Ye neither kenned me in the school
Nor ken me in the kirk;

5   It's clear to me there isna place
Aneath a coo for twa,
If that your lips must touch my face,
Then swear ye never saw.

The milkin' trick's no in yer way,
10   Ye needna try again,
Ye'd pinch my fingers a' the day,
An' wadna git a drain;

They arena like my lady's sma',
But nane that had his wits
15   Wad grip an' squeeze them thumbs an' a',
An' think them Crumles' teats!

So up an' leave me wi' the coo,
Syne in your Sunday claes
Ye ken not me, I ken not you,
20   My lord o' workadays.

[1889]

The Sonsy Milkmaid. *Sonsy*] plump, buxom, comely and pleasant.
3. kenned] recognised.
4. kirk] church (Scottish).
6.] Beneath a cow for two.
9.] The knack of milking is not in your line.
12. drain] drink.
13. sma'] small.
16. Crumles] the name of the cow.
18.] Since in your Sunday clothes.

CHRISTINA ROSSETTI (1830–1894)

A great deal more is known about Christina Rossetti's life than about that of any of the other poets in this volume. This is not just owing to the amount of respect earned by her work during her lifetime, although that was considerable. It is also because she was born into a family containing two highly gifted male children as well as a sister and herself. The boys grew up to be extremely well-known figures, one (William Michael) a literary critic and editor and the other (Dante Gabriel) a famous artist and poet. Naturally this made the literary market peculiarly receptive to the productions of the family's outstanding female member, and it also encouraged archivists to preserve her manuscripts for posterity, along with those of her brothers, in a way that was quite unusual for female writers. Yet there still remains a deep sense of hiddenness at the core of her life. Christina Georgina Rossetti was born in London in 1830, the daughter of Gabriele Rossetti, Italian patriot and professor of Italian at King's College, London, and his wife Frances, *née* Polidori, who had been brought up in England but was of Italian descent. She was educated largely by her mother, and shared many of her brothers' intellectual interests, although she declined joining the Pre-Raphaelite Brotherhood, as their group of fellow bohemian artists and writers chose to call themselves. She did, however, occasionally serve as artist's model to her brother, and he in turn lent her his advice on her poetry. She published some early poems in their magazine, *The Germ*, under the pseudonym Ellen Alleyne. She wrote over 900 poems in English and 60 in Italian: most were religious and devotional (pious but rarely sentimental), though some were love poems (usually stressing sadness, loss, and death, subverting conventional romantic views), or ballads (often focusing shrewdly on jealousy and betrayal).

Her childhood seems to have been happy and secure in the midst of her extraordinarily gifted family. The children were all encouraged to read and write early, and played rhyming games from the time they were very small, so it is not surprising that Rossetti grew up with a finely tuned sense of metric proprieties and possibilities. The family fortunes shifted when their father's health deteriorated badly and he was unable to continue teaching. William and Maria both went out to work, as did Mrs Rossetti, who took up teaching herself. Dante Gabriel still enjoyed art school, however. Christina stayed at home to be with her increasingly difficult father, who was sinking under near-blindness, paranoia, and depression. Partly as a result of the stress of the situation (Marsh [1994a] raises the possibility of sexual abuse, pp. 258–9), she suffered a nervous breakdown in adolescence – her doctor diagnosed a form of 'religious mania' – and from it she emerged as a fairly withdrawn, painfully shy young woman, never to regain the light-hearted impulsive high spirits she had had as a child.

She seems to have schooled herself very severely to repress all signs of egotism – 'Learning "Not to be first"', as she put it (in her poem 'The Lowest Room') – despite her growing skill as a poet and her notable beauty as a woman. Religion

111

(of the high church Anglican variety) remained of key importance to her throughout her life. Her engagement to a member of the Pre-Raphaelite Brotherhood, painter James Collinson, was broken off in 1850 before she turned 21. He left the PRB, reconverted to Catholicism and joined a religious order (though he later left it again). Christina was devastated, and although she had subsequent admirers, including her brother William's friend, the scholar Charles Cayley, who proposed to her in 1866, she was never drawn into another engagement. In the same year (1850), she composed *Maude* (not published until after her death), a story which treats the inner struggles of a young woman poet. Unlike her sister Maria, who first taught and later joined a religious sisterhood, Christina Rossetti was not drawn to either vocation, and in fact could never bring herself to work for a living outside the home. However, in early 1859 she took up charitable work for 'fallen women' in the St Mary Magdalene Penitentiary at Highgate. Here she worked with young women who had been 'rescued' from prostitution in the hope that religious teaching and example could reclaim their lives for honest service. Although she never talked much about her work there, it became very important to her, and the experience surely coloured some of her subsequent writing, including her most well-known poem, 'Goblin Market' (see p. 114 below).

Her brothers remained her acutest critics, but after her first foray into print in *The Germ*, Christina handled her publications herself. She had poems accepted in *Macmillan's Magazine*, including 'Up-Hill', which caused a stir, and then Macmillan published her first volume, *Goblin Market and Other Poems*, in 1862. This volume was received like a breath of fresh air over a rather stale poetic landscape, and almost overnight Rossetti became famous. She took her writing very seriously, and would never be pressed to publish before she felt a piece was ready. Macmillan remained her major publisher. As a literary figure she became more formidable as she grew older, her ill health and shyness causing her to lead an almost reclusive life. However, in the 1860s she did travel abroad, to France and to Italy, where she felt an instant sense of blossoming and warmth. Her immediate family provided her with most of her emotional sustenance, and she remained very close to her siblings and devoted to her mother. She also formed friendships outside the family and knew a number of other women writers, including especially the religious poet, essayist and mystic Dora Greenwell, as well as Adelaide Procter and Jean Ingelow (whose many editions she admitted to envying) and, close to the end of her life, a younger and most fervent admirer, the poet Lisa Wilson. She herself remained a staunch admirer of Elizabeth Barrett Browning throughout her career, and thought highly also of Augusta Webster and of Emily Dickinson, whose work she encountered only late in her life. Rossetti suffered from poor health for most of her life, later contracting a disease of the thyroid, and finally dying painfully of breast cancer.

Macmillan published *The Prince's Progress and Other Poems* (1866), *A Pageant and Other Poems* (1881) and a new and enlarged edition of *Poems* (1890), but *Sing-Song: A Nursery Rhyme Book* was brought out simultaneously by Routledge in London and Roberts Bros., Boston, in 1872. Although designed literally as a set of nursery songs for young children, the volume does repay further study both for the quality of the lyrics and for their tone of self-address, as though her own childhood self is being invoked. Rossetti also published a number of prose pieces which have attracted more attention recently than they did at the time. In the main, however, Rossetti's tendency to religious poetry increased as she grew older, whether because it gave voice to her deepest concerns, or, as has been suggested, because she felt a growing negative pressure from the materialism of the age which had to be countered. It is this religious and devotional aspect of her lyric gift which led to her downgrading during a large part of the twentieth century, coupled with the limpid transparency of her language and imagery, which failed to provide modernist critics, obsessed with ambiguities, with the grist they were seeking. More recently, however, the true strangeness and complexity of her work has earned her the critical respect which she was long denied.

The lyric mode is Rossetti's main strength, and her best achievements are unsurpassed. This has always been recognised by other writers (from Gerard Manley Hopkins to Virginia Woolf) if not by critics. Her religious devotion was one aspect which told against her in many circles, but her apparent lack of social and political engagement has seen her reputation dented in other directions also. In 1878, Augusta Webster tried to persuade Rossetti to lend her name and public support to the cause of female suffrage. Despite her admiration for Webster, Rossetti declined, although the correspondence shows that she had very mixed, even muddled, feelings about the issues. Of course she was aware of gender inequalities in social and political life, but in the inner life of the soul, she felt very strongly that gender had no place, since both male and female were equal in Christ. This perception of an ideal, however, did not prevent her writing poems such as 'The Iniquities of the Fathers upon the Children' on the issue of the unfair taint of illegitimacy; nor does it appear to be central to the consciousness that produced 'Monna Innominata' and 'Goblin Market'. The former, published in her 1881 volume, A Pageant, was a 'sonnet of sonnets', that is, 14 poems of 14 lines, written in simultaneous imitation and subversion of traditional sequences of love sonnets. Rossetti's speaker is not the male poet apostrophising his silent female beloved, but the female lover making her own poems addressed to an unattainable male beloved. Rossetti wrote an introduction to this sequence which makes her subversive intention quite clear, and invokes EBB's Sonnets from the Portuguese as a forerunner. By far her most powerful production, however, remains 'Goblin Market', a poem which has delighted and intrigued readers of all ages ever since its first publication, and been many times reprinted, in formats varying from illustrated books for children, to its infamous appearance in an issue of Playboy (1965), with rather different illustrations.

Between 1980 and 1990, the three volumes of R. W. Crump's splendid variorum edition of Rossetti's complete poems were issued. Previously, the most authoritative edition available had been that published posthumously by William Michael Rossetti in 1904. However, it was neither complete nor free of brotherly editorial intervention. Crump's edition made possible many new scholarly directions in the readings of Rossetti's poems, and it is to be hoped that in time, all of the poets in this volume will be available in such reliably edited modern editions.

Text: The poems chosen are from Goblin Market and Other Poems (1862), The Prince's Progress and Other Poems (1866), Goblin Market, The Prince's Progress and Other Poems (1875) and New Poems, Hitherto Unpublished or Uncollected (1896). Dates of first publication in volume form are given in square brackets at the foot of each poem. The copy-text used in each case is *The Complete Poems of Christina Rossetti: A Variorum Edition*, 3 vols, ed. R. W. Crump, Baton Rouge and London: Louisiana State University Press, 1979–90.

Goblin Market

MORNING and evening
Maids heard the goblins cry:
'Come buy our orchard fruits,
Come buy, come buy:
5   Apples and quinces,
Lemons and oranges,
Plump unpecked cherries,
Melons and raspberries,
Bloom-down-cheeked peaches,
10   Swart-headed mulberries,
Wild free-born cranberries,

Goblin Market] Originally titled *A Peep at the Goblins* (after Anna Bray's *A Peep at the Pixies*, 1854), this poem was composed in 1859. For a good account of Bray's influence as well as that of others, see Marsh, 1994a, pp. 230–1. The rhythm Rossetti chose for her poem may well have been influenced by an early reading of a popular poem written for children by Poet Laureate Robert Southey (1774–1843). This was 'The Cataract of Lodore. Described in rhymes for the nursery', which builds a kind of word game of the sound and motion of the torrent, e.g. 'Rising and leaping, / Sinking and creeping, / Swelling and sweeping, / Showering and springing, / Flying and flinging, / Writhing and ringing, / Eddying and whisking, / Spouting and frisking, / Turning and twisting,' etc. etc. Printed in Southey's *Poetical Works* (1838).

2. Maids] Girls, unmarried women (virgins).

2–4.] The 'crying' of wares in the streets and markets was a common sound.

3. orchard fruits] The Garden of Eden was supposed to contain every kind of tree bearing fruit that is good to eat. The description of fruits that follows (ll. 5–30) is full of symbolic associations. For example, apples are commonly associated with the fruit eaten in the Garden of Eden due to a pun on its Latin name, *malus*, which means both 'apple' and 'bad'; the orange tree symbolises purity and the chastity of the Virgin Mary; grapes are suggestive of paradise (Deuteronomy 8: 8) and carry connotations of the wine of the Eucharist and the blood of Christ, 'the true vine'; while the pomegranate has double significance, associated sometimes with the biblical apple but also symbolic of God's bountiful love and the resurrection, having been promised to the faithful children of Israel when they entered the promised land (Deuteronomy 8: 8). A number of Dante Gabriel Rossetti's paintings depict young women holding pomegranates.

9.] i.e. peaches fresh-picked with the 'bloom' – a delicate powdery deposit on just-picked fruit – still adhering to the 'down', or soft fuzz on the 'cheeks' of the fruit. Several critics have commented upon the ways in which such descriptions implicitly liken the fruit to young women.

10. Swart] Dusky; black.

Crab-apples, dewberries,
Pine-apples, blackberries,
Apricots, strawberries; –
15   All ripe together
In summer weather, –
Morns that pass by,
Fair eves that fly;
Come buy, come buy:
20   Our grapes fresh from the vine,
Pomegranates full and fine,
Dates and sharp bullaces,
Rare pears and greengages,
Damsons and bilberries,
25   Taste them and try:
Currants and gooseberries,
Bright-fire-like barberries,
Figs to fill your mouth,
Citrons from the South,
30   Sweet to tongue and sound to eye;
Come buy, come buy.'

Evening by evening
Among the brookside rushes,
Laura bowed her head to hear,
35   Lizzie veiled her blushes:
Crouching close together
In the cooling weather,
With clasping arms and cautioning lips,

15–16.] The listed fruits do not in reality all ripen together: citrus, for example, is a winter fruit. Thus the reader is alerted to the unnatural attraction of the fruit, and its symbolic associations. Cf. the forbidden fruit with which the serpent tempts Eve (Genesis 3: 1–6), and the passage in Revelation 18: 14 where the 'fruits that thy soul lusted after' depart with the fall of Babylon. Cf. also Shakespeare's *Midsummer Night's Dream*, where Titania's elves feed similar luscious fruits to Bottom.

22. bullaces] wild plums.

23–4.] *Greengages* and *damsons* are both kinds of plum; *bilberries* are similar to blueberries.

27. barberries] red berries with a sharp taste.

34–5.] The name *Laura* suggests the figure immortalised by the Italian poet Petrarch (1304–1374) as his Muse; *Lizzie* was the name by which Rossetti's sister-in-law Elizabeth Siddal (1829–1862) was known. Originally Dante Gabriel Rossetti's model and mistress, later his wife, she was also an artist and poet, and died early from an overdose of laudanum (an opium derivative), to which she was addicted. That Rossetti believed herself descended from Laura is attested by the entry she wrote on Petrarch in the *Imperial Dictionary of Universal Biography* (1857–63), vol. 3, pp. 542–4.

With tingling cheeks and finger tips.
40 'Lie close,' Laura said,
Pricking up her golden head:
'We must not look at goblin men,
We must not buy their fruits:
Who knows upon what soil they fed
45 Their hungry thirsty roots?'
'Come buy,' call the goblins
Hobbling down the glen.
'Oh,' cried Lizzie, 'Laura, Laura,
You should not peep at goblin men.'
50 Lizzie covered up her eyes,
Covered close lest they should look;
Laura reared her glossy head,
And whispered like the restless brook:
'Look, Lizzie, look, Lizzie,
55 Down the glen tramp little men.
One hauls a basket,
One bears a plate,
One lugs a golden dish
Of many pounds weight.
60 How fair the vine must grow
Whose grapes are so luscious;
How warm the wind must blow
Thro' those fruit bushes.'
'No,' said Lizzie: 'No, no, no;
65 Their offers should not charm us,
Their evil gifts would harm us.'
She thrust a dimpled finger
In each ear, shut eyes and ran:
Curious Laura chose to linger
70 Wondering at each merchant man.
One had a cat's face,
One whisked a tail,
One tramped at a rat's pace,
One crawled like a snail,

---

41. *Pricking up*] Unusual usage: normally only used of ears.

46. *'Come buy'*] Alicia Suskin Ostriker observes that the goblins' refrain 'shrewdly brings the Christian trope of selling one's soul into juxtaposition with the marriage market and the unspeakable Victorian fact of female sexuality as commodity' (Ostriker 1993, pp. 69–70).

47. *Hobbling*] Limping; also a suggestion of 'hobgoblin': a bogey, bugbear or tricksy sprite (like Shakespeare's Puck in *Midsummer Night's Dream*).

75   One like a wombat prowled obtuse and furry,
        One like a ratel tumbled hurry skurry.
        She heard a voice like voice of doves
        Cooing all together:
        They sounded kind and full of loves
80   In the pleasant weather.

        Laura stretched her gleaming neck
        Like a rush-imbedded swan,
        Like a lily from the beck,
        Like a moonlit poplar branch,
85   Like a vessel at the launch
        When its last restraint is gone.

        Backwards up the mossy glen
        Turned and trooped the goblin men,
        With their shrill repeated cry,
90   'Come buy, come buy.'
        When they reached where Laura was
        They stood stock still upon the moss,
        Leering at each other,
        Brother with queer brother;
95   Signalling each other,
        Brother with sly brother.
        One set his basket down,
        One reared his plate;
        One began to weave a crown
100   Of tendrils, leaves and rough nuts brown
        (Men sell not such in any town);
        One heaved the golden weight
        Of dish and fruit to offer her:
        'Come buy, come buy,' was still their cry.
105   Laura stared but did not stir,
        Longed but had no money:
        The whisk-tailed merchant bade her taste

---

75. *wombat*] Australian burrowing marsupial, heavily built with short legs and a rudimentary tail, somewhat like a small bear. Dante Gabriel Rossetti obtained one for his menagerie of exotic animals kept in the garden of the house at Cheyne Walk, London, where he lived from 1862.   *obtuse*] suggests blunt in shape, as well as stupid.

76. *ratel*] honey-badger (from S. Africa or India).

82.] i.e. (Laura stretches her neck) like a swan craning to see over tall rushes in which it makes its bed (nest).

83. *beck*] brook or stream.

In tones as smooth as honey,
The cat-faced purr'd,
110   The rat-paced spoke a word
Of welcome, and the snail-paced even was heard;
One parrot-voiced and jolly
Cried 'Pretty Goblin' still for 'Pretty Polly;' –
One whistled like a bird.

115   But sweet-tooth Laura spoke in haste:
'Good folk, I have no coin;
To take were to purloin:
I have no copper in my purse,
I have no silver either,
120   And all my gold is on the furze
That shakes in windy weather
Above the rusty heather.'
'You have much gold upon your head,'
They answered all together:
125   'Buy from us with a golden curl.'
She clipped a precious golden lock,
She dropped a tear more rare than pearl,
Then sucked their fruit globes fair or red:
Sweeter than honey from the rock,
130   Stronger than man-rejoicing wine,
Clearer than water flowed that juice;
She never tasted such before,
How should it cloy with length of use?
She sucked and sucked and sucked the more
135   Fruits which that unknown orchard bore;
She sucked until her lips were sore;
Then flung the emptied rinds away
But gathered up one kernel-stone,

117.] i.e. to accept the fruit without being able to pay for it would be stealing: a breach of trust.

120. furze] gorse, an evergreen shrub with yellow flowers that grows on wasteland. Occasionally considered unlucky when offered as a gift or taken indoors, although another belief associates gorse flowers with kissing.

126–7. a golden lock . . . a tear more rare than pearl] The lock of hair is commonly symbolic of virginity; cf. Pope's satire in *The Rape of the Lock* (1712; 1714). The pearl is symbolic of that which is most valuable or precious; cf. Matthew 13: 46, where heaven is likened to the 'one pearl of great price'. In the Middle Ages, the pearl was often a figure for purity or chastity, an association that strengthened during the eighteenth and nineteenth centuries.

129–30.] Cf. Psalm 81: 16: 'with honey out of the rock should I have satisfied thee'; Psalm 104: 15: 'wine [that] maketh glad the heart of man'.

And knew not was it night or day
140   As she turned home alone.

Lizzie met her at the gate
Full of wise upbraidings:
'Dear, you should not stay so late,
Twilight is not good for maidens;
145   Should not loiter in the glen
In the haunts of goblin men.
Do you not remember Jeanie,
How she met them in the moonlight,
Took their gifts both choice and many,
150   Ate their fruits and wore their flowers
Plucked from bowers
Where summer ripens at all hours?
But ever in the noonlight
She pined and pined away;
155   Sought them by night and day,
Found them no more but dwindled and grew grey;
Then fell with the first snow,
While to this day no grass will grow
Where she lies low:
160   I planted daisies there a year ago
That never blow.
You should not loiter so.'
'Nay, hush,' said Laura:
'Nay, hush, my sister:
165   I ate and ate my fill,
Yet my mouth waters still;
Tomorrow night I will
Buy more:' and kissed her:
'Have done with sorrow;
170   I'll bring you plums tomorrow
Fresh on their mother twigs,
Cherries worth getting;
You cannot think what figs

---

147. Jeanie] There may be an indirect reference here to Dante Gabriel Rossetti's poem about a prostitute, 'Jenny'. 'Jenny' was published in *Poems* (1870) but, as Dante Gabriel indicated in an author's note, many of the poems in this volume were written between 1847 and 1853. Susan Brown discusses 'Jenny', and Augusta Webster's poem 'A Castaway'; see Brown (1991).

160. daisies] An emblem of deceit; cf. Ophelia in Shakespeare's *Hamlet* (III.v.180), who gives the queen a daisy. Alternatively, daisies can be symbolic of innocence, thus unable to grow on the fallen woman's grave.

My teeth have met in,
175 What melons icy-cold
Piled on a dish of gold
Too huge for me to hold,
What peaches with a velvet nap,
Pellucid grapes without one seed:
180 Odorous indeed must be the mead
Whereon they grow, and pure the wave they drink
With lilies at the brink,
And sugar-sweet their sap.'

Golden head by golden head,
185 Like two pigeons in one nest
Folded in each other's wings,
They lay down in their curtained bed:
Like two blossoms on one stem,
Like two flakes of new-fall'n snow,
190 Like two wands of ivory
Tipped with gold for awful kings.
Moon and stars gazed in at them,
Wind sang to them lullaby,
Lumbering owls forbore to fly,
195 Not a bat flapped to and fro
Round their rest:
Cheek to cheek and breast to breast
Locked together in one nest.

Early in the morning
200 When the first cock crowed his warning,
Neat like bees, as sweet and busy,
Laura rose with Lizzie:
Fetched in honey, milked the cows,
Aired and set to rights the house,
205 Kneaded cakes of whitest wheat,
Cakes for dainty mouths to eat,
Next churned butter, whipped up cream,

178–9.] i.e. peaches with a soft, downy skin, like the surface of cloth; seedless grapes with a transparent look to them.

180. mead] meadowland (poetic).

187.] Beds were often enclosed by bed-curtains, both for privacy and to exclude draughts. It was common for sisters to share a bed in Victorian families. Nonetheless, several critics have drawn attention to the suggestions of same-sex eroticism in the poem.

Fed their poultry, sat and sewed;
Talked as modest maidens should:
210 Lizzie with an open heart,
Laura in an absent dream,
One content, one sick in part;
One warbling for the mere bright day's delight,
One longing for the night.

215 At length slow evening came:
They went with pitchers to the reedy brook;
Lizzie most placid in her look,
Laura most like a leaping flame.
They drew the gurgling water from its deep;
220 Lizzie plucked purple and rich golden flags,
Then turning homewards said: 'The sunset flushes
Those furthest loftiest crags;
Come, Laura, not another maiden lags,
No wilful squirrel wags,
225 The beasts and birds are fast asleep.'
But Laura loitered still among the rushes
And said the bank was steep.

And said the hour was early still,
The dew not fall'n, the wind not chill:
230 Listening ever, but not catching
The customary cry,
'Come buy, come buy,'
With its iterated jingle
Of sugar-baited words:
235 Not for all her watching
Once discerning even one goblin
Racing, whisking, tumbling, hobbling;
Let alone the herds
That used to tramp along the glen,
240 In groups or single,
Of brisk fruit-merchant men.
Till Lizzie urged, 'O Laura, come;
I hear the fruit-call but I dare not look:
You should not loiter longer at this brook:
245 Come with me home.

---

220. flags] irises. Purple, the royal colour, in ecclesiastical terms denotes mourning or penitence.
224. wags] stirs or moves.

The stars rise, the moon bends her arc,
Each glowworm winks her spark,
Let us get home before the night grows dark:
For clouds may gather
250   Tho' this is summer weather,
Put out the lights and drench us thro';
Then if we lost our way what should we do?'

Laura turned cold as stone
To find her sister heard that cry alone,
255   That goblin cry,
'Come buy our fruits, come buy.'
Must she then buy no more such dainty fruit?
Must she no more such succous pasture find,
Gone deaf and blind?
260   Her tree of life drooped from the root:
She said not one word in her heart's sore ache;
But peering thro' the dimness, nought discerning,
Trudged home, her pitcher dripping all the way;
So crept to bed, and lay
265   Silent till Lizzie slept;
Then sat up in a passionate yearning,
And gnashed her teeth for baulked desire, and wept
As if her heart would break.

Day after day, night after night,
270   Laura kept watch in vain
In sullen silence of exceeding pain.
She never caught again the goblin cry:
'Come buy, come buy;' –
She never spied the goblin men
275   Hawking their fruits along the glen:
But when the noon waxed bright
Her hair grew thin and gray;
She dwindled, as the fair full moon doth turn
To swift decay and burn
280   Her fire away.

---

258. *succous*] containing juice or sap.

260. *Her tree of life*] The sacred tree of life referred to in the Bible represented fertility (ongoing life) as well as eternal life (Genesis 3: 9, 22, 24; cf. Ezekiel 31: 8). The emphasis of the Eden story, however, is more on this tree as a tree of knowledge (of good and evil).

275. *Hawking*] Offering goods for sale in the street.

One day remembering her kernel-stone
She set it by a wall that faced the south;
Dewed it with tears, hoped for a root,
Watched for a waxing shoot,
285   But there came none;
It never saw the sun,
It never felt the trickling moisture run:
While with sunk eyes and faded mouth
She dreamed of melons, as a traveller sees
290   False waves in desert drouth
With shade of leaf-crowned trees,
And burns the thirstier in the sandful breeze.

She no more swept the house,
Tended the fowls or cows,
295   Fetched honey, kneaded cakes of wheat,
Brought water from the brook:
But sat down listless in the chimney-nook
And would not eat.

Tender Lizzie could not bear
300   To watch her sister's cankerous care
Yet not to share.
She night and morning
Caught the goblins' cry:
'Come buy our orchard fruits,
305   Come buy, come buy:' –
Beside the brook, along the glen,
She heard the tramp of goblin men,
The voice and stir
Poor Laura could not hear;
310   Longed to buy fruit to comfort her,
But feared to pay too dear.
She thought of Jeanie in her grave,
Who should have been a bride;
But who for joys brides hope to have
315   Fell sick and died
In her gay prime,
In earliest Winter time,

---

290. *drouth*] drought (poetic).

300. *cankerous*] literally, ulcerous; i.e. a sore that eats away at the flesh.

314. *for*] instead of.

With the first glazing rime,
With the first snow-fall of crisp Winter time.

320 Till Laura dwindling
Seemed knocking at Death's door:
Then Lizzie weighed no more
Better and worse;
But put a silver penny in her purse,
325 Kissed Laura, crossed the heath with clumps of furze
At twilight, halted by the brook:
And for the first time in her life
Began to listen and look.

Laughed every goblin
330 When they spied her peeping:
Came towards her hobbling,
Flying, running, leaping,
Puffing and blowing,
Chuckling, clapping, crowing,
335 Clucking and gobbling,
Mopping and mowing,
Full of airs and graces,
Pulling wry faces,
Demure grimaces,
340 Cat-like and rat-like,
Ratel- and wombat-like,
Snail-paced in a hurry,
Parrot-voiced and whistler,
Helter skelter, hurry skurry,
345 Chattering like magpies,
Fluttering like pigeons,
Gliding like fishes, –
Hugged her and kissed her,
Squeezed and caressed her:
350 Stretched up their dishes,
Panniers, and plates:

---

318. glazing rime] glass-like covering of hoar frost, or frozen dew.

320–1. Laura dwindling . . . Death's door] The similarity of Laura's symptoms to those of the anorectic have been pointed out by Paula Marantz Cohen (1985) and Deborah Ann Thompson (1992).

336.] i.e. grimacing (like monkeys).

351. Panniers] Baskets.

'Look at our apples
Russet and dun,
Bob at our cherries,
355   Bite at our peaches,
Citrons and dates,
Grapes for the asking,
Pears red with basking
Out in the sun,
360   Plums on their twigs;
Pluck them and suck them,
Pomegranates, figs.' –

'Good folk,' said Lizzie,
Mindful of Jeanie:
365   'Give me much and many:' –
Held out her apron,
Tossed them her penny.
'Nay, take a seat with us,
Honour and eat with us,'
370   They answered grinning:
'Our feast is but beginning.
Night yet is early,
Warm and dew-pearly,
Wakeful and starry:
375   Such fruits as these
No man can carry;
Half their bloom would fly,
Half their dew would dry,
Half their flavour would pass by.
380   Sit down and feast with us,
Be welcome guest with us,
Cheer you and rest with us.' –
'Thank you,' said Lizzie: 'But one waits
At home alone for me:
385   So without further parleying,
If you will not sell me any
Of your fruits tho' much and many,
Give me back my silver penny
I tossed you for a fee.' –

---

354. Bob at] Snatch at with the mouth.

385. parleying] converse as with an enemy, under a truce, for the discussion of terms.

390 They began to scratch their pates,
No longer wagging, purring,
But visibly demurring,
Grunting and snarling.
One called her proud,
395 Cross-grained, uncivil;
Their tones waxed loud,
Their looks were evil.
Lashing their tails
They trod and hustled her,
400 Elbowed and jostled her,
Clawed with their nails,
Barking, mewing, hissing, mocking,
Tore her gown and soiled her stocking,
Twitched her hair out by the roots,
405 Stamped upon her tender feet,
Held her hands and squeezed their fruits
Against her mouth to make her eat.

White and golden Lizzie stood,
Like a lily in a flood, –
410 Like a rock of blue-veined stone
Lashed by tides obstreperously, –
Like a beacon left alone
In a hoary roaring sea,
Sending up a golden fire, –
415 Like a fruit-crowned orange-tree
White with blossoms honey-sweet
Sore beset by wasp and bee, –
Like a royal virgin town
Topped with gilded dome and spire
420 Close beleaguered by a fleet
Mad to tug her standard down.

---

390. pates] heads or skulls (comic usage).

409. lily] The Madonna lily, as its name suggests, is symbolic of the Virgin Mary's purity, an association emphasised by the reference to 'blue' (the Madonna's colour) in the following line. In Dante Gabriel Rossetti's painting 'The Girlhood of Mary Virgin', for which Christina was the model, Mary is depicted embroidering a lily (see Peterson, 1994, pp. 209–10). Arum lilies are traditionally used to decorate churches at Easter, creating an association with the passion, also appropriate here.

415–17.] See note on l. 3 above. The association of orange blossom with weddings and the orange tree with fertility highlights the sexual connotations of the goblin assault.

418.] i.e. like a walled medieval fortress, unconquered and unbreached.

421. standard] flag raised on a pole.

One may lead a horse to water,
Twenty cannot make him drink.
Tho' the goblins cuffed and caught her,
425   Coaxed and fought her,
Bullied and besought her,
Scratched her, pinched her black as ink,
Kicked and knocked her,
Mauled and mocked her,
430   Lizzie uttered not a word;
Would not open lip from lip
Lest they should cram a mouthful in:
But laughed in heart to feel the drip
Of juice that syrupped all her face,
435   And lodged in dimples of her chin,
And streaked her neck which quaked like curd.
At last the evil people
Worn out by her resistance
Flung back her penny, kicked their fruit
440   Along whichever road they took,
Not leaving root or stone or shoot;
Some writhed into the ground,
Some dived into the brook
With ring and ripple,
445   Some scudded on the gale without a sound,
Some vanished in the distance.

In a smart, ache, tingle,
Lizzie went her way;
Knew not was it night or day;
450   Sprang up the bank, tore thro' the furze,
Threaded copse and dingle,
And heard her penny jingle
Bouncing in her purse,
Its bounce was music to her ear.
455   She ran and ran
As if she feared some goblin man
Dogged her with gibe or curse
Or something worse:

---

436. *quaked like curd*] trembled like the creamy cheese-like substance made from milk.

445. *scudded*] darted nimbly.

447. *smart*] hurt or affliction, physical or mental.

But not one goblin skurried after,
460   Nor was she pricked by fear;
The kind heart made her windy-paced
That urged her home quite out of breath with haste
And inward laughter.

She cried 'Laura,' up the garden,
465   'Did you miss me?
Come and kiss me.
Never mind my bruises,
Hug me, kiss me, suck my juices
Squeezed from goblin fruits for you,
470   Goblin pulp and goblin dew.
Eat me, drink me, love me;
Laura, make much of me:
For your sake I have braved the glen
And had to do with goblin merchant men.'

475   Laura started from her chair,
Flung her arms up in the air,
Clutched her hair:
'Lizzie, Lizzie, have you tasted
For my sake the fruit forbidden?
480   Must your light like mine be hidden,
Your young life like mine be wasted,
Undone in mine undoing
And ruined in my ruin,
Thirsty, cankered, goblin-ridden?' –
485   She clung about her sister,
Kissed and kissed and kissed her:
Tears once again
Refreshed her shrunken eyes,
Dropping like rain
490   After long sultry drouth;
Shaking with aguish fear, and pain,
She kissed and kissed her with a hungry mouth.

---

461. *windy-paced*] as fast as the wind.

468–73.] Cf. Jesus' words at the Last Supper, as in Matthew 26: 26–8; Mark 14: 22–4; Luke 22: 17–20.

479. *the fruit forbidden*] God forbade Adam and Eve to eat the fruit of the tree (of knowledge) in the Garden of Eden; Eve, tempted by the serpent, ate (Genesis 3: 6).

490. *drouth*] drought (poetic).

491. *aguish*] feverish.

Her lips began to scorch,
That juice was wormwood to her tongue,
495 She loathed the feast:
Writhing as one possessed she leaped and sung,
Rent all her robe, and wrung
Her hands in lamentable haste,
And beat her breast.
500 Her locks streamed like the torch
Borne by a racer at full speed,
Or like the mane of horses in their flight,
Or like an eagle when she stems the light
Straight toward the sun,
505 Or like a caged thing freed,
Or like a flying flag when armies run.

Swift fire spread thro' her veins, knocked at her heart,
Met the fire smouldering there
And overbore its lesser flame;
510 She gorged on bitterness without a name:
Ah! fool, to choose such part
Of soul-consuming care!
Sense failed in the mortal strife:
Like the watch-tower of a town
515 Which an earthquake shatters down,
Like a lightning-stricken mast,
Like a wind-uprooted tree
Spun about,
Like a foam-topped waterspout
520 Cast down headlong in the sea,
She fell at last;
Pleasure past and anguish past,
Is it death or is it life?

493ff.] The following images of daemonic female power suggest the frenzies of the female worshippers of Dionysus, the Maenades (or Bacchantes). Dionysus or Bacchus, the god of wine, was originally the god of all fruitfulness.

494. wormwood] the plant *Artemisia absinthium*, proverbial for its bitter taste. Cf. Proverbs 5: 3–5; Revelation 8: 11, 10: 9–10. Shelley O'Reilly notes that 'wormwood juice' is also a colloquial term for absinthe, a bitter green liqueur, which was believed during the nineteenth century to stimulate creativity. The abuse of absinthe resulted in the disease absinthism, characterised by addiction, hyper-excitability, hallucinations, brain damage, sleeplessness, tremors and convulsions (O'Reilly, 1996). It is significant that the first taste of goblin fruit is sweet, the second bitter. In *Seek and Find* (1879), Rossetti wrote that 'we often make mistakes between mercies and judgments, putting bitter for sweet, and sweet for bitter (Is. v.20)'.

495. the feast] An indication that Rossetti is using (in radical ways) the concept of the Eucharist.

Life out of death.
525   That night long Lizzie watched by her,
Counted her pulse's flagging stir,
Felt for her breath,
Held water to her lips, and cooled her face
With tears and fanning leaves:
530   But when the first birds chirped about their eaves,
And early reapers plodded to the place
Of golden sheaves,
And dew-wet grass
Bowed in the morning winds so brisk to pass,
535   And new buds with new day
Opened of cup-like lilies on the stream,
Laura awoke as from a dream,
Laughed in the innocent old way,
Hugged Lizzie but not twice or thrice;
540   Her gleaming locks showed not one thread of grey,
Her breath was sweet as May
And light danced in her eyes.

Days, weeks, months, years
Afterwards, when both were wives
545   With children of their own;
Their mother-hearts beset with fears,
Their lives bound up in tender lives;
Laura would call the little ones
And tell them of her early prime,
550   Those pleasant days long gone
Of not-returning time:
Would talk about the haunted glen,
The wicked, quaint fruit-merchant men,
Their fruits like honey to the throat
555   But poison in the blood;
(Men sell not such in any town:)
Would tell them how her sister stood
In deadly peril to do her good,

544–5.] Critics frequently comment on the absence of husbands in this description of the sisters' lives.

548.] Ostriker links Laura's retelling of the tale 'with the very similar conclusion of "The Ancient Mariner", that the poetic voice finds its best habitation in the throats of fortunately fallen and reformed sinners' (see Ostriker, 1993, p. 70).

And win the fiery antidote:
560   Then joining hands to little hands
Would bid them cling together
'For there is no friend like a sister
In calm or stormy weather;
To cheer one on the tedious way,
565   To fetch one if one goes astray,
To lift one if one totters down,
To strengthen whilst one stands.'

[1862]

A Birthday

My heart is like a singing bird
    Whose nest is in a watered shoot;
My heart is like an apple tree
    Whose boughs are bent with thickset fruit;
5   My heart is like a rainbow shell
    That paddles in a halcyon sea;
My heart is gladder than all these
    Because my love is come to me.

Raise me a dais of silk and down;
10   Hang it with vair and purple dyes;

---

559. *the fiery antidote*] Homoeopathic medicine treats disease by administering minute doses of the offending substance; cf. the Latin adage *similia similibus curantur*: likes are cured by likes.

562.] Rossetti may be alluding to Proverbs 18: 24: 'and there is a friend that sticketh closer than a brother'.

A Birthday. 1. *bird*] The bird is frequently used as a symbol for the soul. Antony H. Harrison cites this poem as a prime example of Rossetti's 'open-ended symbolic modes of expression' (Harrison, 1985, p. 234).

2. *watered shoot*] a fresh vigorous new shoot from a main stem, normally called a 'water' shoot.

3. *apple tree*] See note to l. 3 of 'Goblin Market', above.

5. *rainbow*] The rainbow is a symbol of divine benevolence, of peace and concord between God and man; cf. the story of Noah, Genesis 9: 12–14.

6. *halcyon sea*] 'Halcyon' is the Greek word for kingfisher: it was believed that while the king-fisher's eggs were incubating on the surface of the sea, the waves would remain calm. Cf. Naden, 'Scientific Wooing', l. 22, p. 246 below.

9. *Raise me*] While the first stanza of 'A Birthday' employs natural images, the second centres on images of craftsmanship.

10. *vair*] grey and white squirrel's fur used to trim robes in the Middle Ages; one of the heraldic furs, represented by bell- or cup-shaped spaces alternately disposed, usually coloured blue and silver.

CHRISTINA ROSSETTI

Carve it in doves and pomegranates,
  And peacocks with a hundred eyes;
Work it in gold and silver grapes,
  In leaves and silver fleurs-de-lys;
15 Because the birthday of my life
  Is come, my love is come to me.

[1862]

My Dream

HEAR now a curious dream I dreamed last night,
Each word whereof is weighed and sifted truth.

I stood beside Euphrates while it swelled
Like overflowing Jordan in its youth:
5 It waxed and coloured sensibly to sight,
Till out of myriad pregnant waves there welled
Young crocodiles, a gaunt blunt-featured crew,
Fresh-hatched perhaps and daubed with birthday dew.
The rest if I should tell, I fear my friend,

---

11. doves and pomegranates] The dove is an emblem of the Holy Spirit, descending at Jesus' baptism; it can also be used to symbolise peace and reconciliation, as when it brings Noah the olive branch. When depicted near an evangelist, apostle or saint, it symbolises divine inspiration. For the symbolism of pomegranates, see the note on 'Goblin Market', l. 3, above.

12.] The peacock could be used as a symbol of pride, but a belief that its flesh did not rot led to its use as a symbol of the resurrection. According to Greek legend, the 'hundred eyes' of the peacock's tail were transplanted by Hera from Argus, 'the all-seeing', after his death.

13.] *Gold* is the colour of divinity and kingship while *silver* suggests purity and innocence. *Grapes* suggest the wine of the Eucharist; Christ is the vine.

14. fleurs-de-lys] the heraldic lily (borne upon the royal arms of France under the old monarchy). As a variety of lily, the fleur-de-lis is a symbol of purity, especially of the Virgin Mary.

Date.] Composed 18 Nov 1857.

My Dream] The Victorian reader's familiarity with a venerable tradition of dream poetry in English, going back to the Old English *Dream of the Rood*, would have alerted him or her to the probability of a poem of this title carrying an allegorical significance.

3–4.] *Euphrates* is the largest river in western Asia, often subject to flooding. Its valley is traditionally believed to be the site of the earliest development of civilisation: it was one of four rivers flowing from Eden (Genesis 2: 14). Hence, perhaps, the reference to 'in its youth'. The *Jordan* is the most important river in Palestine, flowing from the Sea of Galilee (in the area of Jesus' ministry) down to the Dead Sea.

5.] i.e. it grew larger and became coloured in a way clear to the sight.

10   My closest friend would deem the facts untrue;
            And therefore it were wisely left untold;
            Yet if you will, why, hear it to the end.

            Each crocodile was girt with massive gold
            And polished stones that with their wearers grew:
15   But one there was who waxed beyond the rest,
            Wore kinglier girdle and a kingly crown,
            Whilst crowns and orbs and sceptres starred his breast.
            All gleamed compact and green with scale on scale,
            But special burnishment adorned his mail
20   And special terror weighed upon his frown;
            His punier brethren quaked before his tail,
            Broad as a rafter, potent as a flail.
            So he grew lord and master of his kin:
            But who shall tell the tale of all their woes?
25   An execrable appetite arose,
            He battened on them, crunched, and sucked them in.
            He knew no law, he feared no binding law,
            But ground them with inexorable jaw:
            The luscious fat distilled upon his chin,
30   Exuded from his nostrils and his eyes,
            While still like hungry death he fed his maw;
            Till every minor crocodile being dead
            And buried too, himself gorged to the full,
            He slept with breath oppressed and unstrung claw.
35   Oh marvel passing strange which next I saw:
            In sleep he dwindled to the common size,
            And all the empire faded from his coat.
            Then from far off a wingèd vessel came,
            Swift as a swallow, subtle as a flame:
40   I know not what it bore of freight or host,
            But white it was as an avenging ghost.
            It levelled strong Euphrates in its course;

---

19. *mail*] armour of overlapping metal plates: protective scales.

22. *flail*] iron weapon armed with spikes.

25. *execrable*] abominable, detestable.

26. *battened*] fed gluttonously. Cf. Tennyson, 'The Kraken' (1830): 'Battening upon huge seaworms in his sleep' (l. 12).

34. *unstrung*] weakened, relaxed.

35. *passing*] exceedingly (archaic).

40. *host*] army.

Supreme yet weightless as an idle mote
It seemed to tame the waters without force
45   Till not a murmur swelled or billow beat:
Lo, as the purple shadow swept the sands,
The prudent crocodile rose on his feet
And shed appropriate tears and wrung his hands.

What can it mean? you ask. I answer not
50   For meaning, but myself must echo, What?
And tell it as I saw it on the spot.

[1862]

Maude Clare

OUT of the church she followed them
   With a lofty step and mien:
His bride was like a village maid,
   Maude Clare was like a queen.

5   'Son Thomas,' his lady mother said,
   With smiles, almost with tears:
'May Nell and you but live as true
   As we have done for years;

'Your father thirty years ago
10   Had just your tale to tell;
But he was not so pale as you,
   Nor I so pale as Nell.'

My lord was pale with inward strife,
   And Nell was pale with pride;
15   My lord gazed long on pale Maude Clare
   Or ever he kissed the bride.

47–8.] 'Crocodile tears' are hypocritical tears. The story is that crocodiles lure travellers to them by moaning and sighing like a person in distress, then shed tears while devouring them. Cf. Shakespeare: 'As the mournful crocodile / With sorrow snares relenting passengers' (*Henry VI* Pt II, III.i). Cf. also Thomas Lovell Beddoes in *Death's Jest-Book* (1850), III.iii.

Date.] Composed 6 Feb 1849.

Maude Clare] Rossetti cut this poem from 43 to 12 stanzas for publication.

2. mien] air, manner.

16. Or] Before (poetical).

'Lo, I have brought my gift, my lord,
　　Have brought my gift,' she said:
'To bless the hearth, to bless the board,
20　　To bless the marriage-bed.

'Here's my half of the golden chain
　　You wore about your neck,
That day we waded ankle-deep
　　For lilies in the beck:

25　'Here's my half of the faded leaves
　　We plucked from budding bough,
With feet amongst the lily leaves, –
　　The lilies are budding now.'

He strove to match her scorn with scorn,
30　　He faltered in his place:
'Lady,' he said, – 'Maude Clare,' he said, –
　　'Maude Clare:' – and hid his face.

She turn'd to Nell: 'My Lady Nell,
　　I have a gift for you;
35　Tho', were it fruit, the bloom were gone,
　　Or, were it flowers, the dew.

'Take my share of a fickle heart,
　　Mine of a paltry love:
Take it or leave it as you will,
40　　I wash my hands thereof.'

'And what you leave,' said Nell, 'I'll take,
　　And what you spurn, I'll wear;
For he's my lord for better and worse,
　　And him I love, Maude Clare.

45　'Yea, tho' you're taller by the head,
　　More wise, and much more fair;
I'll love him till he loves me best,
　　Me best of all, Maude Clare.'

[1862]

19. *board*] table spread for a repast: here, for a marriage feast.
24. *beck*] stream. Wading for lilies is the picture of innocence, as lilies symbolise purity.
35–6.] i.e. the freshness of an innocent first love is vanished.

Date.] 'Maude Clare' was probably composed sometime between 8 Dec 1857 and 14 April 1858.

Song

WHEN I am dead, my dearest,
  Sing no sad songs for me;
Plant thou no roses at my head,
  Nor shady cypress tree:
5   Be the green grass above me
  With showers and dewdrops wet;
And if thou wilt, remember,
  And if thou wilt, forget.

I shall not see the shadows,
10   I shall not feel the rain;
I shall not hear the nightingale
  Sing on, as if in pain:
And dreaming through the twilight
  That doth not rise nor set,
15   Haply I may remember,
  And haply may forget.

[1862]

A Better Resurrection

I HAVE no wit, no words, no tears;
  My heart within me like a stone
Is numbed too much for hopes or fears;

Song. *4.*] The *cypress* was a symbol of mourning.

11. nightingale] The nightingale has long been a figure for the poet: its song is associated with pain. In antiquity, the nightingale was thought of as a mother weeping for her children; it has also been interpreted as a cry for help from a soul in purgatory, while Christians often interpreted it as suggesting the longing for paradise or heaven.

15. Haply] Perhaps (poetical).

Date.] Composed 26 Nov 1848.

A Better Resurrection. *Title.*] Hebrews 11: 35: 'Women received their dead raised to life again: and others were tortured, not accepting deliverance; that they might obtain a better resurrection.' This poem was composed on 2 June 1849. It was placed by Rossetti in the devotional section of her volume, as were 'The World' and 'Old and New Year Ditties'.

2.] 'And I will take the stony heart out of their flesh, and will give them an heart of flesh' (Ezekiel 11: 19).

Look right, look left, I dwell alone;
5   I lift mine eyes, but dimmed with grief
No everlasting hills I see;
My life is in the falling leaf:
O Jesus, quicken me.

My life is like a faded leaf,
10   My harvest dwindled to a husk;
Truly my life is void and brief
And tedious in the barren dusk;
My life is like a frozen thing,
No bud nor greenness can I see:
15   Yet rise it shall – the sap of Spring;
O Jesus, rise in me.

My life is like a broken bowl,
A broken bowl that cannot hold
One drop of water for my soul
20   Or cordial in the searching cold;
Cast in the fire the perished thing,
Melt and remould it, till it be
A royal cup for Him my King:
O Jesus, drink of me.

[1862]

6.] 'The blessings of thy father have prevailed above the blessings of my progenitors unto the utmost bound of the everlasting hills' (Genesis 49: 26).

7. *falling leaf*] Cf. Isaiah 34: 4: 'And all the host of heaven shall be dissolved, and the heavens shall be rolled together as a scroll: and all their host shall fall down, as the leaf falleth off from the vine.' Contrast the godly: 'And he shall be like a tree planted by the rivers of water, that bringeth forth his fruit in his season; his leaf also shall not wither; and whatsoever he doeth shall prosper' (Psalm 1: 3). Cf. also *Macbeth* V.iii.22–3: 'my way of life / Is fallen into the sear, the yellow leaf'.

8. *quicken me*] give (or restore) life to me.

9.] 'But we are all as an unclean thing, and all our righteousnesses are as filthy rags; and we all do fade as a leaf; and our iniquities, like the wind, have taken us away' (Isaiah 64: 6). 'And by the river upon the bank thereof . . . shall grow all trees . . . whose leaf shall not fade' (Ezekiel 47: 12).

17.] 'Or ever the silver cord be loosed, or the golden bowl be broken . . . Then shall the dust return to the earth as it was' (Ecclesiastes 12: 6–7).

20. *cordial*] a restorative or invigorating medicine.

24.] A reversal of the form of the Eucharist, as in Matthew 26: 26–8; Mark 14: 22–4; Luke 22: 17–20.

The World

By day she wooes me, soft, exceeding fair:
    But all night as the moon so changeth she;
    Loathsome and foul with hideous leprosy
And subtle serpents gliding in her hair.
5   By day she wooes me to the outer air,
    Ripe fruits, sweet flowers, and full satiety:
    But thro' the night, a beast she grins at me,
A very monster void of love and prayer.
By day she stands a lie: by night she stands
10   In all the naked horror of the truth
With pushing horns and clawed and clutching hands.
Is this a friend indeed; that I should sell
    My soul to her, give her my life and youth,
Till my feet, cloven too, take hold on hell?

[1862]

Old and New Year Ditties

3

PASSING away, saith the World, passing away:
Chances, beauty and youth sapped day by day:
Thy life never continueth in one stay.

The World] The World, the Flesh and the Devil stand together to represent the material, the sensual and the altogether evil. Cf. 'From all the deceits of the world, the flesh, and the devil, Good Lord, deliver us', The Litany (Book of Common Prayer).

1. wooes] Archaic spelling.

11–14.] The Devil is commonly represented as having horns and cloven feet.

Date.] Composed on 21 Oct 1853.

Old and New Year Ditties] W. M. Rossetti notes that the three lyrics under this composite title were composed in three separate years, and were originally titled: [1] 'The end of the year' (1856); [2] 'New Year's Eve' (1860); [3] 'The knell of the year' (1860). He comments: 'I have always regarded this last as the very summit and mountain-top of Christina's work' (Rossetti, ed. Rossetti, 1904, p. 472).

1. PASSING away] Cf. Hemans's poem 'Passing Away': 'It is written on the rose, / In its glory's full array – / Read what those buds disclose – / "Passing away".' See also Webster's 'Passing Away' (1867), p. 147 below. Cf. Ecclesiastes 1: 4: 'One generation passeth away, and another generation cometh: but the earth abideth for ever'; Psalm 144: 4: 'Man is like to vanity: his days are as a shadow that passeth away'; 1 Corinthians 7: 31: 'for the fashion of this world passeth away'; 1 John 2: 17: 'And the world passeth away, and the lust thereof: but he that doeth the will of God abideth for ever'; Matthew 24: 35: 'Heaven and earth shall pass away, but my words shall not pass away'. See also Mark 13: 31 and Luke 21: 33.

Is the eye waxen dim, is the dark hair changing to grey
5   That hath won neither laurel nor bay?
I shall clothe myself in Spring and bud in May:
Thou, root-stricken, shalt not rebuild thy decay
On my bosom for aye.
Then I answered: Yea.

10   Passing away, saith my Soul, passing away:
With its burden of fear and hope, of labour and play;
Hearken what the past doth witness and say:
Rust in thy gold, a moth is in thine array,
A canker is in thy bud, thy leaf must decay.
15   At midnight, at cockcrow, at morning, one certain day
Lo the bridegroom shall come and shall not delay:
Watch thou and pray.
Then I answered: Yea.

Passing away, saith my God, passing away:
20   Winter passeth after the long delay:
New grapes on the vine, new figs on the tender spray,
Turtle calleth turtle in Heaven's May.
Tho' I tarry, wait for Me, trust Me, watch and pray.
Arise, come away, night is past and lo it is day,
25   My love, My sister, My spouse, thou shalt hear Me say.
Then I answered: Yea.

[1862]

---

4. *waxen*] grown.

5. *neither laurel nor bay*] Two words for essentially the same thing: the leaves of the bay-laurel tree were used as an emblem of distinction in poetry.

7.] Cf. Matthew 3: 10: 'every tree which bringeth not forth good fruit is hewn down, and cast into the fire'.

8. *for aye*] for ever.

13.] Cf. Matthew 6: 19: 'Lay not up for yourselves treasures upon earth, where moth and rust doth corrupt . . .'.   *array*] apparel, clothing.

16.] Cf. Matthew 25: 6: 'Behold, the bridegroom cometh; go ye out to meet him' (from the parable of the wise and foolish virgins).

17.] Cf. Mark 14: 38: 'Watch ye and pray, lest ye enter into temptation.'

21–2.] Cf. Song of Solomon 2: 11–17. *Fig* trees and *grape* vines are traditionally held to symbolise peace and prosperity. *Turtles*, i.e. turtle-doves, are known for their affection to their mates.

23.] Cf. Matthew 26: 41: 'Watch and pray, that ye enter not into temptation: the spirit is willing, but the flesh is weak.'

25. *My love, My sister, My spouse*] Cf. Song of Solomon 4: 10: 'How fair is thy love, my sister, my spouse!'

Long Barren

Thou who didst hang upon a barren tree,
My God, for me;
   Tho' I till now be barren, now at length,
   Lord, give me strength
5   To bring forth fruit to Thee.

Thou who didst bear for me the crown of thorn,
Spitting and scorn;
   Tho' I till now have put forth thorns, yet now
   Strengthen me Thou
10   That better fruit be borne.

Thou Rose of Sharon, Cedar of broad roots,
Vine of sweet fruits,
   Thou Lily of the vale with fadeless leaf,
   Of thousands Chief,
15   Feed Thou my feeble shoots.

[1866]

Long Barren] It is worth comparing the sonnet by G. M. Hopkins, 'Thou art indeed just, Lord', which also takes the form of a prayer for relief from aridity. Hopkins had met Christina Rossetti by August 1864. He was sufficiently intrigued by Rossetti's poem 'The Convent Threshold' to write his own poem in response, 'A Voice from the World: Fragments of "An Answer to Miss Rossetti's *Convent Threshold*" ' (composed *c.* June 1864–Jan 1865). For connections between the two poets, see Bump (1980). Composed on 21 Feb 1865, 'Long Barren' appeared in the devotional section of *The Prince's Progress and Other Poems* (1866).

1. a barren tree] i.e. the cross. Cf. 1 Peter 2: 24: 'Who his own self bare our sins in his own body on the tree'; Acts 5: 30: 'The God of our fathers raised up Jesus, whom ye slew and hanged on a tree'.

6–7.] Cf. Matthew 27: 29–30; Mark 15: 17–19.

11–14.] These lines are metaphorically complex: for example, the Rose of Sharon can be at once the Bride of the Song of Songs (see Song of Solomon 2: 1), the Virgin Mary, or Christ himself. Much of this stanza draws upon imagery from the Song, which has borne various allegorical interpretations over time. The one closest to Rossetti's seems to be the tradition begun by St Bernard, of reading the Song as an expression of the soul's search for God, using imagery to speak of the heart of the mystical life. For the 'lily of the vale' see Song of Solomon 2: 1; for 'of thousands Chief', see Song of Solomon 5: 10 ('My beloved is white and ruddy, the chiefest among ten thousand'). For 'the cedar of broad roots' see Hosea 14: 5; for the 'vine of sweet fruits', see John 15: 1–2; for 'the fadeless leaf' see Ezekiel 47: 12.

Autumn Violets

KEEP love for youth, and violets for the spring:
　　Or if these bloom when worn-out autumn grieves,
　　Let them lie hid in double shade of leaves,
　Their own, and others dropped down withering;
5　For violets suit when home birds build and sing,
　　Not when the outbound bird a passage cleaves;
　　Not with dry stubble of mown harvest sheaves,
　But when the green world buds to blossoming.
　Keep violets for the spring, and love for youth,
10　　Love that should dwell with beauty, mirth, and hope:
　　Or if a later sadder love be born,
　Let this not look for grace beyond its scope,
But give itself, nor plead for answering truth –
　　A grateful Ruth tho' gleaning scanty corn.

[1875]

Two Thoughts of Death

1

HER heart that loved me once is rottenness
　　Now and corruption; and her life is dead
　　That was to have been one with mine she said.
　The earth must lie with such a cruel stress
5　On her eyes where the white lids used to press;
　　Foul worms fill up her mouth so sweet and red;
　　Foul worms are underneath her graceful head.
　Yet these, being born of her from nothingness
　These worms are certainly flesh of her flesh. –
10　　How is it that the grass is rank and green,

Autumn Violets] In 1875 Christina Rossetti noted that she and sister poet Dora Greenwell were sharing the experience of aging. Rossetti copied out 'Autumn Violets' and inscribed it to her friend (Gray, 1999, p. 145).

14. Ruth] See Ruth 2: 10. There may be an ironic implication here: Ruth's gleaning led to her marriage to Boaz (by which she became an ancestor of the house of David, and hence of Christ).

Two Thoughts of Death. *10. rank and green*] 'Rank' can mean coarse, gross, lustful, while 'green' can signify both fresh growth and decay.

And the dew dropping rose is brave and fresh
Above what was so sweeter far than they?
Even as her beauty hath passed quite away
   Their's too shall be as tho' it had not been.

2

15   So I said underneath the dusky trees:
   But because I still loved her memory
   I stooped to pluck a pale anemone
And lo! my hand lighted upon heartsease
Not fully blown: while with new life from these
20   Fluttered a starry moth that rapidly
   Rose toward the sun: sunlighted flashed on me
Its wings that seemed to throb like heart pulses.
Far far away it flew far out of sight,
   From earth and flowers of earth it passed away
25   As tho' it flew straight up into the light.
   Then my heart answered me: Thou fool to say
   That she is dead whose night is turned to day,
And whose day shall no more turn back to night.

[1896]

In an Artist's Studio

ONE face looks out from all his canvasses,
   One selfsame figure sits or walks or leans;

---

11. brave] showy or handsome (as well as courageous).

17–18.] *Anemone* and *heartsease* are both flowers which grow easily in the wild as well as under cultivation. The red anemone, in Christian tradition, is said to owe its stained colour to the blood that trickled from the cross; the origin of the name 'heartsease', a smaller kind of pansy, is obscure, but can here be taken literally.

20. starry moth] The epithet 'starry' here emphasises the transcendent capacity of the moth, which emerges from the seeming death of its chrysalis to a 'resurrection' of sorts, as a winged creature ascending away from the earth.

28.] In manuscript, the last line reads: 'And no more shall her day turn back to night'. In her notes on the poem, Crump observes that the revisions appear to be in William Michael Rossetti's hand (Rossetti, ed. Crump, 1990, vol. 3, p. 430). Scholars frequently question W. M. Rossetti's editing of his sister's work after her death.

Date.] Composed on 16 March 1850.

In an Artist's Studio] It is often assumed that this poem refers to Rossetti's sister-in-law Elizabeth ('Lizzie') Siddal (see note on 'Goblin Market', ll. 34–5, above). However, Rossetti had first-hand experience of being an artist's model, posing for Dante Gabriel's paintings of the Virgin Mary,

We found her hidden just behind those screens,
That mirror gave back all her loveliness.
5   A queen in opal or in ruby dress,
    A nameless girl in freshest summer greens,
    A saint, an angel; – every canvass means
The same one meaning, neither more nor less.
He feeds upon her face by day and night,
10   And she with true kind eyes looks back on him
Fair as the moon and joyful as the light:
    Not wan with waiting, not with sorrow dim;
Not as she is, but was when hope shone bright;
    Not as she is, but as she fills his dream.

[1896]

'The Girlhood of Mary Virgin' (1848–9) and 'Ecce Ancilla Domini!' (1849–50), as well as for Holman Hunt's painting of Christ, 'The Light of the World' (1851–3), which now hangs in St Paul's. Hunt's painting is based on Revelation 3: 20: 'Behold, I stand at the door, and knock'; Rossetti published a poem with this text as its title in the *English Woman's Journal* (1861). See Rossetti, ed. Marsh (1994), p. 431.

11.] Cf. Robert Browning's 'Andrea del Sarto' (*Men and Women*, 1855): 'My face, my moon, my everybody's moon, / Which everybody looks on and calls his' (ll. 29–30).

Date.] Composed on 24 Dec 1856.

AUGUSTA WEBSTER (1837–1894)

Julia Augusta Webster (*née* Davies) published first under the pseudonym 'Cecil Home' and later as Augusta Webster. She was born in Poole, Dorset, the daughter of Vice-Admiral George Davies and his wife Julia (Hume). She was unusually well educated for a girl, attending school first at Banff in Scotland (where her father was stationed at Banff Castle from 1844 to 1848), then at Penzance in Cornwall, and after 1851 in Cambridge, where her father was appointed chief constable, and later in Paris and Geneva also. Most of her childhood was spent living on board her father's ship in various ports, but she was a brilliant girl, and by the time she reached Cambridge, where she studied at the School of Art, and learned Latin and Greek to help a younger brother with his schoolwork, she was also able to learn Spanish and Italian. After her marriage in 1863 to Thomas Webster, a fellow and later law lecturer at Trinity College, Cambridge, she became a successful translator as well as a poet, novelist, dramatist and essayist. Webster published in 1866 a verse translation of Aeschylus's *Prometheus Bound*, which plunged her directly into the public territory of classical learning more usually occupied by males; Elizabeth Barrett, however, had been a notable role model with her own version of *Prometheus Bound* published in 1833. Like EBB, Webster was outstanding in her determination to tackle the field of classical learning on equal terms with her male peers. In 1868 she followed up with a fine translation of Euripides' *Medea* – not a heroine for the faint-hearted, and certainly not regarded in Victorian times as a fitting subject for treatment by a female pen.

But before reaching this level of assurance, she had published under her pseudonym three original works – two volumes of verse, *Blanche Lisle, and Other Poems* (1860) and *Lilian Gray* (1864), and a novel, *Lesley's Guardians* (1864). The novel, while interesting, was not a success, being too rambling and improbable, with an ambitious theme revolving about that perennial obsession of so many women poets in the period, beginning (in this volume) with Felicia Hemans – namely, how to reconcile the needs of the artist with the needs of the woman. The novel's treatment of the theme suggests Webster's own involvement in this dilemma at an early stage in her career. The heroine, Lesley, who is half-French – reflecting her author's continental education, perhaps – is initially disappointed in love:

> Nevertheless she had her happiness; she began to feel the inspiration of her art; her life went out into it more and more; and though it might be doubted whether this growing gift of genius were not in itself a sadness, yet it was sorrow's greatest rival.
>
> (vol. 1, p. 116)

By the end of the novel, however, she has located and married a more suitable man, one who, Lesley thinks, will solve her dilemma by accommodating her needs as an artist. In the end, of course, her satisfaction must come vicariously; she has the 'delight of watching the development of talent like hers, and more, in her second boy' (vol. 3, p. 279). Webster moved in a far more feminist direction in her subsequent work, and ironically, perhaps, in the light of this fictional ending, she herself never produced a boy, instead having a daughter, whom she celebrated memorably in her wonderful sonnet sequence *Mother and Daughter*. This unique piece of work was, sadly, never completed before her death from cancer at the age of 53, but it was published posthumously in a volume edited by W. M. Rossetti in 1895. By that time Webster had left far behind her the girlhood ideology producing the notion that, in the end, women must leave artistic endeavour to men, and had herself become not only a well-respected and influential writer and reviewer, but also a firm supporter of improved educational opportunities for women.

Well-respected as her work was, however, it never earned her the wider recognition she deserved. This is probably because her chief creative talent lay in drama, particularly drama based on acute psychological observation of character, and serious theatre was especially difficult for women to break into. Her four plays, *The Auspicious Day* (verse drama, 1872), *Disguises: A Drama* (1879), *In a Day: A Drama* (1882) and *The Sentence: A Drama* (1887), all seem to have been written as closet dramas – to be read, rather than performed. Yet *In a Day*, a domestic drama set in ancient Greece, did receive at least one staging, with Webster's actress daughter playing the female lead, a slave whose master falls in love with her, and whose philosopher father meditates with acute insight on the meanings of freedom while the action goes forward. William Rossetti, along with most readers at the time, judged *The Sentence* to be her best play, asserting its merits in his introductory essay to the volume containing Webster's sonnet sequence:

> Mrs Webster's reputation rests securely upon several volumes of verse – highly remarkable verse, at once feminine and in a right sense masculine – including four Dramas . . . to me *The Sentence* appears the one supreme thing . . . amid the work of *all* British poetesses [he does not except his sister Christina Rossetti, who also greatly admired the work]. Taking into account its importance in scale and subject, and its magnificence in handling, it beats everything else.

It is interesting to speculate upon the meaning of the phrase 'and in a right sense, masculine': presumably, it alluded to a quality of rational thinking which is very strong in Webster's writing. To a modern reader, however, some of the other plays, which may be more open to feminist interpretation, hold at least equal interest. In all of them, however, the main interest lies in the way they combine the setting up of a complex ethical dilemma with astute character analysis.

In fact, Webster's creative talent lay with character study, which is why she was so strongly drawn in her poetry to the form of the dramatic monologue. This form, of course, was strongly associated with Robert Browning by the time Webster began publishing, and like most of the other poets in this volume, she had clearly read his work with admiration. Florence Boos is one recent critic who has noted the derivative nature of Webster's verse-making, particularly her debt to Browning in *Dramatic Studies*, published in 1866, the first of her volumes of verse to be issued under her own name.[1] But to focus on this debt might lead one to overlook the

---

[1] See Boos's article on Webster in the *Dictionary of Literary Biography* 35 (1985), pp. 280–4.

extent to which Webster is actually being original – that is, in conducting an implicit dialogue with other poets, whereby she questions their attitudes and their conclusions. For example, in one of the first monologues in *Dramatic Studies*, 'The Painter', Webster sets a scene very like that of Browning's 'Andrea del Sarto', with an artist husband regretting the constraints of marriage which have prevented the production of a masterpiece; yet, unlike del Sarto's wife, this wife, Ruth, does all she can to encourage his art. 'The Flood of Is in Brittany' (see p. 160 below) may suggest the influence of popular poet Jean Ingelow (who was a friend of Webster's), but its manner of recounting the legend is far more tough-minded, less flowery and sentimental, than Ingelow's style. Again, in 'A Castaway' (see p. 154), on the daring theme of prostitution, Webster constructs a monologue voiced by the kind of woman who is only the silenced object of contemplation in D. G. Rossetti's poem 'Jenny'. Where Rossetti's speaker congratulates himself, as it were, for his kindness to a mere prostitute, Webster's speaker, the prostitute herself, reveals her own mixed feelings at the role she plays in society, and at the hypocrisy, not only of her male clients, but also of middle-class women who used to be her peers before her 'fall'. The poem also draws attention to the sheer waste and sense of bitter frustration among those women who were denied a proper education in Victorian society. Similarly her Medea poem, also reprinted here, articulates a kind of rebellion too often unspoken in so-called polite society, as well as giving an unusually pointed vignette of the Jason-figure in his inability to deal with his own grief, living on the beach with his beloved boat like some modern 'macho' bloke sleeping out with his motorbike or surfboard, unable to cope with the reality of his life and loss.

Again, while a sonnet sequence was not in itself a new genre – indeed, it was a popular form of display among late nineteenth-century poets – the idea of shifting its ground away from the traditional pair of heterosexual lovers to a same-sex love between mother and daughter carries some of the force of breaking a taboo. Many of the sonnets have the air of being written while under sentence of death (she knew she was seriously ill), which gives the poignancy of an imminent parting to the theme of mutual love. It is clear that the mother's love for the daughter is unconditional, felt in the bones, and it has the air of a last lingering look by the possessive lover at the body of the beloved before it is snatched away. This generates an intense awareness of the fragility of life which is very powerful.

Webster may not have been one of the most formally innovative of poets, but she was wonderfully inventive in the way she exploited genre. Preferring to follow speech rhythms rather than formal metric cadences, she was able to cut through a lot of the 'beautification' convention still clinging to Victorian poetry and open it up in ways that enabled her to focus on issues of particular interest to herself and other women.

Text: The poems chosen are from *A Woman Sold* (1867), *Portraits* (1870), *A Book of Rhyme* (1881), *Selections* (1893) and *Mother and Daughter. An Uncompleted Sonnet-Sequence* (1895). The date of first publication in volume form is given in square brackets at the foot of each poem. In each case, the copy-text is the first edition, with the exception of 'Where Home Was', first published in *A Book of Rhyme*, which is taken from *Selections* (1893).

Passing Away

PASSING away from you, love,
And you look so sad, sitting there by my bed,
And I know you are thinking 'How will it be?
'She is the meaning of living to me,
5   'How can I live with her dead?'

Passing away from you, love,
Growing weaker and weaker every day:
Soon you will sit near me, ah! so alone,
For I shall not turn to you, I your own,
10   I shall not heed what you say.

Passing away from you, love,
It will not be long now before the last:
We are thinking about it, feign as we will,
While I seem to sleep and you are so still,
15   Our clasped hands holding fast.

One same thought in our minds,
How strangely lone you will feel in your home
When I have gone out of your waking days
And you dream of our life in a sorrowful maze
20   When the desolate evenings come.

But, love, it cannot be lost,
The life that is ours, that I leave to you yours,
As something far more than a memory;
We know it something too real to die,
25   It is love, and love endures.

It will follow you into the new;
You cannot part it from you, chance what will,
You could not live as if I had not been;
So to you long hence when my grave is green,
30   Love, I must be somewhat still.

Passing Away] Cf. Christina Rossetti's poem from 'Old and New Year Ditties', published in 1862, which begins, 'Passing away, saith the World, passing away' (see p. 138 above). The substance of this poem can be compared with Robert Browning's influential 'Any Wife to Any Husband', from *Men and Women* (1855).

19. *maze*] state of bewilderment.

Passing away from you, love,
And the weakness and weariness grow into pain,
So that the last would seem dropping asleep
If it were not for you. But one rests in God's keep,
35   So I think you will find me again.

[1867]

Medea in Athens [*extract*]

[Note: Webster had published her translation of Euripides' play *Medea* in 1866. Medea was a figure who aroused a lot of interest around this time: see, for example, William Morris, *The Life and Death of Jason*, 1867, and Amy Levy, 'Medea', 1884. Webster's poem is not an extract from her translation, but an imaginative elaboration of what happened to Medea after she quit Corinth for Athens, having murdered her sons and Glaucè, Jason's intended second wife, as well as Glaucè's father, King Creon. As the poem opens, Medea has just received news of Jason's death which happened as she had foretold. The extract printed below occurs at the beginning of the original text, which extends to half as long again.]

DEAD is he? Yes, our stranger guest said dead –
said it by noonday, when it seemed a thing
most natural and so indifferent
as if the tale ran that a while ago
5   there died a man I talked with a chance hour
when he by chance was near me. If I spoke
'Good news for us but ill news for the dead
when the gods sweep a villain down to them,'
'twas the prompt trick of words, like a pat phrase
10   from some one other's song, found on the lips
and used because 'tis there: for through all day
the news seemed neither good nor ill to me.

And now, when day with all its useless talk
and useless smiles and idiots' prying eyes
15   that impotently peer into one's life,
when day with all its seemly lying shows
has gone its way and left pleased fools to sleep,
while weary mummers, taking off the mask,

Medea in Athens. 2.] Note Webster's unusual practice of avoiding capital letters to begin each line of her blank verse poem.

18. mummers] Actors who wore disguises and played in dumb-shows.

discern that face themselves forgot anon
20   and, sitting in the lap of sheltering night,
learn their own secrets from her – even now
does it seem either good or ill to me?
No, but mere strange.

And this most strange of all
that I care nothing.

Nay, how wild thought grows.
25   Meseems one came and told of Jason's death:
but 'twas a dream. Else should I, wondering thus,
reck not of him, nor with the virulent hate
that should be mine against mine enemy,
nor with that weakness which sometimes I feared
30   should this day make me, not remembering Glaucè,
envy him to death as though he had died mine?

Can he be dead? It were so strange a world
with him not in it.

Dimly I recall
some prophecy a god breathed by my mouth.
35   It could not err. What was it? For I think
it told his death.

Has a god come to me?
Is it thou, my Hecate? How know I all?
For I know all as if from long ago:
and I know all beholding instantly.
40   Is not that he, arisen through the mists? –
a lean and haggard man, rough round the eyes,
dull and with no scorn left upon his lip,
decayed out of his goodliness and strength;

---

27. *reck not of*] set no store by, take no notice of.

36.] [Author's note]: Σὺ δ ', ὥσπερ εἰκὸς κα Ὑθανεῖ κακὸς κακῶς,
Ἀργοῦς κάρα σὸν λειψάυψ πεπληγμένος.
EUR. *Med.* 1386, 7.
The Loeb edition translates the lines as 'Thou, as is meet, foul wretch, shall foully die, / By Argo's wreckage smitten on the skull'. In her own translation (1868), Webster gives: 'For thee, as is most fit, thou, an ill man, / Shall die an ill death, thy head battered in / By the ruins of thine Argo'. This is Medea's prophecy of Jason's death.

37. *my Hecate*] goddess of magic, ghosts and witchcraft (and therefore Medea's deity). Hecate's temple had been the scene of Medea's betrothal to Jason.

149

a wanned and broken image of a god;
45 dim counterfeit of Jason, heavily
wearing the name of him and memories.

And lo, he rests with lax and careless limbs
on the loose sandbed wind-heaped round his ship
that rots in sloth like him, and props his head
50 on a half-buried fallen spar. The sea,
climbing the beach towards him, seethes and frets,
and on the verge two sunned and shadowed clouds
take shapes of notched rock-islands; and his thoughts
drift languid to the steep Symplegades
55 and the sound of waters crashing at their base.
And now he speaks out to his loneliness
'I was afraid and careful, but she laughed:
"Love steers" she said: and when the rocks were far,
grey twinkling spots in distance, suddenly
60 her face grew white, and, looking back to them,
she said, "Oh love, a god has whispered me
'twere well had we died there, for strange mad woes
are waiting for us in your Greece": and then
she tossed her head back, while her brown hair streamed
65 gold in the wind and sun, and her face glowed
with daring beauty, "What of woes", she cried,
"if only they leave time for love enough?"
But what a fire and flush! It took one's breath!'
And then he lay half musing, half adoze,
70 shadows of me went misty through his sight.

And bye and bye he roused and cried 'Oh dolt!
Glaucè was never half so beautiful.'
Then under part-closed lids remembering her,
'Poor Glaucè, a sweet face, and yet methinks
75 she might have wearied me:' and suddenly,

---

44. *wanned*] pallid, sickly. 'Wan' is normally an adjective.

48. *his ship*] *Argo*, the ship in which Jason voyaged with the Argonauts in search of the Golden Fleece, only obtained by the help of Medea.

50. *spar*] any piece of the wooden mast or rigging structure on a sailing ship.

54. *the steep Symplegades*] two islands of dangerous rocks at the entrance of the Euxine (now the Black) Sea, one on the side of Asia, the other Europe. Jason and the Argonauts had been the first to establish their position and form.

71. *dolt*] idiot, blockhead.

smiting the sand awhirl with his angry hand,
scorned at himself 'What god befooled my wits
to dream my fancy for her yellow curls
and milk-white softness subtle policy?
80   Wealth and a royal bride: but what beyond?
Medea, with her skills, her presciences,
man's wisdom, woman's craft, her rage of love
that gave her to serve me strength next divine,
Medea would have made me what I would;
85   Glaucè but what she could. I schemed amiss
and earned the curses the gods send on fools.
Ruined, ruined! A laughing stock to foes!
No man so mean but he may pity me;
no man so wretched but will keep aloof
90   lest the curse upon me make him wretcheder.
Ruined!'

        And lo I see him hide his face
like a man who'll weep with passion: but to him
the passion comes not, only slow few tears
of one too weary. And from the great field
95   where the boys race he hears their jubilant shout
hum through the distance, and he sighs 'Ah me!
she might have spared the children, left me them: –
no sons, no sons to stand about me now
and prosper me, and tend me bye and bye
100   in faltering age, and keep my name on earth
when I shall be departed out of sight.'

        And the shout hummed louder forth: and whirring past
a screaming sea-bird flapped out to the bay,
and listlessly he watched it dip and rise
105   till it skimmed out of sight, so small a speck
as a mayfly on the brook; and then he said
'Fly forth, fly forth, bird, fly to fierce Medea
where by great Ægeus she sits queening it,
belike a joyful mother of new sons;
110   tell her she never loved me as she talked,
else had no wrong at my hand shewn so great:

---

81. presciences] foreknowledge of events.

108. Ægeus] mythical king of Attica (ancient Greece), whom Medea took for her next lover after Jason; here (perhaps for Victorian sensibilities) she married him.

tell her that she breaks oaths more than I broke,
even so much as she seemed to love most –
she who fits fondling in a husband's arms
115   while I am desolate.' And again he said
'My house is perished with me – ruined, ruined!'

    At that he rose and muttering in his teeth
still 'ruined, ruined', slowly paced the sands:
then stood and, gazing on the ragged hulk,
120   cried 'Oh loathed tool of fiends, that, through all storms
and sundering waters, borest me to Medea,
rot, rot, accursed thing', and petulant
pashed at the side –

            Lo, lo! I see it part!
a tottering spar – it parts, it falls, it strikes!
125   He is prone on the sand, the blood wells from his brow,
he moans, he speaks, 'Medea's prophecy'.
See he has fainted.

            Hush, hush! he has lain
with death and silence long: now he wakes up –
'Where is Medea? Let her bind my head.'
130   Hush, hush! A sigh – a breath – He is dead.

           *   *   *   *   *   *

            Medea!
What, is it thou? What, thou, this whimpering fool,
this kind meek coward! Sick for pity art thou?
Or did the vision scare thee? Out on me!
135   do I drivel like a slight disconsolate girl
wailing her love?

            No, not one foolish tear
that shamed my cheek welled up for any grief
at his so pitiful lone end. The touch
of ancient memories and the woman's trick
140   of easy weeping took me unawares:
but grief! Why should I grieve?

---

116. *My house is perished with me*] i.e. I am the last of my line, without heirs to my name.

123. *pashed*] struck blows.

And yet for this,
that he is dead. He should still pine and dwine,
hungry for his old lost strong food of life
vanished with me, hungry for children's love,
145　hungry for me. Ever to think of me –
with love, with hate, what care I? hate is love –
Ever to think and long. Oh it was well!
Yea, my new marriage hope has been achieved:
for he *did* count me happy, picture me
150　happy with Ægeus; he *did* dream of me
as all to Ægeus that I was to him,
and to him nothing; and *did* yearn for me
and know me lost – we two so far apart
as dead and living, I an envied wife
155　and he alone and childless. Jason, Jason,
come back to earth; live, live for my revenge.

But lo the man is dead: I am forgotten.
Forgotten; something goes from life in that –
as if oneself had died, when the half self
160　of one's true living time has slipped away
from reach of memories, has ceased to know
that such a woman is.

A wondrous thing
to be so separate having been so near –
near by hate last and once by so strong love.
165　Would love have kept us near if he had died
in the good days? Tush, I should have died too:
we should have gone together, hand in hand,
and made dusk Hades glorious each to each.

Ah me, if then when through the fitful seas
170　we saw the great rocks glimmer, and the crew
howled 'We are lost! lo the Symplegades!'
too late to shun them, if but then some wave,
our secret friend, had dashed us from our course,
sending us to be shivered at the base,
175　well, well indeed! And yet what say I there?

---

142. dwine] waste away.

168. dusk Hades] Dusk is an unusual form of dusky: dim or gloomy. Hades is the Greek name
for the abode of the dead.

Ten years together were they not worth cost
of all the anguish? Oh me, how I loved him!
Why did I not die loving him?

*   *   *   *   *   *   *

[Note: The poem continues for another 90 lines, extending Medea's soliloquy into
a relentless blaming of Jason for making her capable of committing crimes against
those she most loves (first her brother, later her boys) coupled with a determina-
tion never to forgive him. She tries to convince herself that the loss of her children
was worthwhile, since Jason has now died 'shamed and childless', but the terms in
which she dwells both on her own loss of her sons and on her determination to
forget Jason reveal the extent to which they all still haunt her. The poem ends:

Go, go, thou mind'st me of my sons,
and then I hate thee worse; go to thy grave
by which none weep. I have forgotten thee.]

[1870]

A Castaway [*extract*]

POOR little diary, with its simple thoughts,
its good resolves, its 'Studied French an hour,'
'Read Modern History,' 'Trimmed up my grey hat,'
'Darned stockings,' 'Tatted,' 'Practised my new song,'
5   'Went to the daily service,' 'Took Bess soup,'

A Castaway] Cf. Webster's earlier poem, 'The Preacher', from her volume *Dramatic Studies* (1866),
which opens with a biblical quote (1 Corinthians 9: 27): ' *"Lest that by any means / When I have
preached to others I myself / Should be a castaway."* If some one now / Would take that text and
preach to us that preach . . .'. 'Castaway' was the term commonly used in Victorian England
to denote an outcast from polite society, viz. a prostitute. Cf. D. G. Rossetti's poem 'Jenny'
(*Poems*, 1870), for a masculine view of the same topic. For a discussion of 'A Castaway' and
'Jenny', see Brown (1991).

1. diary] It is not clear whether the speaker, in quoting from her girlhood diary, is actually
holding it in her hand, or merely remembering its contents. In either case, these give a good
notion of the conventional occupations of a 'young lady' of the middle classes. In various
essays written for *The Examiner* and collected as *A Housewife's Opinions* (1879), Webster ques-
tions the obligatory investment of women's time in useless occupations. In 'Pianist and
Martyr', for example, she criticises the custom whereby society measures the worth of young
women according to how many hours they practise their piano playing, without any regard
to their individual talents.

4. tatted] i.e. made tatting, a kind of lace-like netted trimming.

'Went out to tea.' Poor simple diary!
and did *I* write it? Was I this good girl,
this budding colourless young rose of home?
did I so live content in such a life,
10 seeing no larger scope, nor asking it,
than this small constant round – old clothes to mend,
new clothes to make, then go and say my prayers,
or carry soup, or take a little walk
and pick the ragged-robins in the hedge?
15 Then for ambition, (was there ever life
that could forego that?) to improve my mind
and know French better and sing harder songs;
for gaiety, to go, in my best white
well washed and starched and freshened with new bows,
20 and take tea out to meet the clergyman.
No wishes and no cares, almost no hopes,
only the young girl's hazed and golden dreams
that veil the Future from her.

    So long since:
and now it seems a jest to talk of me
25 as if I could be one with her, of me
who am . . . me.

    And what is that? My looking-glass
answers it passably; a woman sure,
no fiend, no slimy thing out of the pools,
a woman with a ripe and smiling lip
30 that has no venom in its touch I think,
with a white brow on which there is no brand;
a woman none dare call not beautiful,
not womanly in every woman's grace.

 Aye let me feed upon my beauty thus,
35 be glad in it like painters when they see
at last the face they dreamed but could not find
look out from their canvas on them, triumph in it,
the dearest thing I have. Why, 'tis my all,
let me make much of it: is it not this,
40 this beauty, my own curse at once and tool

---

14. ragged-robins] the popular name for a well-known English flower.

to snare men's souls – (I know what the good say
of beauty in such creatures) – is it not this
that makes me feel myself a woman still,
some little pride, some little –

                              Here's a jest!
45   what word will fit the sense but modesty?
A wanton I but modest!

                    Modest, true;
I'm not drunk in the streets, ply not for hire
at infamous corners with my likenesses
of the humbler kind; yes, modesty's my word –
50   'twould shape my mouth well too, I think I'll try:
'Sir, Mr What-you-will, Lord Who-knows-what,
my present lover or my next to come,
value me at my worth, fill your purse full,
for I am modest; yes, and honour me
55   as though your schoolgirl sister or your wife
could let her skirts brush mine or talk of me;
for I am modest.'

                    Well, I flout myself:
but yet, but yet –

                         Fie, poor fantastic fool,
why do I play the hypocrite alone,
60   who am no hypocrite with others by?
where should be my 'But yet'? I am that thing
called half a dozen dainty names, and none
dainty enough to serve the turn and hide
the one coarse English word that lurks beneath:
just that, no worse, no better.

65   And, for me,
I say let no one be above her trade;
I own my kindredship with any drab
who sells herself as I, although she crouch
in fetid garrets and I have a home

---

46. *wanton*] a loose woman.
47–9.] i.e. I am not a streetwalker.
57. *flout*] mock, jeer at.
67. *drab*] strumpet, whore.

70   all velvet and marqueterie and pastilles,
        although she hide her skeleton in rags
        and I set fashions and wear cobweb lace:
        the difference lies but in my choicer ware,
        that I sell beauty and she ugliness;
75   our traffic's one – I'm no sweet slaver-tongue
        to gloze upon it and explain myself
        a sort of fractious angel misconceived –
        our traffic's one: I own it. And what then?
        I know of worse that are called honourable.
80   Our lawyers, who, with noble eloquence
        and virtuous outbursts, lie to hang a man,
        or lie to save him, which way goes the fee:
        our preachers, gloating on your future hell
        for not believing what they doubt themselves:
85   our doctors, who sort poisons out by chance,
        and wonder how they'll answer, and grow rich:
        our journalists, whose business is to fib
        and juggle truths and falsehoods to and fro:
        our tradesmen, who must keep unspotted names
90   and cheat the least like stealing that they can:
        our – all of them, the virtuous worthy men
        who feed on the world's follies, vices, wants,
        and do their businesses of lies and shams
        honestly, reputably, while the world
95   claps hands and cries 'good luck,' which of their trades,
        their honourable trades, barefaced like mine,
        all secrets brazened out, would shew more white?

        And whom do I hurt more than they? as much?
        The wives? Poor fools, what do I take from them
100   worth crying for or keeping? If they knew
        what their fine husbands look like seen by eyes
        that may perceive there are more men than one!
        But, if they can, let them just take the pains
        to keep them: 'tis not such a mighty task
105   to pin an idiot to your apron-string;

---

70. *marqueterie and pastilles*] furniture with elaborate inlaid designs and lozenges of perfumed
paste for burning to sweeten a room.

75–6.] i.e. our trade is the same – I have no sweet slobbering flattery to gloss it over . . . .

86. *how they'll answer*] how they (i.e. the poisons) will succeed.

97. *brazened out*] faced impudently.

and wives have an advantage over us,
(the good and blind ones have), the smile or pout
leaves them no secret nausea at odd times.
Oh, they could keep their husbands if they cared,
110 but 'tis an easier life to let them go,
and whimper at it for morality.

Oh! those shrill carping virtues, safely housed
from reach of even a smile that should put red
on a decorous cheek, who rail at us
115 with such a spiteful scorn and rancorousness,
(which maybe is half envy at the heart),
and boast themselves so measurelessly good
and us so measurelessly unlike them,
what is their wondrous merit that they stay
120 in comfortable homes whence not a soul
has ever thought of tempting them, and wear
no kisses but a husband's upon lips
there is no other man desires to kiss –
refrain in fact from sin impossible?
125 How dare they hate us so? what have they done,
what borne, to prove them other than we are?
What right have they to scorn us – glass-case saints,
Dianas under lock and key – what right
more than the well-fed helpless barn-door fowl
130 to scorn the larcenous wild-birds?

[1870]

Where Home Was

'TWAS yesterday; 'twas long ago:
    And for this flaunting grimy street
And for this crowding to and fro,
    And thud and roar of wheels and feet,
5   Were elm-trees and the linnet's trill,
        The little gurgles of the rill,

---

112. carping] fault-finding; nit-picking.
128. Dianas] Diana was goddess of chastity as well as queen of the hunt.
130. larcenous] thievish.

158

And breath of meadow-flowers that blow
Ere roses make the summer sweet.

'Twas long ago; 'twas yesterday:
10   Our peach would just be new with leaves,
The swallow pair that used to lay
      Their glimmering eggs beneath our eaves
         Would flutter busy with their brood,
         And, haply, in our hazel-wood,
15   Small village urchins hide at play
      And girls sit binding blue-bell sheaves.

Was the house here, or there, or there?
      No landmark tells. All changed; all lost;
As when the waves that fret and tear
20   The fore-shores of some level coast
         Roll smoothly where the sea-pinks grew.
         All changed, and all grown old anew;
And I pass over, unaware,
      The memories I am seeking most.

25   But where these huddled house-rows spread,
      And where this thickened air hangs murk
And the dim sun peers round and red
      On stir and haste and cares and work,
         For me were baby's daisy-chains,
30   For me the meetings in the lanes,
The shy good-morrows softly said
      That paid my morning's lying lurk.

Oh lingering days of long ago,
      Not until now you passed away.
35   Years wane between and we unknow;
      Our youth is always yesterday.
         But, like a traveller home who craves
         For friends and finds forgotten graves,
I seek you where you dwelt, and, lo,
40   Even farewells not left to say.

[1881]

Where Home Was. *26. hangs murk*] hangs murkily; i.e. thick, dark, heavy.

32. lying lurk] a puzzling phrase: probably means lying idle.

35. unknow] forget.

The Flood of Is in Brittany

CRESTS of foam where the milch-kine fed,
    Where the green corn whitened and tanned;
Crests of foam and breakers ahead,
    And the deeps run smooth over rocks and sand.
5   Will the flood-tide back at the churchyard slope?
       Mercy, God, from thy sea!
'Twill check at the church and the graves. There's hope.
       Christ, let some land yet be!
The surf came sprinkling over the graves:
10   Then, human speed to the speed of waves,
And the drowning sank to the blessèd dead.

Fly who can! No moment to breathe:
    If the homes wreck, life is worth most.
Sound from the front of surges that seethe!
15   'Tis the sea rolling in from the other coast.
Sea from the west! Sea from the south!
     'Husband! snatched in the tide!'
'Child, thy mother?' 'She kissed my mouth,
    And sat with baby and cried,
20   For she could not carry him any more.'
'Brother, farewell, lest neither reach shore.'
Flood, flood right and left! Is there footing beneath?

The Flood of Is in Brittany] Webster takes the outline of her narrative from a Breton legend, possibly dating back to the fifth–sixth centuries, the period of the Breton emigration from Britain. There is more than one version of this tale but they all relate the submersion of the city of Is beneath the waves of the Bay of Douarnanez as punishment for the debauched and excessive behaviour of its inhabitants. According to the legend, the city of Is was built on land reclaimed from the sea, surrounded by dykes to which King Grallon held the keys. One night, after King Grallon leaves a feast to sleep, Dahut steals the keys and opens the dykes. Versions differ over whether Dahut acts completely of her own accord or whether she is encouraged by a lover; one version has Satan steal the keys from Dahut. The sea rushes in and everyone dies except for Grallon, who is warned miraculously of the danger by a saint, in this version St Gwenolé, the founder of the first monastery in Brittany. Dahut attempts to escape death by throwing herself onto her father's horse, thereby overburdening the horse and placing the king at risk. In the legend, St Gwenolé finally rescues Grallon by striking Dahut with his crosier and causing her to fall off. Here, the king casts his daughter off. See Doan (1981). A version of this legend, called 'The Drowning of Kaer-Is', was included in *Ballads and Songs of Brittany*, translated from the *Barsaz Breiz* of Vicomte Hersant de Villemarqué by Tom Taylor (1865). In A. S. Byatt's novel *Possession* (1990), the nineteenth-century poet Christabel LaMotte writes a poem based on this legend.

1. milch-kine] milk cows (archaic).

Grallon rode, rode, and said no word,
    Till the white foam splashed at his knee.
25 'Cling more close, my tender pet-bird;
    No fear but stout Gael save thee and me.'
St. Gwenolé rode behind the king,
    Muttered low in his prayer,
'Can God will the life of this wanton thing,
30   She that scoffed everywhere?'
Foremost and fastest the great tide raced;
Dahut, clasped firm to her father's waist,
Prayed in her terror, and never stirred.

Speed of horse to the flood-tide's speed:
35   And the high land seemed ever more far.
Grallon cried out, and patted his steed,
    'Hurry thee, Gael, or we drown where we are.'
Spake St. Gwenolé, riding at Grallon's hand,
    'Gael bears weight of sin:
40 She that has brought God's doom on thy land
    Sits him; the tide will win.'
Quoth Grallon, 'Thou'rt holy, and I forgive;
None else could have spoken thus and live.'
But proud fair Dahut gave scarcely heed.

45 Gael forced through amid the brunt
    Where the waves lashed at side and flanks.
St. Gwenolé's horse plunged on to the front,
    St. Gwenolé cried, 'Douarnenez banks!
We'd reach them yet, if Gael bore one.
50   Grallon, God bids, obey:
Thy kingdom drowns for the sins she has done;
    Cast the sinner away.'
King Grallon spoke slowly, 'She's my child.'
Fair Dahut lifted her head and smiled;
55 And 'twas 'Wait till Douarnenez, priest, for my thanks.'

23–33.] King Grallon, father of Dahut, rides his horse Gael, holding his daughter, while St Gwenolé rides behind.

48. *Douarnenez*] a fishing port in Brittany, on the western coast of France.

Dead and drowning came on with the scud;
  And the swimmers clutched wrack and drift;
Mark's hill tore and slipped with a thud,
  And the sea made a whirling pool in the rift.
60 Gwenolé's horse had the water shoal;
  Grallon's kept losing his feet,
Swam, but once shrieked like a human soul:
  Grallon's had two in seat.
On a moment's ground Grallon gave him halt,
65 Looked back. Oh, the Heavens for Dahut's fault
No city, no landmarks – bare trackless flood.

'Heart! Dear father: Gael must swim.'
  It was Dahut's voice at his ear.
Close she sat and clinging to him
70 She the thing of the world he held dear.
Her little fingers were knitted so tight,
  Grallon needed his strength:
But 'twixt such a two was no equal strife;
  'Twas but a minute's length.
75 'Father!' she cried, and then, 'Murderer!'
Then fell. So her sins were revenged on her;
And the flood-tide stayed at a low rock rim.

[1893]

---

58. *Mark's hill*] The Mark referred to here is Mark, King of Cornwall, and deceived husband in the legend of Tristan and Isolde; Mark's Hill is the supposed location of one of his dwellings, east of Douarnenez. Mark's Hill is not mentioned in the likely sources of Webster's poem, but Tristan was said to have gone wandering in Brittany after his affair with Isolde (promised bride to his uncle, Mark) was discovered. Here he met and married another Isolde although he did not love her. There is a strong connection between Brittany and Arthurian legend; in particular, the Bretons contributed the idea of Arthur's immortality and destined return. According to one version of the legend, Tristan's native land was Lyonesse, also associated with the submersion of land beneath the sea, a common motif in folk tales of Celtic origin. During the nineteenth century, there was a revival of interest in the story of Tristan and Isolde: e.g. Matthew Arnold, *Tristram and Iseult* (1852), Richard Wagner, *Tristan und Isolde* (1865), Alfred Tennyson, 'The Last Tournament' (1871, part of *Idylls of the King*) and Algernon Swinburne, *Tristram of Lyonesse* (1882).

From Mother and Daughter.
An Uncompleted Sonnet-Sequence

II

THAT she is beautiful is not delight,
   As some think mothers joy, by pride of her,
   To witness questing eyes caught prisoner
And hear her praised the livelong dancing night;
5   But the glad impulse that makes painters sight
   Bids me note her and grow the happier;
   And love that finds me as her worshipper
Reveals me each best loveliness aright.

   Oh goddess head! Oh innocent brave eyes!
10   Oh curved and parted lips where smiles are rare
   And sweetness ever! Oh smooth shadowy hair
Gathered around the silence of her brow!
   Child, I'd needs love thy beauty stranger-wise:
   And oh the beauty of it, being thou!

VI

SOMETIMES, as young things will, she vexes me,
   Wayward, or too unheeding, or too blind.
   Like aimless birds that, flying on a wind,
Strike slant against their own familiar tree;
5   Like venturous children pacing with the sea,
   That turn but when the breaker spurts behind
   Outreaching them with spray: she in such kind
Is borne against some fault, or does not flee.

   And so, may be, I blame her for her wrong,
10   And she will frown and lightly plead her part,
   And then I bid her go. But 'tis not long:
   Then comes she lip to ear and heart to heart.
And thus forgiven her love seems newly strong,
   And, oh my penitent, how dear thou art!

Mother and Daughter] Webster and her husband had only one child, unusually for Victorian families. This child grew up to become an actress, and performed in one of her mother's plays (*In a Day*) at Terry's Theatre, London, in 1890. The sonnet sequence remained uncompleted at Webster's death, and was first published a year later, in 1895, edited by W. M. Rossetti.

II.2. joy] Used here as a verb.

VI.7. in such kind] in such a way.

VII

HER father lessons me I at times am hard,
    Chiding a moment's fault as too grave ill,
    And let some little blot my vision fill,
Scanning her with a narrow near regard.
5   True. Love's unresting gaze is self-debarred
    From all sweet ignorance, and learns a skill,
    Not painless, of such signs as hurt love's will,
That would not have its prize one tittle marred.

Alas! Who rears and loves a dawning rose
10   Starts at a speck upon one petal's rim:
Who sees a dusk creep in the shrined pearl's glows,
    Is ruined at once: 'My jewel growing dim!'
I watch one bud that on my bosom blows,
    I watch one treasured pearl for me and him.

XI

Love's Mourner

'TIS men who say that through all hurt and pain
    The woman's love, wife's, mother's, still will hold,
    And breathes the sweeter and will more unfold
For winds that tear it, and the sorrowful rain.
5   So in a thousand voices has the strain
    Of this dear patient madness been retold,
    That men call woman's love. Ah! they are bold,
Naming for love that grief which *does* remain.

Love faints that looks on baseness face to face:
10   Love pardons all; but by the pardonings dies,
    With a fresh wound of each pierced through the breast.
And there stand pityingly in Love's void place

VII.1. lessons] rebukes; admonishes.

5. is self-debarred] prohibits or excludes itself.

8. tittle] the smallest part.

10. Starts at] recoils from.

XI. Title.] This sonnet, along with the previous one, No. X, 'Love's Counterfeit', sits oddly in the 'Mother and Daughter' sequence, prompting the question whether Webster would really have intended such a placement.

5. strain] melody, tune.

Kindness of household wont familiar-wise,
And faith to Love – faith to our dead at rest.

XVI

SHE will not have it that my day wanes low,
    Poor of the fire its drooping sun denies,
    That on my brow the thin lines write good-byes
Which soon may be read plain for all to know,
5   Telling that I have done with youth's brave show;
    Alas! and done with youth in heart and eyes,
    With wonder and with far expectancies,
Save but to say 'I knew such long ago.'

She will not have it. Loverlike to me,
10   She with her happy gaze finds all that's best,
She sees this fair and that unfretted still,
    And her own sunshine over all the rest:
So she half keeps me as she'd have me be,
And I forget to age, through her sweet will.

XX

THERE's one I miss. A little questioning maid
    That held my finger, trotting by my side,
    And smiled out of her pleased eyes open wide,
Wondering and wiser at each word I said.
5   And I must help her frolics if she played,
    And I must feel her trouble if she cried;
    My lap was hers past right to be denied;
She did my bidding, but I more obeyed.

Dearer she is to-day, dearer and more;
10   Closer to me, since sister womanhoods meet;
Yet, like poor mothers some long while bereft,
I dwell on toward ways, quaint memories left,
    I miss the approaching sound of pit-pat feet,
The eager baby voice outside my door.

12–13.] i.e. in the place previously filled by love, now gone, stands instead a kindness based on everyday familiarity.

XVI.1–2.] i.e. she (the daughter) will not accept that the mother's life is waning, lacking now in the energies its failing strength rejects.

11. unfretted] free of care and distress; also, unmarked by 'fretwork' or etched lines.

XX.12. toward] promising well for the future.

165

XXVII

Since first my little one lay on my breast
   I never needed such a second good,
   Nor felt a void left in my motherhood
She filled not always to the utterest.
5   The summer linnet, by glad yearnings pressed,
     Builds room enough to house a callow brood:
     I prayed not for another child – nor could;
My solitary bird had my heart's nest.

But she is cause that any baby thing
10   If it but smile, is one of mine in truth,
     And every child becomes my natural joy:
And, if my heart gives all youth fostering,
     Her sister, brother, seems the girl or boy:
     My darling makes me mother to their youth.

[1895]

XXVII.5. linnet] songbird.
6. callow] unfledged.

ADAH ISAACS MENKEN (1839?–1868)

Adah Isaccs Menken, also known as Bertha Theodore and Dolores McCord, among other names, was actor first, poet second (though in many ways she would probably have preferred it the other way round). She grew up in America, and later invented many different versions of her early life according to the exigency of the moment, or the needs of her publicity machine – she was adept at the latter, never missing a photo opportunity (a remarkable number of these survive). It has been plausibly suggested that her actual parentage was neither Jewish nor Spanish (two roles she perfected) but Creole (mother) and 'free man of color' (father) (Mankowitz, 1982, p. 34). After establishing herself on the stage in the south-western states, she moved to California, and then headed east, triumphing in many venues before reaching the pinnacle on Broadway, and catching and discarding husbands (some bigamously) as she went. In April 1864 she finally reached London, where she had long been hoping to break into the theatre world. This she was to accomplish, although not, perhaps, in the way she might have wished for. Always a colourful figure, full of verve and passion, though with a deep strain of melancholy which comes out most forcefully in her poetry, she created something of a sensation wherever she went. The fact that her one book of poetry, *Infelicia* (1868), was published in London, thus appearing in the context of the English poetry of the day, rather than to an American public, makes it a worthwhile inclusion in this volume. Its very differences from the other poets represented here serve to highlight their special qualities, as well as Menken's.

She began writing fairly early, and was contributing her own column, 'Fugitive Pencillings', to the *Liberty Gazette* in Texas in the 1850s. In it, she often fulminated against the subordinate role of women: 'Oh! mothers! believe me, there are other missions in the world for women, other than that of wife and mother' (Mankowitz, 1982, p. 38). She also published some of her early verses in this paper. Later, after marriage with Alexander Menken, a Cincinnati Jew, she moved on from an espousal of the feminist cause to take up the cudgels against anti-Semitism, learning both Hebrew and German, studying the Books of the Prophets and publishing essays on such subjects as the Jew in Parliament (*The Israelite*, 3 Sept 1858), about the Rothschild controversy in London. She also gave lectures and dramatic readings. Her poetry was influenced by her great admiration for writers like Edgar Allan Poe (1809–1849) and Walt Whitman (1819–1892), whom she met while acting on the New York stage, and on whose work she apparently published an essay in which she hailed him as 'the American philosopher, who is centuries ahead of his contemporaries' (Mankowitz, 1982, p. 80; no location is given).

During the 1860s, when she made her stage debut in London, she was one of the most celebrated actresses around, her name turning up in comic songs, skits and parodies, as well as being plastered on playbills across the theatre district. Never a classical actor – she preferred to *ad lib* rather than follow Shakespeare's lines – she specialised in the kind of theatre spectacular that was the forerunner of modern

American musical extravaganzas. In London, there was a long tradition which combined circus performance with theatrical production at places like Astley's, the scene of her spectacular opening performance in *Mazeppa* (a romantic melodrama adapted from Byron's poem) on 3 Oct 1864. Loving the adulation she received, she nevertheless resented the scandalous notoriety that accompanied it, particularly after the overwhelming success of her most famous trousers role, that of the 'hero' bound naked to the back of a live horse thundering across the stage in *Mazeppa*. This notorious act she performed time and again for an insatiable public. She had first performed it, to enormous acclaim, in California, where it made a great impression on the young Mark Twain, who wrote a description of it (quoted in Mankowitz, 1982, pp. 120–1). Menken had learned her not inconsiderable horsemanship skills from a military man in Texas.

The literary men of London at that time – including Charles Dickens – appear to have been particularly taken with Menken, and she was often escorted by the novelist Charles Reade as well as by members of the bohemian group surrounding Dante Gabriel Rossetti. Never short of courage, Menken also consented to become Swinburne's lover for a time, urged on by Rossetti and other interested parties.[1] The story goes that Swinburne's friends had become increasingly concerned at his lack of interest in the opposite sex, and chose an actress who was something of a sex symbol to rectify matters. She was certainly sexually experienced, having married at least four husbands during her earlier life in America, and oddly enough, she seems to have retained a genuine affection for the diminutive alcoholic poet after bedding him to order – as he did for her. After her death, he wrote to a friend of his grief, adding: 'She was most loveable as a friend, as well as as a mistress.'[2]

William Michael Rossetti was to include four of Menken's poems ('Infelix', 'One Year Ago', 'Aspiration' and 'Answer Me') in his anthology *American Poems* (1872), commenting that:

> The poems contained in her single published volume are mostly unformed rhapsodies ... more than half unintelligible to the reader. Yet there are touches of genius which place them in a very different category from many so-called poems of more regular construction and more definable deservings. They really express a life of much passion, and not a little aspiration, a life deeply sensible of loss, self-baffled, and mixing the wail of humiliation with that of indignation – like the remnants of a defeated army, hotly pursued. It is this life that cries out in the disordered verses, and these have a responsive life of their own.
>
> (quoted in Northcott, 1921, pp. 42–3)

Menken seems to have published her poems in magazines as she wrote them, keeping the proofs so that she could eventually put out a collection. This she prepared for the press in 1868, but was too ill to correct proofs, an office undertaken by Swinburne's secretary, John Thomson (ibid., p. 39). She died – from 'an abscess in her side' in Paris in August – before publication, so she did not see that her publisher (John Camden Hotten) omitted his own name and that of the printer from the title-page – no doubt from alarm at the contents. She was also spared the brunt of

[1] See the letter to Swinburne from Thomas Purnell, dated 4 Dec 1867, in the BL, Ashley A 3428, fols. 112–113.

[2] See BL, ibid., fols. 50–51, letter cited by Edmund Gosse.

reviewers' scorn – most, unsurprisingly, attacked her work *ad feminam*. Nevertheless, her small volume went through a number of mostly pirated editions in England and America before its last appearance in 1902 (a copy of which is followed here). History does not record Dickens's reaction to having the volume dedicated to him: a letter reproduced in facsimile in the volume, purporting to give his permission, is a clever amalgam of two separate Dickens letters (see *The Letters of Charles Dickens*, ed. Graham Storey [1999], Oxford, vol. 11, pp. 71, 458). Of her own poems, Menken wrote: 'I have written these wild soul-poems in the stillness of midnight and when waking to the world the next day they were to me the deepest mystery' (quoted from an unnamed source by Mankowitz, 1982, p. 199).

Nor are they always crystal clear to her modern readers: often straining after dramatic effect and besprinkled with archaisms and scriptural quotations (or adaptations), their rolling rhythms and free verse format comes as a shock after the more restrained techniques of her sister poets. Yet perhaps this is the previously unheard voice of Dante Rossetti's 'Jenny' – or one very like her, giving vent to feelings so long suppressed that they burst forth like a volcano exploding. Would such a woman, exposed as she was to the seamy side of Victorian society, usually carefully closed off to female curiosity, have been able to avoid an almost overpowering sense of anger at what she saw? No doubt her freer American upbringing (interestingly regarded in England as placing Menken inevitably on the side of the struggle for women's rights) as well as her actressy taste for melodrama had a strong influence on her poetic voice; but her famed melancholy, reflected in her title and remarked upon by reviewers ('Tears, so to speak, bedew every page' [Quoted from the *Pall Mall Gazette* by Mankowitz, 1982, p. 199]), can perhaps be regarded with a hindsight drawn from modern psychology, more in the light of suppressed rage than true sadness. At times, of course, the rage is not suppressed: the poem 'Judith' embodies a kind of revenge drama, an outpouring of anger against the injustice of female victimisation. It is no coincidence that Menken draws so extensively on the language and imagery of the Old Testament as a vehicle for expressing anger: it adds a weight of authority to outpourings that might otherwise sound merely 'shrill' (to use a word favoured by anti-feminists).

As an actress, Menken would have been placed in an especially good position to observe the Victorian double standard in operation 'behind the scenes', as it were, and she has her Judith-figure (see 'Judith', p. 170 below) reserve her fiercest scorn for male hypocrisy as she gloats in triumph over her enemy in a scene which is not only bloodthirsty in the extreme, but also uncannily reminiscent, to a modern reader at least, of Freudian fears of the castrating female. In fact, the climax of the poem is so excessive in its visualisation of female power run amok, that it could serve as a perfect argument against female emancipation. Small wonder, then, that it turned the stomachs of contemporary reviewers. In fact, none of the traditional female virtues of submissiveness, modesty and chastity are evident in Menken's work. Not only is her verse erotically charged, it is also defiantly egocentric in its Nietzschean grasp of individual power. Yet always behind the defiance, like a mirror image, runs a thread of masochistic despair at the same time: 'Beware! that soaring path is lined with shrouds' ('Aspiration', p. 180). Even the boldest of the women poets publishing in England at this time could not, it seems, fully escape from the oppressive gender constraints.

169

Menken certainly did her best, however, to defy convention – literary as well as social – in her writing. If one looks for neat line lengths, melodious rhyme, even logically developed metaphor, Menken will not satisfy. But: if one can enter into her rebellious spirit, take on her outsider's view of her society, and follow her associative, impressionistic, iconoclastic method of improvising verse – a m̲ od̲ which was not to find further favour until the modernist movement in the early twentieth century (Mina Loy, for example, is surely a descendant) – then Menken certainly offers a unique voice from the period.

Text: The poems chosen are from *Infelicia* (1868). The copy-text used is *Infelicia* (Philadelphia 1902).

Judith

'Repent, or I will come unto thee quickly, and will fight thee with the sword
of my mouth.' – REVELATION ii. 16.

I

ASHKELON is not cut off with the remnant of a valley.
  Baldness dwells not upon Gaza.
  The field of the valley is mine, and it is clothed in verdure.

Judith] Judith, whose name is the feminine form of the word for 'Jewish', is the eponymous heroine of the apocryphal Book of Judith. When the Samarian town Bethulia was besieged by the Assyrian general Holofernes and his army, Judith used her considerable charm to gain access to Holofernes. She cut his head off with a sword while he lay drunkenly asleep, then departed with his head concealed in her handmaid's sack. Safely back with her people, she was received as a heroine and Holofernes's head was publicly displayed, becoming a symbol of God's deliverance of the Israelites. The following morning when their army advanced, the Assyrians fled. The apocryphal Judith is portrayed as a saint-like woman who murdered to save her people and for her God. Her story was incorporated into rabbinical literature. Early Christian writers used Judith as an exemplum of chaste widowhood, and of God's power at work through the weak and humble, in which capacity she has been linked to Esther and Susannah, but in the nineteenth century there was a new interest in the sexual dimensions of the story, already foreshadowed in paintings by Michaelangelo, Caravaggio and Gentileschi. In this poem, Menken chooses to emphasise Judith's strength and prophetic powers of delivery as well as her 'unfeminine' sexuality.

Epigraph.] The phrase 'sword of the mouth' appears in ll. 8 and 36 of the poem. See also Isaiah 49: 2 and Revelation 19: 21.

1–3.] *Ashkelon* was a city on the Mediterranean, in the land of the Philistines, close to Gaza. (For the Philistines, see next note.) It was frequently denounced by the prophets. *Gaza* was another of the five chief cities of the Philistines, a strategic base on the highway connecting Egypt with Syria and Mesopotamia. Cf. Jeremiah 47: 5: 'Baldness is come upon Gaza; Ashkelon is cut off with the remnant of their valley: how long wilt thou cut thyself?' According to Jeremiah, these are the words of the Lord, given to him in order that he might warn other nations against their pursuit of ungodly lives. But contrast Zephaniah 2: 4: 'For Gaza shall be forsaken, and Ashkelon a desolation . . .'.

The steepness of Baal-perazim is mine;
5   And the Philistines spread themselves in the valley of Rephaim.
They shall yet be delivered into my hands.
For the God of Battles has gone before me!
The sword of the mouth shall smite them to dust.
I have slept in the darkness –
But the seventh angel woke me, and giving me a sword of flame, points
10   to the blood-ribbed cloud, that lifts his reeking head above the mountain.
Thus am I the prophet.
I see the dawn that heralds to my waiting soul the advent of power.
     Power that will unseal the thunders!
     Power that will give voice to graves!
15   Graves of the living;
      Graves of the dying;
      Graves of the sinning;
      Graves of the loving;
      Graves of the despairing;
20   And oh! graves of the deserted!
These shall speak, each as their voices shall be loosed.
And the day is dawning.

4–5.] *Baal-perazim* was a place near the *valley of Rephaim*, south-west of Jerusalem and north of Bethlehem. In 2 Samuel and 1 Chronicles, it is inhabited by Philistines. These were a group of people who settled on the south-western coastal strip of Canaan, forming the nation of Philistia. Their inland expansion resulted in conflict with the Israelite tribes who formed themselves into a kingdom in response. They are represented in the Old Testament as ungodly and uncovenanted, worshipping false gods. In the nineteenth century, the term was used to represent the materialistic masses as opposed to the culturally enlightened few. See, for example, Matthew Arnold's 'Sweetness and Light' from *Culture and Anarchy* (1869).

7. the God of Battles] Cf. 2 Chronicles 20: 15: 'Be not afraid nor dismayed by reason of this great multitude; for the battle is not yours, but God's'; 2 Chronicles 32: 8: 'With him is an arm of flesh; but with us is the Lord our God to help us, and to fight our battles.' The reference might simply be to the Old Testament God. Cf. the phrase 'Lord of Hosts' or 'Lord God of Hosts'.

9.] Cf. Job 17: 13: 'If I wait, the grave is mine house: I have made my bed in the darkness.'

10–11.] See Revelation 10: 7; 11: 15; 16: 17 for the seventh angel. Seven is the number symbolic of wholeness. References to Revelation were popular among nineteenth-century women poets, perhaps because it deals with radical social upheaval in which, famously, 'the last shall be first' (Matthew 20: 16).   *a sword of flame*] See Genesis 3: 24: 'So he drove out the man; and he placed at the east of the garden of Eden Cherubims, and a flaming sword which turned every way, to keep the way of the tree of life.'   *the blood-ribbed cloud . . . his reeking head*] a sign of the approaching dawn. 'Reeking' means stinking: in this context, and in view of what is to follow, there is a strong suggestion of blood, as in 'reeking with blood'. There are many prophets in the Bible and Menken has already alluded to Jeremiah. However, the references in the preceeding l. 10 suggest that here Judith is comparing herself to John of Patmos, author of Revelation.

13–14.] There are a number of references to thunder in Revelation. See, for example, 10: 3–4; 19: 6. For a reference to the resurrection of the dead in Revelation, see chs. 19–20. One of the memorable images in Revelation is the gradual 'unsealing' of the book with seven seals (Revelation 5–6, 8).

II

Stand back, ye Philistines!

Practice what ye preach to me;

25   I heed ye not, for I know ye all.

Ye are living burning lies, and profanation to the garments which with stately steps ye sweep your marble palaces.

Your palaces of Sin, around which the damning evidence of guilt hangs like a reeking vapor.

Stand back!

I would pass up the golden road of the world.

30   A place in the ranks awaits me.

I know that ye are hedged on the borders of my path.

Lie and tremble, for ye well know that I hold with iron grasp the battle axe.

Creep back to your dark tents in the valley.

Slouch back to your haunts of crime.

35   Ye do not know me, neither do ye see me.

But the sword of the mouth is unsealed, and ye coil yourselves in slime and bitterness at my feet.

---

24. Practice what ye preach] John Armstrong (1709–1779), *Art of Preserving Health* (1774), book 4, l. 305. Now proverbial. The context suggests that the Philistines are being rebuked for the hypocrisy of their moral doctrine – perhaps an oblique reference to men preaching chastity to women and ignoring it themselves.

26. living burning lies] Cf. Proverbs 16: 27: 'An ungodly man diggeth up evil: and in his lips there is as a burning fire.' The book of Jeremiah is distinguished by clashes between Jeremiah and other prophets, whom God accuses of lying: 'Then the Lord said unto me, the prophets prophesy lies in my name: I sent them not, neither have I commanded them, neither spake unto them: they prophesy unto you a false vision and divination, and a thing of nought, and the deceit of their heart' (Jeremiah 14: 14).

27. palaces of Sin] Cf. 'the synagogue of Satan' (Revelation 2: 9).

29. golden road] Gold is the most frequently mentioned metal in the Bible, having a double significance. It is used as a symbol of purity, divinity, kingship and worship: it is offered by the Magi to the infant Jesus (Matthew 2: 11), while St John of Patmos's vision of 'the holy city, new Jerusalem' observes that 'the city was pure gold, like unto clear glass', 'the street of the city was pure gold' (Revelation 21: 1, 18, 21). But gold is also associated with idolatrous worship and materialism (Exodus 32: 2–24). In Isaiah 14: 4, Babylon is referred to as 'the golden city'.

30. A place in the ranks] A reference either to the speaker's assumption of the status of prophet or as one of the redeemed, referred to in Revelation 7: 3–17. Cf. note on l. 44 below.

31. hedged] Cf. Lamentations 3: 7; Job 3: 23; Hosea 2: 6. In each of these cases it is God who hedges in his subjects.

36–7.] Cf. Genesis 3: 14: 'And the Lord God said unto the serpent, Because thou hast done this, thou art cursed above all cattle, and above every beast of the field; upon thy belly thou shalt go, and dust shalt thou eat all the days of thy life.' Later Christian exegesis identified the serpent with Satan and his eventual defeat with the second coming of Christ.

I mix your jeweled heads, and your gleaming eyes, and your hissing tongues with the dust.

My garments shall bear no mark of ye.

When I shall return this sword to the angel, your foul blood will not stain its edge.

40   It will glimmer with the light of truth, and the strong arm shall rest.

III

Stand back!

I am no Magdalene waiting to kiss the hem of your garment.

It is mid-day.

See ye not what is written on my forehead?

45   I am Judith!

I wait for the head of my Holofernes!

Ere the last tremble of the conscious death-agony shall have shuddered, I will show it to ye with the long black hair clinging to the glazed eyes, and the great mouth opened in search of voice, and the strong throat all hot and reeking with blood, that will thrill me with wild unspeakable joy as it courses down my bare body and dabbles my cold feet!

My sensuous soul will quake with the burden of so much bliss.

Oh, what wild passionate kisses will I draw up from that bleeding mouth!

50   I will strangle this pallid throat of mine on the sweet blood!

---

40. the strong arm] Cf. Jeremiah 21: 5, in which God says: 'And I myself will fight against you with an outstretched hand and with a strong arm, even in anger, and in fury, and in great wrath.'

42. Magdalene waiting to kiss the hem of your garment] During the nineteenth century the name Magdalene (or Magdalen – see Levy's poem of that name) came to stand for an unwed mother or repentant prostitute, her repentance being regarded as her most gratifying feature. Kissing the hem of Jesus' garments made people whole; cf. Matthew 9: 20; 14: 36. There is a confusion of Marys in the New Testament. Menken's reference suggests that she may be conflating Mary Magdalene with either the woman with the issue of blood who touched Christ's garment (Matthew 9: 20–2), or the woman who anointed Christ's feet (Matthew 26: 6–13; Luke 7: 36–50). She is also introducing anachronism in having an Old Testament figure cite the New Testament.

43. mid-day] Traditionally, midday was the hour of the fall and of the crucifixion, and was also identified with God's judgment (the 'sol iusticiae' or sun of righteousness).

44. written on my forehead] Revelation 14: 1 reveals the name on the foreheads of the redeemed to be that of God, in contrast to the unredeemed, who bear the mark of the beast (Revelation 14: 9).

47. my bare body and dabbles] A reference to the fact – in Menken's version at least – that Judith seduces Holofernes before she kills him.   *dabbles*] splatters, splashes.

I will revel in my passion.

At midnight I will feast on it in the darkness.

For it was that which thrilled its crimson tides of reckless passion through the blue veins of my life, and made them leap up in the wild sweetness of Love and agony of Revenge!

I am starving for this feast.

55   Oh forget not that I am Judith!

And I know where sleeps Holofernes.

Myself

'La patience est amère; mais le fruit en est doux!'

I

AWAY down into the shadowy depths of the Real I once lived.

I thought that to seem was to be.

But the waters of Marah were beautiful, yet they were bitter.

I waited, and hoped, and prayed;

5   Counting the heart-throbs and the tears that answered them.

Through my earnest pleadings for the True, I learned that the mildest mercy of life was a smiling sneer;

---

51. my passion] Menken appears to be conflating aspects from the story of Salome, seen in the nineteenth century as the archetypal *femme fatale*, who danced for the head of John the Baptist. Cf. Browning's use of the image in 'Fra Lippo Lippi', and later, more outrageously, Oscar Wilde's in his play *Salome* (1893). Since the primary meaning of 'passion' is the suffering of pain (cf. 'Christ's passion' as a term for the crucifixion), Menken may be suggesting another polemical contrast between Old Testament and New Testament values.

Myself] Cf. Walt Whitman's 'Song of Myself'. The American poet Whitman (1819–1892) worked in printing, teaching, politics and journalism before producing *Leaves of Grass* (1855; several enlarged and revised editions throughout his lifetime). He held contradictory beliefs in democratic equality and the individual as a rebel against society's restrictions. His poetry was influenced by his highly sensitive and sensuous nature as well as by the Transcendentalists, in particular Emerson, who portrayed the individual as an impersonal seer. Whitman moved away from traditional rhythm towards a freer verse, in which he influenced Menken. During the 1870s he was much acclaimed by William Rossetti, Swinburne and others, who also favoured the dramatic talents of Menken. 'Song of Myself' was included, without a title, in the first edition of *Leaves of Grass* but was then titled 'Poem of Walt Whitman, an American' in 1856. It didn't appear as 'Song of Myself' until 1881.

Epigraph.] 'Patience is bitter, but its fruit is sweet.' The quotation is from Jean-Jacques Rousseau, *Émile* (1762).

3. Marah] Marah was on the east of the Red Sea, in the peninsula of Sinai. It is where the Israelites stopped, having crossed the Red Sea, to find that the only water was bitter. 'Marah' is Hebrew for 'bitter': see Exodus 15: 23 and Ruth 1: 20. Marah is used primarily as a figure for bitterness, including bitterness of the heart.

And that the business of the world was to lash with vengeance all who
dared to be what their God had made them.

Smother back tears to the red blood of the heart!

Crush out things called souls!

10   No room for them here!

II

Now I gloss my pale face with laughter, and sail my voice on with the
tide.

Decked in jewels and lace, I laugh beneath the gaslight's glare, and quaff
the purple wine.

But the minor-keyed soul is standing naked and hungry upon one of
Heaven's high hills of light.

Standing and waiting for the blood of the feast!

15   Starving for one poor word!

Waiting for God to launch out some beacon on the boundless shores of
this Night.

Shivering for the uprising of some soft wing under which it may creep,
lizard-like, to warmth and rest.

Waiting! Starving and shivering!

III

Still I trim my white bosom with crimson roses; for none shall see the
thorns.

---

11. gloss] veil, cover up.

12–13.] The contrast between the body decked with finery (suggesting whoredom) and the
naked soul before God is pointed in many places in the Old Testament: see, for example,
Ezekiel 16: 39; 23: 29; Job 1: 21; 1 Corinthians 4: 11. 'The gaslight's glare' is possibly sug-
gestive of prostitution, as well as the theatre (the two were closely associated at this time).
Alternatively, 'gaslight's glare' may simply suggest a high-society party (in keeping with the
'jewels and lace').

13. naked] For 'naked', see also Whitman: 'I will go to the bank by the wood and become
undisguised and naked' ('Song of Myself', l. 19).

14. the blood of the feast] the Eucharist.

16. the boundless shores of this Night] Contrast Job's expression of faith: 'He hath compassed
the waters with bounds, until the day and night come to an end' (Job 26: 10).

17. some soft wing] A common biblical image of God's protection: see for example Ruth 2: 12:
'The Lord recompense thy work, and a full reward be given thee of the Lord God of Israel, under
whose wings thou art come to trust'; Psalm 17: 18: 'Keep me as the apple of thy eye, hide me
under the shadow of thy wings.'

19. crimson roses; for none shall see the thorns] The implication is that the crimson colour of the
roses will disguise the bleeding caused by the thorns. In Genesis 3: 18, 'thorns . . . and thistles'
are attributed to the fall.

I bind my aching brow with a jeweled crown, that none shall see the
20 iron one beneath.

My silver-sandaled feet keep impatient time to the music, because I cannot
be calm.

I laugh at earth's passion-fever of Love; yet I know that God is near to
the soul on the hill, and hears the ceaseless ebb and flow of a hopeless love,
through all my laughter.

But if I can cheat my heart with the old comfort, that love can be forgotten,
is it not better?

After all, living is but to play a part!

25 The poorest worm would be a jewel-headed snake if she could!

IV

All this grandeur of glare and glitter has its night-time.

The pallid eyelids must shut out smiles and daylight.

Then I fold my cold hands, and look down at the restless rivers of a love
that rushes through my life.

Unseen and unknown they tide on over black rocks and chasms of Death.

30 Oh, for one sweet word to bridge their terrible depths!

O jealous soul! why wilt thou crave and yearn for what thou canst not have?

And life is so long – so long.

V

With the daylight comes the business of living.

The prayers that I sent trembling up the golden thread of hope all come
back to me.

35 I lock them close in my bosom, far under the velvet and roses of the world.

For I know that stronger than these torrents of passion is the soul that
hath lifted itself up to the hill.

What care I for his careless laugh?

I do not sigh; but I know that God hears the life-blood dripping as I, too,
laugh.

20.] The iron crown of Lombardy is the crown of the ancient Longobardic kings, said to have
been bestowed by Pope Gregory the Great. After various tribulations, it was restored to the
King of Italy by the Emperor of Austria in 1866 (two years before this poem was published). It
has an inner fillet of iron which is said to have been beaten out of a nail from the True Cross
which was given to Constantine by his mother, St Helena. The outer circlet is of beaten gold,
set with precious stones.

22. the hill] Possibly a reference to Calvary.

24.] Cf. Shakespeare, As You Like It, II.iv.139–40: 'All the world's a stage, / And all the men
and women merely players'.

25. the poorest worm] Cf. Job 25: 5: 'How much less man, that is a worm? and the son of man,
which is a worm?'

I would not be thought a foolish rose, that flaunts her red heart out to the sun.

40   Loving is not living!

VI

Yet through all this I know that night will roll back from the still, gray plain of heaven, and that my triumph shall rise sweet with the dawn!

When these mortal mists shall unclothe the world, then shall I be known as I am!

When I dare be dead and buried behind a wall of wings, then shall he know me!

When this world shall fall, like some old ghost, wrapped in the black skirts of the wind, down into the fathomless eternity of fire, then shall souls uprise!

When God shall lift the frozen seal from struggling voices, then shall we
45   speak!

When the purple-and-gold of our inner natures shall be lighted up in the Eternity of Truth, then will love be mine!

I can wait.

Genius

> 'Where'er there's a life to be kindled by love,
>   Wherever a soul to inspire,
> Strike this key-note of God that trembles above
>   Night's silver-tongued voices of fire.'

GENIUS is power,

The power that grasps in the universe, that dives out beyond space, and grapples with the starry worlds of heaven.

41.] Cf. Job 7: 4: 'When I lie down, I say, When shall I arise, and the night be gone? and I am full of tossings to and fro unto the dawning of the day.'

43. *wall of wings*] possibly a screen of angels' wings.

44.] The book of Revelation (or Apocalypse) in the New Testament prophesies a universal destruction which will make way for a heaven on earth for those who are chosen.

45. *the frozen seal*] Possibly a reference to the mysterious seven seals of the Apocalypse. The book in the Apocalypse cannot be fully read until all seven seals are open. In this context, lifting the frozen seal may simply be a metaphor for the gaining of spiritual enlightenment.

46. *purple-and-gold*] Purple is the liturgical colour symbolising sorrow or penance (but can also represent kingship), gold is the colour of glory and rejoicing.

Genius. *Title.*] A term which took on its modern meaning (of creative powers of inspiration and originality) during the eighteenth century, and which was much favoured by English and German Romantics in the early nineteenth century.

Epigraph.] Untraced.

If genius achieves nothing, shows us no results, it is so much the less genius.

The man who is constantly fearing a lion in his path is a coward.

The man or woman whom excessive caution holds back from striking
5 the anvil with earnest endeavor, is poor and cowardly of purpose.

The required step must be taken to reach the goal, though a precipice be the result.

Work must be done, and the result left to God.

The soul that is in earnest, will not stop to count the cost.

Circumstances cannot control genius: it will nestle with them: its power will bend and break them to its path.
10 This very audacity is divine.

Jesus of Nazareth did not ask the consent of the high priests in the temple when he drove out the 'money-changers;' but, impelled by inspiration, he knotted the cords and drove them hence.

Genius will find room for itself, or it is none.

Men and women, in all grades of life, do their utmost.

If they do little, it is because they have no capacity to do more.

I hear people speak of 'unfortunate genius,' of 'poets who never penned
15 their inspirations;' that

'Some mute inglorious Milton here may rest;'

of 'unappreciated talent,' and 'malignant stars,' and other contradictory things.

It is all nonsense.

Where power exists, it cannot be suppressed any more than the earthquake can be smothered.

As well attempt to seal up the crater of Vesuvius as to hide God's given
20 power of the soul.

'You may as well forbid the mountain pines
To wag their high tops, and to make no noise
When they are fretten with the gusts of heaven,'

---

4. a lion in his path] In John Bunyan's *Pilgrim's Progress* (1678), Christian meets Mistrust and Timorous who have turned back because of two lions in the way, but he successfully passes between them.

11.] See Matthew 21: 12 and Mark 11: 15.

16.] Thomas Gray (1716–1771), 'Elegy Written in a Country Churchyard' (1750), l. 59.

21–3.] See Leonard MacNally (1779), *The Apotheosis of Punch; A Satirical Masque: With a Monody on the Death of the late Master Punch*, London, scene 3, ll. 112–14. MacNally (1752–1820) was a poet and political informer.

as to hush the voice of genius.

25   There is no such thing as unfortunate genius.

If a man or woman is fit for work, God appoints the field.

He does more; He points to the earth with her mountains, oceans, and cataracts, and says to man, *'Be great!'*

He points to the eternal dome of heaven and its blazing worlds, and says: 'Bound out thy life with beauty.'

He points to the myriads of down-trodden, suffering men and women, and says: 'Work with me for the redemption of these, my children.'

He lures, and incites, and thrusts greatness upon men, and they will not
30   take the gift.

Genius, on the contrary, loves toil, impediment, and poverty; for from these it gains its strength, throws off the shadows, and lifts its proud head to immortality.

Neglect is but the fiat to an undying future.

To be popular is to be endorsed in the To-day and forgotten in the To-morrow.

It is the mess of pottage that alienates the birth-right.

Genius that succumbs to misfortune, that allows itself to be blotted by the slime of slander – and other serpents that infest society – is so much
35   the less genius.

The weak man or woman who stoops to whine over neglect, and poverty, and the snarls of the world, gives the sign of his or her own littleness.

Genius is power.

The eternal power that can silence worlds with its voice, and battle to the death ten thousand arméd Hercules.

Then make way for this God-crowned Spirit of Night, that was born in that Continuing City, but lives in lowly and down-trodden souls!
40   Fling out the banner!

Its broad folds of sunshine will wave over turret and dome, and over the thunder of oceans on to eternity.

---

28. *Bound out*] Mark out the bounds of.

30. *thrusts greatness upon*] Cf. Shakespeare, *Twelfth Night*, II.v.158: 'But be not afraid of greatness: some men are born great, some achieve greatness, and some have greatness thrust upon them.'

32. *fiat*] Latin: 'let it be done'. A fiat is an authorisation. Menken may be referring to Jesus' statement that 'many that are first shall be last; and the last shall be first' (Matthew 19: 30). Cf. Matthew 20: 16; Mark 30: 31; Luke 14: 10.

34. *mess of pottage*] literally, a serving of porridge or thick soup. Cf. Geneva Bible, chapter heading to Genesis 25: 'Esau selleth his birthright for a mess of pottage'.

38. *Hercules*] a hero of superhuman strength, from Greek mythology.

39. *that Continuing City*] Cf. Hebrews 13: 14: 'For here we have no continuing city, but seek one to come.'

'Fling it out, fling it out o'er the din of the world!
   Make way for this banner of flame,
That streams from the mast-head of ages unfurled,
45   And inscribed by the deathless in name.
And thus through the years of eternity's flight.
   This insignia of soul shall prevail,
The centre of glory, the focus of light;
   O Genius! proud Genius, all hail!'

Aspiration

Poor, impious Soul! that fixes its high hopes
   In the dim distance, on a throne of clouds,
And from the morning's mist would make the ropes
   To draw it up amid acclaim of crowds –
5   Beware! That soaring path is lined with shrouds;
   And he who braves it, though of sturdy breath,
May meet, half way, the avalanche and death!

O poor young Soul! – whose year-devouring glance
   Fixes in ecstasy upon a star,
10   Whose feverish brilliance looks a part of earth,
   Yet quivers where the feet of angels are,
And seems the future crown in realms afar –
   Beware! A spark *thou* art, and dost but see
Thine own reflection in Eternity!

42–9.] Untraced: it is possible that Menken made it up herself.

Aspiration] 'Aspiration' is a word with several meanings: inspiration; the act of breathing; desiring something higher than oneself. While the third meaning appears to be the most appropriate to the theme of poetic ambition that is developed here, the other two are both pertinent also, given that the theme is expressed in the form of a poem, designed for the (breathing) human voice. The particular form of this poem is of course a sonnet, unusually divided into two seven-line parts. According to Mankowitz (1982, p. 108), Dante Gabriel Rossetti particularly admired this poem, regarding it (along with 'Answer Me', below) as Menken's best. Cf. Pfeiffer's poem of the same title, on a similar theme, published eight years later, in 1876 (p. 95).

1. impious] Presumably the soul is labelled 'impious' because its aspirations concern its own aggrandisement rather than any union with a greater being.

8. year-devouring] i.e. overriding any constraints of time in the press of its ambition.

13–14.] The warning is to the Soul for its lack of self-awareness, its inability to realise its own insignificance in the face of eternity, like a spark that will soon be extinguished, and is in pursuit only of its own reflection.

A Memory

I SEE her yet, that dark-eyed one,
  Whose bounding heart God folded up
In His, as shuts when day is done,
  Upon the elf the blossom's cup.
On many an hour like this we met,
  And as my lips did fondly greet her,
I blessed her as love's amulet:
  Earth hath no treasure, dearer, sweeter.

The stars that look upon the hill,
  And beckon from their homes at night,
Are soft and beautiful, yet still
  Not equal to her eyes of light.
They have the liquid glow of earth,
  The sweetness of a summer even,
As if some Angel at their birth
  Had dipped them in the hues of Heaven.

They may not seem to others sweet,
  Nor radiant with the beams above,
When first their soft, sad glances meet
  The eyes of those not born for love;
Yet when on me their tender beams
  Are turned, beneath love's wide control,
Each soft, sad orb of beauty seems
  To look through mine into my soul.

A Memory] The anonymous memoir of Menken which opens *Infelicia* states that this poem was originally entitled 'Laulerack', and was written in memory of an Indian maiden who figured in one of the extraordinary adventures that characterised the younger Menken's life in America. Apparently, while she was living at Liberty, Texas, and writing for the *Liberty Gazette*, she one day joined a hunting party on an expedition which ended in disaster when they were ambushed by Indians. Menken was helped to escape by the young Indian girl, also captive of the tribe, who paid with her life when she was shot by some rangers. Mankowitz (1982) also relates this story, commenting that however unlikely it may seem, the facts of Texas history at that time abound with such events that rival fiction. He also notes: 'The poem has also been said to contain strongly homosexual elements. But in the complex erotic history of Adah Menken, there is not a single close relationship with a woman recorded. One senses in the poem more a profound need in Menken for "sisterhood", and for a real and positive mother' (p. 45).

2. *Whose bounding heart*] Perhaps a reference to the description Menken is supposed to have given of the Indian girl, 'who ran more like a deer than a human being' (quoted in Mankowitz, 1982, p. 43).

7. *amulet*] charm. 'Love's Amulet' is the title of a poem by John Payne (1842–1916).

25   I see her now that dark-eyed one,
              Whose bounding heart God folded up
          In His, as shuts when day is done,
              Upon the elf the blossom's cup.
          Too late we met, the burning brain,
30   The aching heart alone can tell,
          How filled our souls of death and pain
              When came the last, sad word, *Farewell!*

Answer Me

I

IN from the night.
The storm is lifting his black arms up to the sky.
Friend of my heart, who so gently marks out the life-track for me, draw near to-night;
Forget the wailing of the low-voiced wind:
Shut out the moanings of the freezing, and the starving, and the dying,
5 and bend your head low to me:
Clasp my cold, cold hands in yours;
Think of me tenderly and lovingly:
Look down into my eyes the while I question you, and if you love me, answer me –
          Oh, answer me!

II

10   Is there not a gleam of Peace on all this tiresome earth?
    Does not one oasis cheer all this desert-world?
    When will all this toil and pain bring me the blessing?
    Must I ever plead for help to do the work before me set?
    Must I ever stumble and faint by the dark wayside?
    Oh the dark, lonely wayside, with its dim-sheeted ghosts peering up
15 through their shallow graves!
    Must I ever tremble and pale at the great Beyond?
    Must I find Rest only in your bosom, as now I do?
          Answer me –
          Oh, answer me!

Answer Me. *15. dim-sheeted ghosts*] i.e. ghosts of the dead, imagined as shrouded corpses.

III

20 Speak to me tenderly.
Think of me lovingly.
Let your soft hands smooth back my hair.
Take my cold, tear-stained face up to yours.
Let my lonely life creep into your warm bosom, knowing no other rest but this.
Let me question you, while sweet Faith and Trust are folding their white
25 robes around me.
Thus am I purified, even to your love, that came like John the Baptist in the Wilderness of Sin.
You read the starry heavens, and lead me forth.
But tell me if, in this world's Judea, there comes never quiet when once the heart awakes?
Why must it ever hush Love back?
30 Must it only labor, strive, and ache?
Has it no reward but this?
Has it no inheritance but to bear – and break?
Answer me –
Oh, answer me!

IV

35 The Storm struggles with the Darkness.
Folded away in your arms, how little do I heed their battle!
The trees clash in vain their naked swords against the door.
I go not forth while the low murmur of your voice is drifting all else back to silence.
The darkness presses his black forehead close to the window pane, and beckons me without.
40 Love holds a lamp in this little room that hath power to blot back Fear.
But will the lamp ever starve for oil?
Will its blood-red flame ever grow faint and blue?
Will it uprear itself to a slender line of light?
Will it grow pallid and motionless?

---

26. *John the Baptist*] a prophet who took up an ascetic life in the Judean wilderness, usually seen as the forerunner of Jesus. He preached that salvation was achieved through an act of repentance, rather than being guaranteed by lineal descent from Abraham. He is the model of the ascetic's rebuke to the worldly.

28. *this world's Judea*] Judea, or Judaea, was the name given to the southern part of Palestine as occupied by the Jewish community under Persian, Greek and Roman rule. In Luke and Acts the term is sometimes used loosely to denote the whole of western Palestine. Its limits were never precisely defined. It is not the same as Judah, another district of Palestine, from which the name Jew is derived, although Menken here appears to suggest that it is.

45   Will it sink rayless to everlasting death?

                  Answer me –

                  Oh, answer me!

V

Look at these tear-drops.

See how they quiver and die on your open hands.

50   Fold these white garments close to my breast, while I question you.

Would you have me think that from the warm shelter of your heart I must go to the grave?

And when I am lying in my silent shroud, will you love me?

When I am buried down in the cold, wet earth, will you grieve that you did not save me?

Will your tears reach my pale face through all the withered leaves that will heap themselves upon my grave?

Will you repent that you loosened your arms to let me fall so deep, and
55 so far out of sight?

Will you come and tell me so, when the coffin has shut out the storm?

                  Answer me –

                  Oh, answer me!

MATHILDE BLIND (1841–1896)

Mathilde Blind was a translator and literary critic as well as a poet. She was born in Mannheim, Germany, as Mathilde Cohen. Her elderly father, a Jewish banker, died soon after her birth, and her mother subsequently married the revolutionary leader Karl Blind. The family was forced to flee from Paris to England in 1849. Mathilde was educated at a London girls' school, and later in Zurich. Here she tried unsuccessfully to gain admission to university lectures, an experience which fired her later enthusiasm for the cause of women's education. She admired Mary Wollstonecraft, publishing an article on her in 1878, and herself lived the life of an independent woman. She never married, travelled widely in Europe and Egypt, and supplemented her private income by writing and lecturing. Although German was her native tongue, and she published translations from Goethe as well as of D. F. Strauss's *The Old Faith and the New* (1873), she was fluent in other languages as well. She wrote a life of the revolutionary heroine Madame Roland (1886) and translated the extraordinary *Journal of Marie Bashkirtseff* (1890) with a dashing careless style that was felt to do justice to the impetuous and candid form of the original. Well educated and well read, Blind was intellectually confident as well as financially generous, and gained a wide circle of friends in the world of the arts, including Ford Madox Brown, Swinburne, the Rossettis (Dante Gabriel and William), the novelist Mona Caird, Eleanor Marx, and others. In later life she loved to give 'literary dinners' in the private room of some well-chosen hotel.

In 1867 she published her first poems, under the pseudonym 'Claude Lake'. They were dedicated to Giuseppe Mazzini, Italian patriot and staunch republican, whom she knew well (through her stepfather, with whom she later fell out) during his long English exile. Her support for Italian revolutionary patriotism was shared by a number of Victorian women poets, most famously including Elizabeth Barrett Browning, whose *Aurora Leigh* Blind had fervently admired. She was also influenced by George Eliot, sharing her sense of moral idealism, and she published a *Life* of Eliot in 1883. She never cared for Eliot's poetry, however, far preferring Shelley and Byron, on both of whom she produced some intelligent, assured and well-informed literary criticism. This was the side of Blind admired by contemporaries like Richard Garnett and Theodore Watts-Dunton as showing her 'masculine' intellect; they were less comfortable with the passionate voice she often adopted in her poetry. Curiously, her poems were sometimes criticised for having too wide a range of interests, where Christina Rossetti, for example, was too narrow. Her one novel, *Tarantella: A Romance* (1885), was an experimental fiction with an absurd plot weighed down by overblown prose: it was deservedly panned by the critics.

Having travelled to Scotland in 1873, Blind was later inspired to write two long poems, which rank among her most important works. Unfortunately it is not practicable to print them here, but both poems are powerful and challenging long dramatic narratives well worthy of the modern reader's attention. The first, *The Prophecy of St Oran* (1881), deals with religious questions from a firmly atheist angle, which earned her some opprobrium from reviewers, although her powers of characterisation were admired. It deconstructs some deep-seated Pauline doctrines, holding them up to display as man-made constructs of superstitious claptrap and, equally harmfully, deeply ingrained misogyny. At the same time, the poem demonstrates the terrible powers given to these constructs in the life of an ascetic religious community. Set in the Hebrides, it deals with the fate of two young lovers who are hounded to death for daring to contravene Church authority. The girl is driven to suicide, while the young monk, Oran, punished with a death sentence for breaking his vows, utters his scourging atheist prophecy at the end of the poem before being buried alive.

The Heather on Fire, published in 1886, while absorbed in a similar theme of struggle against repressive authority, dramatises it quite differently. This time it is the shameful story of the Highland clearances which grips Blind's imagination. Her Scottish travels would have showed her the numbers of razed villages from which the inhabitants had been cruelly driven to forced emigration earlier in the century, betrayed by their own chiefs, in order to make way for a vast increase in the more profitable business of grazing sheep. In addition, 1884 saw the publication of the report of the Crofters' Commission on the state of the Highlands. The English public in general remained indifferent to its revelations of cruelty and injustice on a grand scale. Blind's non-English background no doubt made it easier for her to look squarely at the ugly facts behind the romantic myths about Highland life. Her poem pulls no punches in its account of the dirty work of driving peasant folk, young and old, in the foulest weather, out of their homes which were then set on fire, and the herding of them onto the beaches to set sail for Canada. In one dramatic section of the poem Blind describes the agonising plight of a crippled old woman whom no-one removed from her home before it was fired.

Another long poem, or rather collection of poems, even more ambitious in its choice of subject-matter, was *The Ascent of Man* (1889). Here the aim was to take the theories of the men of science – in particular, Charles Darwin, whose *Descent of Man* had been published in 1871 – and give them an imaginative spin in the direction of the poetic spirit. Blind was convinced by Darwin's theories, but she wanted to imbue them with her own brand of revolutionary optimism and social critique: hence the spirit of reversal implied in her title. The work uses a kind of imaginative impressionism that is the reverse of realistic: it follows the history of the human species from its murky beginnings in time up to the flowering of human creative and artistic achievement, weaving in a critique of the state of contemporary civilisation. Blind was disappointed by its lukewarm reception: her bold project of romanticising her atheism and socialism failed to win public acclaim.

Blind's poetry in general was admired for its imaginative scope, the apparent sincerity of its passion, and for its fine moments of intensity and authenticity. But it was also criticised for its lapses in linguistic tact (no doubt partly occasioned by her non-English-speaking background), its occasional over-earnestness, its blemishes of form. Yet while critics such as Theodore Watts-Dunton, literary editor of *The*

Athenaeum, praised her as a 'woman of genius', he also sensed her particular isolation as a woman who, while not claiming for herself the dubious notoriety of the title of 'New Woman' (i.e. militant feminist), was understandably irritated by 'female fetters' (*The Athenaeum*, 5 Dec 1896, p. 792). Despite such apparently sympathetic assessment, however, we can sense in his remarks an unease with the side of Blind that was strongly 'woman-identified', to use a modern expression, and that remained indignant at their continuing oppression. He accused her, also, of being in later life 'greedy of fame': something always to be abhorred in women. Yet Arthur Symons published her *Poetical Works* in 1900: not many female poets had that honour accorded them.

Many of her poems, one suspects, did not appeal to male readers because they were not especially designed for them. 'The Message' (see p. 194 below) is a case in point. Included here more for its interest as part of a Victorian 'sub-genre', the 'fallen woman' poem (see also Levy's 'Magdalen' and Webster's 'The Castaway'), than for its intrinsic poetic quality (it is rather prosaic in form, and points a very heavy temperance moral), it certainly caused reviewers to turn up their noses in distaste. 'A hospital tale of a harlot's death-bed', sniffed Eric Robertson, reviewer for *The Academy* (12 Dec 1891, p. 531). Much more universally admired were her passionate love poems; and indeed, it was the combination of passion and thoughtfulness in Blind that was most prized by her critics. Perhaps we can add to that, her sense of *com*passion, a quality that distinguishes many of her poems whether they deal with the Arab's love for his horse ('A Fantasy', p. 203), the urban squalor of a city like Manchester ('Manchester by Night', p. 188), the pains of childbirth ('Motherhood', p. 189), or the oppression of Muslim women ('Mourning Women', p. 205). Although her experiments with poetic form were not always successful, they work very well indeed when they do come off, combining vivid enlivening imagery with an unusual pleasure for the ear.

Towards the end of her life, she wrote in her Commonplace Book words revealing the darker side of her lifelong determination to be an independent woman: 'I have been an exile in this world. Without a God, without a country, without a family.' She bequeathed her estate to Newnham College, Cambridge, to found a scholarship for women.

Text: The texts chosen are from *The Prophecy of Saint Oran and Other Poems* (1881), *The Ascent of Man* (1889), *Dramas in Miniature* (1891), *Songs and Sonnets* (1893) and *Birds of Passage: Songs of the Orient and Occident* (1895). Dates of first publication in volume form are given in square brackets at the foot of each poem.

Manchester by Night

O'ER this huge town, rife with intestine wars,
Whence as from monstrous sacrificial shrines
Pillars of smoke climb heavenward, Night inclines
Black brows majestical with glimmering stars.
5   Her dewy silence soothes life's angry jars:
And like a mother's wan white face, who pines
Above her children's turbulent ways, so shines
The moon athwart the narrow cloudy bars.

Now toiling multitudes that hustling crush
10   Each other in the fateful strife for breath,
And, hounded on by diverse hungers, rush
Across the prostrate ones that groan beneath,
Are swathed within the universal hush,
As life exchanges semblances with death.

[1881]

Haunted Streets

Lo, haply walking in some clattering street –
Where throngs of men and women dumbly pass,
Like shifting pictures seen within a glass
Which leave no trace behind – one seems to meet,
5   In roads once trodden by our mutual feet,
A face projected from that shadowy mass
Of faces, quite familiar as it was,
Which beaming on us stands out clear and sweet.

Manchester by Night] Manchester was a key centre for cotton manufacturing in the period, and the type of the northern industrial city for numerous Victorian writers (e.g. Dickens, Gaskell).

1. intestine] domestic or civil.

5. angry jars] discord or physical shock.

14. semblances] appearances, images.

Haunted Streets. *1. haply*] by chance.

3. glass] looking-glass; mirror.

5. our mutual feet] An odd usage: literally means: the feet we have in common, but the meaning seems to be, equally by each of our pairs of feet.

The face of faces we again behold
10   That lit our life when life was very fair,
And leaps our heart toward eyes and mouth and hair:
Oblivious of the undying love grown cold,
Or body sheeted in the churchyard mould,
We stretch out yearning hands and grasp – the air.

[1881]

Motherhood

(From Part II of *The Ascent of Man*)

FROM out the font of being, undefiled,
   A life hath been upheaved with struggle and pain;
   Safe in her arms a mother holds again
That dearest miracle – a new-born child.
5   To moans of anguish terrible and wild –
   As shrieks the night-wind through an ill-shut pane –
   Pure heaven succeeds; and after fiery strain
Victorious woman smiles serenely mild.

Yea, shall she not rejoice, shall not her frame
10   Thrill with a mystic rapture! At this birth,
The soul now kindled by her vital flame
      May it not prove a gift of priceless worth?
Some saviour of his kind whose starry fame
      Shall bring a brightness to the darkened earth.

[1889]

14.] An allusion to the ghosts in Book 6 of Virgil's *Aeneid*, 'stretching out their arms to the further shore'.

Motherhood. *Volume Title: The Ascent of Man*] The allusion is to Charles Darwin's *The Descent of Man* (1871). Blind's poem series gives a positive twist to Darwin's evolutionary theories.

1. font of being] fountain or source of existence; or, more specifically with reference to childbirth, the depths of the body: womb.

9–14.] The sestet of this sonnet seems to universalise the ecstasy of the Virgin Mary at being chosen to give birth to the Messiah. Cf. Elizabeth Barrett Browning's 'Only a Curl' (*Last Poems*, 1862), in which giving birth is compared to the apocalypse, and described as 'The motherhood's advent in power' (l. 35).

On a Forsaken Lark's Nest

Lo, where left 'mid the sheaves, cut down by the iron-fanged reaper,
Eating its way as it clangs fast through the wavering wheat,
Lies the nest of a lark, whose little brown eggs could not keep her
As she, affrighted and scared, fled from the harvester's feet.

5 Ah, what a heartful of song that now will never awaken,
Closely packed in the shell, awaited love's fostering,
That should have quickened to life what, now a-cold and forsaken,
Never, enamoured of light, will meet the dawn on the wing.

Ah, what pæans of joy, what raptures no mortal can measure,
10 Sweet as honey that's sealed in the cells of the honey-comb,
Would have ascended on high in jets of mellifluous pleasure,
Would have dropped from the clouds to nest in its gold-curtained
    home.

Poor, pathetic brown eggs! Oh, pulses that never will quicken!
Music mute in the shell that hath been turned to a tomb!
15 Many a sweet human singer, chilled and adversity-stricken,
Withers benumbed in a world his joy might have helped to illume.

[1889]

The Red Sunsets, 1883

THE twilight heavens are flushed with gathering light,
  And o'er wet roofs and huddling streets below
  Hang with a strange Apocalyptic glow
On the black fringes of the wintry night.

On a Forsaken Lark's Nest. *1. sheaves*] tied bundles of cut stalks complete with ears of grain. *iron-fanged reaper*] Mechanical harvesters were in general use in England from about 1870.

9. pæans] songs of praise or thanksgiving.

16. illume] poetic form of illumine.

The Red Sunsets, 1883] The volcanic eruption of Krakatoa near Java and Sumatra in what is now Indonesia, in August 1883, was one of the most gigantic ever recorded; fine particles carried around the earth in the upper atmosphere caused particularly brilliant sunsets for some time afterwards. This is the second of two sonnets entitled 'The Red Sunsets, 1883' (1889). In *Songs and Sonnets* (1893) the order was reversed and this became the first of the pair.

3. Apocalyptic glow] Suggests the destructive aspect of the Apocalypse (the prophetic revelations of St John) with a sense of fiery doom for the wicked.

5 Such bursts of glory may have rapt the sight
   Of him to whom on Patmos long ago
   The visionary angel came to show
  That heavenly city built of chrysolite.

  And lo, three factory hands begrimed with soot,
10   Aflame with the red splendour, marvelling stand,
  And gaze with lifted faces awed and mute.
   Starved of earth's beauty by Man's grudging hand,
  O toilers, robbed of labour's golden fruit,
   Ye, too, may feast in Nature's fairyland.

[1889]

A Winter Landscape

  ALL night, all day, in dizzy, downward flight,
   Fell the wild-whirling, vague, chaotic snow,
   Till every landmark of the earth below,
  Trees, moorlands, roads, and each familiar sight
5 Were blotted out by the bewildering white.
   And winds, now shrieking loud, now whimpering low,
   Seemed lamentations for the world-old woe
  That death must swallow life, and darkness light.

  But all at once the rack was blown away,
10   The snowstorm hushing ended in a sigh;
   Then like a flame the crescent moon on high
  Leaped forth among the planets; pure as they,
  Earth vied in whiteness with the Milky Way:
   Herself a star beneath the starry sky.

[1889]

---

6. *Patmos*] The small Greek island to which John was exiled, and where he wrote his Gospel and Book of Revelation (or Apocalypse) inspired by his vision of the New Jerusalem.

8. *chrysolite*] 'And I John saw the holy city, new Jerusalem, coming down from God out of heaven' (Revelation 21: 2). The foundations of the city were of precious stones, including chrysolite, a sort of golden topaz.

13. *robbed of labour's golden fruit*] An anti-capitalist reference to the comparatively poor rewards for labour.

A Winter Landscape. 9. *rack*] a mass of cloud driven by the wind.

13. *Milky Way*] a galaxy; figuratively, a path leading to heaven.

From Love in Exile

Note: This series of love poems was first published in *The Ascent of Man* (1889). In *Songs and Sonnets* (1893) it was reprinted with some additions: three poems were taken from *The Prophecy of Saint Oran* (1881), where they had appeared under the title 'Love Trilogy', and were placed at the head of the series; other poems were added from *Dramas in Miniature* (1891), and there were also some omissions. In his edition of Blind's *Poetical Works* (1900) Arthur Symons further enlarged and rearranged the series, reinstating some of the omitted poems. The 1889 text, from which the poems selected here are taken, included the following epigraph from Tennyson's elegy *In Memoriam* (1850):

> 'Whatever way my ways decline,
> I felt and feel, tho' left alone,
> His being washing in my own,
> The footsteps of his life in mine.'
> Lord Tennyson.

I

THOU walkest with me as the spirit-light
   Of the hushed moon, high o'er a snowy hill,
Walks with the houseless traveller all the night,
   When trees are tongueless and when mute the rill.
5 Moon of my soul, O phantasm of delight,
   Thou walkest with me still.

The vestal flame of quenchless memory burns
   In my soul's sanctuary. Yea, still for thee
My bitter heart hath yearned, as moonward yearns
10   Each separate wave-pulse of the clamorous sea:
My Moon of love, to whom for ever turns
   The life that aches through me.

Love in Exile. *I.*] As a result of the additions to the series (see above), this poem became no. 4 in 1893.

4. *rill*] small stream or rivulet.

5. *phantasm*] ghost, or counterfeit likeness.

7. *vestal flame*] the sacred flame brought by Aeneas from Troy and tended by virgin priestesses in the temple of Vesta (goddess of the hearth) at Rome.

10. *wave-pulse of the clamorous sea*] A reference to the moon's control of the tides.

II

I WAS again beside my Love in a dream:
    Earth was so beautiful, the moon was shining;
The muffled voice of many a cataract stream
    Came like a love-song, as, with arms entwining,
5   Our hearts were mixed in unison supreme.

The wind lay spell-bound in each pillared pine,
    The tasselled larches had no sound or motion,
As my whole life was sinking into thine –
    Sinking into a deep, unfathomed ocean
10   Of infinite love – uncircumscribed, divine.

Night held her breath, it seemed, with all her stars:
    Eternal eyes that watched in mute compassion
Our little lives o'erleap their mortal bars,
    Fused in the fulness of immortal passion,
15   A passion as immortal as the stars.

There was no longer any thee or me;
    No sense of self, no wish or incompleteness;
The moment, rounded to Eternity,
    Annihilated time's destructive fleetness:
20   For all but love itself had ceased to be.

IV

I WOULD I were the glow-worm, thou the flower,
    That I might fill thy cup with glimmering light;
I would I were the bird, and thou the bower,
    To sing thee songs throughout the summer night.

5   I would I were a pine tree deeply rooted,
    And thou the lofty, cloud-beleaguered rock,
Still, while the blasts of heaven around us hooted,
    To cleave to thee and weather every shock.

I would I were the rill, and thou the river;
10   So might I, leaping from some headlong steep,
With all my waters lost in thine for ever,
    Be hurried onwards to the unfathomed deep.

II.] No. 6 in 1893.

3. cataract] waterfall.

IV.] No. 9 in 1893.

I would – what would I not? O foolish dreaming!
  My words are but as leaves by autumn shed,
15   That, in the faded moonlight idly gleaming,
  Drop on the grave where all our love lies dead.

[1889]

The Message

FROM side to side the sufferer tossed
  With quick impatient sighs;
Her face was bitten as by frost,
The look as of one hunted crossed
5   The fever of her eyes.

All seared she seemed with life and woe,
  Yet scarcely could have told
More than a score of springs or so;
Her hair had girlhood's morning glow,
10   And yet her mouth looked old.

Not long for her the sun would rise,
  Nor that young slip of moon,
Wading through London's smoky skies,
Would dwindling meet those dwindling eyes,
15   Ere May was merged in June.

May was it somewhere? Who, alas!
  Could fancy it was May?
For here, instead of meadow grass,
You saw, through naked panes of glass,
20   Bare walls of whitish gray.

Instead of songs, where in the quick
  Leaves hide the blackbirds' nests,
You heard the moaning of the sick,
And tortured breathings harsh and thick
25   Drawn from their labouring chests.

The Message. *6. seared*] burned, as by a hot iron; rendered incapable of moral feeling or conscience (see 1 Timothy 4: 2).

8. a score] i.e. twenty.

21. quick] living, growing.

She muttered, 'What's the odds to me?'
    With an old cynic's sneer;
And looking up, cried mockingly,
'I hate you, nurse! Why, can't you see
30   You'll make no convert here?'

And then she shook her fist at Heaven,
    And broke into a laugh!
Yes, though her sins were seven times seven,
Let others pray to be forgiven –
35   She scorned such canting chaff.

Oh, it was dreadful, sir! Far worse
    In one so young and fair;
Sometimes she'd scoff and swear and curse;
Call me bad names, and vow each nurse
40   A fool for being there.

And then she'd fall back on her bed,
    And many a weary hour
Would lie as rigid as one dead;
Her white throat with the golden head
45   Like some torn lily flower.

We could do nothing, one and all
    How much we might beseech;
Her girlish blood had turned to gall:
Far lower than her body's fall
50   Her soul had sunk from reach.

Her soul had sunk into a slough
    Of evil past repair.
The world had been against her; now
Nothing in heaven or earth should bow
55   Her stubborn knees in prayer.

---

33. seven times seven] See Matthew 18: 21: 'How often shall . . . I forgive him? till seven times?'

35. canting chaff] hypocritical rubbish.

47. How much] i.e. however much.

48. gall] intensely bitter secretion from the liver.

51. slough] marshy ground. See John Bunyan, *Pilgrim's Progress* (1678): 'They drew near to a very miry slough . . . The name of the slough was Despond.'

Yet I felt sorry all the same,
   And sometimes, when she slept,
With head and hands as hot as flame,
I watched beside her, half in shame,
60   Smoothed her bright hair and wept.

To die like this – 'twas awful, sir!
   To know I prayed in vain;
And hear her mock me, and aver
That if her life came back to her
65   She'd live her life again.

Was she a wicked girl? What then?
   She didn't care a pin!
She was not worse than all those men
Who looked so shocked in public, when
70   They made and shared her sin.

'Shut up, nurse, do! Your sermons pall;
   Why can't you let me be?
Instead of worrying o'er my fall,
I wish, just wish, you sisters all
75   Turned to the likes of me.'

I shuddered! I could bear no more,
   And left her to her fate;
She was too cankered at the core;
Her heart was like a bolted door,
80   Where Love had knocked too late.

I left her in her savage spleen,
   And hoarsely heard her shout,
'What does the cursed sunlight mean
By shining in upon this scene?
85   Oh, shut the sunlight out!'

---

63. *aver*] assert.

78. *cankered*] rotten, ulcerated.

81. *savage spleen*] irritable temper.

Sighing, I went my round once more,
    Full heavy for her sin;
Just as Big Ben was striking four,
The sun streamed through the open door,
90   As a young girl came in.

She held a basket full of flowers –
    Cowslip and columbine;
A lilac bunch from rustic bowers,
Strong-scented after morning showers,
95   Smelt like some cordial wine.

There, too, peeped Robin-in-the-hedge,
    There daisies pearled with dew,
Wild parsley from the meadow's edge,
Sweet-william and the purple vetch,
100   And hyacinth's heavenly blue.

But best of all the spring's array,
    Green boughs of milk-white thorn;
Their petals on each perfumed spray
Looked like the wedding gift of May
105   On nature's marriage morn.

And she who bore those gifts of grace
    To our poor patients there,
Passed like a sunbeam through the place:
Dull eyes grew brighter for her face,
110   Angelically fair.

---

88. Big Ben] clock famous for its accuracy, housed in the tower at the eastern end of the Houses of Parliament at Westminster, London.

93. rustic bowers] *Cowslips* are wild flowers, then commonly found in meadows; *columbines* and *lilac* are cultivated flowers often found in cottage gardens.

95. cordial] restorative.

96–100.] *Robin-in-the-hedge* is a ground-ivy; *sweet-william* a species of pink; *vetch* grows as a weed in cornfields; the *hyacinth* is a fragrant flower growing from a bulb.

102. milk-white thorn] i.e. hawthorn, or may-blossom, often grown as a hedge along country lanes; the symbol of 'good hope' in the language of flowers.

She went the round with elf-like tread,
  And with kind words of cheer,
Soothing as balm of Gilead,
Laid wild flowers on each patient's bed,
115   And made the flowers more dear.

At last she came where Nellie Dean
  Still moaned and tossed about –
'What does the cursed sunlight mean
By shining in upon this scene?
120   Will no one shut it out?'

And then she swore with rage and pain,
  And moaning tried to rise;
It seemed her ugly words must stain
The child who stood with heart astrain,
125   And large blue listening eyes.

Her fair face did not blush or bleach,
  She did not shrink away;
Alas! she was beyond the reach
Of sweet or bitter human speech –
130   Deaf as the flowers of May.

Only her listening eyes could hear
  That hardening in despair,
Which made that other girl, so near
In age to her, a thing to fear
135   Like fever-tainted air.

She took green boughs of milk-white thorn
  And laid them on the sheet,
Whispering appealingly, 'Don't scorn
My flowers! I think, when one's forlorn,
140   They're like a message, Sweet.'

---

113. *balm of Gilead*] 'Is there no balm in Gilead?' (Jeremiah 8: 22): is there no remedy, no consolation?

116. *Nellie Dean*] The name of the servant at Wuthering Heights, in the novel by Emily Brontë; this appears to be a coincidental identification.

How heavenly fresh those blossoms smelt,
　　Like showers on thirsty ground!
The sick girl frowned as if repelled,
And with hot hands began to pelt
145　　And fling them all around.

But then some influence seemed to stay
　　Her hands with calm control;
Her stormy passion cleared away,
The perfume of the breath of May
150　　Had passed into her soul.

A nerve of memory had been thrilled,
　　And, pushing back her hair,
She stretched out hungry arms half filled
With flower and leaf, and panting shrilled,
155　　'Where are you, mother, where?'

And then her eyes shone darkly bright
　　Through childhood in a mist,
As if she suddenly caught sight
Of some one hidden in the light
160　　And waited to be kissed.

'Oh, mother dear!' we heard her moan,
　　'Have you not gone away?
I dreamed, dear mother, you had gone,
And left me in the world alone,
165　　In the wild world astray.

'It was a dream; I'm home again!
　　I hear the ivy-leaves
Tap-tapping on the leaded pane!
Oh, listen! how the laughing rain
170　　Runs from our cottage eaves!

'How very sweet the things do smell!
　　How bright our pewter shines!
I am at home; I feel so well:
I think I hear the evening bell
175　　Above our nodding pines.

---

172. pewter] Pewter was an alloy of tin and lead, widely used for dishes, platters, mugs and bowls where silver would have been too expensive.

174. the evening bell] i.e. the church bell calling to evening service.

'The firelight glows upon the brick,
   And pales the rising moon;
And when your needles flash and click,
My heart, my heart, that felt so sick,
180   Throbs like a hive in June.

'If only father would not stay
   And gossip o'er his brew;
Then, reeling homewards, lose his way,
Come staggering in at break of day
185   And beat you black and blue!

'Yet he can be as good as gold,
   When mindful of the farm,
He tills the field and tends the fold:
But never fear; when I'm grown old
190   I'll keep him out of harm.

'And then we'll be as happy here
   As kings upon their throne!
I dreamed you'd left me, mother dear;
That you lay dead this many a year
195   Beneath the churchyard stone.

'Mother, I sought you far and wide,
   And ever in my dream,
Just out of reach you seemed to hide;
I ran along the streets and cried,
200   "Where are you, mother, where?"

'Through never-ending streets in fear
   I ran and ran forlorn;
And through the twilight yellow-drear
I saw blurred masks of loafers leer,
205   And point at me in scorn.

'How tired, how deadly tired, I got;
   I ached through all my bones!
The lamplight grew one quivering blot,
And like one rooted to the spot,
210   I dropped upon the stones.

---

188. fold] pen or enclosure for domestic animals.

'A hard bed make the stones and cold,
      The mist a wet, wet sheet;
And in the mud, like molten gold,
The snaky lamplight blinking rolled
215   Like guineas at my feet.

'Surely there were no mothers when
      A voice hissed in my ear,
"A sovereign! Quick! Come on!" – and then
A knowing leer! There were but men,
220   And not a creature near.

'I went – I could not help it. Oh,
      I didn't want to die!
With now a kiss and now a blow,
Strange men would come, strange men would go;
225   I didn't care – not I.

'Sometimes my life was like a tale
      Read in a story-book;
Our blazing nights turned daylight pale,
Champagne would fizz like ginger-ale,
230   Red wine flow like a brook.

'Then like a vane my dream would veer:
      I walked the street again;
And through the twilight yellow-drear
Blurred clouds of faces seemed to peer,
235   And drift across the rain.'

She started with a piercing scream
      And wildly rolling eye:
'Ah me! it was no evil dream
To pass with the first market-team –
240   That thing of shame am I.

---

218. *A sovereign*] a gold coin initially worth 20 shillings; by this time a smaller version worth 10 shillings was in circulation.

231. *vane*] i.e. weathervane: an ornamental plate of metal designed to turn with the wind and point its changing direction.

236. *started*] jumped.

'Where were you that you could not come?
   Were you so far above –
Far as the moon above a slum?
Yet, mother, you were all the sum
245   I had of human love.

'Ah yes! you've sent this branch of May,
   A fair light from the past.
The town is dark – I went astray.
Forgive me, mother! Lead the way;
250   I'm going home at last.'

In eager haste she tried to rise,
   And struggled up in bed,
With luminous, transfigured eyes,
As if they glassed the opening skies,
255   Fell back, sir, and was dead.

[1891]

Many Will Love You

MANY will love you; you were made for love;
For the soft plumage of the unruffled dove
   Is not so soft as your caressing eyes.
You will love many; for the winds that veer
5   Are not more prone to shift their compass, dear,
   Than your quick fancy flies.

Many will love you; but I may not, no;
Even though your smile sets all my life aglow,
   And at your fairness all my senses ache.
10   You will love many; but not me, my dear,
Who have no gift to give you but a tear
   Sweet for your sweetness' sake.

[1891]

---

254. *glassed*] mirrored.

Many Will Love You. 5. *to shift their compass*] to change their direction.

A Fantasy

I was an Arab,
　　I loved my horse;
Swift as an arrow
　　He swept the course.

5　　Sweet as a lamb
　　He came to hand;
He was the flower
　　Of all the land.

Through lonely nights
10　　I rode afar;
God lit His lights –
　　Star upon star.

God's in the desert;
　　His breath the air:
15　Beautiful desert,
　　Boundless and bare!

Free as the wild wind,
　　Light as a foal;
Ah, there is room there
20　　To stretch one's soul.

Far reached my thought,
　　Scant were my needs:
A few bananas
　　And lotus seeds.

A Fantasy. 2.] Nomadic tribes of Arabs living in the desert depended on their swift war horses for survival, and the Arabian horse is famous for its intelligence and powers of endurance as well as its capacity for a special relationship with a human.

16. *Boundless and bare!*] See Shelley's 'Ozymandias' (1818), ll. 12–14: '. . . Round the decay / Of that colossal wreck, boundless and bare / The lone and level sands stretch far away.'

23–4. *bananas . . . lotus seeds*] Bananas were cultivated in parts of Egypt, though they were not normally associated with the Arabian desert. Dates might have been more appropriate, but would not have scanned so well. Although 'lotus' is a name given to many plants, e.g. by the Egyptians to the water lily, it traditionally symbolises the eminence of divine intellect; but it also carried the connotation from Homeric myth that eating of its fruit induced a dreamy forgetfulness of home and duty. See Tennyson's poem 'The Lotos-Eaters' (1832).

25   Sparkling as water
                  Cool in the shade,
               Ibrahim's daughter,
                  Beautiful maid.

               Out of thy Kulleh,
30   Fairest and first,
               Give me to drink
                 Quencher of thirst.

               I am athirst, girl;
                 Parched with desire,
35   Love in my bosom
                 Burns as a fire.

               Green thy oasis,
                 Waving with Palms;
               Oh, be no niggard,
40   Maid, with thy alms.

               Kiss me with kisses,
                 Buds of thy mouth,
               Sweeter than Cassia
                 Fresh from the South.

45   Bind me with tresses,
                 Clasp with a curl;
               And in caresses
                 Stifle me, girl.

               I was an Arab
50   Ages ago!
               Hence this home-sickness
                 And all my woe.

               [1895]

---

27. *Ibrahim's*] Not a biblical reference; rather, a generic 'Arab' name.

29. *Kulleh*] a lamb-skin cap.

39. *niggard*] miser.

40. *alms*] charity to the poor.

43. *Cassia*] a kind of cinnamon.

Scarabæus Sisyphus

I'VE watched thee, Scarab! Yea, an hour in vain
    I've watched thee, slowly toiling up the hill,
    Pushing thy lump of mud before thee still
With patience infinite and stubborn strain.
5   Strive as thou mayst, spare neither time nor pain,
    To screen thy burden from all chance of ill;
    Push, push, with all a beetle's force of will,
Thy ball, alas! rolls ever down again.

Toil without end! And why? That after thee
10   Dim hosts of groping Scarabs too shall climb
This self-same height? Accursèd progeny
    Of Sisyphus, what antenatal crime
Has doomed us too to roll incessantly
    Life's Stone, recoiling from the Alps of time?

[1895]

Mourning Women

ALL veiled in black, with faces hid from sight,
    Crouching together in the jolting cart,
    What forms are these that pass alone, apart,
In abject apathy to life's delight?
5   The motley crowd, fantastically bright,
    Shifts gorgeous through each dazzling street and mart;
    Only these sisters of the suffering heart
Strike discords in this symphony of light.

Scarabæus Sisyphus] The beetle (*Scarabæus sacer*) was the emblem of the pinciple of life and creative power, which the Egyptians worshipped under such manifold forms. It was supposed to have no female, and to roll the eggs which produce its offspring into a kind of ball, sparing no effort to place them in safety [Author's note]. 'Scarabaeus sacer', or sacred scarab, the Latin name for the ancient Egyptian dung-beetle, is here being played upon by the substitution of Sisyphus for sacer. Sisyphus was doomed in hell to roll a large stone uphill until it reached the summit and fell down again. The Egyptian scarabs actually roll their dung-balls uphill and let them roll down in order to compact the matter around their eggs.

Mourning Women. 1.] Muslim women clothe themselves in black from head to toe and veil their faces, as a sign of subservience.

5. *motley*] i.e. dressed in variegated bright colours.

Most wretched women! whom your prophet dooms
10   To take love's penalties without its prize!
Yes; you shall bear the unborn in your wombs,
    And water dusty death with streaming eyes,
And, wailing, beat your breasts among the tombs;
    But souls ye have none fit for Paradise.

[1895]

Noonday Rest

THE willows whisper very, very low
    Unto the listening breeze;
Sometimes they lose a leaf which, flickering slow,
    Faints on the sunburnt leas.

5   Beneath the whispering boughs and simmering skies,
    On the hot ground at rest,
Still as a stone, a ragged woman lies,
    Her baby at the breast.

Nibbling around her browse monotonous sheep,
10   Flies buzz about her head;
Her heavy eyes are shuttered by a sleep
    As of the slumbering dead.

The happy birds that live to love and sing,
    Flitting from bough to bough,
15   Peer softly at this ghastly human thing
    With grizzled hair and brow.

O'er what strange ways may not these feet have trod
    That match the cracking clay?
Man had no pity on her – no, nor God –
20   A nameless castaway!

9–14.] The sestet alludes to the doctrine (believed to be Islamic) that women do not have souls and therefore will be denied entry into paradise.

9. *your prophet*] Mahommed.

Noonday Rest. 4. *leas*] poetic word for grassland.
16. *grizzled*] grey-haired.

But Mother Earth now hugs her to her breast,
    Defiled or undefiled;
And willows rock the weary soul to rest,
    As she, even she, her child.

Hampstead Heath.

[1895]

Hampstead Heath] Hampstead Heath, here identified as the scene of the poem, was at this time a large tract of uncultivated heathland on high ground to the north of London.

'MICHAEL FIELD' [KATHARINE HARRIS BRADLEY (1846–1914) AND EDITH EMMA COOPER (1862–1913)]

'Michael Field' was the pseudonym used by two women poets, Katharine Harris Bradley and Edith Emma Cooper, who wrote and published together, as one person, throughout most of their lives. Katharine's elder sister was Emma's mother, making them aunt and niece. Katharine did publish a first volume of poems (*The New Minnesinger*) on her own in 1875, under the pseudonym 'Arran Leigh' (no doubt partly inspired by Barrett Browning's *Aurora Leigh*, still renowned after 20 years). In 1881 she published a second volume, *Bellerophon*, this time with her niece, as 'by Arran and Isla Leigh'. The collaboration had begun.

Deeply romantic and idealistic in their aspirations, the pair formed what they termed a 'fellowship' with each other, and resolved to devote their lives to art. They aimed principally at what seemed to them the highest form of poetry, blank verse drama in the Elizabethan manner, no matter how currently unfashionable that might be. *Callirhöe, Fair Rosamund* was their first publication as Michael Field: these two dramas were published in one volume in 1884. For a while Michael Field enjoyed great success: each new work was received with acclaim, and a new young talent hailed by hardened old reviewers. Robert Browning was an early admirer who became a friend, but unfortunately, despite repeated exhortations from Bradley in particular to make sure he kept their identity secret: 'the world will not tolerate [what we have to say] from a woman's lips . . .', he did let slip that Michael Field was female, and the bubble of his popularity was burst. The deeper half of their secret, which Browning did not disclose about his 'two dear Greek women', as he called them, and which was not suspected until much later, was that Michael Field was not only female, but *two* females. Once Edith became an adult, the two women also became lovers. They lived together for the rest of their lives, but their love affair was not without vicissitudes.

In terms of their poetry, they took care to promote the idea that they always wrote as one: each could pick up the other's thought, or line, where it had been left off. In this romantic collaboration, they prided themselves on being 'closer married' even than the Brownings, who never attempted joint poetic production. However, the reality appears to have been somewhat different: evidence from their journals reveals that, while the many plays that they wrote were joint efforts, the lyric poems (of which between them they published eight volumes) were almost always composed by one or other individually. The journals, which have not yet been published (except in excerpted form),[1] are a treasure trove for the researcher, although dauntingly detailed, allusive and voluminous. The two women appear to have shaped

---

[1] As *Works and Days*, a title drawn from the Greek poet Hesiod. This volume was edited by Michael Field's literary executor, T. Sturge Moore, in 1933. The original 28 volumes of the handwritten diary are held in the British Library, London.

their lives, dedicated to poetry and to each other, as if they were precious works of art. A private income enabled them to enjoy such luxuries as European travel, a house of their own (called The Paragon, on the river in Richmond), an independent, even eccentric, way of life dedicated to aesthetic and spiritual goals, and a determination to see each of their published volumes produced as beautifully as possible. This last they achieved by having their work privately printed in limited editions, beautifully bound. Unfortunately, however, such preciosity told against them in the long run, for their books are so exceedingly rare as to be unobtainable outside major library collections. Only one or two of their dramas were ever produced on the stage: like much nineteenth-century verse drama, Browning's and Tennyson's included, it is far too much interested in the language of poetry and too little concerned with the language of character and action.

The devotion of the two women to each other seems to have been accepted by their families as totally normal, even admirable, but they themselves became increasingly anxious about its appearance in the eyes of the world, particularly after the trial of Oscar Wilde on charges of homosexuality in 1895. The other factor which made them self-conscious was their conversion to the Roman Catholic church in 1907. Edith was the first to join, then Katharine felt she had no choice but to follow, albeit somewhat reluctantly. Previously they had enjoyed their own form of worship which was a kind of paganism, Greek-based (they both learned Greek: Katharine even attended classes at Newnham College, Cambridge, during 1874) but largely of their own invention. They seem to have envisioned themselves, in some sense, as wild libertarian Maenads, or Bacchantes, handmaidens of the god Dionysus or Bacchus. Such a self-fashioning proved far more empowering for their writing lives than were the later restrictions of the Christian faith, at least in its Catholic manifestation. It is tempting to see Katharine mourning the lost days of their pagan freedom together in her little poem 'Palimpsest' (see p. 227 below). However, as in everything they undertook together, their embrace of the Catholic faith was wholehearted, and one imagines it must have helped them accept the cancer that eventually took their lives – Edith first, then Katharine less than a year later (having kept her own illness a secret from the beloved younger woman).

One of their most inspired productions during their pagan phase was the volume of lyrics titled *Long Ago* (1889). This was a collection based on the recent re-issue of the works of the sixth-century Greek poet Sappho in a straightforward translation, along with a memoir, in 1885 by Henry Thornton Wharton. This translation was an important milestone because, for the first time, it did not bowdlerise the same-sex love poems written by Sappho by altering the pronouns 'she' and 'her' to 'he' and 'him', thus restoring, for all to see, the lesbian poet (who came, literally, from the isle of Lesbos) to her original meaning. Although her work only survived in fragments, Sappho had for centuries been renowned for the fiery eroticism of her love lyrics, but hitherto, only Greek scholars had understood the nature of the sexual desires they expressed. For Michael Field, the revelation acted as a catalyst to creativity. The lyrics of *Long Ago* each took as epigraph and starting point a line from one of Sappho's lyrics, and then improvised an expansion on that theme. Several examples are included in the selection given here. To Michael Field's contemporaries, it seemed like a very bold experiment, almost as though it were an attempt to gild the lily: Sappho was so universally admired as a master songwriter. But to Michael Field, it was more like an act of homage, a celebration of all that Sappho might mean to the woman poet once she had been freed from the appropriation of pusillanimous translators. However, it is important to realise also that Michael Field never adopted a proselytising position for same-sex relationships. On the contrary, the model of heterosexuality is heightened into a romantic ideal in his poetry, with the voice of the poet always appropriating masculinity and, in the love lyrics, always addressing a female beloved. Both these women poets unconsciously valued the greater power the masculine role carried in the literary world (they each had a male nickname – Katharine was Michael and Edith was Henry), and neither had much sympathy for other women poets, at one time claiming that they only admired Dorothy Wordsworth among their sisters. Although this claim was exaggerated – they liked and admired Alice Meynell, for example, and they published a sonnet to Christina Rossetti – they were certainly what we would now call 'male-identified', and not in any sense politically engaged in the struggles for women's rights.

Yet, paradoxically, some of their finest lyrics were written from within a bodily sense of being a woman. The beautiful flower lyrics included here ('Irises', 'Tiger-Lilies', 'Cyclamens': see pp. 224–5) show an intense erotic awareness of female sexuality from the inside, as it were. These flower lyrics are an example of what has long been recognised as a strong female genre, culminating in the twentieth century in the famous 'tulip' and 'poppy' poems of Sylvia Plath. All Victorian women poets would have been aware of traditional symbolic associations of flowers in literature, and of their being regarded as somehow a female province. But where the earlier women poets, among them Rossetti, tended to use what was known as 'the language of flowers' in an emblematic way, Michael Field broke out into an early kind of Imagism, anticipating Amy Lowell's experiments in the twentieth-century modernist period. In their poems, flower descriptions are used to symbolise female sexual desire. Expression of female desire also becomes the subject for one of the *Long Ago* lyrics, no. LII, titled 'Tiresias: but that I know by experience' (see p. 215). The poem rehearses in a new way the age-old debate presented in Greek myth as the argument between Zeus and Hera as to whether the man or the woman derives the most pleasure from sexual intercourse; an argument which Tiresias was called upon to settle as he had experienced both in his transformation from one sex to the other. Michael Field's poem on the subject focuses on the different kinds of pleasure that flow from the two different roles, that of seduced and seducer, showing also how those roles can merge and swap under the pressures of sexual desire. But the poem also openly celebrates female sexual pleasure in a way that was quite extraordinary in the period. This is part of the positive result of a poet's (or poets') choice to ignore current fashion; the more negative result was that they built themselves an exquisite ivory tower, in which they flourished and died forgotten. Much more interest has been taken in their work recently, however, and researchers will be helped by the publication in 1998 of an index to Michael Field's works put out by Ivor Treby, albeit only in a limited edition, just like the works of his subject.

Text: The poems chosen are from *Long Ago* (1889), *Sight and Song* (1892), *Underneath the Bough* (1893; 1898), *Wild Honey from Various Thyme* (1908), *A Selection from the*

Poems of Michael Field, ed. T. Sturge Moore (1923), and *The Wattlefold* (1930). The date of first publication in volume form is given in square brackets at the foot of each poem. The copy-texts used are the first editions except in the case of *Underneath the Bough*, for which the (revised and enlarged) 1898 American edition has been used.

Long Ago

XIV

Τὸ μέλημα τοὐμόν·

ATTHIS, my darling, thou did'st stray
A few feet to the rushy bed,
When a great fear and passion shook
My heart lest haply thou wert dead;
It grew so still about the brook,
As if a soul were drawn away.

Anon thy clear eyes, silver-blue,
Shone through the tamarisk-branches fine;
To pluck me iris thou had'st sprung
Through galingale and celandine;
Away, away, the flowers I flung
And thee down to my breast I drew.

My darling! Nay, our very breath
Nor light nor darkness shall divide;
Queen Dawn shall find us on one bed,
Nor must thou flutter from my side
An instant, lest I feel the dread,
Atthis, the immanence of death.

[1889]

Long Ago] The poems following are selected from a numbered sequence from the volume titled *Long Ago*, an experimental work devoted to the Greek poet Sappho, in which each poem explored the Sapphic theme indicated by its Greek epigraph. Translations for some of the epigraphs have been kindly supplied by Dr Yopie Prins.

XIV. Epigraph.] 'My Darling'.

1. ATTHIS] One of Sappho's pupils. Some of Sappho's poems suggest that there was a break between the two women. See Loeb, *Lyra Graeca*, vol. 1, #83: '[So I shall never see Atthis more,] and in sooth I might as well be dead.'

8. tamarisk] a graceful evergreen shrub originally from southern Europe, but later much planted by the seashore in the south of England.

10. galingale] an English species of sedge (rush-like plants).   *celandine*] a kind of meadow flower.

XXIV

Ψάπφοι, τί τὰν πολύολβον Ἀφρόδιταν;

WHY should I praise thee, blissful Aphrodite?
    Wrong hast thou wrought
Thy Sappho, thy flower-weaving one, who brought
The fair, white goat, and poured the milky bowl,
        Using thy mighty,
Malignant craft to baulk me of my goal;
    Though all my days
And starless nights I crown thee with my lays:
    Why should I praise,
Why should I praise thee, blissful Aphrodite?

Why should I praise thee, blissful Aphrodite?
    Thou dost not guide,
Rather with conflict dire my mind divide;
For me the trembling boy grows honey-pale,
    While for the mighty
Fervours of Phaon's breast, without avail,
    My mad heart prays.
Win him, O Queen, who shunned to seek my gaze!
    Then will I praise,
Then will I praise thee, blissful Aphrodite.

[1889]

XXXIII

Ταῖς κάλαις ὔμμιν [τὸ] νόημα τῶμον οὐ διάμειπτον·

MAIDS, not to you my mind doth change;
Men I defy, allure, estrange,

XXIV. Epigraph.] 'Sappho, why [praise] bountiful Aphrodite?' Cf. Loeb, *Lyra Graeca*, vol. 1, #126: 'Why, Sappho, [do you disdain] Aphrodite of the many blessings?'

1. Aphrodite] goddess of the sea, of love, beauty, flowers and seasons. Pronounced to rhyme with 'mighty'.

4. fair, white goat] See Loeb, *Lyra Graeca*, vol. 1, #7 and 8: 'and to thee I [will burn the rich] fat of a white goat'. The note on this fragment indicates that white goats were sacrificed to Aphrodite.

8. lays] songs.

16. Phaon] Sappho's faithless male lover.

XXXIII. Epigraph.] 'To you lovely women my mind does not change.' Cf. Loeb, *Lyra Graeca*, vol. 1, #14: 'Towards you pretty ones this mind of mine can never change.'

Prostrate, make bond or free:
Soft as the stream beneath the plane
5   To you I sing my love's refrain;
Between us is no thought of pain,
          Peril, satiety.

Soon doth a lover's patience tire,
But ye to manifold desire
10   Can yield response, ye know
When for long, museful days I pine,
The presage at my heart divine;
To you I never breathe a sign
Of inward want or woe.

15   When injuries my spirit bruise,
Allaying virtue ye infuse
With unobtrusive skill:
And if care frets ye come to me
As fresh as nymph from stream or tree,
20   And with your soft vitality
          My weary bosom fill.

[1889]

XXXIV

Οὔ τι μοι ὔμμες.

'SING to us Sappho!' cried the crowd,
    And to my lyre I sprang;
Apollo seized me, and aloud
    Tumultuous I sang.
5   I did not think of who would hear;
I knew not there were men who jeer;
Nor dreamed I there were mortals born
To make the poet's heart forlorn.

---

4. plane] Either a reference to a plane tree, or possibly, 'plane' could mean the same as 'plain' (see *OED*).

12.] i.e. [you] guess the omen at my heart.

XXXIV. Epigraph.] 'You are nothing to me.' Cf. Loeb, *Lyra Graeca*, vol. 1, #49: 'It is not you who are . . . to me. . . .'

3. Apollo] god of music and poetry, thought to inspire both poets and prophets by divine possession.

There is a gift the crowd can bring,
10   A rapture, a content;
Pierian roses scarcely fling
        So ravishing a scent
As that with which the air is stirred
When hearts of heavenly things have heard –
15   Sigh, and let forth the odour steal
Of that which in themselves they feel.

But now no subtle incense rose;
        I heard a hostile sound
And looked – oh, scornfuller than those
20   'Mong men I ne'er have found.
I paused: the whistling air was stilled;
Then through my chords the godhead thrilled,
And the quelled creatures knew their kind
Ephemeral through foolish mind.

25   They saw their ghosts in Hades' grove
        A dismal, flitting band;
They felt they were shut out from love
        And honour in their land;
For never in the Muses' strain
30   Of them memorial would remain;
And spell-bound they received the curse
Of the great King's derided verse.

[1889]

---

11. *Pierian*] belonging to the Muses (Pieria is the reputed home of the Muses). See Loeb, *Lyra Graeca*, vol. 1, #71: 'Sappho, to a woman of no education: "When you are dead you will lie unremembered for evermore; for you have no part in the roses that come from Pieria; nay, obscure here, you will move obscure in the house of Death, and flit to and fro among such of the dead as have no fame." '

23–4.] i.e. these men knew themselves to be ephemeral because of their inferior spirit (see previous notes).

25. *Hades' grove*] the abode of departed spirits.

29–30.] Contrast Sappho's confidence about her own reputation: 'But I have received true prosperity from the golden Muses, and when I die I shall not be forgot' (Loeb, *Lyra Graeca*, vol. 1, #11).

31–2. *the great King*] Apollo. See also note to l. 3, above.

XXXV

Ἀλλα, μὴ μεγαλύνεο δακτυλίῳ πέρι·

COME, Gorgo, put the rug in place,
    And passionate recline;
I love to see thee in thy grace,
    Dark, virulent, divine.
5   But wherefore thus thy proud eyes fix
    Upon a jewelled band?
Art thou so glad the sardonyx
    Becomes thy shapely hand?

Bethink thee! 'Tis for such as thou
10   Zeus leaves his lofty seat;
'Tis at thy beauty's bidding how
    Man's mortal life shall fleet;
Those fairest hands – dost thou forget
    Their power to thrill and cling?
15   O foolish woman, dost thou set
    Thy pride upon a ring?

[1889]

LII

Ἔγων δ᾽ ἐμαύτᾳ τοῦτο σύνοιδα·

[Tiresias: but that I know by experience]

CLIMBING the hill a coil of snakes
Impedes Tiresias' path; he breaks

XXXV. Epigraph.] 'But do not pride yourself on a ring.' Cf. Loeb, *Lyra Graeca*, vol. 1, #51: 'But come, be not so proud of a ring.'

1. Gorgo] a wealthy female rival of Sappho's.

7. sardonyx] a precious stone, striped white and brown.

10. Zeus] king of the gods.

LII. Epigraph.] 'And in my own self I know this.' Cf. Loeb, *Lyra Graeca*, vol. 1, #15: 'and as for me, I am conscious of this'.

Title.] Added by T. Sturge Moore. Tiresias was a soothsayer. Tradition stated that while walking on Mount Cyllene, the young Tiresias saw two serpents mating, whereupon he either separated the serpents, wounded them, or killed the female (Field's poem favours the latter interpretation). As a result of this action he became a woman. Several years later at the same spot he again saw

His staff across them – idle thrust
That lays the female in the dust,
5   But dooms the prophet to forego
His manhood, and, as woman, know
The unfamiliar, sovereign guise
Of passion he had dared despise.

Ah, not in the Erinnys' ground
10 Experience so dire were found
As that to the enchanter known
When womanhood was round him thrown:
He trembled at the quickening change,
He trembled at his vision's range,
15 His finer sense for bliss and dole,
His receptivity of soul;
But when love came, and, loving back,
He learnt the pleasure men must lack,
It seemed that he had broken free
20 Almost from his mortality.

Seven years he lives as woman, then
Resumes his cruder part 'mong men,
Till him indignant Hera becks
To judge betwixt the joys of sex,
25 For the great Queen in wrath has heard
By her presumptuous lord averred
That, when he sought her in his brave,
Young godhead, higher bliss he gave
Than the unutterable lure
30 Of her veiled glances could procure
For him, as balmy-limbed and proud
She drew him to Olympia's cloud.

---

the serpents mating. Having intervened in the same way, he became a man again. When Hera and Zeus were quarrelling over which sex experienced the greater pleasure in love-making, they consulted Tiresias, who had experienced both. He replied that if the enjoyment of love was constituted out of ten parts, the woman possessed nine, the man one. Hera was so furious that she struck Tiresias blind but Zeus gave him the gift of prophecy and the privilege of living for seven human generations.

9. *Erinnys*] goddesses, identified by the Romans with the Furies. They were depicted as winged spirits with serpents in their hair and lived in Erebus, the darkest pit of the Underworld. They tortured their victims, sometimes striking them with madness.

32. *Olympia's cloud*] 'Olympia' appears to be used here as a variation of Olympus, the mountain home of the gods. Clouds obscured the gods from mortal view.

'In marriage who hath more delight?'
She asks; then quivers and grows white,
35 As sacrilegious lips reveal
What woman in herself must feel –
And passes an avenging hand
Across his subtle eyelids bland.

Deep-bosomed Queen, fain would'st thou hide
40 The mystic raptures of the bride!
When man's strong nature draweth nigh
'Tis as the lightning to the sky,
The blast to idle sail, the thrill
Of springtide when the saplings fill.
45 Though fragrant breath the sun receives
From the young rose's softening leaves,
Her plaited petals once undone
The rose herself receives the sun.

Tiresias, ere the goddess smite,
50 Look on me with unblinded sight,
That I may learn if thou hast part
In womanhood's secluded heart:
Medea's penetrative charm
Own'st thou to succour and disarm,
55 Hast thou her passion inly great
Heroes to mould and subjugate?
Can'st thou divine how sweet to bring
Apollo to thy blossoming
As Daphne; or, as just a child
60 Gathering a bunch of tulips wild,
To feel the flowery hillside rent
Convulsive for thy ravishment?

---

38. *bland*] in the sense of smooth to the touch (now archaic).

53. *Medea*] Medea was known for her magic skills. She fell in love with Jason, leader of the Argonauts, and helped him to obtain the golden fleece. As his wife she also restored Jason's kingdom to him by arranging for the death of the usurper, Pelias. When Jason deserted her she killed Glaucé, his intended second wife, Glaucé's father and her own two sons. See Augusta Webster's poem 'Medea in Athens', p. 148 above.

59–62. *Daphne . . . ravishment?*] Daphne, whose name means 'laurel' in Greek, was a nymph desired by Apollo. When being chased by him, she begged for help to escape his clutches and was turned into a laurel tree. The child ravished while gathering flowers is Persephone, daughter of Zeus and Demeter, who was taken by Hades to be his queen in the Underworld.

Thou need'st not to unlock thine eyes,
Thy slow ironic smile replies:
65   Thou hast been woman, and although
The twining snakes with second blow
Of golden staff thou did'st assail,
And, crushing at a stroke the male,
Had'st virtue from thy doom to break,
70   And lost virility re-take –
Thou hast been woman, and her deep,
Magnetic mystery dost keep;
Thou hast been woman, and can'st see
Therefore into futurity:
75   It is not that Zeus gave thee power
To look beyond the transient hour,
For thou hast trod the regions dun,
Where life and death are each begun;
Thy spirit from the gods set free
80   Hath communed with Necessity.
Tilphusa's fountain thou may'st quaff
And die, but still thy golden staff
Will guide thee with perceptive hand
Among the Shades to understand
85   The terrors of remorse and dread,
And prophesy among the dead.

[1889]

LXV

πολυ ἴδριδι

PROMETHEUS fashioned man,
Then ruthful, pitying

---

67. golden staff] Athena was said to have given Tiresias a staff to guide him in his blindness. Sometimes it is specified as golden.

81. Tilphusa's fountain] One account of Tiresias's death attributed it to drinking from the spring of Telphusa.

84–6.] 'Shades' refers to the dead. Tiresias was reputedly the only shade to keep his intelligence after death, and Odysseus journeyed to Hades to consult him and hear his prophecy.

LXV. Epigraph.] 'of much knowledge'.

1.] According to Greek legend, Prometheus was employed by Zeus to make men from mud and water; out of pity, he then stole fire from heaven and gave it to them.

His creature when the snowy storms began
To numb, the frost to harass and to cling,

5   Towards the sun's golden wheel
        He clomb, and, as the blaze
Burned past, taught of Athene, sprang to steal
A scintillating fragment from the rays.

        With wisdom-guided torch
10   Dipped in the heavenly flame
Back he returned to each unlighted porch,
And filled the homes with joy where'er he came.

        Zeus marked the flickering brand,
        And earthward bent to urge
15 Two countervailing evils through the land:
One was the fever with its fiery scourge;

        One was Pandora's face,
        Her smiles and luring feet –
'Woman,' he said, 'shall scorch man's petty race,
20 And fill his senses with insidious heat.'

        But, Phaon, tremble thou
        Whom beauty cannot fire,
Who livest with no rage upon thy brow,
Unstricken by complaint or by desire.

25   Remember what thou art,
        Think of the wrath above,
Scathless to stand is not a mortal's part:
O fool, accept the furious curse of love!

[1889]

_____

7. *Athene*] Pallas Athene, patron goddess of Athens, and goddess of wisdom.

13. *marked*] noted.   *brand*] torch.

15. *countervailing*] equivalent.

17. *Pandora*] Her name means the all-gifted, as each of the gods supposedly gave her some power which was to bring about the ruin of men.

21. *Phaon*] Sappho's faithless male lover.

27. *Scathless*] Unharmed.

L'Indifférent

Watteau
The Louvre

HE dances on a toe
As light as Mercury's:
Sweet herald, give thy message! No,
He dances on; the world is his,
5   The sunshine and his wingy hat;
His eyes are round
Beneath the brim:
To merely dance where he is found
Is fate to him
10   And he was born for that.

He dances in a cloak
Of vermeil and of blue:
Gay youngster, underneath the oak,
Come, laugh and love! In vain we woo;
15   He is a human butterfly; –
No soul, no kiss,
No glance nor joy!
Though old enough for manhood's bliss,
He is a boy,
20   Who dances and must die.

[1892]

L'Indifférent] *Watteau* (1684–1721) was a French painter of the Rococo period and style. His work was influenced by the *commedia dell'arte* and the opera ballet, and frequently concerned itself with the ephemeral. There was a resurgence of interest in his work in nineteenth-century England. 'L'Indifférent' ('The Indifferent One') was painted *c*.1716. The *Louvre* is the national museum and art gallery of France, located in Paris. It has one of the richest collections of paintings in the world, representing all periods of European art up to Impressionism in the early twentieth century. In June 1890 Bradley and Cooper toured art galleries in France, Switzerland and Italy, collecting materials for *Sight and Song* (1892).

2–5.] Mercury was the messenger of the gods, usually depicted wearing winged hat and winged sandals.

12. vermeil] poetical word for scarlet.

La Gioconda

Leonardo da Vinci
The Louvre

HISTORIC, side-long, implicating eyes;
A smile of velvet's lustre on the cheek;
Calm lips the smile leads upward; hand that lies
Glowing and soft, the patience in its rest
5   Of cruelty that waits and doth not seek
For prey; a dusky forehead and a breast
Where twilight touches ripeness amorously:
Behind her, crystal rocks, a sea and skies
Of evanescent blue on cloud and creek;
10   Landscape that shines suppressive of its zest
For those vicissitudes by which men die.

[1892]

'Thanatos, thy praise I sing'

THANATOS, thy praise I sing,
Thou immortal, youthful king!
Glorious offerings I will bring;
For men say thou hast no shrine,
5   And I find thou art divine
As no other god: thy rage
Doth preserve the Golden Age,
What we blame is thy delay;
Cut the flowers ere they decay!

La Gioconda] *Leonardo da Vinci* (1429–1519) was an Italian painter, draftsman, sculptor, architect and engineer, whose skill epitomised the ideal of Renaissance humanism. His painting 'La Gioconda' ('The Mona Lisa', 1503–6) is one of the most famous paintings of the Renaissance, said to have revolutionised portrait painting. The subject is the wife of a Florentine merchant named Francesco di Bartolommeo del Giocondo: Madonna, or Mona, Lisa del Giocondo. For the *Louvre*, see the note on 'L'Indifférent' above.

9. evanescent] on the point of vanishing, so carrying here a double suggestion of a disappearing colour and disappearing objects.

'Thanatos, thy praise I sing'. *1.* THANATOS] Death, son of Night, here represented as 'youthful' because of his power to preserve youth by cutting life short.

7. the Golden Age] a mythical period when life was idyllic.

10   Come, we would not derogate,
          Age and nipping pains we hate,
          Take us at our best estate:
          While the head burns with the crown,
          In the battle strike us down!
15   At the bride-feast do not think
          From thy summons we should shrink;
          We would give our latest kiss
          To a life still warm with bliss.

          Come and take us to thy train
20   Of dead maidens on the plain
          Where white lilies have no stain;
          Take us to the youths, that thou
          Lov'st to choose, of fervid brow,
          Unto whom thy dreaded name
25   Hath been simply known as Fame:
          With these unpolluted things
          Be our endless revellings.

          [1893]

'A girl'

          A GIRL,
          Her soul a deep-wave pearl
        Dim, lucent of all lovely mysteries;
          A face flowered for heart's ease,
5   A brow's grace soft as seas
          Seen through faint forest-trees:
          A mouth, the lips apart,
       Like aspen-leaflets trembling in the breeze
          From her tempestuous heart.

10.] We would not take away from your force.

12. *at our best estate*] in our prime.

'A girl'. 2. *deep-wave*] Variation on 'deep sea'.

3. *lucent of*] luminous with.

4. *heart's ease*] both the heart-shaped flower of this name, and the more literal meaning.

10   Such: and our souls so knit,
               I leave a page half-writ –
               The work begun
             Will be to heaven's conception done,
               If she come to it.

[1893]

'It was deep April, and the morn'

IT was deep April, and the morn
   Shakspere was born;
The world was on us, pressing sore;
My Love and I took hands and swore,
5   Against the world, to be
Poets and lovers evermore,
To laugh and dream on Lethe's shore,
To sing to Charon in his boat,
Heartening the timid souls afloat;
10 Of judgment never to take heed,
But to those fast-locked souls to speed,
Who never from Apollo fled,
Who spent no hour among the dead;
   Continually
15   With them to dwell,
Indifferent to heaven and hell.

[1893]

10–14.] A reference to the poets' claim that they worked as one on their manuscripts.

'It was deep April, and the morn'. 1–2.] Shakespeare's birthday is traditionally celebrated on 23 April. This poem was later given the title 'Prologue', upon its reprinting in *A Selection from the Poems of Michael Field*, ed. T. Sturge Moore (1923).

7. *Lethe's shore*] In Greek myth, Lethe was the river of forgetfulness in Hades, the place of the dead.

8. *Charon*] the name of the ferryman who conveyed the shades of the departed across the River Styx in Hades.

12. *Apollo*] See note to *Long Ago* XXXIV, l. 3.

16.] Cf. Baudelaire's poem 'Lesbos' from *Les Fleurs du Mal* (1857). One stanza ends: 'Et l'amour se rira de l'Enfer et du Ciel!' – 'And love will laugh at hell and heaven!' Michael Field had certainly read his Baudelaire, as Angela Leighton points out when she makes this comparison (Leighton, 1992b, p. 210).

Irises

IN a vase of gold
And scarlet, how cold
The flicker of wrinkled grays
In this iris-sheaf! My eyes fill with wonder
5   At the tossed, moist light, at the withered scales under
And among the uncertain sprays.

The wavings of white
On the cloudy light,
And the finger-marks of pearl;
10   The facets of crystal, the golden feather,
The way that the petals fold over together,
The way that the buds unfurl!

[1893]

Cyclamens

THEY are terribly white:
There is snow on the ground,
And a moon on the snow at night;
The sky is cut by the winter light;
5   Yet I, who have all these things in ken,
Am struck to the heart by the chiselled white
Of this handful of cyclamen.

[1893]

Constancy

'I am pure! I am pure! I am pure!'

I LOVE her with the seasons, with the winds,
As the stars worship, as anemones

Cyclamens] Cyclamens are flowers which grow from tubers, prized for their early spring blooms.
They are often grown indoors, in pots.

5. *in ken*] in view.

Constancy. *Epigraph*] Ivor Treby gives *The Book of the Dead* as source (Treby, 1998, p. 175).
This ancient Egyptian work of religion and magic exists in a variety of texts. The epigraph was
omitted from the next printing of the poem, in *Wild Honey* (1908).

2. *anemones*] flowers that open their petals to the sun.

Shudder in secret for the sun, as bees
Buzz round an open flower: in all kinds
5   My love is perfect, and in each she finds
Herself the goal; then why, intent to tease
And rob her delicate spirit of its ease,
Hastes she to range me with inconstant minds?
If she should die, if I were left at large
10   On earth without her – I, on earth, the same
Quick mortal with a thousand cries, her spell
She fears would break. And I confront the charge
As sorrowing, and as careless of my fame
As Christ intact before the infidel.

[1898]

Tiger-lilies

LILIES, are you come!
    I quail before you as your buds upswell;
    It is the miracle
Of fire and sculpture in your brazen urns
5   That strikes me dumb, –
Fire of midsummer that burns,
    And as it passes,
Flinging rich sparkles on its own clear blaze,
Wreathes with the wreathing tongues and rays,
10   Great tiger-lilies, of your deep-cleft masses!
        It is the wonder
        I am laid under
        By the firm heaves
And overtumbling edges of your liberal leaves.

[1898]

12–14.] A reference to Christ's steadfastness in the face of mockery and physical abuse by his Jewish captors (see Luke 22: 63–5). 'Careless of his fame' reminds the reader that Christ's acceptance of such treatment was a prelude to his willingness to be crucified.

Renewal

As the young phoenix, duteous to his sire,
Lifts in his beak the creature he has been,
And, laying o'er the corse broad vans for screen,
Bears it to solitudes, erects a pyre,
And, soon as it is wasted by the fire,
Grides with disdainful claw the ashes clean;
Then spreading unencumbered wings serene
Mounts to the aether with renewed desire:

So joyously I lift myself above
The life I buried in hot flames to-day;
The flames themselves are dead – and I can range
Alone through the untarnished sky I love,
And I trust myself, as from the grave one may,
To the enchanting miracles of change.

[1898]

A Flaw

To give me its bright plumes, they shot a jay:
On the fresh jewels, blood! Oh, sharp remorse!
The glittering symbols of the little corse
I buried where the wood was noisome, blind,
Praying that I might nevermore betray
The universe, so whole within my mind.

[1908]

Renewal] An allusion to the legend in which the aged phoenix (a mythical bird) sings his own dirge and burns himself to ashes, from which a new, younger self is reborn. Here, however, the young bird appears to be burning the body of his 'father' bird.

3. corse] poetic for corpse.   *van*] poetic for wing.

6. Grides] Scrapes (archaic).

A Flaw. *1.*] Women's hats were often lavishly decorated with birds' feathers in the later nineteenth century. The *jay* is a fairly common European bird noted for the livid flashes of blue and white in its black plumage. Such outrage at the barbarity of fashion was not uncommon at this period; cf. Robert Browning's 'The Lady and the Painter', in *Asolando* (1889). But note also the comparative indifference to the fate of the fox used for adornment in 'Second Thoughts' (below).

3. corse] corpse (poetic).

4. noisome] ill-smelling.

Onycha

THERE is a silence of deep gathered eve,
There is a quiet of young things at rest;
In summer, when the honeysuckles heave
Their censer boughs, the forest is exprest.
5   What singeth like an orchard cherry-tree
Of its blown blossom white from tip to root,
Or solemn ocean moving silently,
Or the great choir of stars for ever mute?
So falleth on me a great solitude;
10   With miser's clutch I gather in the spell
Of loving thee, unwooing and unwooed;
And, as the silence settles, by degrees
Fill with thy sweetness as a perfumed shell
Sunk inaccessible in Indian seas.

[1908]

A Palimpsest

. . . THE rest
Of our life must be a palimpsest –
The old writing written there the best.

In the parchment hoary
5   Lies a golden story.
As 'mid secret feather of a dove,
As 'mid moonbeams shifted through a cloud:

Onycha] Onycha is a kind of seashell having a distinctive incense-like smell when burnt.
It denotes one of the ingredients used in the Mosaic ritual to construct the altar of incense.
See Exodus 30: 34–8.

4. *Their censer boughs*] i.e. their boughs swinging like the incense vessels used in some Roman
Catholic and High Anglican church rituals.

A Palimpsest] A palimpsest is a parchment which has been twice written upon, the recent
writing covering the earlier. The particular reference here seems to be the poets' conversion to
Catholicism, which necessitated an 'over-writing' of their earlier hedonistic paganism.

4. *hoary*] mouldy, musty.

Let us write it over,
O my lover,
10   For the far Time to discover,
As 'mid secret feathers of a dove,
As 'mid moonbeams shifted through a cloud!

[1908]

Second Thoughts

I THOUGHT of leaving her for a day
In town, it was such iron winter
At Durdans, the garden frosty clay,
The woods as dry as any splinter,
5   The sky congested. I would break
From the deep, lethargic, country air
To the shining lamps, to the clash of the play,
And, to-morrow, wake
Beside her, a thousand things to say.
10   I planned – O more – I had almost started; –
I lifted her face in my hands to kiss, –
A face in a border of fox's fur,
For the bitter black wind had stricken her,
And she wore it – her soft hair straying out
15   Where it buttoned against the gray, leather snout:
In an instant we should have parted;
But at sight of the delicate world within
That fox-fur collar, from brow to chin,
At sight of those wonderful eyes from the mine,
20   Coal pupils, an iris of glittering spa,
And the wild, ironic, defiant shine
As of a creature behind a bar
One has captured, and, when three lives are past,
May hope to reach the heart of at last,

Second Thoughts] This poem was not published in the authors' lifetime. Clearly it was written by Katharine Bradley and addressed to Edith Cooper.

3. Durdans] The name of the house in Reigate, Surrey, where the two poets lived 1890–9.

12–15.] Late Victorian fashion encouraged women to decorate themselves in animal skins complete with paws, snout, etc. Foxes were traditionally hunted as vermin, hence, perhaps, the lack of compunction shown here, compared with that felt for the jay in 'A Flaw' (above).

20. spa] probably 'spar', a lustrous crystalline mineral.

25 All that, and the love at her lips, combined
To shew me what folly it were to miss
A face with such thousand things to say,
And beside these, such thousand more to spare,
For the shining lamps, for the clash of the play –
30 O madness; nor for a single day
Could I leave her! I stayed behind.

[1923]

Wheat-miners

BURTHEN of my anger on my soul,
Spacious anger, tragic goal; –
Earth corn-bearing, rich, defenceless,
Used by libertines with senseless
5 Passion, not for golden wheat,
Got from out the cornfields vast and sweet
Of that quarter where the sun
Sets in gold when day is done;
Earth impregnated by men,
10 Violators, in their ken
Nothing gold but money; naught
Treasureable, worth a thought
Save what they can work and mine
From the wheat-farms, till these shine
15 With their lustrous corn no more
Than a gold-reef's worked-out store.
Sensual, malicious greed
Of wild infidels, who heed
Nothing holy in the womb
20 Of the prairie-land they doom
By the lust with which they reap

Wheat-miners] This is a protest poem directed at the exploitative cropping methods of American farmers in the mid-West prairies who strip the land of its riches just as miners do.

1. BURTHEN] Burden (poetic).

10. ken] perception.

16. gold-reef] a vein of gold-bearing rock.

18. infidels] from a Christian point of view, an adherent of a religion opposed to Christianity; a disbeliever in religion or divine revelation generally.

From its soil a yearly harvest deep;
Through each year the ruined earth grows thin
With the wasting of such wastrels' sin
25 While she crowns the greed that makes her teem
And there is no mercy, not a gleam
On her of man's love by night nor day;
Only she must bear that he may reap;
Only flaunt what potency she may;
30 Only hide her weakness, bold and gay,
From the horror of a certain end –
He would leave her wan, debauched, cast by,
With the future of her past, to die.
Christ, avenge her; creature of Thy Hands,
35 Earth, the mother of Thy element,
Of Thy Flesh come down from Heaven and blent
With the corn of autumn-ripened lands,
Thy last Incarnation while time wheels.
Blessed Sacrament, to Whom man kneels,
40 For his spirit's feeding evermore
Till earth's cornfields to the trumpet's roar
Shrivel in the beatific fire
Of the Presence all earth's ends desire;
Mercy on Thy wheat-farms of the West!
45 By Thy fierce rejecting Hand expressed
That turns devils back to Hell,
And the souls that must with devils dwell,
Turn away the miners of Thy wheat:
Turn away those mouths that never eat
50 Of Thy Love, marauders; rend their prey
From their clutches; drive the horde away!
Send forth eaters of Thy living Bread
Venerators of Thy wheat, instead
Of these enemies, who breathe a curse
55 On the soil, the loaf, the wafer! God
Plant in liberal grace to till the sod
Peasant farmers, Catholic, averse
From vile lucre, simple men content
Rather with the welfare and the wealth

---

24. *wastrel*] a good-for-nothing, idle, disreputable person, likely to be a spendthrift.
35. *element*] one of the simple substances of which all material bodies are compounded.
36–9.] A reference to the Eucharist.
58. *lucre*] gain or profit.

60 Of their fields and lustre of their health
    Than with gain that means true treasure spent.
    Catholic, they love Thy Mother
    Earth, their Mother, Mother of Thy flesh
    In Thy Holy Host's corn-woven mesh –
65 Blessed Sacrament of earthly wheat
    Save the corn-farms lust would make effete!
    Consecrated let full harvests wave
    Round a people Thou dost feed to save.
    Composed 1913

    [1930]

Will You Crucify Your King?

    'CRUCIFY Him, Crucify Him!' Hark,
    The ground-swell of men's voices, dark
    With rage they cannot comprehend;
    The darkness comprehends not; light
5   Will never blend with! Hark!
        'Crucify, Crucify!' –
        Unlit, yelling sky;
        Horizons that unite
        To choke what beats upon their walls,
10   As lunatics determinate calls,
        Within a madhouse by a waste . . .
    'Crucify Him! Crucify Him!' Haste!
        It is one will, the will of man,
        His obduracy and his plan;
15   His root-desire,
        His blood-fanged fire;
        All pulses of his heart
        Together, none apart;

Will You Crucify Your King?] See Mark 15: 12–14: 'And Pilate answered and said again unto them, What will ye then that I shall do unto him whom ye call the King of the Jews? And they cried out again, Crucify him. Then Pilate said unto them, Why, what evil hath he done? And they cried out the more exceedingly, Crucify him.' See also Matthew 27; Luke 23: 21.

2. *ground-swell*] a deep swell or heavy rolling of the sea, used here to describe the crowd.

4–5.] A reference to John 1: 5: 'And the light shineth in darkness; and the darkness comprehended it not.'

10. *determinate*] clearly defined.

The cruel set of roof and street that cry

20   For many One must die.

      'Crucify,
Crucify Him, Crucify Him!' – Small,
How slight the Victim, the pursuit of all . . .
One white, thin Man – and all the people cry

25   That He must die . . .
      The people and all prophecy!
Christ, is it I – ?
Not I, who raised that shriek I heard,
Among the voices to insistence stirred?

30   No, no, not I!
But yet I heard a 'Crucify!'
      I heard it roll my lips apart;
      I felt it sever from my heart –
      My very self am one and loud

35   With the immitigable crowd.

Have pity, O my King!
This is a desperate thing –
My sins – all, all is loss
And death, unless Thy Cross

40   Is my demand, my single shout!
Wildly I join the rout:
Yea, I am calling through the ground-swell dire,
The roar of low, destructive fire,
That surges higher and higher,

45   Reaching the Judgement-Seat where one in ruth
And cowardice sits and mumbles 'What is Truth?'
Composed 1913

[1930]

20.] A reference to Caiaphas the High Priest in John 11: 50: 'it is expedient for us, that one man should die for the people, and that the whole nation perish not' (repeated at 18: 14).

35. immitigable] that cannot be softened or appeased; implacable.

42. ground-swell] See note 2 above.

45. Judgement-Seat] the seat on which a judge sits when pronouncing judgment. Here, the throne of Pontius Pilate.   *ruth*] compassion, pity; more rarely, repentance, remorse.

46. 'What is Truth?'] Cf. John 18: 37–8: 'Pilate therefore said unto him, Art thou a king then? Jesus answered, Thou sayest that I am a king. To this end was I born, and for this cause came I into the world, that I should bear witness unto the truth. Every one that is of the truth heareth my voice. Pilate saith unto him, What is truth? . . .' Pilate then asks the crowd whether they would have him release Jesus or Barabbas and the crowd votes for the latter.

'Loved, on a sudden thou didst come to me'

LOVED, on a sudden thou didst come to me
   On our own doorstep, still I see thee stand
In thy bleared welcome, with the grim command
From Heaven that we must sever presently;
5   And no farewell was in the misery . . .
So you condemned me; did not understand
O lovely and gay-coloured tulip-land,
I would not break on thee my wrathful sea;
   Back to the flood-gates, firm to my defence –
10   So hard, as thou complainest, so apart;
But had I not held tight from thee my sense,
My memory, my will against my heart,
But one defeat, the rupture of one sigh
How little of the world had been left dry!
Composed April 19th, 1911

[1930]

Lovers

LOVERS, fresh plighting lovers in our age
Lovers in Christ – so tender at the heart
The pull about the strings as they engage –
One thing is plain: – that we can never part.
5   O Child, thou hauntest me in every room;
Not for an instant can we separate;
And thou or I, if absent in a tomb
Must keep unqualified our soul's debate.
Death came to me but just twelve months ago
10   Threatening thy life; I counted thee as dead –
Christ by thy bier took pity of my woe
And lifted thee and on my bosom spread;

'Loved, on a sudden . . .'. *3. bleared*] misty, dim (as with tears).

4.] The reference is to the day Edith came home from the doctor with the news of her incurable cancer.

7–8.] i.e. Holland, always vulnerable to flooding from the sea.

Lovers. *1.*] i.e. they have repledged themselves to each other in their (old) age.

And did not then retire and leave us twain:
Together for a little while we stood
15   And looked on Him, and chronicled His pain,
The wounds for us that started in their blood –
We, with one care, our common days shall spend,
As on that noble sorrow we attend.
Composed 1912

[1930]

'Lo, my loved is dying, and the call'

Lo, my loved is dying, and the call
Is come that I must die,
All the leaves are dying, all
Dying, drifting by.
5   Every leaf is lonely in its fall,
Every flower has its speck and stain;
The birds from hedge and tree
Lisp mournfully,
And the great reconciliation of this pain
10   Lies in the full, soft rain.
Composed Oct, 1913

[1930]

'Lo, my loved is dying . . .'. *1–2.*] Katharine Bradley has by now had her own cancer diagnosed.
Composition date] Two months before Edith's death on 13 Dec.

CONSTANCE NADEN (1858–1889)

Constance Naden, poet, essayist and philosopher, was born in Edgbaston, a suburb of Birmingham, to Thomas Naden, later President of the Birmingham Architectural Association, and his wife Caroline, who died within two weeks of her daughter's birth. As a result of the loss of her mother, the baby Constance was handed over by her father to be raised by her mother's parents, who were very comfortably off. In fact, her father also lived with his parents-in-law at that time. She appears to have led a sheltered if rather solemn childhood, attending a private day school run by the Unitarian Misses Martin, between the ages of eight and sixteen, and mentally digesting the contents of her grandfather's extensive library. The young Naden showed a remarkable intellectual precocity, which she nevertheless kept hidden from her schoolfellows. She is said, however, to have entertained the younger girls with a succession of marvellous stories. Her talents were unusual in that they ranged across both the sciences and the arts, with an acute power of deductive reasoning complemented by a strong sense of aesthetic design. She was sometimes held in awe by her contemporaries for her unswerving adherence to the pursuit of truth as well as for her quiet but mischievous sense of fun.

From 1879 to 1881 Naden attended classes in botany, science, art and languages (at which she was particularly brilliant, translating ancient Greek into modern German at sight) at the Birmingham and Midland Institute, and from 1881 was enrolled at the Mason College of Science where she studied a wide range of scientific subjects, from zoology to physics. Here she came under the influence of Herbert Spencer's evolutionary philosophy, which confirmed her new-found atheism, and possibly influenced her to place a greater importance on her scientific work than on her poetry (Spencer, an early sociologist, had a contempt for the humanities). At college Naden entered a communal intellectual life with gusto, becoming a mainstay of the debating society, for example – but, having no need to earn a living, she declined to study specifically for a degree, preferring instead to pursue independent scholarship, in which she won great distinction, and a number of prestigious prizes.

Unlike some of the other women poets in this anthology, there is quite a lot of biographical material available on Naden. This may be because her status as an intellectual woman, like that of George Eliot, was widely accepted not only among her woman friends, but also by her male peers – scientists, philosophers and sociologists. One of the latter who was a great admirer and encourager of Naden's intellectual powers (they met in 1876) was Dr Robert Lewins, a Scottish surgeon retired from service in the British army who developed a philosophical doctrine he called 'Hylo-Idealism', to which he managed to convert the young Naden. It is a doctrine which places all value on the self as perceiver and therefore shaper of the universe. Lewins published part of the correspondence he held on the subject with Naden, as *Humanism versus Theism; or, Solipsism (Egoism) = Atheism* (1887). The title gives some indication of the radical nature of Lewins's theories, and of the radical intellectual position Naden was taking up when she espoused them. The major account of Naden's life (1890) was by William R. Hughes, who knew Naden for the last six years of her life. Titled *Constance Naden: A Memoir*, it contained an introduction by one learned professor, additions by another, and further additions by Lewins. Robert Lewins appears to have believed he held a major stake in Naden's posthumous reputation, for he had a hand in every memoir of her that was published. Hughes's memoir roundly criticises Herbert Spencer for his publicly expressed view that Naden's death from the after-effects of an operation to remove ovarian cysts was the inevitable outcome of over-taxing with mental tasks 'the feminine organization'.

In the same year, 1890, Lewins published a collection of impressively learned essays by Naden titled *Induction and Deduction*. In the following year, George McCrie published a further collection, dedicated to Robert Lewins, and titled *Further Reliques of Constance Naden: Being Essays and Tracts for our Times* (1891). Naden's essays still make interesting reading, on subjects like 'Scientific Idealism', 'The Greek Cosmologists', 'Evolutionary Ethics' and 'The Evolution of a Sense of Beauty'. They have a cool, humorous and pithy style all their own. McCrie points out that Naden was already an atheist before she met Lewins (others had apparently argued that he drew her down that path). Lewins's collection contains another memoir, this time written by a close woman friend. Madeline Daniell had known Naden since mid-1887, had travelled through Europe and India with her, and had then shared her home in London, being with her when she died.

Although Naden was remembered chiefly for her scientific and philosophical essays, she also produced a considerable body of verse over her short lifetime. She published her first volume of poems, *Songs and Sonnets of Springtime*, in 1881, boldly signed with her full name, and dedicated to the grandparents who had brought her up (her grandmother died in 1881). The covers of this volume, as well as her later volume, *A Modern Apostle* (1887), and her posthumously published *Complete Poetical Works* (1894), each bear the identical design of a graceful S-shaped spray of flowered vine (taken from her own painting of a convolvulus), with a single flower and leaf from the same vine appearing on the spine. Noted as a young woman for her intensely accurate flower paintings (one was accepted for publication by the Birmingham Society of Artists), she must have had a hand in the design of her book covers. It is worth noting that her second volume of verse, *A Modern Apostle*, was declined by an 'eminent' London firm, even when she offered to pay costs, on the grounds that 'it would discredit their establishment' (Hughes, 1890, p. 31). Women and atheism were an alarming mix, it seems.

The style and interests of Naden's poetry put her in a similar bracket to Kendall. Each displays considerable wit and sense of humour in the treatment of scientific subjects, especially geology and its impact on religion, and in this, they may both have been influenced by Andrew Lang (1844–1912), a Scottish poet, anthropologist, historian and Greek scholar, whose work had a wide impact and to whose light, clever, topical poetry many women were drawn (Levy and Watson as well as Kendall and Naden, for example). Naden, however, was more philosophically inclined in her poetry than either Lang or Kendall – more given to speculative musing and disinclined to be personal. Like most comic poets, however, she exploits conventional forms with strong rhyme schemes, though she is not as adept as Kendall in the choice of splendidly nonsensical end-rhymes. Some of her best work is in the series playfully titled 'Evolutionary Erotics' (see p. 246 below), which deals with the eternal conflict between romantic, idealistic notions of life and their factual scientific counterparts. The flaws in both positions are mocked pretty equally.

But some of her poems are more serious: 'The Sister of Mercy', for example (see p. 238), is about not responding to an offer of sexual love, and the consequences of that:

> Nay, tell me not thy strong young heart will break
> If to thy prayer such cold response I make;
> It will not break – hearts cannot break, I know,
> Or this weak heart had broken long ago.

(ll. 21–4)

Here the opposition between the pull of rationality and the pull of feeling is nicely staggered by the last line, which suddenly reverses the rational trend of the argument by falling back upon the evidence of feeling. Naden's verse is more pessimistic than Kendall's. It sees and struggles against human egotism. Yet, perhaps oddly, where Kendall will question her own position of privilege in society, Naden does not. She takes it entirely for granted. This may have been because Naden was so well accepted in the male world of the scientifically learned that she acted, in a sense, as an honorary man. Like a man, she had the means to do many things normally denied to women of her time and place – she travelled extensively in Europe and Asia, she owned her own home in London (where she moved after the death of her Birmingham grandmother in 1887), and she was free to choose her own pursuits in life. But although she may have taken for granted her upper-middle-class social status and privilege, it would be wrong to conclude that she was unaware of women less fortunate than herself. For example, in 1889, just a year before she died, Naden lectured for the Women's Liberal Association in favour of the suffrage for women; in the same year, she campaigned to raise funds for a new Hospital for Women. Her death at 31 cut short not only her own career, but also her plans for charitable work for other women. Although her poetry-writing was only one strand of Naden's many interests, it was marked with a unique stamp that makes it an important contribution to any wider view of Victorian cultural production.

Text: The poems chosen are from *Songs and Sonnets of Springtime* (1881) and *A Modern Apostle, The Elixir of Life and Other Poems* (1887). The date of first publication in volume form is given in square brackets at the foot of each poem. The copy-text is *The Complete Poetical Works of Constance Naden* (1894).

The Sister of Mercy

SPEAK not of passion, for my heart is tired,
I should but grieve thee with unheeding ears;
Speak not of hope, nor flash thy soul inspired
In haggard eyes, that do but shine with tears.
5   Think not I weep because my task is o'er;
This is but weakness – I must rest to-day:
Nay, let me bid farewell and go my way,
Then shall I soon be patient as before.
Yes, thou art grateful, that I nursed thee well;
10   This is not love, for love comes swift and free:
Yet might I long with one so kind to dwell,
Cared for as in thy need I cared for thee:
And sometimes when at night beside thy bed
I sat and held thy hand, or bathed thy head,
15   And heard the wild delirious words, and knew
Even by these, how brave thou wert, and true,
Almost I loved – but many valiant men
These hands have tended, and shall tend again;
And now thou art not fevered or distressed
20   I hold thee nothing dearer than the rest.
Nay, tell me not thy strong young heart will break
If to thy prayer such cold response I make;
It will not break – hearts cannot break, I know,
Or this weak heart had broken long ago.
25   Ah no! I would not love thee, if I could;
And when I cry, in some rebellious mood,
'To live for others is to live alone;
Oh, for a love that is not gratitude,
Oh, for a little joy that is my own!'
30   Then shall I think of thee, and shall be strong,
Knowing thee noblest, best, yet undesired:
Ah, for what other, by what passion fired,
Could I desert my life-work, loved so long?
I marvel grief like thine can move me still,
35   Who have seen death, and worse than death, ere now –

The Sister of Mercy] The Sisters of Mercy was a Roman Catholic sisterhood founded in Dublin in 1827, but it was also a name widely used in the nineteenth century for members of any religious community engaged in nursing or other similar work.

20.] i.e. I do not care for you more than for any of the others I have tended.

Nay, look not glad, rise up; thou shalt not bow
Thy knee, as if these tears thy hope fulfil:
Farewell! I am not bound by any vow;
This is the voice of mine own steadfast will.

[1881]

The Pantheist's Song of Immortality

BRING snow-white lilies, pallid heart-flushed roses,
    Enwreathe her brow with heavy-scented flowers;
In soft undreaming sleep her head reposes,
    While, unregretted, pass the sunlit hours.

5   Few sorrows did she know – and all are over;
    A thousand joys – but they are all forgot:
Her life was one fair dream of friend and lover;
    And they were false – ah, well, she knows it not.

Look in her face, and lose thy dread of dying;
10   Weep not, that rest will come, that toil will cease:
Is it not well, to lie as she is lying,
    In utter silence, and in perfect peace?

Canst thou repine that sentient days are numbered?
    Death is unconscious Life, that waits for birth:
15   So didst thou live, while yet thy embryo slumbered,
    Senseless, unbreathing, e'en as heaven and earth.

Then shrink no more from Death, though Life be gladness,
    Nor seek him, restless in thy lonely pain:
The law of joy ordains each hour of sadness,
20   And firm or frail, thou canst not live in vain.

---

38. *not bound by any vow*] i.e. not bound by any sense of obligation; or, perhaps more specifically, a reference to the speaker's being a lay sister in the community.

The Pantheist's Song of Immortality] The pantheist doctrine is that God is everything and everything is God: it denies the transcendence of God. The philosophers Spinoza (1632–1677) and Hegel (1770–1831) each held pantheist doctrines, which for them solved the problem of dualism (mind *v.* matter). For Naden, Mind (and Soul) was the product of Matter: her own brand of pantheism led her into atheism.

13.] i.e. can you really fret that the life in which we feel things will come to an end?

19. *ordains*] decrees.

What though thy name by no sad lips be spoken,
    And no fond heart shall keep thy memory green?
Thou yet shalt leave thine own enduring token,
    For earth is not as though thou ne'er hadst been.

25   See yon broad current, hasting to the ocean,
    Its ripples glorious in the western red:
Each wavelet passes, trackless; yet its motion
    Has changed for evermore the river bed.

Ah, wherefore weep, although the form and fashion
30   Of what thou seemest, fades like sunset flame?
The uncreated Source of toil and passion,
    Through everlasting change abides the same.

Yes, thou shalt die: but these almighty forces,
    That meet to form thee, live for evermore:
35   They hold the suns in their eternal courses,
    And shape the tiny sand-grains on the shore.

Be calmly glad, thine own true kindred seeing
    In fire and storm, in flowers with dew impearled;
Rejoice in thine imperishable being,
40   One with the Essence of the boundless world.

[1881]

Love Versus Learning

ALAS, for the blight of my fancies!
    Alas, for the fall of my pride!
I planned, in my girlish romances,
    To be a philosopher's bride.

5   I pictured him learned and witty,
    The sage and the lover combined,
Not scorning to say I was pretty,
    Nor only adoring my *mind*.

---

23. token] sign.

31.] i.e. the life-force (seen as endemic in all matter, not as part of the creation of a god).

Love Versus Learning. 6. sage] man of profound wisdom.

No elderly, spectacled Mentor,
10   But one who would worship and woo;
Perhaps I might take an inventor,
    Or even a poet would do.

And tender and gay and well-favoured,
    My fate overtook me at last:
15 I saw, and I heard, and I wavered,
    I smiled, and my freedom was past.

He promised to love me for ever,
    He pleaded, and what could I say?
I thought he must surely be clever,
20   For he is an Oxford M.A.

But now, I begin to discover
    My visions are fatally marred;
Perfection itself as a lover,
    He's neither a sage nor a bard.

25 He's mastered the usual knowledge,
    And says it's a terrible bore;
He formed his opinions at college,
    Then why should he think any more?

My logic he sets at defiance,
30   Declares that my Latin's no use,
And when I begin to talk Science
    He calls me a dear little goose.

He says that my lips are too rosy
    To speak in a language that's dead,
35 And all that is dismal and prosy
    Should fly from so sunny a head.

---

9. *Mentor*] a wise and faithful guide and counsellor (named after the friend of Telemachus, the son of Odysseus in Homer's *Odyssey*).

20. *Oxford M.A.*] i.e. he has the degree of Master of Arts from the University of Oxford (actually, the Oxford MA was notoriously 'bought' rather than earned, since it was automatically awarded to any holder of the BA (Bachelor of Arts) degree after a statutory period).

24. *sage . . . bard*] a wise man nor a poet.

35. *prosy*] prosaic, dull.

He scoffs at each grave occupation,
    Turns everything off with a pun;
And says that his sole calculation
40   Is how to make two into one.

He says Mathematics may vary,
    Geometry cease to be true,
But scorning the slightest vagary
    He still will continue to woo.

45 He says that the sun may stop action,
        But he will not swerve from his course;
    For love is his law of attraction,
        A smile his centripetal force.

His levity's truly terrific,
50   And often I think we must part,
But compliments so scientific
    Recapture my fluttering heart.

Yet sometimes 'tis very confusing,
    This conflict of love and of lore –
55 But hark! I must cease from my musing,
    For that is his knock at the door!

[1881]

Moonlight and Gas

THE poet in theory worships the moon,
    But how can he linger, to gaze on her light?
With proof-sheets and copy the table is strewn,
    A poem lies there, to be finished to-night.

---

43. *vagary*] divergence from decorum: caprice or freak of fancy. Pronounced here with the accent on the second syllable to rhyme with 'vary', by way of burlesque licence.

48. *centripetal*] proceeding from the exterior to the centre (i.e. the opposite to centrifugal).

49.] i.e. his agility of mind (or possibly, his frivolity) is truly terrifying.

54. *lore*] instruction.

Moonlight and Gas. *Title*.] Gas lighting was in common use in middle-class households by the 1880s.

3. *copy*] manuscript prepared for printing.

5   He silently watches the queen of the sky,
        But orbs more prosaic must dawn for him soon –
      The gas must be lighted; he turns with a sigh,
        Lets down his venetians and shuts out the moon.

      'This is but a symbol,' he sadly exclaims,
10   'Heaven's glory must yield to the lustre of earth;
      More golden, less distant, less pure are the flames
        That shine for the world over sorrow and mirth.
      When Wisdom sublime sheds her beams o'er the night,
        I turn with a sigh from the coveted boon,
15   And choosing instead a more practical light
        Let down my venetians and shut out the moon.'

      He sits to his desk and he mutters 'Alas,
        My muse will not waken, and yet I must write!'
      But great is Diana: venetians and gas
20   Have not been sufficient to banish her quite.
      She peeps through the blinds and is bright as before,
        He smiles and he blesses the hint opportune,
      And feels he can still, when his labour is o'er,
        Draw up his venetians and welcome the moon.

      [1881]

The Two Artists

      'EDITH is fair,' the painter said,
        'Her cheek so richly glows,
      My palette ne'er could match the red
        Of that pure damask rose.

---

6. *orbs more prosaic*] the spherical globes of the gas lights.

8. *venetians*] adjustable window blinds.

19. *Diana*] The goddess of hunting, associated with fertility, she was commonly regarded as a moon goddess. This line contains a pun on the phrase 'Great is Diana of the Ephesians!' (Acts 19: 28).

The Two Artists. 3. *palette*] originally, the thin flat tablet of wood or porcelain used by the artist to mix colours upon; here, used in the later transferred sense, of the set of colours used by the artist for a particular work.

4. *damask rose*] Initially from Damascus, these are double pink or light red roses prized for their rich perfume.

5   'Perchance, the evening rain-drops light,
            Soft sprinkling from above,
        Have caught the sunset's colour bright,
            And borne it to my love.

        'In distant regions I must seek
10   For tints before unknown,
        Ere I can paint the brilliant cheek
           That blooms for me alone.'

        All this his little sister heard,
           Who frolicked by his side;
15   To check such theories absurd,
           That gay young sprite replied:

        'Oh, I can tell you where to get
           That pretty crimson bloom,
        For in a bottle it is set
20   In Cousin Edith's room.

        'I'm sure that I could find the place,
           If you want some to keep;
        I watched her put it on her face –
           She didn't see me peep!

25   'So nicely she laid on the pink,
           As well as *you* could do,
        And really, I almost think
           She is an artist, too.'

        The maddened painter tore his hair,
30   And vowed he ne'er would wed,
        And never since, to maiden fair,
           A tender word has said.

---

10. *before*] earlier.

17–20.] Female 'painting' was a traditional subject of satire; see e.g. Alexander Pope's *The Rape of the Lock* (1712; 1714), which does it fairly gently, and Jonathan Swift's 'The Lady's Dressing Room' (1730), which does it extremely harshly. Here, the point is as much male impercipience as female vanity.

Bright ruby cheeks, and skin of pearl,
  He knows a shower may spoil,
35 And when he wants a blooming girl
  Paints one himself in oil.

[1881]

Love's Mirror

I LIVE with love encompassed round,
  And glowing light that is not mine,
  And yet am sad; for, truth to tell,
  It is not I you love so well;
5 Some fair Immortal, robed and crowned,
  You hold within your heart's dear shrine.

Cast out the Goddess! let me in;
  Faulty I am, yet all your own,
  But this bright phantom you enthrone
10 Is such as mortal may not win.

And yet this beauty that you see
  Is like to mine, though nobler far;
  Your radiant guest resembles me
E'en as the sun is like a star.

15 Then keep her in your heart of hearts,
  And let me look upon her face,
  And learn of that transcendent grace,
Till all my meaner self departs,

And, while I love you more and more,
20   My spirit, gazing on the light,
  Becomes, in loveliness and might,
The glorious Vision you adore.

[1887]

Love's Mirror. 4–6.] i.e. you love not the 'real' me, but a goddess of your own creation. Compare Rossetti's poem 'In an Artist's Studio', p. 142 above.

18. *meaner*] less noble, more small-minded.

245

Evolutional Erotics

[1] Scientific Wooing

I WAS a youth of studious mind,
Fair Science was my mistress kind,
    And held me with attraction chemic;
No germs of Love attacked my heart,
5   Secured as by Pasteurian art
    Against that fatal epidemic.

For when my daily task was o'er
I dreamed of H_2SO_4,
    While stealing through my slumbers placid
10   Came Iodine, with violet fumes,
And Sulphur, with its yellow blooms,
    And whiffs of Hydrochloric Acid.

My daily visions, thoughts, and schemes
With wildest hope illumed my dreams,
15   The daring dreams of trustful twenty:
I might accomplish my desire,
And set the river Thames on fire
    If but Potassium were in plenty!

Alas! that yearnings so sublime
20   Should all be blasted in their prime
    By hazel eyes and lips vermilion!

Evolutional Erotics] This is the heading given to a group of four comic poems, based loosely on an exploration of the impact of evolutionary theories on human courtship rituals.

Scientific Wooing. *3. chemic*] poetic and rhetorical for chemical.

5. Pasteurian] Louis Pasteur (1822–1895), French chemist and microbiologist whose discoveries led to the development of a number of vaccines against disease.

8. H₂SO₄] the chemical symbol for sulphuric acid.

10–12.] *Iodine*, one of the non-metallic elements, vaporises into a deep violet colour; *sulphur*, a brittle crystalline solid, is well known for its bright yellow colour (its popular name is brimstone); *hydrochloric acid* contains hydrogen and chlorine in chemical combination and is a colourless gas with a pungent, highly irritating odour.

17. set the river Thames on fire] do something marvellous, work wonders. See also Kendall, 'Failures' (p. 325 below), l. 15.

18. Potassium] one of the elements: if thrown into water, it unites with the hydrogen and causes the liberated oxygen to burst into flames.

21. vermilion] bright red or scarlet.

Ye gods! restore the halcyon days
While yet I walked in Wisdom's ways,
   And knew not Mary Maud Trevylyan!

25   Yet nay! the sacrilegious prayer
Was not mine own, oh fairest fair!
   Thee, dear one, will I ever cherish;
Thy worshipped image shall remain
In the grey thought-cells of my brain
30   Until their form and function perish.

Away with books, away with cram
For Intermediate Exam!
   Away with every college duty!
Though once Agnostic to the core,
35   A virgin Saint I now adore,
   And swear belief in Love and Beauty.

Yet when I meet her tranquil gaze,
I dare not plead, I dare not praise,
   Like other men with other lasses;
40   She's never kind, she's never coy,
She treats me simply as a boy,
   And asks me how I like my classes!

I covet not her golden dower –
Yet surely Love's attractive power
45   Directly as the mass must vary –
But ah! inversely as the square
Of distance! shall I ever dare
   To cross the gulf, and gain my Mary?

---

22. halcyon days] 'Halcyon' is the Greek word for kingfisher: the ancient Greeks believed that while the kingfisher's eggs were incubating on the surface of the sea, the waves would remain calm. Hence this expression, meaning times of happiness and prosperity.

31. cram] To 'cram' for an examination is to stuff the memory with facts: used as a noun, as here, it can mean either the action of cramming, or the matter to be crammed.

32. Intermediate Exam!] Intermediate education usually referred to a course of study beyond the elementary and including Latin and Greek as well as mathematics and science.

34. Agnostic] Term coined by T. H. Huxley in 1869, which came into wider currency in the 1870s, used to describe those who hold that the ultimate origin of all things must be some cause unknown and unknowable.

43. her golden dower] Either a direct reference to money or property which she would bring to her husband upon marriage, or a figurative reference to her beauty.

45–7.] A play on the mathematical jargon used to describe theorems.

So chill she seems – and yet she might
50   Welcome with radiant heat and light
       My courtship, if I once began it;
    For is not e'en the palest star
    That gleams so coldly from afar
       A sun to some revolving planet?

55   My Mary! be a solar sphere!
    Envy no comet's mad career,
       No arid, airless lunar crescent!
    Oh for a spectroscope to show
    That in thy gentle eyes doth glow
60   Love's vapour, pure and incandescent!

Bright fancy! can I fail to please
    If with similitudes like these
       I lure the maid to sweet communion?
    My suit, with Optics well begun,
65   By Magnetism shall be won,
       And closed at last in Chemic union!

At this I'll aim, for this I'll toil,
    And this I'll reach – I will, by Boyle,
       By Avogadro, and by Davy!
70   When every science lends a trope
    To feed my love, to fire my hope,
       Her maiden pride must cry *'Peccavi!'*

I'll sing a deep Darwinian lay
    Of little birds with plumage gay,

---

58. spectroscope] an instrument used for examining spectra, i.e. the coloured band into which a beam of light is decomposed by means of a prism.

64. Optics] the science of sight (involving, in physics, the study of light).

65. Magnetism] both the laws and properties of a magnet, and (figuratively) personal charm.

68–9.] Robert *Boyle* (1627–1691), natural philosopher and chemist, was one of the founders of the Royal Society; both he and Amedeo *Avogadro* (1776–1856), Italian physicist, discovered important laws of physics (respectively named after them) relating to the properties of gases; Sir Humphry *Davy* (1778–1829), another natural philosopher and chemist, invented the miner's safety-lamp.

72. cry 'Peccavi!'] to acknowledge oneself in the wrong (literally: I have sinned).

73. Darwinian lay] Perhaps not simply a reference to Charles Darwin, but also to his grandfather, Erasmus Darwin (1731–1802), a physician who studied botany and published a poem, 'The Botanic Garden', in two parts (1789; 1791). It contained a section called 'Loves of the Plants'. A 'lay' is a song.

75   Who solved by courtship Life's enigma;
        I'll teach her how the wild-flowers love,
        And why the trembling stamens move,
            And how the anthers kiss the stigma.

        Or Mathematically true
80   With rigorous Logic will I woo,
            And not a word I'll say at random;
        Till urged by Syllogistic stress,
        She falter forth a tearful 'Yes,'
            A sweet *'Quod erat demonstrandum!'*

[2] The New Orthodoxy

        So, dear Fred, you're not content
        Though I quote the books you lent,
        And I've kept that spray you sent
            Of the milk-white heather;
5   For you fear I'm too 'advanced'
        To remember all that chanced
        In the old days, when we danced,
            Walked, and rode together.

        Trust me, Fred, beneath the curls
10   Of the most 'advanced' of girls,
        Many a foolish fancy whirls,
            Bidding Fact defiance,
        And the simplest village maid
        Needs not to be much afraid
15   Of her sister, sage and staid,
            Bachelor of Science.

77–8.] The references are to the parts of the flower controlling fertilisation and reproduction: the *stamen* is the male part, the *anthers* contain the pollen, the *stigma* is the female part that receives the pollen.

82. Syllogistic] refers to a particular kind of tight argument used as a term in logic.

84. 'Quod erat demonstrandum'] Latin term, often expressed simply as QED – literally 'Which was to be demonstrated': a term appended to the theorems of Euclid. In schoolboy parlance, 'Quite Easily Done'.

The New Orthodoxy] The scenario depicted in this poem is a reversal of the familiar nineteenth-century situation (in life and literature) in which a woman refuses to marry an eligible suitor because his religious faith is in question. Christina Rossetti broke off her engagement to the Pre-Raphaelite poet James Collinson when he rejoined the Roman Catholic church.

4. milk-white heather] White heather was considered a lucky charm.

Ah! while yet our hope was new
Guardians thought 'twould never do
That Sir Frederick's heir should woo
    Little Amy Merton:
So the budding joy they snatched
From our hearts, so meetly matched –
You to Oxford they despatched,
    Me they sent to Girton.

Were the vows all writ in dust?
No – you're one-and-twenty – just –
And you write – 'We will, we must
    Now, at once, be married!'
Nay, you plan the wedding trip!
Softly, sir! there's many a slip
Ere the goblet to the lip
    Finally is carried.

Oh, the wicked tales I hear!
Not that you at Ruskin jeer,
Nor that at Carlyle you sneer,
    With his growls dyspeptic:
But that, having read in vain
Huxley, Tyndall, Clifford, Bain,
All the scientific train –
    You're a hardened sceptic!

Things with fin, and claw, and hoof
Join to give us perfect proof
That our being's warp and woof

20
25
30
35
40

---

22. *meetly*] properly, fittingly.

24. *Girton*] a college for women, founded by Emily Davies in 1869 and transferred to Cambridge University in 1873. Women who studied there were not at this time eligible to take degrees.

30–2.] A jocular elaboration of the proverbial saying 'There's many a slip 'twixt cup and lip': success is never certain.

34–6.] John *Ruskin* (1819–1900) and Thomas *Carlyle* (1795–1881) were both trenchant critics of a society based on democratic materialism. Carlyle did indeed suffer from dyspepsia.

38.] Thomas Henry *Huxley* (1825–1895), John *Tyndall* (1820–1893), William Kingdon *Clifford* (1845–1879) and Alexander *Bain* (1818–1903), a disparate grouping of well-known scientists and mathematicians who contributed as much to philosophy as to 'hard' science, and who were commonly regarded as among those responsible for seeking to draw the populace away from traditional religious belief.

43. *warp and woof*] terms taken from weaving, referring to the threads running lengthwise (warp) which are crossed by the weaving (woof).

We from near and far win;
45   Yet your flippant doubts you vaunt,
And – to please a maiden aunt –
You've been heard to say you can't
    Pin your faith to Darwin!

Then you jest, because Laplace
50   Said this Earth was nought but gas
Till the vast rotating mass
    Denser grew and denser:
Something worse they whisper too,
But I'm sure it *can't* be true –
55   For they tell me, Fred, that you
    Scoff at Herbert Spencer!

Write – or telegraph – or call!
Come yourself and tell me all:
No fond hope shall me enthrall,
60   No regret shall sway me:
Yet – until the worst is said,
Till I know your faith is dead,
I remain, dear doubting Fred,
Your believing
         AMY.

[3] Natural Selection

I HAD found out a gift for my fair,
    I had found where the cave-men were laid;
Skull, femur, and pelvis were there,
    And spears, that of silex they made.

---

48. Darwin] Charles Darwin (1809–1882), famous for his theory of evolution as propounded in *The Origin of Species* (1859).

49–56.] Pierre Simon, Marquis de *Laplace* (1749–1827), French mathematician and astronomer, popularly known as 'the French Newton', and commonly supposed to be an atheist: his theories uncovered many new facts about the workings of the solar system. That referred to here was known as the 'nebular hypothesis' and was in fact first put forward by Immanuel Kant (1724–1804). *Herbert Spencer* (1820–1903) was the founder of evolutionary philosophy.

Natural Selection. *Title.*] The so-called Law of Natural Selection was propounded by Charles Darwin in his evolutionary theory: it is commonly known as 'the law of the jungle' or 'survival of the fittest'.

3. femur] thigh-bone.

4. silex] flint.

5　　　But he ne'er could be true, she averred,
　　　　　Who would dig up an ancestor's grave –
　　　And I loved her the more when I heard
　　　　　Such filial regard for the Cave.

　　　My shelves, they are furnished with stones
10　　　　All sorted and labelled with care,
　　　And a splendid collection of bones,
　　　　　Each one of them ancient and rare;

　　　One would think she might like to retire
　　　　　To my study – she calls it a 'hole!'
15　　　Not a fossil I heard her admire,
　　　　　But I begged it, or borrowed, or stole.

　　　But there comes an idealess lad,
　　　　　With a strut, and a stare, and a smirk;
　　　And I watch, scientific though sad,
20　　　　The Law of Selection at work.

　　　Of Science he hasn't a trace,
　　　　　He seeks not the How and the Why,
　　　But he sings with an amateur's grace,
　　　　　And he dances much better than I.

25　　　And we know the more dandified males
　　　　　By dance and by song win their wives –
　　　'Tis a law that with *Aves* prevails,
　　　　　And even in *Homo* survives.

　　　Shall I rage as they whirl in the valse?
30　　　　Shall I sneer as they carol and coo?
　　　Ah no! for since Chloe is false,
　　　　　I'm certain that Darwin is true!

27–8.] Aves: plural of 'avis', bird (Latin). Homo: man. Birds, as warm-blooded vertebrates, were regarded as the earliest precursors of man.

29. valse] the French form of the German word 'waltz': a dance in three-time, fashionable from the late eighteenth century.

32. Darwin] See note to Title above.

[4] Solomon Redivivus, 1886

WHAT am I? Ah, you know it,
 I am the modern Sage,
Seer, savant, merchant, poet –
 I am, in brief, the Age.

5 Look not upon my glory
 Of gold and sandal-wood,
But sit and hear a story
 From Darwin and from Buddh.

Count not my Indian treasures,
10 All wrought in curious shapes,
My labours and my pleasures,
 My peacocks and my apes;

For when you ask me riddles,
 And when I answer each,
15 Until my fifes and fiddles
 Burst in and drown our speech,

Oh then your soul astonished
 Must surely faint and fail,
Unless, by me admonished,
20 You hear our wondrous tale.

Solomon Redivivus. *Title.*] Literally, Solomon brought back to life (Latin). Solomon was third king of Israel who died around 930 BC and was noted for his wisdom and his great wealth. He figures largely in the Old Testament books 1 and 2 Kings and, of course, in the remarkable Song of Solomon.

2–3.] A *sage* is a wise man; a *savant*, a learned one.

6. sandal-wood] an ointment made of powdered sandalwood, a sweet-smelling timber, especially associated with Solomon's temple.

8.] For *Darwin*, see note to 'The New Orthodoxy', l. 48 above; *Buddh* is a shortening of Buddha (in Sanscrit, 'the enlightened'), the founder of the religion of Buddhism.

12.] *Peacocks* and *apes* were reputed appurtenances of kingly existence. In 1 Kings 10: 22 and 2 Chronicles 9: 22 they are listed amongst Solomon's treasures, contributing to the fact that 'king Solomon exceeded all the kings of the earth for riches and for wisdom' (1 Kings 10: 23).

13. riddles] Solomon's wisdom often expressed itself in riddles and proverbs; he was also famed as a solver of riddles (e.g. those of the Queen of Sheba).

15. fifes . . . fiddles] kinds of flute and violin.

We were a soft Amoeba
   In ages past and gone,
Ere you were Queen of Sheba,
   And I King Solomon.

25   Unorganed, undivided,
   We lived in happy sloth,
And all that you did I did,
   One dinner nourished both:

Till you incurred the odium
30   Of fission and divorce –
A severed pseudopodium
   You strayed your lonely course.

When next we met together
   Our cycles to fulfil,
35   Each was a bag of leather,
   With stomach and with gill.

But our Ascidian morals
   Recalled that old mischance,
And we avoided quarrels
40   By separate maintenance.

Long ages passed – our wishes
   Were fetterless and free,
For we were jolly fishes,
   A-swimming in the sea.

---

21. *Amoeba*] a microscopic animal having no constant form; the first link in the evolutionary chain.

23. *Queen of Sheba*] Legendary for her beauty and power, she was reputed to have had an affair with Solomon, although the splendour of his palaces and his wisdom, which she had thought to test, left her feeling as though 'there was no more spirit in her' (1 Kings 10: 5). Her state visit to him formed the subject for a number of nineteenth-century paintings.

29–30.] i.e. until you incurred the opprobrium, or scandal, of separation and divorce. 'Fission' is a technical term in biology for cell division.

31. *pseudopodium*] protrusion from a protozoa (an animal of single cell), sometimes called a 'false footstalk'.

37. *Ascidian*] i.e. of the Ascidia, a group of molluscs well described in the preceding two lines (35–6).

45 We roamed by groves of coral,
    We watched the youngsters play –
The memory and the moral
    Had vanished quite away.

Next, each became a reptile,
50   With fangs to sting and slay;
No wiser ever crept, I'll
    Assert, deny who may.

But now, disdaining trammels
    Of scale and limbless coil,
55 Through every grade of mammals
    We passed with upward toil.

Till, anthropoid and wary
    Appeared the parent ape,
And soon we grew less hairy,
60   And soon began to drape.

So, from that soft Amoeba,
    In ages past and gone,
You've grown the Queen of Sheba,
    And I King Solomon.

[1887]

The Pessimist's Vision

I DREAMED, and saw a modern Hell, more dread
    Than Dante's pageant; not with gloom and glare,
    But all new forms of madness and despair
Filled it with complex tortures, some Earth-bred,

---

53. *trammels*] originally, trammel-net, used for catching birds or fish. Here, it means fetters or restrictions.

57. *anthropoid*] man-like; cf. an anthropoid ape.

60. *drape*] dress, clothe ourselves.

The Pessimist's Vision. 2. *Dante's pageant*] Referring to the work of the great Italian poet Dante Alighieri (1265–1321). His *Divina Commedia* describes Hell, Heaven and Purgatory with their imagined inhabitants.

5 Some born in Hell: eternally full-fed
   Ghosts of all foul disease-germs thronged the air:
   And as with trembling feet I entered there,
  A Demon barred the way, and mocking said –

  'Through our dim vales and gulfs thou need'st not rove;
10 From thine own Earth and from its happiest lot
   Thy lust for pain may draw full nourishment,
   With poignant spice of passion; knowest thou not
  Fiends wed for hate as mortals wed for love,
   Yet find not much more anguish? Be content.'

[1887]

Poet and Botanist

FAIR are the bells of this bright-flowering weed;
  Nectar and pollen treasuries, where grope
  Innocent thieves; the Poet lets them ope
And bloom, and wither, leaving fruit and seed
5 To ripen; but the Botanist will speed
  To win the secret of the blossom's hope,
  And with his cruel knife and microscope
Reveal the embryo life, too early freed.

Yet the mild Poet can be ruthless too,
10 Crushing the tender leaves to work a spell
   Of love or fame; the record of the bud
  He will not seek, but only bids it tell
  His thoughts, and render up its deepest hue
   To tinge his verse as with his own heart's blood.

[1887]

Poet and Botanist *3. Innocent thieves*] i.e. bees and other insects who feed on the flower.

ROSAMUND MARRIOTT WATSON (1860–1911)

Rosamund Marriott Watson, also known as Graham R. Tomson, underwent a number of name changes during her writing career which may have served to track her marital adventures but did no service to the consolidation of a literary career. Hence her work disappeared from view very quickly after her death. Born in a suburb of London as Rosamund Ball, youngest daughter of an accountant and his wife, she was encouraged to read widely while growing up and began writing at an early age. Her father, a book-lover with an extensive private library, also wrote verse. Her mother died of uterine cancer in 1874 when Rosamund was 13; her father died in 1883. Her first publications (verse and journalism), signed 'Mrs G. Armytage', came after her marriage in 1879 to George Armytage, an attractive and wealthy Australian. The 19-year-old Rosamund was herself a stunningly attractive as well as highly intelligent woman. In 1884, when this early marriage was already showing signs of strain, she published her first volume of poetry, *Tares*, anonymously. When this marriage ended in divorce in 1887, she lost custody of her two daughters along with her husband. She then married the artist Arthur Graham Tomson, two months later had a son she called Graham, and began to publish under the pseudonym 'Graham R. Tomson'.

This period marked the high point in her literary career. She became well known in literary circles, and her work was favourably reviewed. *The Bird-Bride: A Volume of Ballads and Sonnets* came out in 1889, *A Summer Night and Other Poems* in 1891, with a frontispiece by Arthur Tomson. She produced other works besides her own poetry – anthologies, designed for the marketplace, of border ballads, of translations from the Greek, of cat poems (illustrated by her husband). Presumably they were in need of money, and her new name was by now well enough known to assure publishers of good sales. As well as male editors, publishers and writers, among whom she was very popular (Henry James, H. G. Wells and Thomas Hardy all admired her), she also moved in circles of women writers. These included Amy Levy, Mathilde Blind, Alice Meynell (poet and essayist), Mona Caird (novelist) and the Americans Elizabeth Pennell (who became a close friend) and Louise Chandler Moulton.

In 1894, however, she left the melancholic Tomson (and her young son) for another handsome energetic Australian, H. B. Marriott Watson, also a writer, with whom she had a son, and lived happily for the rest of her life. Although they did not marry, Rosamund took the name Marriott Watson for all her publications from 1895. After her death from cancer in 1911, her *de facto* husband produced her posthumous collected *Poems of Rosamund Marriott Watson* (1912), which he had desperately tried to get through the press before she died.

In telling contrast with the pattern suggested by this outline of a life – a woman seemingly determined to seek her own sexual fulfilment at any price, and apparently succeeding – much of her poetry is underwritten by a piercing sense of grief, anger, and loss, especially, as might be expected, the loss of children. No woman at this period who was divorced on the grounds of her adultery would have been able to keep her children. Even for an exceptionally talented woman living late in the century and inhabiting artistic, even bohemian, circles as she did, with friends as influential as novelist and poet Thomas Hardy, scholar and writer Andrew Lang,[1] literary editor W. E. Henley and 'nineties' publisher John Lane, both society and the law would have taken their toll, and it is scarcely surprising that she eschewed marriage in her last relationship. Even the tolerant circle of writers for John Lane's famous *Yellow Book*, with whom she had mixed most comfortably, while accepting her first divorce well enough, found it hard to swallow her second.

Watson's poetry is variable in quality, which is not surprising for one who published five volumes of poetry in the six years from 1898. Her best work, however, is marked by a clarity of insight married to a fine technical discipline, which gives it its uniquely haunting quality. Looking for a *métier* in which she can evoke emotion without over-personalising it, she often draws for her subject-matter on myth and legend (for example, 'Ballad of the Bird-bride' [see p. 260 below], 'A Ballad of the Were-wolf' [p. 271], and 'The Moor Girl's Well' [p. 268]). As a result, archetypes rather than individuals inhabit her verse, which lends it a detachment that seems to imprint the emotional intensity all the more deeply upon the mind of the reader. At the same time, her feminist revisions of traditional mythic subject-matter lend her work a freshness that is still striking to the modern reader. The ballad form – very fashionable in the 1880s and 1890s – was clearly a favourite (she published a selection of north country ballads in 1888[2]); the primitive force of the chilling tale or bloodthirsty story with a twist, couched in a mock-medieval style or Scottish dialect, provided an outlet from social 'niceness' that must have been welcome. Under the cover of apparently traditional forms, she was able to articulate the sense of torn loyalties surrounding subjects like marital breakdown and divorce, and the ensuing loss of children. Had she written of such subjects more directly, they would scarcely have been as acceptable. Less bloody and more melancholic than the ballads is her haunting and mysterious poem 'Vespertilia' (see p. 273), named for a creature of the twilight, a kind of bat, but also carrying the idea of a ghost returning from the dead. In it, Watson explores a theme that seems to be largely autobiographical, and is based on the idea of regret for lost love which, when it returns to us after all, we turn away from and reject, only to mourn the loss bitterly when it is finally too late.

Magic and nature are heavily entwined in her verses, which can lend them a mannerist feel, especially when she utilises a high-flown vocabulary studded with archaisms and poeticisms. 'The Moor Girl's Well' suffers a little from this style: 'thy loathly hold', 'the steely deep'; but it can be argued that such phrases are a

---

[1] Lang (1844–1912), poet, classical scholar, anthropologist, journalist, and Scottish historian, who became fascinated with the origins of folk tales, was a lively and original thinker and witty verse-writer, who popularised a revival of old French verse forms, like the ballade, rondeau, triolet, etc. He was particularly influential for a number of younger women poets, including Levy, Kendall, Webster and Watson.

[2] *Ballads of the North Countrie*, ed. with intro. and notes by Graham R. Tomson (London: Walter Scott, 1888), reissued later that year as *Border Ballads*.

necessary signal to the reader of the poem's kind. Influenced no doubt by Keats's well-known poem about a snake-woman sexual temptress, 'Lamia', it may well be following in that tradition for its language. Watson's snake-woman differs markedly from Keats's, however, in the sympathy with which her plight of enchantment is portrayed and the failure of love delineated. Another poem which reads like an answer to an earlier male poet is 'An Enchanted Princess' (see p. 267). Here the starting-point is surely the Tennysonian ideal of the passive 'feminine' woman, worshipped as a princess by all of nature. Unlike Tennyson's 'Mariana', however, in which the refrain urges a masochistic finale onto the heroine (who endlessly wishes she were dead), Watson's poem gives a sharper and grimmer view of unrequited love. But others of her poems veer right away from literary language, and have a stark dramatic quality using a speaking voice ('Old Pauline', p. 260 below, for example). Yet others show evidence of a lively sense of humour – 'Betty Barnes, the Book-burner' (p. 264) gives a witty catalogue of the destruction wreaked by an ignorant woman on the works of learned men, and one that is not without an undercurrent of revenge. She also writes some striking poems about the (sub)urban environment of London, marking a shift towards a use of cityscape that was to become one of the hallmarks of early modernism: 'Of the Earth, Earthy' (p. 265) celebrates the 'Charm of the motley' on the 'dun, dim pavement trod by myriad feet'. 'Aubade' (p. 266) is another example, and with its uneven line-lengths and run-on lines, as well as its persistent striding rhythm and almost total lack of metaphor, has a disruptive force and adventurous spareness of form which is very modern. By contrast, some of Watson's later poems appear to be seeking a more traditional simplicity of form coupled with a certain sense of nostalgia for lost innocence and for the predictability of regular verse patterns: 'A Ruined Altar' (p. 280) and 'The White Lady' (p. 281) are examples of this more resigned sadness in her work, which contrasts strongly with the wild restlessness of some of her earlier pieces. This probably means that the earlier work will be more valued by modern readers, simply because of its unique perspective on the troubled and torturous underside of the Victorian domestic ideal, written by one who, unusually for a Victorian woman poet, had chosen to plunge herself into a string of heterosexual relationships, producing a total of four children, at the same time as projecting herself with a strong sense of ambition into the literary marketplace.

The American critic Linda K. Hughes has produced a number of articles on this poet, and her work has been a major source for the information about Watson's life contained in this note.

Text: Poems chosen are from *Tares* (1884),[3] *The Bird-Bride: A Volume of Ballads and Sonnets* (1889), *A Summer Night and Other Poems* (1891), *Vespertilia* (1895) and *After Sunset* (1904). Dates of first publication in volume form are shown in square brackets at the foot of each poem. The copy-text used is *The Poems of Rosamund Marriott Watson* (1912).

---

[3] Tares are weeds in a cornfield. The title of the volume is self-deprecating, alluding to the parable of the tares as the image of evil sown among the wheat by the Devil (Matthew 13: 24–30).

Old Pauline

So your boys are going to Paris? That's how I lost my own.
Lonely? Ah yes, but I know it, the old are always alone.
You remember my boys, Euphrasie? No? Was it before your day?
Each, when his turn came, kissed me, and cried; but they went away.
How I longed for them, always, vainly! and thought of them, early
5   and late;
I would start and look round in the pasture if any one clicked the gate.
But a greater sorrow fell on me: my Marie, with eyes so blue,
Grew restless, poor bird! in the home-nest – she must seek her
    fortune too.
And, once the desire is on them, 'tis a fever, they cannot stay;
And Marie, my poor little Marie! well, I missed her one bright
10   spring day.
'Twas *then* that my heart broke, 'Phrasie, for my children gay and tall,
For fair, vile, glittering Paris had taken them all.
Yet the good God is merciful always; I live, and I have no pain,
Only the old dumb longing for the children home again.
15 Still I watch the road to the city, up the glistening sun-set track,
But they never come back, Euphrasie – never come back!

[1884]

Ballad of the Bird-bride

(Eskimo)

THEY never come back, though I loved them well;
  I watch the South in vain;

Old Pauline. *3. Euphrasie*] *Euphrasia* is the species name for the plant known as eyebright. It has been reputed to be good for sore eyes.

16. they never came back] Watson lost her children as a result of her divorce (see headnote).

Ballad of the Bird-bride. *(Eskimo)*] Linda K. Hughes locates the probable sources of this poem in Northern mythology and folklore, claiming that 'this tale is clearly a variant of the swan-maiden story common to European and Arabic tradition'. Hughes points the reader to a contrastive working of the motif in William Morris's 'Land East of the Sun and West of the Moon' in *The Earthly Paradise* (1868–70) as well as to 'the probable source of both Morris' and Tomson's poems, Sabine Baring-Gould's *Curious Myths of the Middle Ages* (1866). Baring-Gould gives the following account of the myth's structure: "1. A man falls in love with a woman of supernatural race. 2. She consents to live with him, subject to one condition. 3. He breaks the condition and loses her. 4. He seeks her, and – α. recovers her; β. never recovers her." ' Hughes, 1994, pp. 101–2.

The snow-bound skies are blear and grey,
Waste and wide is the wild gull's way,
5   And she comes never again.

Years agone, on the flat white strand,
    I won my sweet sea-girl:
Wrapped in my coat of the snow-white fur,
I watched the wild birds settle and stir,
10   The grey gulls gather and whirl.

One, the greatest of all the flock,
    Perched on an ice-floe bare,
Called and cried as her heart were broke,
And straight they were changed, that fleet bird-folk,
15   To women young and fair.

Swift I sprang from my hiding-place
    And held the fairest fast;
I held her fast, the sweet, strange thing:
Her comrades skirled, but they all took wing,
20   And smote me as they passed.

I bore her safe to my warm snow house;
    Full sweetly there she smiled;
And yet, whenever the shrill winds blew,
She would beat her long white arms anew,
25   And her eyes glanced quick and wild.

But I took her to wife, and clothed her warm
    With skins of the gleaming seal;
Her wandering glances sank to rest
When she held a babe to her fair, warm breast,
30   And she loved me dear and leal.

---

3. blear] misty, dim; often used of watering eyes.

19. skirled] shrieked; cried out with shrill voices (Scottish and northern dialect).

20. smote] struck.

21.] Cf. Keats, 'La Belle Dame Sans Merci' (1819): 'I set her on my pacing steed / And nothing else saw all day long' (ll. 21–2).

30. leal] truly.

Together we tracked the fox and the seal,
   And at her behest I swore
That bird and beast my bow might slay,
For meat and for raiment, day by day,
35   But never a grey gull more.

A weariful watch I kept for aye
   'Mid the snow and the changeless frost:
Woe is me for my broken word!
Woe, woe's me for my bonny bird,
40   My bird and the love-time lost!

Have ye forgotten the old keen life?
   The hut with the skin-strewn floor?
O winged white wife, and children three,
Is there no room left in your hearts for me,
45   Or our home on the low sea-shore?

Once the quarry was scarce and shy,
   Sharp hunger gnawed us sore,
My spoken oath was clean forgot,
My bow twanged thrice with a swift, straight shot,
50   And slew me sea-gulls four.

The sun hung red on the sky's dull breast,
   The snow was wet and red;
Her voice shrilled out in a woeful cry,
She beat her long white arms on high,
55   'The hour is here,' she said.

She beat her arms, and she cried full fain
   As she swayed and wavered there.
'Fetch me the feathers, my children three,
Feathers and plumes for you and me,
60   Bonny grey wings to wear!'

---

34. *raiment*] clothing.

36. *for aye*] for ever.

56. *fain*] very eagerly, gladly.

60. *Bonny*] Bright, comely.

262

They ran to her side, our children three,
    With the plumage black and grey;
Then she bent her down and drew them near,
She laid the plumes on our children dear,
65   'Mid the snow and the salt sea-spray.

'Babes of mine of the wild wind's kin,
    Feather ye quick, nor stay.
Oh, oho! but the wild winds blow!
Babes of mine, it is time to go:
70   Up, dear hearts, and away!'

And lo! the grey plumes covered them all,
    Shoulder and breast and brow.
I felt the wind of her whirling flight:
Was it sea or sky? was it day or night?
75   It is always night-time now.

Dear, will you never relent, come back?
    I loved you long and true.
O winged white wife, and our children three,
Of the wild wind's kin though ye surely be,
80   Are ye not of my kin too?

Aye, ye once were mine, and, till I forget,
    Ye are mine forever and aye,
Mine, wherever your wild wings go,
While shrill winds whistle across the snow
85   And the skies are blear and grey.

[1889]

69–70.] Cf. Matthew Arnold, 'The Forsaken Merman' (1849): 'Come, dear children, let us away'.
85. blear] See note to l. 3, above.

Betty Barnes, the Book-burner

WHERE is that baleful maid
  Who Shakspeare's quartos shred?
Whose slow diurnal raid
  The flames with *Stephen* fed?
5   Where is *Duke Humphrey* sped?
Where is the *Henries'* book?
  They all are vanishèd
With Betty Barnes the Cook.

And now her ghost, dismayed,
10   In woeful ways doth tread –
(Though once the grieving shade
  Sir Walter visited) –
Where culprits sore bestead,
In dank or fiery nook,
15   Repent their deeds of dread
With Betty Barnes the Cook.

Betty Barnes, the Book-burner. *Title.*] *The Oxford Companion to English Literature* gives Betsy Baker as the name of the cook who unwittingly burnt the major part of her employer John Warburton's (1682–1759) priceless collection of manuscripts, using them in her kitchen as firelighters and pie-tin liners. Watson's source was probably Walter Scott's 'Introductory Epistle' to *The Fortunes of Nigel* (1822) in which Scott, 'speaking in a feigned voice and assumed character', recounts a meeting with 'the spirit of Betty Barnes . . . that unhappy Elizabeth or Betty Barnes, long cook-maid to Mr. Warburton, the painful collector, but ah! the too careless custodier, of the largest collection of ancient plays ever known – of most of which the titles only are left to gladden the Prolegomena of the Variorum Shakespeare. Yes, stranger, it was these ill-fated hands that consigned to grease and conflagration the scores of small quartos, which, did they now exist, would drive the whole Roxburghe Club out of their senses; it was these unhappy pickers and stealers that singed fat fowls and wiped dirty trenchers with the lost works of Beaumont and Fletcher, Massinger, Jonson, Webster – what shall I say? even of Shakespeare himself!'

1. baleful] either: full of active evil, or: unhappy, sorrowing. Here both senses apply.

3. diurnal] daily.

4–6.] *Stephen, Duke Humphrey* and the *Henries* are all titles reputed to be of plays by Shakespeare. A letter from Frederick Thornhill to the *Gentleman's Magazine* of 1815 (see vol. 2, pp. 217–22 and p. 424) lists the contents of Warburton's lost collection. Included were *Duke Humphrey. Tragedy,* a *History of King Stephen* and *Henry the 1st and 2nd,* all plays entered on the book of the Stationers' Company on 29 June 1660. Humphrey, Duke of Gloucester (1391–1447), was himself a famous book collector whose original library forms the oldest part of the Bodleian in Oxford.

12. Sir Walter] Sir Walter Scott (1771–1832), Scottish novelist. See note on title, above.

13. bestead] hard pressed.

There Bagford's evil trade
　　Is duly punishèd;
There fierce the flames have played
20　　　Round Caliph Omar's head;
　　The biblioclastic dead
Have diverse pains to brook,
　　'Mid rats and rainpools led
With Betty Barnes the Cook.

25　　Caxton! Be comforted,
　　　For those who wronged thee – look;
They break affliction's bread
　　　With Betty Barnes the Cook.

[1889]

Of the Earth, Earthy

NEVER for us those dreams aforetime shown
Of white-winged angels on a shining stair,
Or seas of sapphire round a jasper throne:
Give us the spangled dust, the turbid street;
5　The dun, dim pavement trod by myriad feet,
Stained with the yellow lamplight here and there;
The chill blue skies beyond the spires of stone:

---

17. *Bagford's evil trade*] John Bagford (1651–1716) was deputed to collect ballads for Robert Harley, Earl of Oxford, but at the same time amassed a private collection for himself.

20. *Caliph Omar*] the second of four caliphs (vice-regents) who succeeded Mahommed; said to have ordered the burning of the library at Alexandria when he captured the city in 640.

21. *biblioclastic*] book-destroying (especially the Bible).

22.] Have various tortures to endure.

25. *Caxton*] William Caxton (1422?–1491) was the first English printer.

27.] They share the food of suffering. The bread of affliction occurs several times in the Bible: e.g. Deuteronomy 16: 3; 2 Kings 22: 27: 'Put this fellow in the prison, and feed him with the bread of affliction and with water of affliction.'

Of the Earth, Earthy. *Title.*] 'The first man is of the earth, earthy': 1 Corinthians 15: 47.

2–4.] Cf. the description of the New Jerusalem in Revelation 21: 10–21. The 'angels on a shining stair' could be a reference to Jacob's dream (Genesis 28: 12) of a ladder to heaven with 'the angels of God ascending and descending on it'.

4. *turbid*] confused, disturbed, muddied: more usually used of liquids or air.

The world's invincible youth is all our own,
Here where we feel life's pulses burn and beat.

10   Here is the pride of Life, be it foul or fair,
        This clash and swirl of streets in the twilight air;
        Beauty and Grime, indifferent, side by side;
        Surfeit and Thirst, Endeavour and Despair,
        Content and Squalor, Lassitude and Care,
15   All in the golden lamplight glorified:
        All quick, all real, hurrying near and wide.

        Life and Life's worst and best be ours to share,
        Charm of the motley! undefined and rare;
        Melodious discord in the heart o' the tune,
20   Sweet with the hoarse note jarring everywhere!

        Let us but live, and every field shall bear
        Fruit for our joy; for Life is Life's best boon.

        [1891]

Aubade

THE lights are out in the street, and a cool wind swings
Loose poplar plumes on the sky;
Deep in the gloom of the garden the first bird sings:
Curt, hurried steps go by
5   Loud in the hush of the dawn past the linden screen,
Lost in a jar and a rattle of wheels unseen
Beyond on the wide highway: –
Night lingers dusky and dim in the pear-tree boughs,
Hangs in the hollows of leaves, though the thrushes rouse,
10   And the glimmering lawn grows grey.
Yours, my heart knoweth, yours only, the jewelled gloom,
Splendours of opal and amber, the scent, the bloom,

---

18. *motley*] mixed, changeable; can also suggest the dress of a fool or court jester.
22. *boon*] a favour, blessing or gift.

Aubade. *Title.*] literally: dawn song; but can suggest the dawn after a night of love-making.
5. *linden*] lime-tree.

266

Yours all, and your own demesne –
Scent of the dark, of the dawning, of leaves and dew;
15   Nothing that was but hath changed – 'tis a world made new –
A lost world risen again.

The lamps are out in the street, and the air grows bright –
Come – lest the miracle fade in the broad, bare light,
The new world wither away:
20   Clear is your voice in my heart, and you call me – whence?
Come – for I listen, I wait, – bid me rise, go hence,
Or ever the dawn turn day.

[1891]

An Enchanted Princess

I FOUND her deep in the forest,
   The beeches and elms between,
A delicate amber plane-tree
   'Mid masses of bronze and green;

5   A sorrowful, spell-bound princess
   Awaiting her lover there.
She said: 'He will know me, surely,
   By the veil of my yellow hair.'

'He seeks me the wide world over,
10   He seeks me the whole year through,
To loosen the charm that binds me –
   My prince, and my lover true!'

She shivered beneath her foliage
   And sighed in the twilight chill:
15   'Ay me; wilt though find me never,
   Thy love that thou seekest still?'

---

13. *demesne*] archaic term for territory.
22. *Or ever*] Before (poetic).

'I saw him,' chirruped a blackird,
  'He passed by this very spot;
He is come and gone, O princess!
20   He passed – and he knew you not.'

The cold wind rustled her branches
  Till the yellow leaves fell slow –
'He is dead and gone, O princess,
  Many a year ago.'

[1891]

The Moor Girl's Well

Where the still sunshine falls
  On faded splendours of old days long done –
The Moorish castle halls
  Void and forsaken, save for wind and sun –
5 Lies a square court-yard fenced with painted walls.
There, where the yellow sunlight lies asleep,
  Bound in a drowsy spell,
Glimmers that silent water, clear and deep,
  Our village maidens call the Moor Girl's Well.

10 Fair are the village maidens – kind and fair –
  And black-browed Manuela smiles on me,
  Driving her white goats homeward leisurely
Up from the pastures through the evening air,
  And I fling back her jest,
15 Laughing, with all the will to woo her – yet
I pass – the words unspoke, mine eyelids wet.
  Why, my heart knoweth best.

An Enchanted Princess. *17–20.*] Cf. Tennyson's *Maud* (1855), Part One, XXII, x: 'The red rose cries, "She is near, she is near;" / And the white rose weeps, "She is late;" / The larkspur listens, "I hear, I hear;" / And the lily whispers, "I wait." '

The Moor Girl's Well. *Title.*] Moors came from North Africa, and conquered Spain in the eighth century; Europeans lumped all Mohammedans together as 'Moors' in the Middle Ages.

1–3.] Cf. Tennyson, *The Princess* (1841): 'The splendour falls on castle walls' (III, IV, 1). This song was added to *The Princess* in 1850.

Through the grey dusk of dawn
    I went one autumn morning, long ago,
20   Forth, with my flock behind me trailing slow;
    And to that castle in the vale below –
I know not why – my vagrant steps were drawn.

And I beheld a woman, fair and young,
    Beside the well-spring in the court-yard bare,
25   Dabbling her slim feet in the water there,
    And singing softly in some outland tongue;
No veil about her golden beauty clung –
    No veil nor raiment rare,
    Save but her dusky hair.

30 Sweetly she smiled on me, and, lisping, spake,
    Even as a child that strives to say aright
Some unlearned language for its teacher's sake;
    Her long eyes pierced me with their diamond light.
    She told me of an old spell laid on her
35 That bound her in the semblance of a snake,
    Lonely and mute as in the sepulchre.

And he who would this bitter bondage break
    Must suffer her in serpent form to cling
Close to his breast, unshrinking, undismayed,
40 And let her cold kiss on his lips be laid
    Thrice without faltering.

All this I promised her, for fervently
    I longed to free her from the evil spell –
Pity and love so swiftly wrought on me!
45   (Scarce I beheld her but I loved her well.)
Then, as I spake, she vanished suddenly,
    And o'er the marble came
A great snake, brighter than a shifting flame;

---

22. *vagrant*] wandering.

24. *well-spring*] fountainhead or source of a stream, rather than a sunken well. Here it is contained within the courtyard by a marble surround (see l. 47, below).

26. *outland*] foreign.

With scales of emerald and of amethyst
50   Her lithe coils dazzled me, and yet the same
Shone her sad eyes; but quickly, ere I wist,
She twined about me, clammy-chill and cold,
Staying my life-breath with her strangling fold;

The bright eyes neared mine own, the thin mouth hissed,
55   And I, nigh swooning, shrank from her embrace.
      'Leave me,' I gasped, and turned aside my face –
'Leave me, and loose me from thy loathly hold!'

The icy bands fell from me; numb with pain,
      Half blind, I sank beside the Moor Girl's Well,
60   Hearing a sough as of the summer rain,
A slow, sad voice from out the depths complain,
      'Redoubled tenfold is the cruel spell.'

And sometimes when the yellow dawn is chill
      The memory grips my heart so that I rise,
65   And go with hurried footsteps down the hill
      Where the lone court-yard lies,
And kneeling gaze into those waters still
      Beneath the quiet skies:
'Only come back and I shall do thy will!'

70   I seek, and still the steely deep denies
The piercing sorrow of her diamond eyes;
I seek, but only see
Mine own gaze back at me.

[1891]

---

51. *ere I wist*] before I knew (archaic).

53. *Staying*] Arresting.

60. *sough*] gentle sigh or murmuring sound.

A Ballad of the Were-wolf

THE gudewife sits i' the chimney-neuk,
　　An' looks on the louping flame;
The rain fa's chill, and the win' ca's shrill,
　　Ere the auld gudeman comes hame.

5　　'Oh, why is your cheek sae wan, gudewife?
　　An' why do ye glower on me?
Sae dour ye luik i' the chimney-neuk,
　　Wi' the red licht in your e'e!

'Yet this nicht should ye welcome me,
10　　This ae nicht mair than a',
For I hae scotched yon great grey wolf
　　That took our bairnies twa.

A Ballad of the Were-wolf. *Title.*] A were-wolf is a man (usually) who takes on the form of a wolf to roam at night and terrify infants. Linda K. Hughes identifies the probable source of this poem as Howard Williams's *Superstitions of Witchcraft* (1865), in which the following account is given: 'A gentleman while hunting was suddenly attacked by a savage wolf of monstrous size. Impenetrable by his shot, the beast made a spring upon the helpless huntsman, who in the struggle luckily, or unluckily for the unfortunate lady, contrived to cut off one of its fore-paws. This trophy he placed in his pocket, and made the rest of his way homewards in safety. On the road he met a friend, to whom he exhibited a bleeding paw, or rather (as it now appeared) a woman's hand, upon which was a wedding-ring. His wife's ring was at once recognized by the other. His suspicions aroused, he immediately went in search of his wife, who was found sitting by the fire in the kitchen, her arm hidden beneath her apron, when the husband, seizing her by the arm, found his terrible suspicions verified. The bleeding stump was there, evidently just fresh from the wound. She was given into custody, and in the event was burned at Riom, in the presence of thousands of spectators.' Hughes, 1994, p. 105.

1. gudewife] familiar Scottish term for wife. The use of Scottish dialect in the poem follows a nineteenth-century fashion that was originally set in train by the popularity of Robert Burns (1759–1796). *chimney-neuk*] chimney-nook or corner.

2. louping] leaping.

3.] The rain falls chill, and the wind calls shrill.

4.] Before the old husband comes home.

7. luik] look.

8. licht] light.

10.] This one night more than all. 'Ae' is Scottish and northern dialect for 'one'.

11. scotched] wounded so as to render harmless.

12. bairnies twa] two little children.

"Twas a sair, sair strife for my very life,
    As I warstled there my lane;
15   But I'll hae her heart or e'er we part,
    Gin ever we meet again.

'An' 'twas ae sharp stroke o' my bonny knife
    That gar'd her haud awa';
Fu' fast she went out-owre the bent
20   Wi'outen her right fore-paw.

'Gae tak' the foot, o' the drumlie brute,
    And hang it upo' the wa';
An' the next time that we meet, gudewife,
    The tane of us shall fa'.'

25   He's flung his pouch on the gudewife's lap,
    I' the firelicht shinin' fair,
Yet naught they saw o' the grey wolf's paw,
    For a bluidy hand lay there.

O hooly, hooly rose she up,
30   Wi' the red licht in her e'e,
Till she stude but a span frae the auld gudeman
    Whiles never a word spak' she.

But she stripped the claiths frae her lang richt arm,
    That were wrappit roun' and roun',
35   The first was white, an' the last was red;
    And the fresh bluid dreeped adown.

---

13. *sair*] painful, difficult.

14.] As I wrestled alone.

15. *or e'er*] before.

16. *Gin*] In case.

18.] That forced her hold to loosen.

19. *out-owre the bent*] across the moorland.

21. *drumlie*] turbid, troubled.

24. *tane*] a contraction of 'that one'; often used tautologically with the definite article, as here. Also used elliptically for 'the one or the other', which also makes sense in this context.

29. *hooly*] slowly and carefully.

31. *span*] an (extended) hand's-breadth.

33. *claiths*] northern pronunciation for 'cloths'.

She stretchit him out her lang right arm,
   An' cauld as the deid stude he.
The flames louped bricht i' the gloamin' licht –
40   There was nae hand there to see! –

[1891]

Vespertilia

IN the late autumn's dusky-golden prime,
   When sickles gleam and rusts the idle plough,
   The time of apples dropping from the bough,
   And yellow leaves on sycamore and lime;
5   O'er grassy uplands far above the sea
   Often at twilight would my footsteps fare,
   And oft I met a stranger-woman there
      Who stayed and spake with me:
   Hard by the ancient barrow smooth and green,
10   Whose rounded burg swells dark upon the sky,
   Lording it high o'er dusky dell and dene,
      We wandered – she and I.

---

38. cauld as the deid] cold as the dead.

39. gloamin'] twilight.

Vespertilia. *Title.*] Vespertilia is literally the (female) bat. The bat's dual nature as a winged mammal has been reflected in many of its symbolic associations. When portrayed as a fallen angel, the Devil is often depicted with bat's wings. While the bat could suggest vigilance in classical culture, in the *Odyssey*, the souls of the dead are described as fluttering around Hell, emitting bat-like cries. It is worth noting that Mary Coleridge used the male form, Vespertilio, as an early pseudonym (see Coleridge headnote, p. 284 below). The mythical vampire bat is traditionally regarded as a dead person returned to life, usually a criminal or heretic. Linda K. Hughes reads this poem in terms of this idea of the revenant (Hughes, 1999). Watson later wrote a poem called 'Revenant' (published posthumously), about revisiting one's house after death (see *Poems* [1912], p. 280).

2. sickles] a sickle is a crescent-shaped blade on a handle for cutting grass or corn. They gleam with use at harvest time.

6. fare] travel.

9. barrow] burial mound, dating from pre-Christian times, still found in certain parts of England.

10. burg] fortress.

11. dene] wooded vale.

Ay, many a time as came the evening hour
And the red moon rose up behind the sheaves,
15 I found her straying by that barren bower,
Her fair face glimmering like a white wood-flower
That gleams through withered leaves.
Her mouth was redder than the pimpernel,
Her eyes seemed darker than the purple air
20 'Neath brows half hidden – I remember well –
'Mid mists of cloudy hair.

And all about her breast, around her head,
Was wound a wide veil shadowing cheek and chin,
Woven like the ancient grave-gear of the dead:
25   A twisted clasp and pin
Confined her long blue mantle's heavy fold
Of splendid tissue dropping to decay,
  Faded like some rich raiment worn of old,
With rents and tatters gaping to the day.
30 Her sandals wrought about with threads of gold,
Scarce held together still, so worn were they,
Yet sewn with winking gems of green and blue,
And pale as pearls her naked feet shone through.

And all her talk was of some outland rare,
35 Where myrtles blossom by the blue sea's rim,
And life is ever good and sunny and fair;
'Long since,' she sighed, 'I sought this island grey –
Here, where the winds moan and the sun is dim,
When his beaked galleys cleft the ocean spray,
40 For love I followed him.'

Once, as we stood, we heard the nightingale
Pipe from a thicket on the sheer hillside,
Breathless she hearkened, still and marble-pale,

---

18. *pimpernel*] a scarlet flower.

24. *grave-gear*] clothes covering a corpse: an Anglo-Saxon term.

34. *outland*] foreign country – here presumably Greece, with its associations of myrtles, blue sea, and galleys.

39. *beaked galleys*] a large, wooden, flat-decked boat with a carved prow like a beak. The identity of the man she followed is left mysterious, thus opening the way for the suggestion that it may be the speaker of the poem (see l. 47).

Then turned to me with strange eyes open wide –
45 'Now I remember! . . . Now I know!' said she,
'Love will be life . . . ah, Love *is* Life!' she cried,
'And thou – thou lovest me?'

I took her chill hands gently in mine own,
'Dear, but no love is mine to give,' I said,
50 'My heart is colder than the granite stone
That guards my true-love in her grassy bed;
My faith and troth are hers, and hers alone,
Are hers . . . and she is dead.'

Weeping, she drew her veil about her face,
55 And faint her accents were and dull with pain;
'Poor Vespertilia! gone her days of grace,
Now doth she plead for love – and plead in vain:
None praise her beauty now, or woo her smile!

    *   *   *   *   *

Ah, hadst thou loved me but a little while,
60   I might have lived again.'

Then slowly as a wave along the shore
She glided from me to yon sullen mound;
My frozen heart, relenting, smote me sore –
Too late – I searched the hollow slopes around,
65 Swiftly I followed her, but nothing found,
   Nor saw nor heard her more.

And now, alas, my true-love's memory,
Even as a dream of night-time half-forgot,
   Fades faint and far from me,
70 And all my thoughts are of the stranger still,
   Yea, though I loved her not:
I loved her not – and yet – I fain would see,
Upon the wind-swept hill,
Her dark veil fluttering in the autumn breeze;
75 Fain would I hear her changeful voice awhile,
Soft as the wind of spring-tide in the trees,
And watch her slow, sweet smile.

Ever the thought of her abides with me
Unceasing as the murmur of the sea;
80   When the round moon is low and night-birds flit,
When sink the stubble-fires with smouldering flame,
Over and o'er the sea-wind sighs her name,
    And the leaves whisper it.

'*Poor Vespertilia*,' sing the grasses sere,
85   '*Poor Vespertilia*,' moans the surf-beat shore;
Almost I feel her very presence near –
    Yet she comes nevermore.

[1895]

Hic Jacet

AND is it possible? – and must it be –
At last, indifference 'twixt you and me?
We who have loved so well,
Must we indeed fall under that strange spell,
5   The tyranny of the grave?

In sullen severance patient and resigned,
By each of each forgotten out of mind –
Dear, is there none to save?
Must you whose heart makes answer to mine own,
10   Whose voice compels me with its every tone,
Must you forget my fealty to claim,
And I – to turn and tremble at your name,
Sunk in dull slumber neath a lichened stone?
Shall not my pulses leap if you be near?
15   Shall these endure, the sun, the wind, the rain,
And naught of all our tenderness remain,
Our joy – our hope – our fear? . . .

---

81. stubble-fires] Cornfields were burnt after harvest to boost the soil for a new crop.

Hic Jacet. *Title*.] 'Here lies' (Latin). Commonly found on tombstones.

11. fealty] obligation of fidelity due from a vassal to a lord.

12–14.] Cf. Tennyson's *Maud* (1855), Part One, XXII, xi: 'My heart would hear her and beat, /
Were it earth in an earthy bed; / My dust would hear her and beat, / Had I lain for a century
dead; / Would start and tremble under her feet, / And blossom in purple and red.'

Sweet, 'tis one thing certain – rail or weep,
Plead or defy, take counsel as we may,
20   It shall not profit us: this, only, pray
Of the blind powers that keep
The harvest of the years we sow and reap,
That naught shall sever nor estrange us – Nay,
Let us live out our great love's little day
25   Fair and undimmed, before we fall on sleep.

[1895]

A Midnight Harvest

Cornish Coast

THE white, white gulls wheel inland,
    The breakers rake and grind;
The swagging clouds go swiftly
    With a shattering gale behind;
5   What are the white gulls crying
    Above the ripened corn?
'O, harvest will be over
    Before the morrow's morn:
No need to whet the sickle,
10   No need to bring the wain,
The storm shall reap on the cliff-side steep,
    And the west wind thresh the grain.'

The white, white gulls whirl gaily,
    They keep a merry coil,
15   But the farmer's heart is heavy
    For all his months of toil:
He hears the white gulls' chorus,

A Midnight Harvest. *Title.*] The ghoulish idea of a shipwreck as a 'harvest' from the sea was explored in a number of nineteenth-century contexts: see, for example, J. M. W. Turner's paintings 'The Shipwreck' (1805), 'Wreckers – Coast of Northumberland, with a Steam Boat assisting a Ship off Shore' (1834), and 'Rough Sea with Wreckage' (c.1830–5).

3. swagging] swaying, sinking, sagging.

9. whet] sharpen.

10. wain] large farm waggon.

<blockquote>
Their cries of joyous scorn:
'O, harvest will be over
20   Or ever comes the morn:
Now go you to your bed, Farmer,
   Lie down and take your ease;
The wind shall reap while you rest and sleep,
   And the storm shall scour the leas.'
</blockquote>

<blockquote>
25   The white, white foam flies upward,
   The black rocks show their teeth,
Dark frowns the towering headland
   They grin and gird beneath;
What are the wild gulls crying
30   Far up the valleys grey!
</blockquote>

<blockquote>
'Hey for the midnight harvest,
   The merry breakers' play!
There'll be harvest out at sea, Farmer,
   And harvest here on land:
35   There'll be rare ripe grain for the hungry main,
   And drowned folk for the strand.'
</blockquote>

[1895]

Serenade

<blockquote>
WHO is it sings the gypsies' song to-night
   To muted strings,
Deep in the linden shade, beyond the light
   My casement flings?
</blockquote>

<blockquote>
5   Can it be Death who sings? Ah no, not he,
   For he is old, –
His voice is like the murmur of the sea
   When light grows cold.
</blockquote>

---

24. *leas*] grasslands.
28. *gird*] encircle; or possibly the meaning is 'jeer' (now archaic).
35. *main*] ocean.

Serenade. 3. *linden*] lime tree.
4. *casement*] window opening outwards.

Who is it sings once more, once more again
10   The gypsy song? –
Song of the open road, the starry plain
        Estranged so long: –

'Come to the woods, come, for the woods are green,
        The sweet airs blow,
15   The hawthorn boughs the forest boles between
        Are white as snow.' . . .

The wet leaves stir; the dim trees dream again
        Of vanished Springs: –
Out in the night, out in the slow, soft rain,
20   My lost youth sings.

[1904]

Die Zauberflöte

A THRUSH is singing on the walnut tree –
        The leafless walnut-tree with silver boughs,
He sings old dreams long distant back to me –
        He sings me back to childhood's happy house.

5   O to be you, triumphant Voice-of-Gold,
        Red rose of song above the empty bowers,
Turning the faded leaves, the hopes grown cold,
        To Springtide's good green world of growing flowers:

Might the great change that turns the old to new
10   Remould this clay to better blossoming,
I would be you, Great-Heart, I would be you,
        And sing like you of Love and Death and Spring.

[1904]

---

15. *hawthorn*] The hawthorn was a symbol of good hope in the language of flowers; also a charm against sorcery.   *forest boles*] tree trunks.

Die Zauberflöte. *Title.*] The magic flute (cf. the opera of this name composed by Wolfgang Amadeus Mozart, 1791).

1.] Cf. Thomas Hardy's poem 'The Darkling Thrush', composed on 31 Dec 1900.

10. Remould this clay] i.e. this flesh (about to rejoin the earth).

ROSAMUND MARRIOTT WATSON

A Ruined Altar

'The hare shall kitle on thy cold hearth-stane.'
– Thomas the Rhymer.

GREEN is the valley, and fair the slopes around it,
    Wide waves of barley shining to the sun;
Softly the stock-doves murmur in the pine trees,
    Deep through the hollow the happy waters run.

5   Roofless and ruinous lies the little homestead,
    All the grey walls of it crumbling to the ground;
Only the hearth-place, steadfast and unshaken,
    Stands, like a tomb, 'mid the lusty leafage round.

Foxglove and hemlock blossom in the garden,
10   Where the bright ragwort tramples on the rose;
Gone is the gate, and lost the little pathway, –
    High on the threshold the gaunt nettle grows.

Here, long ago, were toil, and thought, and laughter,
    Poor schemes for pleasures, piteous plans for gain,
15   Love, fear, and strife – for men were born and died here –
    Strange human passion, bitter human pain.

Now the square hearth-place, shrouded deep in shadow,
    Holds in its hollow wild things of the wood;
Here comes the hawk, and here the vagrant swallow
20   Nests in the niche where cup and trencher stood.

Shy furry forms, that hide in brake and covert,
    Leap on the stone where leapt the yellow flame;
Up the wide chimney, black with vanished smoke-wreaths,
    Clambers the weed that wreathes the mantel-frame.

A Ruined Altar. *Title.*] The analogy of the hearthstone of a house with an altar ironically invokes the high Victorian ideal of the sacred status of the family hearth, presided over by the pure woman; an ideal which, as this poem suggests, had not withstood the stresses of the later nineteenth century.

Epigraph. kitle] give birth (to kittens: i.e. baby hares). Thomas the Rhymer was Thomas Ercildoune, 13th–century border poet and prophet.

3. stock-doves] wild pigeons.

9–10.] *Foxgloves* and *roses* are cultivated flowers, while *hemlock* and *ragwort* are weeds.

20. trencher] wooden platter used for meat.

21. brake] thicket of bushes.   *covert*] undergrown wood, the refuge of wildlife.

25 But when cometh Winter and all the weeds are withered
   In these bare chambers open to the rain,
Then, when the wind moans in the broken chimney,
   And the hare shivers in the sodden lane,

Then the old hearth-nook mourns the folk that filled it,
30   Mourns for the cheer of the red and golden blaze;
Heaped with the snow-drifts, standing bleak and lonely,
   Dreams of the dead and their long-forgotten days.

[1904]

The White Lady

THE white stone lady on the grass
   Beneath the walnut tree,
She never smiles to see me pass,
   Or blows a kiss to me.

5 She holds a cup in both her hands
   With doves upon its brink,
And ho, so very still she stands
   The thrushes come to drink.

She will not listen when I speak,
10   She never seemed to know,
When once I climbed to kiss her cheek
   And brush away the snow.

She never took the daisy ring
   I gave her yesterday;
15 She never cares to hear me sing,
   Or watch me at my play.

The White Lady. *Title.*] A 'White Lady', from Teutonic myth, is a kind of spectre of death. She particularly forebodes the death of a child or maiden, whose souls she receives. The White Lady of Avenal, in Scott's *The Monastery* (1820), is based upon the legend. Cf. Mary Coleridge's 'The White Women', p. 301 below.

13. daisy ring] presumably the same as 'daisy chain', a necklace of daisies strung together.

But, still she looks through sun or rain,
    Towards the golden door,
As though some child should come again
20   Who often came before.

Some little child who went away,
    Before they knew of me,
Another child who used to play
    Beneath the walnut tree.

[1904]

MARY ELIZABETH COLERIDGE (1861–1907)

Mary Elizabeth Coleridge was a novelist, literary critic and essayist as well as a poet. Although it was her novels which brought her fame in her lifetime, it is her poetry which has best withstood the test of time. Her father was great-grandson of Samuel Taylor Coleridge's elder brother; Sara Coleridge (1802–1852), also a writer, was her great-aunt. Such eminent forebears were not likely to be unintimidating to a young woman aspiring to be a writer herself, and Mary Coleridge always insisted on a pseudonym for the publication of her verse, although she agreed to sign her novels. Nor did she seek to publish her poetry, but was rather persuaded into it, and then only very small selections.

Born in London, growing up in the staid middle-class environs of South Kensington, she lived a protected life as one of two daughters of a keen amateur musician who was a lawyer by profession. Arthur Duke Coleridge was a fine singer and a popular host who enjoyed the friendship of a number of artists, musicians and poets, including Millais, Ruskin, Holman Hunt, Fanny Kemble, Tennyson and Browning (Mary's favourite poet). Mary was well educated at home, learning a number of languages including Hebrew (taught her by her father) and ancient Greek (taught by the ex-Etonian teacher William Cory, with whom she studied Plato). Evidently she felt little pressure to marry, preferring the society of her family and a number of close female friends with whom she discussed her writing and her inner life. She consciously revered the art of friendship, and the five who called themselves the Quintette remained friends all their lives. One, Margaret Duckworth, married Henry Newbolt, another writer, who was welcomed to their literary discussions and later edited Coleridge's collected poems, published in 1908 after her death, and including a majority of the poems she herself had not seen fit to publish.

Unlike the young Virginia Stephen (later Woolf), who was born into a similar environment 20 years later, Mary Coleridge does not appear to have been drawn to rebel against parental authority or fret at suffocating social convention. There is no evidence that she was ever attracted by the feminist cause, or by political radicalism of any sort. Yet the dutiful daughter of everyday life releases disturbing imagery of spiritual angst and awareness of human violence in the poetry she wrote primarily for herself and her friends, rather than for publication. Her poems are often very private, rather than just personal, and like the reclusive American poet Emily Dickinson, with whom she is often compared, her intelligence exults in ambiguity and indirection. But she is less radical than Dickinson, in that her verse follows traditional forms, particularly the sonnet and the ballad.

Wanting some occupation that would do good, yet hating the sense of patronage implicit in philanthropy, in 1895 Coleridge began to teach grammar and then literature at the Working Women's College, a task she came to enjoy greatly. In 1896 her first volume of 48 poems, *Fancy's Following*, was published by a private press in Oxford. This came about through her friend Violet Hodgkin, who showed some of

Coleridge's poems to her (Violet's) relative, Robert Bridges. He was instantly able to recognise her genius, and persuaded her not only to allow him to arrange publication of 125 copies, but also to help her to 'correct' her poems first. He helped to polish, but not to shape them, and she was duly grateful. The pseudonym she chose for publication was 'Anodos', the name of the hero of George Macdonald's *Phantastes* (1858) who undertakes a mystical quest for Platonic perfection. As one critic has shown, this pseudonym also points back to Plato himself, who uses the term 'anodos' in his *Republic* to denote the movement of the psyche from the dimness of the cave into the world of sunlight (Battersby, 1996, p. 254). Her original title had been 'Verses by Vespertilio', meaning the bat, a creature inhabiting two worlds, of darkness and of day, and often used as a symbol of melancholy (ibid.), or as an image of a ghost returning from the dead (see Rosemary Marriott Watson's poem 'Vespertilia', p. 273). The following year, she issued another small collection, *Fancy's Guerdon*, consisting of eleven poems from the first volume, along with seven new ones, through the publisher Elkin Mathews; it was not a success. Only when her poems appeared for the first time under her own name, in the posthumous edition edited by Newbolt which contained many more poems taken from notebooks and letters, did her poetry find readers.

Characteristically, her poetry has a deceptively simple surface, emphasised by the almost childlike nursery-poem forms she favoured. Coleridge tends to use rhyme quite conventionally, metre less so. For an example of her subtle use of metre, see her sonnet 'True to myself' (p. 290 below), where the sonnet form is stitched up tightly within a limited range of rhyme endings, echoing the speaker's struggle to keep 'Fear, sorrow, love' tightly under control and hidden from view. Not a songlike poet, she inserts unexpected dissonances that will disconcert any complacent reading. Her style is meditative, and even her sonnets remain understated and low-keyed. She always prefers to suggest through imagery rather than to state her purpose directly.

Like Rosemary Watson and Christina Rossetti, she likes to exploit the genre of the 'mystery' ballad, dealing with a mythic subject in a non-referential space so that it is very hard for the reader to hang any meaning onto it, let alone an unambiguous one. This method is richly suggestive. In the poem 'Wilderspin', for example (see p. 296), its protagonist, a (male) weaver, appears to play with a kind of gender-reversed Lady of Shalott. But how gender-reversed is it really? All the images suggest that the little red house is a site of female significance, perhaps a vulva or womb: a jewelled room, amber grapes, flowing torrent, even the cup of sheeny cider. The weaver is using this space as a trap, he is explicitly likened to a black spider, a predator, lying in wait. Nothing is explained. Another equally mysterious example is 'Master and Guest' (p. 288), a chilling poem in ballad style that plays on ambiguities, teasing the reader as the poem's female narrator is teased by the evil-looking guest, whose identity is never specified. He could be her dead husband returned in a different guise, or he could be the Devil himself playing tricks: the point is, the woman's belief in the sanctity of her marriage is completely undermined by his appearance. The subject of marriage is treated in her poem of that name with a delicate double edge (see p. 294), where every apparent positive in favour of marriage is immediately undercut by a lament for the loss of the soul's single integrity as well as the young girl's unfettered sense of fun and freedom.

Marriage is always viewed sceptically in Coleridge. So is Christianity. Here Coleridge moves right away from the devotional poetry of Rossetti and yet does not go as far as the post-Darwinian poets like Blind, Kendall and Naden. Coleridge is concerned in poems like 'Our Lady' (p. 291) to demystify – or even desanctify – Christianity, and also to cut down to size the false gentility inherent in the ideal of fine ladyhood. In 'He Came Unto His Own' (see p. 289), Christ's role in the poem is ambiguous: ballad tradition has it that anything declared unequivocally true is likely to be false (see l. 22). The poem suggests another take on the notion that Christ was of the common folk. 'Doubt' (p. 292) is an uncompromising poem about religious doubt with a characteristic twist in its tail. The last two lines turn the poem around to suggest that the speaker's faith is still intact enough, after all, to enable him or her (gender is unspecified here, and in a sense, irrelevant) to pity those 'others' with no belief in God or Satan. Yet up till then, it has seemed that the speaker is torn between the two impossible extremes of too much darkness and too much light.

There is often a curiously misogynist strain in Coleridge's writing which comes through in her essays as well. This suggests that she, like many other intelligent women of her generation, viewed the exaggerated trivialisation of the feminine role with distaste:

Woman with a big W bores me supremely . . . It is a mere abstraction born of monks and the mists of the North. A woman I know, but what on earth is Woman? She has done her best to spoil history, poetry, novels, essays, and Sir Thomas Browne and Thoreau are the only things safe from her; that's why I love them.

(Coleridge, 1910, p. 234)

At the same time, her writing can indicate to us the limits of what was acceptable for nicely brought up young women of the period in its frequent suggestion of a layer of painful self-suppression. 'The Other Side of a Mirror' is one of her most striking poems (see p. 287 below). It created a stir in the late twentieth century when Sandra Gilbert and Susan Gubar used it as the mainspring of their new feminist poetics (Gilbert and Gubar, 1979a, p. 15; see also the critique of their reading by Christine Battersby, 1996). The mirror is a time-honoured image of femininity, but here it is used subversively to reflect not beauty, but ugliness, fear and distress. These disquieting attributes, normally repressed in the 'good' Victorian female, are here represented as inhabiting another, private, realm, co-existent with the public realm, but not usually accessible from it. An early poem by W. B. Yeats (a poet admired by Coleridge), 'The Two Trees' (1893), plays interestingly with a similar idea from another perspective.

Coleridge's poetry retains its interest for the modern reader not for any narrative or storytelling power, but rather for its sympathetic quality of being a modern sensibility musing on life's poignant moments. We sense that for this poet, privacy is almost a fetish; she wants to erect a smokescreen between herself and the reader. Paradoxically, this gives a sense of submerged force, with the added suggestion of a strong erotic drive. She writes about sorrow, but she is not a sad poet like Rossetti, and her sense of humour can be mischievous at times (though so too can Rossetti's, of course). But there remains always an intriguing feeling of unease in Coleridge, a sense of doubleness, of split subjectivity, of heightened self-consciousness.

Newbolt's granddaughter, Theresa Whistler, edited a new and revised version of the *Collected Poems* in 1954, adding further poems from manuscript sources. However, she states her belief that Mary's father, Arthur Coleridge, destroyed most of his daughter's manuscripts after Newbolt had completed his edition in 1907, the year of Mary's untimely death from appendicitis.

Text: Poems chosen are from *Fancy's Following* (1896), *Fancy's Guerdon* (1897), *The Garland* (1899) and *Poems* (1908). Date of first publication in volume form is given in square brackets at the foot of each poem. The copy-text used is *Poems* (1908).

To Memory

STRANGE Power, I know not what thou art,
Murderer or mistress of my heart.
I know I'd rather meet the blow
Of my most unrelenting foe
5   Than live – as now I live – to be
Slain twenty times a day by thee.

Yet, when I would command thee hence,
Thou mockest at the vain pretence,
Murmuring in mine ear a song
10   Once loved, alas! forgotten long;
And on my brow I feel a kiss
That I would rather die than miss.

[1896]

To Memory. *1. Strange Power*] Cf. S. T. Coleridge: 'I pass, like night, from land to land; / I have strange power of speech' ('The Rime of the Ancient Mariner', ll. 586–7). This may or may not be a conscious echo; STC's usage of the phrase refers to the mariner's tormented need to repeat his story, thus implying that memory is a cruel power, which has some relevance for this poem. Cf. John Milton, *Samson Agonistes* (1671), ll. 1003–5: '*Chor.* Yet beauty, though injurious, hath strange power, / After offence returning, to regain / Love once possessed . . .'.

2. mistress] Memory was traditionally female (from the muse Mnesmosyne).

11–12.] Cf. the last stanza of Robert Browning's 'Subiety', from *Asolando* (1889): 'Perhaps but a memory, after all! / – Of what came once when a woman leant / To feel for my brow where her kiss might fall. / Truth ever, truth only the excellent!' (ll. 21–4).

The Other Side of a Mirror

I SAT before my glass one day,
   And conjured up a vision bare,
Unlike the aspects glad and gay,
   That erst were found reflected there –
5   The vision of a woman, wild
   With more than womanly despair.

Her hair stood back on either side
   A face bereft of loveliness.
It had no envy now to hide
10   What once no man on earth could guess.
It formed the thorny aureole
   Of hard unsanctified distress.

Her lips were open – not a sound
   Came through the parted lines of red.
15   Whate'er it was, the hideous wound
   In silence and in secret bled.
No sigh relieved her speechless woe,
   She had no voice to speak her dread.

And in her lurid eyes there shone
20   The dying flame of life's desire,
Made mad because its hope was gone,
   And kindled at the leaping fire
Of jealousy, and fierce revenge,
   And strength that could not change nor tire.

The Other Side of a Mirror] Gilbert and Gubar (1979a) based their argument about feminist poetics on their reading of this poem.

1. I sat before my glass] The mirror is a time-honoured image of femininity, but here it is being used subversively to reflect not beauty, but ugliness, fear and distress, normally repressed into another realm. Cf. W. B. Yeats, 'The Two Trees', from *The Rose* (1893): 'Gaze no more in the bitter glass' (l. 21). Hardy may conceivably have echoed this poem in 'I look into my glass' (1898).

4. erst] earlier, first.

11. thorny aureole] an aureole is a halo: a golden circle of radiant light around the head. 'Thorny aureole' is an ironic reference to the crown of thorns.

19. lurid] either ghastly pale or with a reddish light; ominously suggestive of violence.

25   Shade of a shadow in the glass,
          O set the crystal surface free!
      Pass – as the fairer visions pass –
          Nor ever more return, to be
      The ghost of a distracted hour,
30   That heard me whisper, 'I am she!'

          [1896]

Master and Guest

      THERE came a man across the moor,
          Fell and foul of face was he.
          He left the path by the cross-roads three,
      And stood in the shadow of the door.

5   I asked him in to bed and board.
          I never hated any man so.
          He said he could not say me No.
      He sat in the seat of my own dear lord.

      'Now sit you by my side!' he said,
10   'Else may I neither eat nor drink.
          You would not have me starve, I think.'
      He ate the offerings of the dead.

      'I'll light you to your bed,' quoth I.
          'My bed is yours – but light the way!'
15   I might not turn aside nor stay;
          I showed him where we twain did lie.

---

25. Shade] Ghost.

Master and Guest. *2. Fell*] Cruel, cunning, ruthless.

3. cross-roads three] Cross-roads used to be places of execution, where criminals and suicides were buried; more usually the meeting of four roads, here the reference to three might suggest a magic number containing beginning, middle and end; or possibly, a back-handed reference to the holy trinity.

8. my own dear lord] ambiguous: could mean either her own dear husband, or her own dear Lord God.

12. the offerings of the dead] Refers to the funeral custom, originally Roman, of preparing a feast for the mourners. Cf. Shakespeare's *Hamlet* (c.1600–1): 'the funeral bak'd meats / Did coldly furnish forth the marriage tables' (I.ii.177–8).

The cock was trumpeting the morn.
   He said: 'Sweet love, a long farewell!
   You have kissed a citizen of Hell,
20   And a soul was doomed when you were born.

'Mourn, mourn no longer for your dear!
   Him may you never meet above.
   The gifts that Love hath given to Love,
Love gives away again to Fear.'

[1896]

'He came unto His own, and His own received Him not'

As Christ the Lord was passing by,
   He came, one night, to a cottage door.
   He came, a poor man, to the poor;
He had no bed whereon to lie.

5   He asked in vain for a crust of bread,
   Standing there in the frozen blast.
   The door was locked and bolted fast.
'Only a beggar!' the poor man said.

Christ the Lord went further on,
10   Until He came to a palace gate.
   There a king was keeping his state.
In every window the candles shone.

---

22. *Him may you never meet above*] Refers equally to her dead husband and to God, the import being that she will never go to heaven.

'He came unto His own . . .'. *Title*.] Cf. John 1: 11, referring to the rejection of Jesus by those he came to save. The story told in this poem reverses the usual stereotype of the poor man being hospitable and the rich inhospitable. Cf. 2 Samuel 12: 1–13, in which Nathan tells the parable of the rich man who, instead of killing one of his own flock to feed a traveller, kills a poor man's only lamb. As Nathan points out, this parallels David's own behaviour when he killed Uriah, the Hittite, in order to take his wife. David already had a number of wives.

6. *frozen blast*] freezing gust of wind.

11. *keeping his state*] holding court.

The king beheld Him out in the cold.
　　He left his guests in the banquet-hall.
15　　　He bade his servants tend them all.
'I wait on a Guest I know of old.'

''Tis only a beggar-man!' they said.
　　'Yes,' he said; 'it is Christ the Lord.'
　　He spoke to Him a kindly word,
20　He gave Him wine and he gave Him bread.

Now Christ is Lord of Heaven and Hell,
　　And all the words of Christ are true.
　　He touched the cottage, and it grew;
He touched the palace, and it fell.

25　The poor man is become a king.
　　Never was man so sad as he.
　　Sorrow and Sin on the throne make three,
He has no joy in mortal thing.

But the sun streams in at the cottage door
30　　That stands where once the palace stood,
　　And the workman, toiling to earn his food,
Was never a king before.

[1896]

'True to myself am I, and false to all'

'To thine own self be true;
And it must follow, as the night the day,
Thou canst not then be false to any man.'

TRUE to myself am I, and false to all.
　　Fear, sorrow, love, constrain us till we die.
　　But when the lips betray the spirit's cry,
The will, that should be sovereign, is a thrall.

---

27. *make three*] the poor man himself makes up the trinity.

'True to myself am I . . .'. *Epigraph.*] Shakespeare, *Hamlet* (*c.*1600–1; I.iii.55–7). This quotation stands in ironic relation to the poem.

4. *thrall*] slave.

5   Therefore let terror slay me, ere I call
        For aid of men. Let grief begrudge a sigh.
        'Are you afraid?' – 'unhappy?' 'No!' The lie
      About the shrinking truth stands like a wall.
      'And have you loved?' 'No, never!' All the while,
10   The heart within my flesh is turned to stone.
      Yea, none the less that I account it vile,
        The heart within my heart makes speechless moan,
        And when they see one face, one face alone,
      The stern eyes of the soul are moved to smile.

[1896]

Our Lady

MOTHER of God! no lady thou:
    Common woman of common earth!
OUR LADY ladies call thee now,
    But Christ was never of gentle birth;
5   A common man of the common earth.

For God's ways are not as our ways.
    The noblest lady in the land
Would have given up half her days,
    Would have cut off her right hand,
10   To bear the Child that was God of the land.

Never a lady did He choose,
    Only a maid of low degree,
So humble she might not refuse
    The carpenter of Galilee.
15   A daughter of the people, she.

---

8. shrinking truth] Both senses of shrinking are appropriate here: retreating or recoiling, and lessening.

12. The heart within my heart] A distinction is being made between the spiritual and physical manifestations of love.

Our Lady. *Title.*] Mother of God, the Virgin Mary. The poem plays on the class-ridden associations of the word 'lady'.

4. gentle birth] born to be a gentleman, belonging to the class defined by its fine manners and inherited wealth.

14. the carpenter of Galilee] Joseph, husband of Mary, was a humble carpenter.

Out she sang the song of her heart.
   Never a lady so had sung.
She knew no letters, had no art;
   To all mankind, in woman's tongue,
20   Hath Israelitish Mary sung.

And still for men to come she sings,
   Nor shall her singing pass away.
'He hath filled the hungry with good things' –
   Oh, listen, lords and ladies gay! –
25   'And the rich He hath sent empty away.'

[1896]

Doubt

Two forms of darkness are there. One is Night,
When I have been an animal, and feared
I knew not what, and lost my soul, nor dared
Feel aught save hungry longing for the light.
5   And one is Blindness. Absolute and bright,
The Sun's rays smote me till they masked the Sun;
The Light itself was by the light undone;
The day was filled with terrors and affright.

Then did I weep, compassionate of those
10   Who see no friend in God – in Satan's host no foes.

[1896]

---

20. Israelitish Mary] The mother of Christ was, of course, an Israelite, or Jew (one of God's chosen people).

23, 25.] Cf. Luke 1: 53: 'He hath filled the hungry with good things; and the rich he hath sent empty away.' These words appear in the Magnificat, the hymn spoken by the Virgin Mary to her cousin Elizabeth, whom she visits after being told that she is to bear the son of God (Luke 1: 46–55).

Doubt. *6. smote*] struck.

7.] i.e. the 'Light' of faith in God was destroyed by the light of reason (or even the mundane light of everyday reality). Alternatively, the very intensity of the 'light' of God blinded her (with terror).

10. host] company, troops.

The Witch

I HAVE walked a great while over the snow,
And I am not tall nor strong.
My clothes are wet, and my teeth are set,
And the way was hard and long.
5   I have wandered over the fruitful earth,
But I never came here before.
Oh, lift me over the threshold, and let me in at the door!

The cutting wind is a cruel foe.
I dare not stand in the blast.
10   My hands are stone, and my voice a groan,
And the worst of death is past.
I am but a little maiden still,
My little white feet are sore.
Oh, lift me over the threshold, and let me in at the door!

15   Her voice was the voice that women have,
Who plead for their heart's desire.
She came – she came – and the quivering flame
Sank and died in the fire.
It never was lit again on my hearth
20   Since I hurried across the floor,
To lift her over the threshold, and let her in at the door.

[1896]

The Witch. *7. lift me over the threshold*] Traditionally, brides are lifted over the threshold by their new husbands, to start life afresh in the married state. Here, however, the title warns us that the 'little maiden' pleading to be lifted over the threshold is in fact a witch, so bringing a curse rather than blessings into the dwelling. The haunting refrain of this eerie short poem hinges on the powerful image of the threshold as a marker of transition between two states of being.

15. Her voice] Although the voice of the first two stanzas (belonging to the maiden/witch) switches in the third stanza to the voice of the house-owner, it is not made at all clear that this switch is anything more than a modulation, thus suggesting that the witch-figure might not be an externalised figure of foreboding so much as a projected aspect of the self.

Awake

THE wailing wind doth not enough despair;
   The Sea, for all her sobbing, hath the Moon,
I cannot find my heart's cry anywhere,
    Fain to complain alone.

5   The whistle of the train that, like a dart,
   Pierces the darkness as it hurries by,
Hath not enough of sadness, and my heart
     Is stifled for a cry.

[1899]

Marriage

No more alone sleeping, no more alone waking,
   Thy dreams divided, thy prayers in twain;
Thy merry sisters to-night forsaking,
    Never shall we see thee, maiden, again.

5   Never shall we see thee, thine eyes glancing,
   Flashing with laughter and wild in glee,
Under the mistletoe kissing and dancing,
      Wantonly free.

There shall come a matron walking sedately,
10   Low-voiced, gentle, wise in reply.
Tell me, O tell me, can I love her greatly?
   All for her sake must the maiden die!

[1899]

Awake. *2. for all her sobbing*] This phrase appears to be deliberately ambiguous, meaning either: despite her sobbing, or: to answer to her sobbing (the moon controls the tides of the sea).
4. Fain] Obliged.
8. for] for want of.

Marriage. *2. divided . . . twain*] In Genesis 2: 24, 'cleave' is used to describe the joining of man and woman in marriage; in Coleridge's poem, marriage is associated with the other meaning of 'cleave', which is to split or rend apart. 'Divided' and 'twain' suggest the division or loss of selfhood.
4.] i.e. she will never be seen again as a maiden or virgin after her marriage.
7. Under the mistletoe] It is an English custom at Christmas to hang mistletoe above a doorway, where a man may kiss any girl beneath it.
8. Wantonly] Lasciviously: but here a more ambivalent association is suggested. Cf. Eve's 'wanton ringlets' in Milton's *Paradise Lost* (1667; Bk iv, l. 306).

On a Bas-relief of Pelops and Hippodameia

Which was wrecked and lay many years under the sea.

THUS did a nameless and immortal hand
  Make of rough stone, the thing least like to life,
  The husband and the wife
That the Most High, ere His creation, planned.
5   Hundreds of years they lay, unsunned, unscanned,
  Where the waves cut more smoothly than the knife,
  What time the winds tossed them about in strife,
And filled those lips and eyes with the soft sand.

Art, that from Nature stole the human form
10   By slow device of brain, by simple strength,
Lent it to Nature's artless force to keep.
So with the human sculptor wrought the storm
  To round those lines of beauty, till at length
A perfect thing was rescued from the deep.

[1899]

In Dispraise of the Moon

I WOULD not be the Moon, the sickly thing,
To summon owls and bats upon the wing;
For when the noble Sun is gone away,
She turns his night into a pallid day.

On a Bas-relief of Pelops and Hippodameia. *Title. Bas-relief*] generally associated with classical art, a sculpture in low relief, where the figures project less than half of their true proportion. *Pelops*] son of Tantalus, King of Phrygia, was restored to life by the king of the gods, Zeus, and one of the Fates after being cooked and served to the gods by his father. He later won the hand of the celebrated beauty *Hippodameia* by defeating her father, Oenomaus, King of Pisa, in a chariot race in which Pelops cheated. The marriage was subsequently cursed and became one of bitterness, crime and revenge.

1. nameless and immortal] i.e. some anonymous classical sculptor, made immortal through his art.

4.] A puzzling line: it seems to imply that God planned marriage for man and woman before he began the task of creating them.

7. What time] i.e. During which time.

9–14.] The artist modelled his figures slowly and carefully from Nature; then Nature took the sculpture and rounded it to smoothness through the action of the sea.

In Dispraise of the Moon. *1. I would not be the Moon*] The speaker is partly reacting against the traditional poetic association of the moon with a woman. Cf. 'Andrea del Sarto' by Robert

5   She hath no air, no radiance of her own,
That world unmusical of earth and stone.
She wakes her dim, uncoloured, voiceless hosts,
Ghost of the Sun, herself the sun of ghosts.

The mortal eyes that gaze too long on her
10   Of Reason's piercing ray defrauded are.
Light in itself doth feed the living brain;
That light, reflected, but makes darkness plain.

[1899]

Wilderspin

In the little red house by the river,
    When the short night fell,
Beside his web sat the weaver,
    Weaving a twisted spell.
5   Mary and the Saints deliver
    My soul from the nethermost Hell!

Browning (*Men and Women*, 1855), in which the speaker refers to his wife as 'My face, my moon, my everybody's moon / Which everybody looks on and calls his' (ll. 27–30). In 'One Word More', from the same collection and addressed to Elizabeth Barrett Browning, Robert Browning called his wife 'my moon of poets' (l. 188), praised by the world.

5–6. no air, no radiance . . . world unmusical] The moon has no atmosphere and emits no light; without air, sound (i.e. music) has no medium through which to travel, and so cannot exist.

7–8.] The *hosts* are the crowds of the dead in Hades; the moon (Artemis, or Diana) is the triple goddess (air, earth, underworld) and so in one of her manifestations is the *sun of ghosts*, i.e. queen of the dead.

9–10.] The moon – especially when full – was traditionally associated with madness; hence 'lunacy'.

12. but] only.

Wilderspin. *Title.*] Wilderspin is not in the OED. To 'wilder' is to go astray, become lost or confused. There may be some association with the word 'widdershins' or 'withershins', which means: the wrong way; in a direction contrary to the path of the sun.

1. the little red house] A Freudian reading might associate this image with the female genitalia.

4.] Cf. Alfred Tennyson, 'The Lady of Shalott' (1832), in which the Lady is trapped by a spell which keeps her at her weaving.

5. Mary and the Saints] the Virgin Mary, sometimes known by her role as Our Lady of Mercy.

6. nethermost Hell] Possibly a reference to Dante Alighieri (1265–1321), Italian poet much admired by the Victorians, who describes the topography of Hell in his best known work, the *Commedia* (later known as *Divina Commedia*, c.1308–21); in the *Inferno*, the lowest (nethermost) level is reserved for the treacherous.

In the little red house by the rushes
　　It grew not dark at all,
For day dawned over the bushes
10　　Before the night could fall.
Where now a torrent rushes,
　　The brook ran thin and small.

In the little red house a chamber
　　Was set with jewels fair;
15　There did a vine clamber
　　Along the clambering stair,
And grapes that shone like amber
　　Hung at the windows there.

Will the loom not cease whirring?
20　　Will the house never be still?
Is never a horseman stirring
　　Out and about on the hill?
Was it the cat purring?
　　Did some one knock at the sill?

25　To the little red house a rider
　　Was bound to come that night.
A cup of sheeny cider
　　Stood ready for his delight.
And like a great black spider,
30　　The weaver watched on the right.

To the little red house by the river
　　I came when the short night fell.
I broke the web for ever,
　　I broke my heart as well.
35　Michael and the Saints deliver
　　My soul from the nethermost Hell!

[1899]

---

27. *sheeny*] shining.

35. *Michael and the Saints*] St Michael the Archangel, associated with prudence, weighs the
souls of the risen dead.

Death

i

O THOU slight word, most like to *breath*, and made
Of a few letters merely, what's in thee,
Terror of flesh, the spirit's ecstasy,
Mysterious, voiceless, shadow of a shade?
5   They that fear nothing else, of thee afraid,
Do call thee *Sleep* and *Passing*. Thou set'st free
Infinite shapes of all a man may be,
Yet at thy nothingness he shrinks dismayed.
If thou wert not, the Poets had been dumb,
10   And Music silent. Yea, majestic Art
Had never sought and found her better part
Nor by the living eyes betrayed the heart.
Great prophecy were an unmeaning hum,
What-is no longer holding what's-to-come.

ii

15   I have wept for those who on this turning earth
Had lived more years than I – who were to me
The aim and goal of my felicity,
The dear reward of effort, crown of worth.
And I have wept for babes who died at birth,
20   Most deeply moved that I should never see
The flower and fruit of all the days to be,
A younger youth than mine, a merrier mirth.
But never ere this day I felt the sting
Of terror lest my burning tears should fall
25   For one who felt when first I felt the spring,
Heard from the wood the self-same cuckoo call,
Heard the same robin in the autumn sing,
Was one with me in life – in love – in all.

Death. *4. shade*] ghost.

6–7.] i.e. death, or the knowledge of mortality, releases man's imagination during life.

12.] A puzzling line: possibly means that *Art* gives away the secrets of the *heart* by its *living eyes*, i.e. its true depiction of life.

13–14.] i.e. without death, any prophecy of life after death would become meaningless.

16–17.] i.e. those older than herself whom she hopes to emulate and thus achieve happiness.

23. never ere this day] This would appear to refer to a specific deathbed: the occasion has not been identified.

iii

Bid me remember, O my gracious Lord,
30   The flattering words of love are merely breath!
O not in roses wreathe the shining sword,
Bid me remember, O my gracious Lord,
      The bitter taste of death!

Wrap not in clouds of dread for me that hour
35   When I must leave behind this house of clay,
When the grass withers and the shrunken flower!
Bid me, O Lord, in that most dreadful hour,
      Not fall, but fly away!

[1908]

Pride

O MORTAL virtue and immortal sin,
How often hast thou led the fool aright,
Sent forth a shivering coward to the fight,
    And made the worst man win!

5   Thine are the laurels giddy Pleasure lost,
The crown that hard Endeavour hardly earned.
And Glory woos thee, whom thy foot hath spurned,
    With all her host.

He that hath thee, tho' poor in seeming wealth,
10   Is not bereft. He that hath all beside,
Lives like a beggar, being poor in pride,
    And dies by stealth.

[1908]

---

35. *house of clay*] the body.

Pride. *1*.] Pride is one of the seven deadly sins; in a different sense, it can also be a sustaining virtue.

5. *laurels*] symbols of victory or poetic genius.   *giddy*] light-headed, frivolous.

6. *hardly*] with difficulty.

7–8.] i.e. Fame (*Glory*) and all that goes along with it, despite being spurned by pride, still seeks out the proud one.

Wasted

THOU show'st thy beauty unto all the men
    That meet thee by the way,
And one day thou shalt render it again
    To death and to decay.

5   Thou giv'st thy wisdom to a chosen few,
    As 'twere some precious book,
Yet were there only two or three that knew
    The art therein to look.

Thou giv'st thy laughter only unto one.
10   He hath no eyes to see.
Give, when his bitter jest with thee is done,
    Thy tears to me!

[1908]

'The fire, the lamp, and I, were alone together'

THE fire, the lamp, and I, were alone together.
Out in the street it was wild and windy weather.

The fire said, 'Once I lived, and now I shine.
I was a wood once, and the wind was mine.'

5   The lamp said, 'Once I lived and was the Sun.
The fire and I, in those old days, were one.'

The fire said, 'Once I lived and saw the Spring.
I die in smoke to warm this mortal thing.'

The lamp said, 'I was once alive and free.
10   In smoke I die to let this mortal see.'

Then I remembered all the beasts that died
That I might eat and might be satisfied.

Wasted. *3. render it again*] a variant on paying the 'debt of Nature', i.e. dying.

'The fire, the lamp, and I . . .'. *10. In smoke*] An oil lamp smokes when it is extinguished.

Then I remembered how my feet were shod,
Thought of the myriad lives on which I trod,

15   And sighed to feel that as I went my way,
I was a murderer ninety times a day.

[1908]

September

Now every day the bracken browner grows,
        Even the purple stars
        Of clematis, that shone about the bars,
Grow browner; and the little autumn rose
5   Dons, for her rosy gown,
        Sad weeds of brown.

Now falls the eve; and ere the morning sun,
        Many a flower her sweet life will have lost,
        Slain by the bitter frost,
10   Who slays the butterflies also, one by one;
        The tiny beasts
        That go about their business and their feasts.

[1908]

The White Women

WHERE dwell the lovely, wild white women folk,
        Mortal to man?
They never bowed their necks beneath the yoke,
They dwelt alone when the first morning broke
5   And Time began.

September. 3.] *Clematis* is a climbing plant; the *bars* may be window bars.

6. weeds] mourning garments.

The White Women. *Title.*] From a legend of Malay, told by Hugh Clifford [Author's note].
Sir Hugh Clifford (1866–1947), author of many works on life in Malaya, co-author of a diction-
ary of the language, and friend of Joseph Conrad, Ford Madox Ford and Rudyard Kipling,
was British Resident there for a number of years between 1888 and 1903.

2.] i.e. fatal to man.

3. *the yoke*] marriage.

Taller are they than man, and very fair,
　　Their cheeks are pale,
At sight of them the tiger in his lair,
The falcon hanging in the azure air,
10　　　　The eagles quail.

The deadly shafts their nervous hands let fly
　　Are stronger than our strongest – in their form
Larger, more beauteous, carved amazingly,
And when they fight, the wild white women cry
15　　　　The war-cry of the storm.

Their words are not as ours. If man might go
　　Among the waves of Ocean when they break
And hear them – hear the language of the snow
Falling on torrents – he might also know
20　　　　The tongue they speak.

Pure are they as the light; they never sinned,
　　But when the rays of the eternal fire
Kindle the West, their tresses they unbind
And fling their girdles to the Western wind,
25　　　　Swept by desire.

Lo, maidens to the maidens then are born,
　　Strong children of the maidens and the breeze,
Dreams are not – in the glory of the morn,
Seen through the gates of ivory and horn –
30　　　　More fair than these.

---

11. nervous] sensitive.

22. the eternal fire] the sun; or, as the next line makes clear, sunset. However, the phrase also suggests hellfire.

26–7.] Kathleen Hickok (1984) asserts of these lines: 'Their love is lesbian, their reproduction parthenogenetic' (p. 169). This might be the implication, but the poem actually states that these are the 'children of the maidens and the breeze'; Zephyrus, the personification in Greek legend of the Western wind (mentioned already, l. 24 above), fathered a number of children, although the fact that the children here are all 'maidens' favours Hickok's theory.

29. gates of ivory and horn] the two gates of dreams. Delusive dreams pass through the Ivory Gate; dreams which come true, through the Gate of Horn. The terms arose from a linguistic pun in Greek.

And none may find their dwelling. In the shade
   Primeval of the forest oaks they hide.
One of our race, lost in an awful glade,
Saw with his human eyes a wild white maid,
35   And gazing, died.

[1908]

'O Earth, my mother! not upon thy breast'

O EARTH, my mother! not upon thy breast
Would I my heavy head in death recline,
Would I lay down these weary limbs of mine
When the great Voice shall call me into rest.
5   Too well have I obeyed thy gay behest,
Too eagerly have worshipped at thy shrine;
The better part of all my life was thine,
I used thee as a lover not a guest.
I would not make with thee my dying bed,
10 Low, low beneath thy lowest let me be;
Far from thy living, farther from thy dead,
From every fetter of remembrance free,
Deep in some ocean cave, and overhead
The ceaseless sounding of thy waves, O Sea!

[1908]

No Newspapers

WHERE, to me, is the loss
   Of the scenes they saw – of the sounds they heard;
A butterfly flits across,
   Or a bird;
5 The moss is growing on the wall,
   I heard the leaf of the poppy fall.

[1908]

---

33. *awful*] full of dread.

'O Earth, my mother! . . .'. 5. *behest*] command.

No Newspapers. 2. *they*] men: newspapers of the period told mainly men's news from a patriarchal viewpoint.

MARY ELIZABETH COLERIDGE

A Clever Woman

YOU thought I had the strength of men,
    Because with men I dared to speak,
And courted Science now and then,
    And studied Latin for a week;
5   But woman's woman, even when
    She reads her Ethics in the Greek.

You thought me wiser than my kind;
    You thought me 'more than common tall;'
You thought because I had a mind,
10   That I could have no heart at all;
But woman's woman you will find,
    Whether she be great or small.

And then you needs must die – ah, well!
    I knew you not, you loved not me.
15   'Twas not because that darkness fell,
    You saw not what there was to see.
But I that saw and could not tell –
    O evil Angel, set me free!

[1908]

Alcestis to Admetus

BUILD over me no marble monument,
To stand for ever high above the throng;
Weave not my name in any wreath of song,
Hang up no picture of my life's event.

A Clever Woman. *Title.*] Cf. Charlotte Yonge's well-known novel for girls, *The Clever Woman of the Family* (1865), which, while far from feminist, does advocate a wider field for women's endeavours.

6.] The principal moral philosophers among the Greeks were Socrates, Plato and Aristotle.

18.] i.e. a plea to the Devil to set the speaker free from the torment of unrequited love that went unnoticed.

Alcestis to Admetus. *Title.*] In the Greek myth, Admetus, King of Pherae, had obtained from the Fates an assurance that he would not die if someone consented to die in his stead. When the fatal moment arrived, his wife, Alcestis, took his place. Some versions say Hercules wrested her from death's grasp and restored her to her husband, but evidently not this one. Robert Browning's 'Balaustion's Adventure' (1872) treated the Alcestis myth, with a female narrator strongly sympathetic to Alcestis and scornful of Admetus.

5   The lasting stone would mock thy brief lament
Witness thy short affection over long,
The steadfast words thy changing passion wrong,
The painted features cry 'Repent! repent!'

       Live and forget me. Farewell! Better so,
10   Than that I should be made the scorn of men,
Who mark the pageantry of grief, the show
Of feeling lighter than the wind, and then,
With lifted eyebrows, smile and whisper 'Lo!
A year is past, Admetus weds again!'

[1908]

Solo

       LEAVE me alone! my tears would make you laugh,
Or kindly turn away to hide a smile.
My brimming granaries cover many a mile;
How should you know that all my corn is chaff?
5   Leave me alone! my tears would make you laugh.

       Leave me alone! my mirth would make you weep.
I only smile at all that you hold dear;
I only laugh at that which most you fear;
I see the shallows where you sound the deep.
10   Leave me alone! my mirth would make you weep.

[1908]

Sadness

       I THINK that Sadness is an idiot born;
She has no eyes to see the sun in heaven,
No ears to hear the music of the earth,
No voice to utter forth her own desire.

[1908]

Solo. *9. sound the deep*] measure the depth of the sea.

Sadness. *1. an idiot born*] Women and idiots were accorded the same rights (or lack of them) under English law for most of the nineteenth century; *Sadness* is here gendered female.

Words

WORDS, dear companions! In my curtained cot
I cooed and twittered like a nesting bird;
And women spoke around me; but no word
Came to my baby lips – I knew you not.

5   Yet laughter did I know. I have not learned
To laugh more gaily since I first began.
The reasons of his mirth are born in man;
But man was born to laugh ere he discerned.

And tears I knew. Who taught me how to cry?
10   Was it my mother's heart that whispered me?
Tears have I wept since then that none could see,
Nor laughed, as then I laughed, ere they were dry.

Words, dear companions! As the spirit grew,
I loved you more and more with every hour.
15   I felt the sweep, the whirlwind of the power
HE gave to man, when man created you.

Words, dear companions! glittering, fair and brave!
Rapt in your rapture I was whirled along,
Strong in the faith of old, the might of song,
20   Struck through the silent portals of the grave.

Words, dear companions! Into you I drove
The dark dumb devil that besets the heart;
Nature in you rose to a heavenly art,
And wrought on earth an airy heaven of love.

25   Ah, when ye leave me, will there yet remain
The laughter and the weeping all untaught?
And will they, in the realm of perfect thought,
Teach me new words to sing of life again?

[1908]

Words. *8. ere he discerned*] i.e. before he was able to discriminate between things.

20. portals] doorway.

22. besets] hems in, encloses.

27. the realm of perfect thought] Although compatible with Christian ideas of the afterlife, this concept may also allude to the Platonic idea that full understanding is only possible after the soul is liberated from the body.

'Some in a child would live, some in a book'

SOME in a child would live, some in a book;
When I am dead let there remain of me
Less than a word – a little passing look,
Some sign the soul had once, ere she forsook
5   The form of life to live eternally.

[1908]

'Some in a child would live . . .'. *4–5.*] Some sign of individuality expressed through the form of life, before that was discarded for eternity.

MAY KENDALL
[EMMA GOLDWORTH] (1861–1943)

May Kendall was born Emma Goldworth Kendall, in Bridlington, Yorkshire, the daughter of James Kendall, a Wesleyan minister, and his wife Eliza (Goldworth Level). Little is known about her early life, but she was clearly well educated and certainly highly intelligent. Poetry constituted only part of her creative output: as well as two volumes of verse, Kendall also published several novels. She was a strong believer in woman's right to an independent life as well as her intellectual equality with men. She never married, but she enjoyed working alongside men and collaborated extensively with two men in particular: Andrew Lang and B. Seebohm Rowntree. Andrew Lang (1844–1912) was a Scottish poet, anthropologist, historian and Greek scholar, whose work had a wide impact and to whose light, clever, topical poetry many women were drawn (Levy and Watson as well as Kendall and Naden, for example). Certainly, something of his deftly jaunty style rubs off on her own verse, along with another comic influence, that of master wordsmith Lewis Carroll. With Lang, Kendall published a book of verses and satirical essays on contemporary society, science and politics, titled *That Very Mab* (1885). Much later in her life, after moving to York, she became involved with the well-known family of Quaker philanthropists, the Rowntrees. She helped Seebohm Rowntree with his study *How the Labourer Lives* (1913), and with his work on the minimum wage, *The Human Needs of Labour* (1918). While Rowntree provided the statistics, Kendall wove a readable narrative spiced with anecdotes. She refused to take any payment for this work, although she was eventually to die in poverty herself and lie in an unmarked grave in York Cemetery.

While still a young woman, however, Kendall published her own two volumes of verse, the first dedicated to her parents and titled *Dreams to Sell* (1887) – the title taken from Thomas Lovell Beddoes's poem 'Dream-Pedlary': 'If there were dreams to sell, / What would you buy? / Some cost a passing-bell, / Some cost a sigh.' Beddoes, who died under strange circumstances in 1851, was a queer, off-beat kind of poet whose work appealed to some of the more quirky Victorians (Robert Browning among them). Kendall's volume reprinted some poems from their first publication in magazines like *Punch* and *Longman's*, but many were new. As a whole, the volume continued Kendall's early predilection for sharp-eyed satire in 'Lay of the Trilobite' (see p. 311 below), which mocks the notion of equating civilisation with progress, and added a socially conscious twist in poems like 'Legend of the Crossing-sweeper', 'Legend of the Maid-of-all-work' and 'Woman's Future' – 'Alas, is it woolwork you take for your mission?' Without being overtly feminist, Kendall was nonetheless prepared to look squarely at some of the more glaring inequities of Victorian society, and was also much more conscious than, say, Naden (whom she often resembles in her poetic interests) of her own position of comparative privilege as a member of the prosperous, well-educated middle classes.

Kendall's second volume, *Songs from Dreamland* (1894), again contained poems reprinted from their original airing in literary magazines. Where her earlier volume had subdivided its contents fairly prosaically into such topics as 'Science', 'Sea and Shore', 'Town and Country', 'Art' and 'In Church', this time Kendall chose rather more whimsical subheadings, such as 'Fantasies', 'Problems', 'On the Windy Side of Care', and 'Looking for Peru' (where 'Peru' seems to be a metaphor for some exotic space situated well beyond the mundane world of everyday existence and containing the promise of hitherto unattainable love). Between the appearance of the two volumes of poetry, Kendall had published three novels. *From a Garrett* appeared in 1887, followed by *Such is Life* (1889) and *White Poppies* (1893). The first two were very much in the 'New Woman' vein, focusing on young, independent heroines. However, the more concise and pointed style of Kendall's verse-writing seems to have better suited her natural talents.

Kendall is certainly one of the most intelligent and witty of the poets in this anthology. She clearly had a particular interest in the scientific debates of the day, and often uses scientific jargon as a clever way of mocking scientific method, undercutting it with its own implements. But then she takes her interest a stage further, and uses these debates as a way of putting contemporary mores to the question. She has a much more objective view of the age than most, with an ability to occupy an outsider's position. For example, one of her poems, 'The Fatal Advertisements' (not included here), imagines Martians viewing earth and puzzling over the meaning of various signs, which the reader, of course, knows to be advertisements (such as 'Linoleum'). Although at first the joke seems slight, almost trivial, there is a sharp point to it, which translates slyly to the human sphere, as the most learned Martians argue earnestly over the meaning of portents they cannot possibly interpret correctly. Her 'Lay of the Trilobite', in deadpan absurdist mode, has a kind of Lewis Carroll feel to it as it plays with the viewpoint of an extinct crustacean from the ocean floor: 'And then, quite natural and free / Out of his rocky bed, / That Trilobite he spoke to me, / And this is what he said'. Again, this is a witty device used to reflect upon the foibles of humanity and the popular delusion that evolution brings an increase in the sum of human happiness. Another poem which takes its voice from a fossil is the 'Ballad of the Ichthyosaurus' (see p. 314), an interesting experiment in that it is a kind of comedic dramatic monologue. The speaker is a fossilised museum piece, the Ichthyosaurus of the title, who muses upon the contrast between his own superseded attribute of splendid vision ('Gigantic and beautiful Eye!') and the (Aryan) human being's evolved brain which he envies while inadvertently revealing its ultimate pointlessness.

Kendall's work is most unconventional in outlook, yet her approach to the craft of verse-writing is not new. Like most comic verse, hers exploits ordinary metrical forms and clear-cut rhyme schemes to comic effect with clever twists of the language. The effect is to puncture the vanities and complacencies of her age with playful mockery. But even while her terminology satirises scientific discourse, it nevertheless partakes of the rationalist's outlook. Kendall's verse places humans as part of nature in an unsentimental way, which is quite unromantic, unwordsworthian, and certainly unpantheistic. Man (or woman for that matter) holds no special chosen place in the scheme of the universe, has no innate superiority to the animal world

– in 'The Philanthropist and the Jelly-fish', for example (see p. 317), the philan-thropist's attempt to anthropomorphise the jellyfish is roundly rebutted by the creature itself (in what is, however, but a more sophisticated version of the same human tendency). The poem laughs at itself as well as (not unkindly) at the moral pretension of its human protagonist.

Not all the poems are comic, however. Many have a serious turn and display an impressive depth of social conscience. Kendall has a very unusual take on class, as she is seemingly able to project herself imaginatively into the minds and feelings of people quite different from herself. The vagrant in the 'Ballad of the Cadger', for example (see p. 320), knows himself to be unappealing as an object of the kind of middle-class philanthropy which seeks only to flatter itself, while in 'Underground' (p. 329), the Porter speaks respectfully enough to the gentleman about to enter his first-class carriage, yet the very degree of respect is suddenly made to appear out of all proportion to the fundamentals of human existence, and throws the arbitrary nature of class difference sharply under the microscope. Kendall's social conscience and awareness of the poor and their viewpoint on the so-called upper classes is unusual among the poets in this volume, all of whom come from the educated middle classes. While she often extends her sympathies to poor men, she is by no means oblivious to the special constraints under which girls and women are obliged to live in Victorian society. The poem 'In the Toy Shop' (p. 330), although it does not treat the topic overtly, shows a telling awareness of gender privilege and its disparities. It focuses on the theme of the 'naughty' (i.e. wilful) child, who *happens* to be female: 'She had "a will that must be broken''; / Her brothers drove her wild'. Yet the apparent 'naughtiness' of the child springs from 'longings all unspoken', which in the context of the poem are strongly suggested to be longings for freedom from the prescribed rules of young ladyhood. The choice offered the poem's protagonist lies between the way of the wooden doll – 'My animation's nil' – and the way of pain and suffering for those of 'nervous tissue', 'striving wildly'. Inter-estingly, the poem remains poised between the two, as the speaker adopts first one role, then the other, without plumping for either. Thus it manages to show a poignant awareness of female disadvantage while also indicating recognition of differences within the gender as well – the doll wishes she were real, and could 'Get cross, and have a will!' just as heartily as the little girl 'of protoplasm' wishes she were made of wood, so that she '*might* be good'. Such an idea of goodness, like all other externally applied moral standards, is of course viewed by Kendall as nothing more than an amusing human delusion, and this quirkily displaced viewpoint is the key to her charm as a poet.

Text: Poems chosen are from *Dreams to Sell* (1887) and *Songs from Dreamland* (1894). In each case, these are the copy-texts for the poems. The date of first publication in volume form is given in square brackets at the foot of each poem.

Lay of the Trilobite

A MOUNTAIN's giddy height I sought,
    Because I could not find
Sufficient vague and mighty thought
    To fill my mighty mind;
5   And as I wandered ill at ease,
    There chanced upon my sight
A native of Silurian seas,
    An ancient Trilobite.

So calm, so peacefully he lay,
10   I watched him even with tears:
I thought of Monads far away
    In the forgotten years.
How wonderful it seemed and right,
    The providential plan,
15   That he should be a Trilobite,
    And I should be a Man!

And then, quite natural and free
    Out of his rocky bed,
That Trilobite he spoke to me,
20   And this is what he said:
'I don't know how the thing was done,
    Although I cannot doubt it;

Lay of the Trilobite. *Title. Lay*] a poetic word for 'song'.　　*Trilobite*] an extinct anthropodous (i.e. having jointed limbs) animal, a tiny creature of the ocean floor. See Kendall's own note to l. 52 below. Interest in their fossilised remains (amongst the earliest known) was at a peak about the time Kendall was writing, as the immense age of these fossils was regarded as a certain indicator that the origin of life on earth was immeasurably earlier than had previously been thought. In chapter 22 of Thomas Hardy's novel *A Pair of Blue Eyes* (1873), Henry Knight is depicted in a hazardous situation, hanging from the edge of a sheer cliff. As he gradually loses faith in being rescued, he notices a trilobite fossil in the cliff face: 'Time closed up like a fan before him. He saw himself at one extremity of the years, face to face with the beginning and all the intermediate centuries simultaneously.'

7. Silurian] the third of the six geological periods of the ancient Palaeozoic era, spanning the time interval from 438 to 408 million years ago.

11. Monads] Around 1830 this term began to be used to describe hypothetical simple organisms assumed to be the foundation of the genealogy of living beings.

But Huxley – he if anyone
Can tell you all about it;

25 'How all your faiths are ghosts and dreams,
How in the silent sea
Your ancestors were Monotremes –
Whatever these may be;
How you evolved your shining lights
30 Of wisdom and perfection
From Jelly-fish and Trilobites
By Natural Selection.

'You've Kant to make your brains go round,
Hegel you have to clear them,
35 You've Mr Browning to confound,
And Mr Punch to cheer them!
The native of an alien land
You call a man and brother,
And greet with hymn-book in one hand
40 And pistol in the other!

'You've Politics to make you fight
As if you were possessed:
You've cannon and you've dynamite
To give the nations rest:

---

23. Huxley] Thomas Henry Huxley (1825–1895) was a powerful supporter of Darwinism and a controversial advocate of the new science. In 1886 he had published *Science and Morals*, where he defines the relation of science to philosophical and religious speculation. He coined the word 'agnostic' to express his own position.

27. Monotremes] Monotremata is the correct plural of monotremus, the lowest order of mammal, having only one opening for the genital, urinary and digestive organs.

33–6.] Immanuel *Kant* (1724–1804), Prussian philosopher, whose *Critique of Pure Reason* (1781) was his best-known work. His metaphysics placed religion and morality outside the province of knowledge into the region of faith. His theories were modified by another German philosopher, Georg Wilhelm Friedrich *Hegel* (1770–1831), who sought to resolve the essential dualism of Kant's thought into a theory of dialectical unity, and find a resolution which could be reconciled with Christian doctrine. Robert *Browning* (1812–1889), husband of Elizabeth Barrett Browning, was long held to be one of the most obscure of English poets in terms of his writing style. *Mr Punch* was the mythical eponymous hero of the famous illustrated comic weekly *Punch, or, The London Charivari*, founded in 1841, and at a height of popularity from about the 1870s.

36–40.] A reference to the hypocritical treatment of black slaves in America. 'Am I not a man and a brother?' was the well-known catch-cry of the abolitionists; here, the reference is probably to missionary and colonial activity in Africa.

45 The side that makes the loudest din
        Is surest to be right,
    And oh, a pretty fix you're in!'
        Remarked the Trilobite.

    'But gentle, stupid, free from woe
50   I lived among my nation,
    I didn't care – I didn't know
        That I was a Crustacean.
    I didn't grumble, didn't steal,
        I *never* took to rhyme:
55   Salt water was my frugal meal,
        And carbonate of lime.'

    Reluctantly I turned away,
        No other word he said;
    An ancient Trilobite, he lay
60   Within his rocky bed.
    I did not answer him, for that
        Would have annoyed my pride:
    I merely bowed, and raised my hat,
        But in my heart I cried: –

65   'I wish our brains were not so good,
        I wish our skulls were thicker,
    I wish that Evolution could
        Have stopped a little quicker;
    For oh, it was a happy plight,
70   Of liberty and ease,
    To be a simple Trilobite
        In the Silurian seas!'

    [1887]

---

52. *Crustacean*] 'He was not a Crustacean. He has since discovered that he was an Arachnid, or something similar. But he says it does not matter. He says they told him wrong once, and they may again' [Author's note]. Initially classified as a Crustacean, trilobites were later relegated to the Arachnida, a species comprising spiders, scorpions and mites.

56. *carbonate of lime*] limestone.

Ballad of the Ichthyosaurus

*(The Ichthyosaurus laments his imperfect advantages.
He aspires after the Higher Life.)*

I ABIDE in a goodly Museum,
　　Frequented by sages profound:
'Tis a kind of a strange mausoleum,
　　Where the beasts that have vanished abound.
5　There's a bird of the ages Triassic,
　　With his antediluvian beak,
And many a reptile Jurassic,
　　And many a monster antique.

Ere Man was developed, our brother,
10　　We swam and we ducked and we dived,
And we dined, as a rule, on each other –
　　What matter, the toughest survived.
Our paddles were fins, and they bore us

Ballad of the Ichthyosaurus. *Title.*] Ichthyosaurus (literally: fish-lizard) is an extinct marine reptile which characterised the Mesozoic period, the third of the great eras into which geological time is divided. It comes after the Palaeozoic period, and consists of the Triassic, Jurassic and Cretaceous periods, and extends from 245 to 66.4 million years ago. Nearly complete skeletons, discovered as fossils, are now in the British Museum, London.

Subtitle. the Higher Life] The capitalised term 'Higher Life' may parody religious beliefs that privileged the life of the soul and mind over bodily existence. Evolutionary theory was perceived to promise progress, not merely change, and in this respect did not automatically preclude adherents of religious faiths. The theorist who seems most pertinent here is Robert Chambers (1802–1871), who anonymously published *Vestiges of the Natural History of Creation* (1844) and its sequel (1845). Chambers believed that evolution was not determined by mechanical causes alone but by an overall design or purpose in nature: that all creation was subject to universal laws ordained by a rational Creator whose plan was evolutionary progress. In this connection, see the reference to the 'providential plan', 'Lay of the Trilobite', l. 14. Chambers devoted the second section of *Vestiges* to describing the development of plants and animals from simple to complex forms by means of transmutation. During his life Chambers was better known as a publisher; with his brother, he published *Chambers Edinburgh Journal* from 1832. The journal claimed to offer everything necessary for the education of the shopkeeper or artisan who aspired to self-improvement, an idea also echoed in Kendall's poem. (See Postlethwaite, 1988; Schwartz, 1988; and Yeo, 1984.) Alternatively, the term might be a pun on 'higher criticism', the attempt to place biblical interpretation on an objective, scientific basis. The controversy over appropriate methods of interpreting the Bible was contemporary with the debate between literalism and geological evidence, especially with respect to the understanding of Genesis.

1. a goodly Museum] the British Museum.

5–7.] The *Jurassic* series of geological strata (to the lower division of which belongs the Ichthyosaurus) comes between the *Triassic* and the more recent Cretaceous (chalky) series (see note to Title). 'Antediluvian' means: before the Flood.

Through water: in air we could fly;
15   But the brain of the Ichthyosaurus
Was never a match for his eye.

Geologists, active and eager,
Its excellence hasten to own,
And praise, with no eulogy meagre,
20   The eye that is plated with bone.
'See how, with unerring precision,
His prey through the wave he could spy.
Oh, wonderful organ of vision,
Gigantic and beautiful Eye!'

25   Then I listen in gloomy dejection,
I gaze, and I wish I could weep;
For what is mere visual perfection
To Intellect subtle and deep?
A loftier goal is before us,
30   For higher endowments we sigh.
But the brain of the Ichthyosaurus
Was never a patch on his eye!

It owned no supreme constitution,
Was shallow, and simple, and plain,
35   While mark but the fair convolution
And size of the Aryan brain.
'Tis furnished for School Board inspections,
And garnished for taking degrees,
And bulging in many directions,
40   As every phrenologist sees.

14.] 'He could not really fly. After so many millions of years, perhaps he may be excused for slipping in a matter of detail' [Author's note]. The Ichthyosaurus has two sets of paddle-like limbs.

20.] The Ichthyosaurus has enormous eyes surrounded by a ring of bony plates for protection during diving.

36. Aryan] Indo-European.

37. School Board inspections] These were instituted in government-funded schools by the Education Act of 1870.

40. phrenologist] Phrenology was the supposed science of the shape of the cranium as an indicator of mental and emotional capacities and propensities. It was at its peak in the second quarter of the nineteenth century.

Sometimes it explodes at high pressure
        Of some overwhelming demand,
But plied in unmerciful measure
        'Tis wonderful what it will stand!
45   In college, in cottage, in mansion,
        Bear witness, the girls and the boys,
How great are its powers of expansion,
        How very peculiar its joys!

Oh Brain that is bulgy with learning,
50   Oh wisdom of women and men,
Oh Maids for a First that are yearning,
        Oh youths that are lectured by Wren!
You're acquainted with Pisces and Taurus,
        And all sorts of beasts in the sky,
55   But the brain of the Ichthyosaurus
        Was never so good as his eye!

Reconstructed by Darwin or Owen,
        We dwell in sweet Bloomsbury's halls,
But we couldn't have passed Little go in
60   The Schools, we'd have floundered in Smalls!
Though so cleverly people restore us,
        We are bound to confess with a sigh
That the brain of the Ichthyosaurus
        Was *never* so good as his eye!

[1887]

---

51. *a First*] first-class honours at university; women were not admitted to degrees at London University until 1878, and at Oxford until 1920. Women were allowed to take degrees at Cambridge in 1921 but were not admitted as full members of the university until 1948.

52. *Wren*] Sir Christopher Wren (1632–1723), as well as being a famous architect, was professor of astronomy at Oxford from 1660. Perhaps used here as a 'type' of a learned Oxbridge don.

53. *Pisces and Taurus*] constellations: respectively the twelfth and second signs of the zodiac.

57. *Darwin or Owen*] Charles Darwin (1809–1882), famous for his theory of evolution as propounded in *The Origin of Species* (1859); Sir Richard Owen (1804–1892), a professor of comparative anatomy and physiology, fiercely opposed Darwin's views. Among his publications was *A History of British Fossil Reptiles* (1849–1884).

58. *sweet Bloomsbury's halls*] The British Museum is located in the area of London known as Bloomsbury.

59–60.] Colloquial names for preliminary examinations at Cambridge (*Little go*) and Oxford (*Smalls*). *The Schools* referred to the Examination Schools.

The Philanthropist and the Jelly-fish

HER beauty, passive in despair,
   Through sand and seaweed shone,
The fairest jelly-fish I e'er
   Had set mine eyes upon.

5   It would have made a stone abuse
   The callousness of fate,
This creature of prismatic hues,
   Stranded and desolate!

Musing I said: 'My mind's unstrung,
10   Joy, hope, are in their grave:
Yet ere I perish all unsung
   One jelly-fish I'll save!'

And yet I fancied I had dreamed
   Of somewhere having known
15   Or met, a jelly-fish that seemed
   As utterly alone.

But ah, if ever out to sea
   That jelly-fish I bore,
Immediately awaited me
20   A level hundred more!

I knew that it would be in vain
   To try to float them all;
And though my nature is humane,
   I *felt* that it would pall.

25   'Yet this one jelly-fish,' I cried,
   'I'll rescue if I may.
I'll wade out with her through the tide
   And leave her in the bay.'

The Philanthropist and the Jelly-fish. *7.*] The transparent jellyfish can brightly reflect varied colours under sunlight, like a glass prism.

9. unstrung] unnerved.

I paused, my feelings to control,
　　To wipe away a tear –
It seemed to me a murmur stole
　　Out of the crystal sphere.

30

She said: 'Your culture's incomplete,
　　Though your intention's kind;
The sand, the seaweed, and the heat
　　I do not really mind.

35

'To wander through the briny deep
　　I own I do not care;
I somehow seem to go to sleep
　　Here, there, or anywhere.

40

'When wild waves tossed me to and fro,
　　I never felt put out;
I never got depressed and low,
　　Or paralysed by doubt.

45

''Twas not the ocean's soothing balm.
　　Ah no, 'twas something more!
I'm just as peaceful and as calm
　　Here shrivelling on the shore.

'It does not matter what may come,
　　I'm dead to woe or bliss:
I haven't a Sensorium,
　　And that is how it is.'

50

[1887]

Woman's Future

COMPLACENT they tell us, hard hearts and derisive,
　　In vain is our ardour: in vain are our sighs:
Our intellects, bound by a limit decisive,
　　To the level of Homer's may never arise.

---

51. Sensorium] seat of nervous sensation; can be used simply to mean 'brain'.

Woman's Future. *4. Homer's*] Homer is the supposed author of two famous early Greek epics,
the *Odyssey* and the *Iliad*.

5   We heed not the falsehood, the base innuendo,
        The laws of the universe, these are our friends.
    Our talents shall rise in a mighty crescendo,
        We trust Evolution to make us amends!

    But ah, when I ask you for food that is mental,
10   My sisters, you offer me ices and tea!
    You cherish the fleeting, the mere accidental,
        At cost of the True, the Intrinsic, the Free.
    Your feelings, compressed in Society's mangle,
        Are vapid and frivolous, pallid and mean.
15 To slander you love; but you don't care to wrangle:
        You bow to Decorum, and cherish Routine.

    Alas, is it woolwork you take for your mission,
        Or Art that your fingers so gaily attack?
    Can patchwork atone for the mind's inanition?
20   Can the soul, oh my sisters, be fed on a *plaque*?
    Is this your vocation? My goal is another,
        And empty and vain is the end you pursue.
    In antimacassars the world you may smother;
        But intellect marches o'er them and o'er you.

25 On Fashion's vagaries your energies strewing,
        Devoting your days to a rug or a screen,
    Oh, rouse to a lifework – do something worth doing!
        Invent a new planet, a flying-machine.
    Mere charms superficial, mere feminine graces,
30   That fade or that flourish, no more you may prize;
    But the knowledge of Newton will beam from your faces,
        The soul of a Spencer will shine in your eyes.

8.] Darwin's evolutionary theory seemed to promise a continual path of improvement for all species.

17. woolwork] the sewing of coloured wools onto a canvas backing to form a design, as in tapestry. By this time, such trivial occupations for otherwise intelligent women were often the butt of attack.

20. plaque] Used to describe a patch in patchwork.

23. antimacassars] coverings (often embroidered) placed over chair backs to protect them from hair oil (of which 'Macassar' was a brand name).

25. vagaries] To be pronounced with stress on the second syllable, in burlesque style.

26. screen] Firescreens were often covered in woolwork.

31–2.] Sir Isaac Newton (1642–1727), philosopher and mathematician, famous for formulating the laws of gravity; Herbert Spencer (1820–1903), the founder of what has been called 'evolutionary philosophy'.

ENVOY

Though jealous exclusion may tremble to own us,
    Oh, wait for the time when our brains shall expand!
35   When once we're enthroned, you shall never dethrone us –
    The poets, the sages, the seers of the land!

[1887]

Ballad of the Cadger

REMEMBER the old hawker
    With trumpery tin ware,
Brooches and pins, and medals
    Containing the Lord's Prayer?

5   For an ideal vagrant
    He would not be one's choice.
He had a leer rapacious,
    And a discordant voice.

I've sometimes spoken with him
10   As he his medals cried,
When for his scanty guerdon
    He trudged along Cheapside.

'Philanthropy, they call it,
    Is all the rage,' said he,
15   'But bless your 'art, the gentry
    'Ud never look at me!

'They wants a blooming orphan,
    Blue eyes and yaller curls,
Or they wants a wasted widder,
20   Or half-starved sewing girls.

ENVOY] i.e. concluding stanza, containing an address to the reader. (Such formality is here being mocked, of course.)

Ballad of the Cadger. *Title.*] A *cadger* is a street-seller or hawker.

2. *trumpery*] worthless, trashy.

11. *guerdon*] reward (poetical).

12. *Cheapside*] In the middle of the nineteenth century, Cheapside in east London rivalled the West End as a major shopping centre.

19. *wasted widder*] starving widow.

'They likes their money's vally,
    It isn't in their beat
To look at an old cadger
    Goes hawking on the street.

25   ' "Go down among the masses!"
    Why, every blessed toff –
It isn't *us* he cares for,
    It's showing hisself off!'

But one day – with his burden
30   He scarce had strength to pace –
He fell, and all the trinkets
    Scattered about the place.

And we knew the end was nearing
    To his life of wants and lies;
35 But we raised him from the pavement,
    And we carried him to Guy's.

Then there hurried to his bedside
    A curate white and spare;
And he looked a poor fanatic,
40   But he was strong in prayer.

For he prayed for this our brother
    Who had so little chance,
Because of want and training
    And adverse circumstance.

45   And he wasn't hard upon him,
    He knew what he'd gone through;
But he prayed as if he meant it,
    As if God meant it too!

---

21. vally] value.

22. in their beat] part of their programme.

26. toff] one of the well-to-do.

36. Guy's] Guy's Hospital, founded by Thomas Guy, opened in 1726 in St Thomas's Street, east London.

And then the pallid curate,
50   Knowing a sign sufficed,
Said, 'raise your hand, my brother,
    If you believe in Christ!'

Then over the hawker's features
    A smile of cunning broke,
55 And his hands seemed groping after
    The medals as he spoke:

'*The Bulwarks of Religion,*
    Penny complete, all there!
Together on a farthing,
60   *The Creed and the Lord's Prayer!'*

[1887]

The Last Performance

THE last time the curtain arises
    On two hours of bliss unalloyed.
My rival his mischief devises –
    What matter? his treachery's void.
5 I scorn him: I know whose the prize is.

I, seeming foredoomed to confusion,
    And he, with so many a spell –
Who would have believed the conclusion?
    'Twas I that she loved passing well.
10 She loved *me* – no idle delusion.

Why, I could have pitied his sinning
    That left me so utterly blest;
And I had small claim to the winning
    Except to have loved her the best,
15 In truth, from the very beginning.

57.] Likely to be the title of a tract or evangelical hymn. *The Bulwarks of Protestantism* by Hugh Stowell Brown (1823–1886) was published in Manchester in 1868.

The Last Performance. *Title.*] i.e. the last stage performance. Here, it is evidently a comedy that has revolved around the conventional triangle of: heroine, hero, villain. The speaker is the hero. In real life the outcome is reversed – the actress who plays the heroine is really in love with the actor who plays the villain.

Two hours! and the comedy's ended
    That gave me the touch of her lips:
While it lasted, the rapture was splendid,
    A glory well worth the eclipse,
20   Like Fate, when the curtain descended.

And Fate leaves the villain in clover,
    The villain who fled in his rage;
And I, the poor fortunate lover,
    Am standing alone on the stage;
25   And all the performance is over.

[1887]

Church Echoes

1. Vicar's Daughter

Down in the depths of this fair church –
A man may find them if he search,
There lie six pews that are called Free,
And there the strange Bohemians be.
5   (Have mercy upon them, miserable offenders.)

We Philistines in cushioned pews
Have prayer-books more than we can use.
They have one prayer-book that they share.
They do not kneel: they sit and stare.
10   (Have mercy upon them, miserable offenders.)

Decorously we meet their view
As if they were an empty pew.
We are above them and beyond,
And reverently we respond.
15   (Have mercy upon them, miserable offenders.)

Church Echoes. 3.] Well-to-do local families would subscribe a certain amount to the church and have the best pews set aside for their exclusive use. The remainder were 'free' pews for anybody to use.

4. Bohemians] gypsies, or social outcasts of some description.

5.] A (mis)quotation from The Book of Common Prayer: 'But thou, O Lord, have mercy upon us miserable offenders'.

6. Philistines] originally, the name of a warlike people of ancient Palestine who harassed the Israelites; later, a term of contempt for ignorant, uncultured people. The term was popularised in England by Matthew Arnold's usage of it in Culture and Anarchy (1869). See also note to ll. 4–5 of Menken's 'Judith', p. 171 above.

2. Charity Child

The Vicar's daughters look so good,
We think that they are made of wood.
Like rests for hymn-books, there they stand,
With each a hymn-book in her hand.

20   Half through the sermon once we tried
To hold our eyelids open wide,
That we might know if they *could* keep
Awake, or sometimes went to sleep.

It was no use, we may be wrong.
25   The Vicar preached so very long;
And keep awake we never could –
We *think* that they are made of wood.

3. Tramp

Hardly includes us in its glance
The Vicar's glassy countenance:
30   The Verger with superior eyes
Surveys us in a still surprise.

But when the organ's notes begin
I heed not any Philistine:
To hear the music is my bliss;
35   And I'm at home where music is.

Through ranks of aliens to and fro
I see the true musician go.
So dim their eyes, they cannot trace
The light unknown upon his face.

40   Here week by week I come, and see
No hand stretched out to welcome me;
And I am in a friendless land –
But music takes me by the hand.

[1887]

Subtitle: Charity Child] a child, usually orphaned, who was raised in the poorhouse.
23.] 'For if they can go to sleep they are *not* made of wood' [Author's note].
30. Verger] attendant who takes care of the church interior.

Failures

AND you have failed, O Poet? Sad!
  Yet failures are a commonplace.
Boast not as though you only had
  Secured a failure in the race.
5 You see them thick on every hand
    As blackberries; but you, you say,
Because your nature was so grand,
    Have failed in a peculiar way.

You weep: 'I had such lofty aims.
10   My soul had yearnings truly great.
Than broken altars, dying flames,
  I had deserved a better fate.
And others gain my heart's desire
    They win the prize I vainly crave;
15 And they will set the Thames on fire
    When I am mouldering in my grave.'

What matter, yet? The years of blight
    The fair and laughing seasons bring
And if you flee or if you fight,
20   It is a very little thing.
Small anguish have *you* undergone,
    Poor fool, to write, with careful art,
Your melancholy sonnets on,
    When some, to fail, would break the heart!

25 Go, look into some dingy street
    Your mood aesthetic scorns to pace.
Mark well the throng; you will not meet
    One happy or one careless face.
Have these not failed, on whom the rain
30   Strikes cheerless from the sky of grey?
No lurking comfort in their pain
    Of subtle self-esteem have they.

Failures. *15.*] i.e. become famous for something extraordinary (proverbial).

17–18.] See Genesis 41, in which Joseph interprets Pharaoh's dreams to signify seven years of plenty followed by seven years of famine.

26. mood aesthetic] The notion of 'the aesthete' gained currency in the late 1870s and early 1880s; it denoted those who regarded themselves as having a superior appreciation of things beautiful, and was satirised, for example, in Gilbert and Sullivan's comic operetta *Patience* (1881).

They live their wasted lives, and die,
    Nor much their destiny bewail,
35   While you to all the world must cry:
    'Alas, but see how *I* can fail!
Compassionate my fruitless tears,
    Peruse the volume of my woes,
The burden of my blighted years,
40   In metre some, and some in prose!'

You fail? Then take it at the worst.
    Shall some not gloriously succeed?
Ah, waive awhile your lot accurst,
    To triumph in a noble deed!
45   Nay, but you grudge the victory,
    Nor heed how the hard fight prevailed.
Through Time's exulting harmony
    You shriek, 'Alas, *but I have failed!'*

[1887]

The Sandblast Girl and the Acid Man

Of all the cities far and wide,
    The city that I most prefer,
Though hardly through the fog descried,
    Is Muggy Manchester.
5   Of all its buildings the most dear,
    I find a stained glass factory –
Because the sandblast girl works here,
    In the same room with me!

---

37. Compassionate] Have pity on.

The Sandblast Girl and the Acid Man. *Title.*] Refers to the manufacturing process for a certain type of decorative glass. In the sandblast process, the surface of the glass is exposed to a stream of sharp sand driven by compressed air. In the etching process, hydrofluoric acid is allowed to eat into the surface. Both methods rely on protecting those parts of the surface which are not to be marked, thus forming the pattern. Both were cheaper – and less artistically valued – than engraving on glass.

4. Muggy Manchester] major industrial city of northern England, known for its unhealthy humid atmosphere, polluted by factory smoke. It was the model for Milton in Elizabeth Gaskell's novel *North and South* (1855) as well as for Coketown in Charles Dickens's *Hard Times* (1854).

It made a most terrific din,
    Of yore, that sandblasting machine,
I cursed the room I laboured in,
    And all the dull routine,
And the *old* sandblast girl, who broke,
    Of coloured glass, so many a sheet,
In fruitless efforts to evoke
    Tracery clear and neat.

That sandblast girl, at last she left –
    They couldn't let her blunders pass.
But Maggie's hands are slim and deft,
    They never break the glass!
From ruby, orange, or from blue,
    The letters stand out clear as pearl.
The fellows say they never knew
    So smart a sandblast girl!

I raise my eyes: I see her stand,
    A sheet of glass her arms embrace;
Out spurts the narrow stream of sand
    On each uncovered space,
Till perfectly the work is done,
    And clear again grows Maggie's brow –
Till a fresh labour is begun,
    She's merely human, now!

And sometimes when her hands are free,
    While with my acid still I work,
She'll give a hasty glance at me,
    Embossing like a Turk.
Her pretty hair so soft and brown
    Is coiled about her shapely head,
And I look up and she looks down,
    And both of us go red!

She has a dress of navy blue,
    A turn-down collar, white and clean
As though no smoke it travelled through,

---

36. like a Turk] i.e. with frenetic energy.

And smuts had never seen.
45   I've noticed that white snowdrops bells
        Have a peculiar look of her!
And nothing but her pallor tells
        Of Muggy Manchester.

Just twenty shillings every week!
50   And always somebody distressed
Wants helping; and you feel a sneak
        If you don't do your best.
Suppose that I began to hoard,
        And steeled my heart, my coffer hid,
55 I wonder if I could afford
        To – Would she, if I did?

She has a mother to support,
        And I've a sister. Trade's not brisk,
And for a working man, in short,
60   Life is a fearful risk.
The Clarion I sometimes read,
        I muse upon in winter nights,
I wonder if they'll e'er succeed
        In putting things to rights!

65   I'm vastly better off than some!
        I think of how the many fare
Who perish slowly, crushed and dumb,
        For leisure, food and air.
'Tis hard, in Freedom's very van,
70   To live and die a luckless churl.
'Tis hard to be an acid man,
        Without a sandblast girl!

[1894]

---

54. *coffer*] money-box.

61. The Clarion] a socialist weekly which was published between 1891 and 1932.

69. *van*] foremost division.

70. *churl*] low-bred fellow.

Underground

(The PORTER speaks.)

A QUARTER of an hour to wait,
    And quite sufficient too,
Since your remarks on Bishopsgate
    Impress the mind as true,
5   Unless you work here soon and late,
    Till 'tis like home to you.

You see, a chap stands what he must,
    He'll hang on anywhere;
He'll learn to live on smoke and dust,
10   Though 'tisn't healthy fare.
We're used to breathing grime in, just
    Like you to breathing air.

And yet 'tis odd to think these trains,
    In half an hour, maybe,
15   Will be right out among green lanes,
    Where the air is pure and free.
Well, sir, There's Bishopsgate remains
    For us, and here are we!

Your train. First class, sir. That's your style!
20   In future, I'll be bound,
You'll stick to hansoms, since you'd spile
    Here in the Undergound.
I've got to wait a little while
    Before *my* train comes round.

[1894]

Underground. *Title.*] Construction of the first underground railway in London began in the 1850s with the Metropolitan line, which travelled partly under and partly above ground.

3. Bishopsgate] Bishopsgate was mentioned in the *City Medical Reports* of 1849 and 1850 as a particularly unhealthy part of the city, distinguished by its cramped and crowded dwellings, poor ventilation and pollution.

21. hansoms] Hansom cabs were horse-drawn vehicles available for hire on the street, the precursor of modern taxicabs.   *spile*] spoil or turn rotten, like a vegetable. The pronunciation represents the London working-class (Cockney) accent.

In the Toy Shop

THE child had longings all unspoken –
　　She was a naughty child.
She had 'a will that must be broken';
　　Her brothers drove her wild.
5　She read the tale, but skipped the moral.
　　She thought: 'One *might* be good,
If one could never scream and quarrel,
　　If one were only wood!'

Meanwhile the doll: 'Ah, fatal chasm!
10　　Although I've real curls,
I am not made of protoplasm,
　　Like other little girls.
You see on every wooden feature
　　My animation's nil.
15　How nice to be a human creature,
　　Get cross, and have a will!'

And what may be the real issue
　　There's none hath understood;
But some of us are nervous tissue,
20　　And some of us are wood.
And some to suffering, striving wildly,
　　Are never quite resigned;
While we of wood yet murmur mildly
　　At being left behind.

[1894]

In the Toy Shop. *11. protoplasm*] a substance constituting the physical basis of life in all plants and animals.

AMY LEVY (1861–1889)

Amy Levy was an Anglo-Jewish poet and novelist who published three volumes of poetry as well as three novels and a number of essays and short stories before her tragically early death by suicide during a bout of depression just before her 28th birthday. She grew up in a close-knit Jewish family that had been settled in England for some time, and she was born and spent most of her life in London. Exceptionally intelligent, she was given an education that was highly unusual for a girl at that time, being sent first to a girls' boarding school and then in 1879 to Newnham College, Cambridge. The university had only recently opened its doors to women, who were still not allowed to take a degree. However, it appears that Levy's family was comfortably well-off, and although she was to make a certain amount from publishing her writing, her main goal in studying at Cambridge seems to have been the further access it gave her to a classical education, rather than fitting her for a career, say, in teaching.

She began writing early, publishing her first volume, *Xantippe and Other Verse*, in 1881. The title poem, a substantial dramatic monologue from the viewpoint of the much-maligned wife of Socrates, gives early evidence of Levy's powers, being witty, skilful with language, iconoclastic and unsentimental. At this stage, Levy's work indicates a strong feminist sympathy for oppressed women, also apparent in another early piece, 'Run to Death', a narrative poem on the rather horrifying subject of a group of aristocrats hunting a gypsy woman for sport (see the first poem reproduced below, p. 334). Later, her writing tended to shy away from any direct engagement with what might be construed as political issues, being more concerned to explore the ambiguities as well as inequalities of gender, and to focus on the universal theme of the modern poet as an alienated soul, acutely aware of the meaninglessness of life's diurnal round.

Levy was among the first generation of women to enjoy the social freedom to live a comparatively independent existence as a single person. Her life in college at university prepared her for a new mobility previously unavailable to respectable middle-class women. She was able to travel about London on her own (see her comic poem 'Ballade of an Omnibus', p. 346 below), visiting her friends (mainly other like-minded, educated women) or going to the British Museum to read and study in the library there. She was also able to travel on the Continent in the company of a female friend, and she set one of her novels, *Miss Meredith* (1889), in Florence, where she spent some time on more than one occasion, and where she met the famous Vernon Lee (pseudonym of Violet Paget, 1856–1935) writer, philosopher and art historian. Lee was a well-known novelist, critic and aesthetician, who had had an early success with the publication of her book *Studies of the Eighteenth Century in Italy* (1880) and, with her austere manner and rather insensitive acute intelligence, had become something of a cult figure for female artists and intellectuals. She lived near Florence with her mother and invalid brother, conducted discreet romantic relationships with other women, and made frequent trips to England. Levy seems to have fallen in love with Lee, but sadly, as apparently with all of her subsequent romantic attachments (all for women), her feelings were not reciprocated.[1] Whether Levy constantly made bad choices in love, or whether there were special difficulties for her in being not only lesbian but also Jewish, and therefore, in some sense, foreign to her English friends, and unrecognised in Jewish circles, we cannot know, but her increasing bouts of severe depression cannot have been helped by her inability to find a partner.

That Levy did feel somewhat alienated from English society, despite being non-religious, and a so-called 'assimilated' Jew, becomes very clear when we read her poetry, particularly those pieces that treat the subject of 'otherness', like 'Run to Death' and 'Medea'. Yet she could not draw any particular comfort from her Judaism either, as its spiritual side held no meaning for her. Like Mathilde Blind, Constance Naden and May Kendall, Levy was certainly one of the new breed of post-Darwinian atheists, which in her case contributed to a modernist sense of social alienation. She did, however, care deeply about the art and craft of writing, and her poetry shows a remarkable level of restraint and sophistication in its adroit manipulation of language. Her detached, ironic lyric voice is distinctive, and separates her from other, more sentimental, poets of melancholy. She admired the German poet Heine and translated some of his work, and shares with him the ability to mingle comedy with sadness in a sudden unexpected turn to a verse, while avoiding unnecessary pathos. It is her keen sense of humour that lightens her work, which would otherwise be totally suffused with melancholy.

Levy was very conscious of herself as a poet of the urban environment, and in this she again shows herself different from many of the other poets in this volume. Women poets in particular were expected to adhere to the convention that their verse should be a kind of pastoral celebration, that a sensitivity to nature was an acceptable female trait. Levy instead chose to celebrate the sturdy London plane-tree (see p. 346) with which she clearly identifies in the poem of that name (also, rather defiantly perhaps, chosen as the title of her last, posthumously published, collection). Like the image she projects of this hardy tree, wrapped in fog and smoke but still loving the town, her poetry feels most at home in a London streetscape, whether it be a square in Bloomsbury (where she spent the last part of her life), or a street in the East End, where she quirkily sets one of her love lyrics ('In the Mile End Road', p. 348).

Comparing Levy's poem 'Magdalen' (see p. 337) with poems on the same theme (that of the 'fallen woman') by other poets in this volume – Webster's 'A Castaway', Blind's 'The Message', Rossetti's 'Maude Clare' – it is Levy's and Rossetti's which are least concerned with the 'social problem' aspect of the topic, and which also present an unbroken defiance of the temptation to repent. Levy's poem, however, unlike Rossetti's more emblematic ballad, goes further than a defiance of social convention. It represents the protagonist as actually relishing her sexual experience, and regarding the trappings of an enforced penitence (presumably in some kind of religious penitentiary similar to the one Rossetti worked in at Highgate) as a fair price

[1] There are letters from Levy to Lee in the Vernon Lee collection at Colby College, Maine.

to pay for 'such bliss' as she enjoyed in love-making. That Levy was strongly aware of the urgent power of bodily desire is further evidenced in the highly charged erotic language of two of her love lyrics printed here – 'Sinfonia Eroica' (one of her finest poems; see p. 336) and 'The First Extra' (p. 352). Both of these poems use the trope of musical ecstasy to portray a moment of orgasmic experience in acceptable terms; both emphasise the simultaneous pain and rapture of unrequited desire, making the orgasmic experience simultaneously onanistically fulfilling and piercingly empty. In 'The First Extra', a deceptively simple little poem which beautifully imitates the swing and sway of a waltz rhythm, the hints of the end of love (the rose fallen from her head unheedingly crushed beneath his feet) precede the orgasmic climax of the last stanza, almost as its precondition:

> O swing, and sway, and swing,
> And rise, and sink, and fall!
> There is no bliss like unto this,
> This is the best of all.
>
> (ll. 13–16)

Clearly Levy was strongly drawn to music:

> Slow on the waiting air swell'd forth a sound
> So wondrous sweet that each man held his breath
>
> (Sinfonia Eroica, ll. 25–6)

– all the more poignant, then, that she was troubled throughout her twenties with increasing deafness. It cannot have helped her tendency to depression. Her inner ear remained strong, however, and she rarely makes an error in her own musical arrangements: her lyric poems. Levy is not drawn to the sonnet form like other women poets of the period, but she does prefer to use rhyme as well as regular metric patterns in her shorter verse, often deploying these with great skill and subtlety. 'Xantippe' and 'Medea' – the first, a substantial dramatic monologue, the second, a drama – both use blank verse. 'Medea', too lengthy to reproduce here, is a particularly powerful poem which has links to Menken's 'Judith' in its defiance of patriarchal law about female submissiveness. In it, Levy figures Medea as a lonely dark spirit, abused and shamefully neglected by her ungrateful husband, driven to infanticide by his public humiliation of her. There is a strong temptation for the reader to infer a reference to Levy's own alienated position as a Jewess living in an apparently civilised, tolerant and friendly but really deeply suspicious and hostile environment whose citizens fail to understand her and are quick to condemn what they cannot appreciate.

In 1888, Levy published her finest novel, *Reuben Sachs*, in which she openly criticised many aspects of the conservative, materialistic and mysogynist Anglo-Jewish society of her own upbringing. It received devastating reviews, particularly from within the Jewish community, and was generally misread and misunderstood as anti-Semitic. In view of all the accumulated evidence – her unhappy love life, her deafness, her lack of appreciation by the critics, and, above all, her tendency to severe depression – it is perhaps not altogether surprising that Amy Levy decided to take her own life (she inhaled the fumes of a charcoal stove). One week earlier, she had corrected proofs for her last book of poems, *A London Plane-Tree* (1889).

Text: Poems chosen are from *Xantippe and Other Verse* (1881), *A Minor Poet and Other Verse* (1884; 2nd edn, with portrait and additional poems reprinted from *Xantippe and Other Verse*, 1891), *A London Plane-Tree and Other Verse* (1889), and *A Ballad of Religion and Marriage* (1915). In each case, the copy-text is the first edition, with the exception of *A Minor Poet and Other Verse*, for which the second edition has been used. Dates of first publication in volume form are shown in square brackets at the foot of each poem.

Run to Death

A True Incident of Pre-Revolutionary French History.

Now the lovely autumn morning breathes its freshness in earth's face,
In the crowned castle courtyard the blithe horn proclaims the chase;
And the ladies on the terrace smile adieux with rosy lips
To the huntsmen disappearing down the cedar-shaded groves,
5   Wafting delicate aromas from their scented finger tips,
And the gallants wave in answer, with their gold-embroidered gloves.
On they rode, past bush and bramble, on they rode, past elm and oak;
And the hounds, with anxious nostril, sniffed the heather-scented air,
Till at last, within his stirrups, up Lord Gaston rose, and spoke –
10   He, the boldest and the bravest of the wealthy nobles there
'Friends,' quoth he, 'the time hangs heavy, for it is not as we thought,
And these woods, tho' fair and shady, will afford, I fear, no sport.
Shall we hence, then, worthy kinsmen, and desert the hunter's track
For the chateau, where the wine cup and the dice cup tempt us back?'
15   'Ay,' the nobles shout in chorus; 'Ay,' the powder'd lacquey cries;
Then they stop with eager movement, reining in quite suddenly;
Peering down with half contemptuous, half with wonder-opened eyes
At a 'something' which is crawling, with slow step, from tree to tree.
Is't some shadow phantom ghastly? No, a woman and a child,

Run to Death] It has not been possible to trace the source for this poem. It is likely that it refers to the reign of Louis XV (1715–1774), who was known for his indifference to most matters, with the significant exceptions of his mistresses and hunting. During his rule he enlarged the hunting grounds of the French kings. Known as 'the Great Hunter', Louis XV's passion for the gratuitous pursuit of hunting (as opposed to the 'appropriate' pursuit of war) earned him a reputation for violence. In 1720, also during Louis XV's reign, severe steps were taken to repress homeless people and beggars and a number of these people were killed. This poem gives a new twist to Tennyson's complacent line in *The Princess* (1847): 'Man is the hunter: woman is his game' (V, l. 147).

2. *crowned*] castellated. Should be stressed on the second syllable: crownéd.

3. *adieux*] goodbyes (Fr.).

15. *powder'd lacquey*] a footman wearing hair powder.

20 Swarthy woman, with the 'gipsy' written clear upon her face;
    Gazing round her with her wide eyes dark, and shadow-fringed, and
        wild,
    With the cowed suspicious glances of a persecuted race.
    Then they all, with unasked question, in each other's faces peer,
    For a common thought has struck them, one their lips dare scarcely
        say, –
25 Till Lord Gaston cries, impatient, 'Why regret the stately deer
    When such sport as yonder offers? quick! unleash the dogs – away!'
    Then they breath'd a shout of cheering, grey-haired man and
        stripling boy,
    And the gipsy, roused to terror, stayed her step, and turned her
        head –
    Saw the faces of those huntsmen, lit with keenest cruel joy –
30 Sent a cry of grief to Heaven, closer clasped her child, and fled!

    O ye nobles of the palace! O ye gallant-hearted lords!
    Who would stoop for Leila's kerchief, or for Clementina's gloves,
    Who would rise up all indignant, with your shining sheathless
        swords,
    At the breathing of dishonour to your languid lady loves!
35 O, I tell you, daring nobles, with your beauty-loving stare,
    Who ne'er long the coy coquetting of the courtly dames withstood,
    Tho' a woman be the lowest, and the basest, and least fair,
    In your manliness forget not to respect her womanhood,
    And thou, gipsy, that hast often the pursuer fled before,
40 That hast felt ere this the shadow of dark death upon thy brow,
    That hast hid among the mountains, that hast roamed the forest o'er,
    Bred to hiding, watching, fleeing, may thy speed avail thee now!

    Still she flees, and ever fiercer tear the hungry hounds behind,
    Still she flees, and ever faster follow there the huntsmen on,
45 Still she flees, her black hair streaming in a fury to the wind,
    Still she flees, tho' all the glimmer of a happy hope is gone.
    'Eh? what? baffled by a woman! Ah, *sapristi!* she can run!'

---

27. *stripling boy*] youth.

31–4.] There is a satirical echo here of Burke's famous paean to Marie Antoinette in *Reflections on the Revolution in France* (1790): 'little did I dream that I should have lived to see disasters fallen upon her in a nation of gallant men, in a nation of men of honour, and of cavaliers. I thought ten thousand swords must have leaped from their scabbards to avenge even a look that threatened her with insult. But the age of chivalry is gone.'

47. sapristi] Euphemism for 'sacristi': 'Good God!', 'damnation!' (Fr.).

Should she 'scape us, it would crown us with dishonour and disgrace;
It is time' (Lord Gaston shouted) 'such a paltry chase were done!'
50　And the fleeter grew her footsteps, so the hotter grew the chase –
Ha! at last! the dogs are on her! will she struggle ere she dies?
See! she holds her child above her, all forgetful of *her* pain,
While a hundred thousand curses shoot out darkly from her eyes,
And a hundred thousand glances of the bitterest disdain.
55　Ha! the dogs are pressing closer! they have flung her to the ground;
Yet her proud lips never open with the dying sinner's cry –
Till at last, unto the Heavens, just two fearful shrieks resound,
When the soul is all forgotten in the body's agony!
Let them rest there, child and mother, in the shadow of the oak,
60　On the tender mother-bosom of that earth from which they came.
As they slow rode back those huntsmen neither laughed, nor sang,
　　nor spoke,
Hap, there lurked unowned within them throbbings of a secret shame.
But before the flow'ry terrace, where the ladies smiling sat,
With their graceful nothings trifling all the weary time away,
65　Low Lord Gaston bowed, and raising high his richly 'broider'd hat,
'Fairest ladies, give us welcome! 'Twas a famous hunt to-day.'
1876

[1881]

Sinfonia Eroica

(To Sylvia.)

My Love, my Love, it was a day in June,
A mellow, drowsy, golden afternoon;
And all the eager people thronging came
To that great hall, drawn by the magic name
5　Of one, a high magician, who can raise
The spirits of the past and future days,
And draw the dreams from out the secret breast,
Giving them life and shape.

---

62. Hap] Short for haply: perhaps.

Sinfonia Eroica *Title.*] i.e. the Heroic Symphony, nickname given to Beethoven's third sympathy, in E. flat (1803–4), reputedly dedicated initially to Napoleon. In this instance, Levy might be playing on the similarity of sound between 'eroica' and 'erotic'.

Subtitle.] *Sylvia* was virtually a generic name in traditional poetry for a female beloved. The poem's speaker is, of course, assumed to be male.

I, with the rest,
Sat there athirst, atremble for the sound;
10   And as my aimless glances wandered round,
Far off, across the hush'd, expectant throng,
I saw your face that fac'd mine.
Clear and strong
Rush'd forth the sound, a mighty mountain stream;
Across the clust'ring heads mine eyes did seem
15   By subtle forces drawn, your eyes to meet.
Then you, the melody, the summer heat,
Mingled in all my blood and made it wine.
Straight I forgot the world's great woe and mine;
My spirit's murky lead grew molten fire;
Despair itself was rapture.
20   <center>Ever higher,</center>
Stronger and clearer rose the mighty strain;
Then sudden fell; then all was still again,
And I sank back, quivering as one in pain.
Brief was the pause; then, 'mid a hush profound,
25   Slow on the waiting air swell'd forth a sound
So wondrous sweet that each man held his breath;
A measur'd, mystic melody of death.
Then back you lean'd your head, and I could note
The upward outline of your perfect throat;
30   And ever, as the music smote the air,
Mine eyes from far held fast your body fair.
And in that wondrous moment seem'd to fade
My life's great woe, and grow an empty shade
Which had not been, nor was not.
And I knew
35   Not which was sound, and which, O Love, was you.

[1884]

Magdalen

ALL things I can endure, save one.
The bare, blank room where is no sun;

Magdalen. *Title.*] Originally a reference to the Mary Magdalene who was a disciple of Christ, 'Magdalen' became a generic term for a fallen woman, in some cases signifying a prostitute. Here, the speaker seems to be located in a religious penitentiary for unwed mothers.

The parcelled hours; the pallet hard;
The dreary faces here within;
The outer women's cold regard;
The Pastor's iterated 'sin'; –
These things could I endure, and count
No overstrain'd, unjust amount;
No undue payment for such bliss –
Yea, all things bear, save only this:
That you, who knew what thing would be,
Have wrought this evil unto me.
It is so strange to think on still –
That you, that *you* should do me ill!
Not as one ignorant or blind,
But seeing clearly in your mind
How this must be which now has been,
Nothing aghast at what was seen.
Now that the tale is told and done,
It is so strange to think upon.

You were so tender with me, too!
One summer's night a cold blast blew,
Closer about my throat you drew
The half-slipt shawl of dusky blue.
And once my hand, on a summer's morn,
I stretched to pluck a rose; a thorn
Struck through the flesh and made it bleed
(A little drop of blood indeed!)
Pale grew your cheek; you stoopt and bound
Your handkerchief about the wound;
Your voice came with a broken sound;
With the deep breath your breast was riven;
I wonder, did God laugh in Heaven?

3. *parcelled hours*] hours divided among set activities, as in the strict routine of conventual life. *pallet*] rough bed or mattress stuffed with straw.

5. *outer women's*] A reference to visitors on charitable missions.

6. *iterated*] repeatedly asserted.

9. *such bliss*] i.e. the bliss of sexual fulfilment.

11–12.] You (i.e. the man) who, unlike the female speaker, had prior knowledge of the consequences of sexual activity, yet still proceeded, to her downfall. It is not made clear in the poem (although strongly hinted at) that the woman has borne an illegitimate child.

26. *a rose; a thorn*] A rose traditionally symbolises sexual desire; thorns are the punishment.

How strange, that *you* should work my woe!
35   How strange! I wonder, do you know
How gladly, gladly I had died
(And life was very sweet that tide)
To save you from the least, light ill?
How gladly I had borne your pain.
40   With one great pulse we seem'd to thrill, –
Nay, but we thrill'd with pulses twain.

Even if one had told me this,
'A poison lurks within your kiss,
Gall that shall turn to night his day:'
45   Thereon I straight had turned away –
Ay, tho' my heart had crack'd with pain –
And never kiss'd your lips again.

At night, or when the daylight nears,
I hear the other women weep;
50   My own heart's anguish lies too deep
For the soft rain and pain of tears.
I think my heart has turn'd to stone,
A dull, dead weight that hurts my breast;
Here, on my pallet-bed alone,
55   I keep apart from all the rest.
Wide-eyed I lie upon my bed,
I often cannot sleep all night;
The future and the past are dead,
There is no thought can bring delight.
60   All night I lie and think and think;
If my heart were not made of stone,
But flesh and blood, it needs must shrink
Before such thoughts. Was ever known
A woman with a heart of stone?

65   The doctor says that I shall die.
It may be so, yet what care I?
Endless reposing from the strife?
Death do I trust no more than life.

---

37. tide] short for the medieval term 'summer-tide', meaning summer-time.
44. Gall] An intensely bitter substance.
45. straight] straight away, immediately.

For one thing is like one arrayed,
70   And there is neither false nor true;
But in a hideous masquerade
All things dance on, the ages through.
And good is evil, evil good;
Nothing is known or understood
75   Save only Pain. I have no faith
In God or Devil, Life or Death.

The doctor says that I shall die.
You, that I knew in days gone by,
I fain would see your face once more,
80   Con well its features o'er and o'er;
And touch your hand and feel your kiss,
Look in your eyes and tell you this:
That all is done, that I am free;
That you, through all eternity,
85   Have neither part nor lot in me.

[1884]

Christopher Found

I

At last; so this is you, my dear!
How should I guess to find you here?
So long, so long, I sought in vain
In many cities, many lands,
5   With straining eyes and groping hands;
The people marvelled at my pain.
They said: 'But sure, the woman's mad;
What ails her, we should like to know,
That she should be so wan and sad,
10   And silent through the revels go?'

---

69. *arrayed*] dressed or decked out.

80. *Con*] Study so closely as to commit to memory.

84–5.] Possibly an oblique reference to the death of her child, as well as to the fact that she has freed herself from loving him.

Christopher Found. *10. revels*] lively and noisy festivities.

They clacked with such a sorry stir!
Was I to tell? were they to know
That I had lost you, Christopher?
Will you forgive me for one thing?
15 Whiles, when a stranger came my way,
My heart would beat and I would say:
'Here's Christopher!' – then lingering
With longer gaze, would turn away
Cold, sick at heart. My dear, I know
20 You will forgive me for this thing.
It is so very long ago
Since I have seen your face – till now;
Now that I see it – lip and brow,
Eyes, nostril, chin, alive and clear;
25 Last time was long ago; I know
This thing you will forgive me, dear.

II

There is no Heaven – this is the best;
O hold me closer to your breast;
Let your face lean upon my face,
30 That there no longer shall be space
Between our lips, between our eyes.
I feel your bosom's fall and rise.
O hold me near and yet more near;
Ah sweet; I wonder do you know
35 How lone and cold, how sad and drear,
Was I a little while ago;
Sick of the stress, the strife, the stir;
But I have found you, Christopher.

III

If only you had come before!
40 (This is the thing I most deplore)
A seemlier woman you had found,
More calm, by courtesies more bound,
Less quick to greet you, more subdued
Of appetite; of slower mood.

11.] They chattered with such a distressing commotion.
15. Whiles] During that time.
41. seemlier] either: handsomer; or: more in conformity with good taste.

341

45   But ah! you come so late, so late!
                 This time of day I can't pretend
                 With slight, sweet things to satiate
                 The hunger-cravings. Nay, my friend,
                 I cannot blush and turn and tremble,
50   Wax loth as younger maidens do.
                 Ah, Christopher, with you, with you,
                 You would not wish me to dissemble?

IV

                 So long have all the days been meagre,
                 With empty platter, empty cup,
55   No meats nor sweets to do me pleasure,
                 That if I crave – is it over-eager,
                 The deepest draught, the fullest measure,
                 The beaker to the brim poured up?

V

                 Shelley, that sprite from the spheres above,
60   Says, and would make the matter clear,
                 That love divided is larger love; –
                 We'll leave those things to the bards, my dear.
                 For you never wrote a verse, you see;
                 And I – my verse is not fair nor new.
65   Till the world be dead, you shall love but me,
                 Till the stars have ceased, I shall love but you.

EPILOGUE

                 Thus ran the words; or rather, thus did run
                 Their purport. Idly seeking in the chest
                 (You see it yonder), I had found them there:

---

50. *Wax loth*] Appear to become unwilling.

52. *dissemble*] pretend.

53. *meagre*] bare, thin.

59–61. *Shelley*] Percy Bysshe Shelley (1792–1822), Romantic poet. By the later part of the nine-teenth century, he was very much seen in these ethereal terms. See the passage from his 'Epipsychidion' (1821) beginning: 'True love in this differs from gold and clay, / That to divide is not to take away' (ll. 160–1).

68. *purport*] meaning.

70   Some blotted sheets of paper in a case,
     With a woman's name writ on it: 'Adelaide.'
     Twice on the writing there was scored the date
     Of ten years back; and where the words had end
     Was left a space, a dash, a half-writ word,
75   As tho' the writer minded, presently
     The matter to pursue.
                    I questioned her,
     That worthy, worthy soul, my châtelaine,
     Who, nothing loth, made answer.
                              There had been
     Another lodger ere I had the rooms,
     Three months gone by – a woman.
80   'Young, sir? No.
     Must have seen forty if she'd seen a day!
     A lonesome woman; hadn't many friends;
     Wrote books, I think, and things for newspapers.
     Short in her temper – eyes would flash and flame
85   At times, till I was frightened. Paid her rent
     Most regular, like a lady.
                         Ten years back,
     They say (at least Ann Brown says), ten years back
     The lady had a lover. Even then
     She must have been no chicken.
                              Three months since
90   She died. Well, well, the Lord is kind and just.
     I did my best to tend her, yet indeed
     It's bad for trade to have a lodger die.
     Her brother came, a week before she died:
     Buried her, took her things, threw in the fire
     The littered heaps of paper.
95   Yes, the sheets,
     They must have been forgotten in the chest; –
     I never knew her name was Adelaide.'

     [1884]

---

75. *minded*] intended.   *presently*] before too long.

77. *châtelaine*] a medieval word for the mistress of a house; here, landlady.

To Lallie

(Outside the British Museum.)

Up those Museum steps you came,
And straightway all my blood was flame,
         O Lallie, Lallie!

The world (I had been feeling low)
5   In one short moment's space did grow
         A happy valley.

There was a friend, my friend, with you;
A meagre dame, in peacock blue
         Apparelled quaintly:

10   This poet-heart went pit-a-pat;
I bowed and smiled and raised my hat;
         You nodded – faintly.

My heart was full as full could be;
You had not got a word for me,
15   Not one short greeting;

That nonchalant small nod you gave
(The tyrant's motion to the slave)
         Sole mark'd our meeting.

Is it so long? Do you forget
20   That first and last time that we met?
         The time was summer;

The trees were green; the sky was blue;
Our host presented me to you –
         A tardy comer.

To Lallie. *Subtitle. the British Museum*] The British Museum (in London), famous for its world-wide collection of antiquities, at this time also contained the library (now the British Library) where Levy did much of her reading.

8. meagre] thin.

10–11.] These two lines signify a male speaker.

18. Sole mark'd] Was the only sign of.

24. A tardy comer] A latecomer.

25   You look'd demure, but when you spoke
      You made a little, funny joke,
                  Yet half pathetic.

      Your gown was grey, I recollect,
      I think you patronized the sect
30   They call 'æsthetic.'

      I brought you strawberries and cream,
      I plied you long about a stream
                  With duckweed laden;

      We solemnly discussed the – heat.
35   I found you shy and very sweet,
                  A rosebud maiden.

      Ah me, to-day! You passed inside
      To where the marble gods abide:
                  Hermes, Apollo,

40   Sweet Aphrodite, Pan; and where,
      For aye reclined, a headless fair
                  Beats all fairs hollow.

      And I, I went upon my way,
      Well – rather sadder, let us say;
45   The world looked flatter.

      I had been sad enough before,
      A little less, a little more,
                  What *does* it matter?

      [1884]

---

30. 'æsthetic'] The notion of 'the aesthete' gained currency in the late 1870s and early 1880s; it
denoted those who regarded themselves as having a superior appreciation of things beautiful,
and was satirised, for example, in Gilbert and Sullivan's comic operetta *Patience* (1881).

33. duckweed] Duckweed floats on still water, carpeting the surface.

39–40.] The British Museum has an extensive collection of classical Greek and Roman statues.
Among them: *Hermes*, messenger of the gods; *Apollo*, god of music and poetry, identified with
the sun; *Aphrodite*, goddess of beauty and love; *Pan*, god of shepherds and huntsmen.

41.] *For aye*] for ever.

A London Plane-tree

GREEN is the plane-tree in the square,
  The other trees are brown;
They droop and pine for country air;
  The plane-tree loves the town.

5   Here from my garret-pane, I mark
  The plane-tree bud and blow,
Shed her recuperative bark,
  And spread her shade below.

Among her branches, in and out,
10   The city breezes play;
The dun fog wraps her round about;
  Above, the smoke curls grey.

Others the country take for choice,
  And hold the town in scorn;
15 But she has listened to the voice
  On city breezes borne.

[1889]

Ballade of an Omnibus

To see my love suffices me.

– Ballades in Blue China.

SOME men to carriages aspire;
On some the costly hansoms wait;
Some seek a fly, on job or hire;
Some mount the trotting steed, elate.

Ballade of an Omnibus. *Title. Ballade*] Originally an Old French verse form, the most common type of ballade comprises three eight-line stanzas (rhymed ababbcbc) and a four-line envoi (bcbc). The last line of each stanza serves as a refrain, repeated also at the end of the envoi. The ballade form was revived in England in the later nineteenth century by a group of poets that included Andrew Lang; often its subject matter was light. Levy's poem fits the ballade form, with the exception of the envoi, which is here rhymed acac. See also her 'Ballad of Religion and Marriage' (p. 354 below).

Epigraph.] Andrew Lang (1844–1912) published *Ballades in Blue China* in 1880 and 1881. This line forms the refrain to 'Ballade Amoureuse' from the 1881 edition.

1–3.] Private *carriages* were kept only by the well-to-do; *hansoms* were the horse-drawn fore-runners of the modern taxicab; a *fly* was a lighter vehicle that could be 'jobbed' (hired for a stretch of time) or hired for a particular journey.

5   I envy not the rich and great,
                      A wandering minstrel, poor and free,
                      I am contented with my fate –
                      An omnibus suffices me.

                      In winter days of rain and mire
10   I find within a corner strait;
                      The 'busmen know me and my lyre
                      From Brompton to the Bull-and-Gate.
                      When summer comes, I mount in state
                      The topmost summit, whence I see
15   Crœsus look up, compassionate –
                      An omnibus suffices me.

                      I mark, untroubled by desire,
                      Lucullus' phaeton and its freight.
                      The scene whereof I cannot tire,
20   The human tale of love and hate,
                      The city pageant, early and late
                      Unfolds itself, rolls by, to be
                      A pleasure deep and delicate.
                      An omnibus suffices me.

25   Princess, your splendour you require,
                      I, my simplicity; agree
                      Neither to rate lower nor higher.
                      An omnibus suffices me.

                      [1889]

London Poets

(In Memoriam.)

THEY trod the streets and squares where now I tread,
With weary hearts, a little while ago;

---

8. *omnibus*] a four-wheeled horse-drawn passenger bus.

15. *Crœsus*] The type of a rich man, from King Croesus of Lydia (560–546 BC).

18. *Lucullus' phaeton*] Lucullus, a Roman statesman of the first century BC who was renowned for luxurious living; a phaeton was a fast, lightweight carriage.

London Poets. *Subtitle. In Memoriam*] literally, in memory. Cf. also the famous long poem 'In Memoriam A. H. H.' published in 1850 by Alfred Tennyson (1809–1892).

When, thin and grey, the melancholy snow
Clung to the leafless branches overhead;
5   Or when the smoke-veiled sky grew stormy-red
In autumn; with a re-arisen woe
Wrestled, what time the passionate spring winds blow;
And paced scorched stones in summer: – they are dead.

The sorrow of their souls to them did seem
10   As real as mine to me, as permanent.
To-day, it is the shadow of a dream,
The half-forgotten breath of breezes spent.
So shall another soothe his woe supreme –
'No more he comes, who this way came and went.'

[1889]

In the Mile End Road

How like her! But 'tis she herself,
   Comes up the crowded street,
How little did I think, the morn,
   My only love to meet!

5   Whose else that motion and that mien?
   Whose else that airy tread?
For one strange moment I forgot
   My only love was dead.

[1889]

---

7. what time] at the time that.

14. 'No more he comes, who this way came and went.'] This has not been located as a quotation.

In the Mile End Road. *Title.*] A long thoroughfare in the east end of London.

6. that airy tread.] Cf. Tennyson's *Maud*, Part One, XXII, xi: 'She is coming, my own, my sweet; / Were it ever so airy a tread, / My heart would hear her and beat, / Were it earth in an earthy bed; / My dust would hear her and beat, / Had I lain for a century dead; / Would start and tremble under her feet, / And blossom in purple and red.'

The Old House

IN through the porch and up the silent stair;
　　Little is changed, I know so well the ways; –
Here, the dead came to meet me; it was there
　　The dream was dreamed in unforgotten days.

5　　But who is this that hurries on before,
　　A flitting shade the brooding shades among? –
She turned, – I saw her face, – O God, it wore
　　The face I used to wear when I was young!

I thought my spirit and my heart were tamed
10　　To deadness; dead the pangs that agonise.
The old grief springs to choke me, – I am shamed
　　Before that little ghost with eager eyes.

O turn away, let her not see, not know!
　　How should she bear it, how should understand?
15　　O hasten down the stairway, haste and go,
　　And leave her dreaming in the silent land.

[1889]

Captivity

THE lion remembers the forest,
　　The lion in chains;
To the bird that is captive a vision
　　Of woodland remains.

5　　One strains with his strength at the fetter,
　　In impotent rage;
One flutters in flights of a moment,
　　And beats at the cage.

The Old House. 5–6.] Cf. *Maud*, Part Two, IV, iii: 'A shadow flits before me, / Not thou, but like to thee: / Ah Christ, that it were possible / For one short hour to see / The souls we loved, that they might tell us / What and where they be.'

16. dreaming in the silent land] Cf. Christina Rossetti's 'Remember' (1862): 'Remember me when I am gone away, / Gone far away into the silent land' (ll. 1–2). Levy wrote an essay on Rossetti's poetry: 'The Poetry of Christina Rossetti', *The Woman's World* 1 (Feb 1888): 178–80.

Captivity. *5. fetter*] usually a chain which shackles a prisoner to the wall by the ankle or wrist.

If the lion were loosed from the fetter,
10 To wander again;
He would seek the wide silence and shadow
  Of his jungle in vain.

He would rage in his fury, destroying;
  Let him rage, let him roam!
15 Shall he traverse the pitiless mountain,
  Or swim through the foam?

If they opened the cage and the casement,
  And the bird flew away;
He would come back at evening, heartbroken,
20 A captive for aye.

Would come if his kindred had spared him,
  Free birds from afar –
There was wrought what is stronger than iron
  In fetter and bar.

25 I cannot remember my country,
  The land whence I came;
Whence they brought me and chained me and made me
  Nor wild thing nor tame.

This only I know of my country,
30 This only repeat: –
It was free as the forest, and sweeter
  Than woodland retreat.

When the chain shall at last be broken,
  The window set wide;
35 And I step in the largeness and freedom
  Of sunlight outside;

Shall I wander in vain for my country?
  Shall I seek and not find?
Shall I cry for the bars that encage me,
40 The fetters that bind?

  [1889]

---

15. *traverse*] journey across.

17. *casement*] a window opening outward on hinges attached to the upright sides of the frame.

20. *for aye*] for ever.

Cambridge in the Long

WHERE drowsy sound of college-chimes
    Across the air is blown,
And drowsy fragrance of the limes,
    I lie and dream alone.

5   A dazzling radiance reigns o'er all –
    O'er gardens densely green,
O'er old grey bridges and the small,
    Slow flood which slides between.

This is the place; it is not strange,
10   But known of old and dear. –
What went I forth to seek? The change
    Is mine; why am I here?

Alas, in vain I turned away,
    I fled the town in vain;
15   The strenuous life of yesterday
    Calleth me back again.

And was it peace I came to seek?
    Yet here, where memories throng,
Ev'n here, I know the past is weak,
20   I know the present strong.

This drowsy fragrance, silent heat,
    Suit not my present mind,
Whose eager thought goes out to meet
    The life it left behind.

25   Spirit with sky to change; such hope,
    An idle one we know;
Unship the oars, make loose the rope,
    Push off the boat and go. . . .

Cambridge in the Long. *Title.*] i.e. Cambridge University in the summer long vacation.

1. college-chimes] Many of the colleges of the university have their own chapels with bell-towers.

3. limes] flowering lime trees.

10. But known of old and dear] Levy attended Newnham College probably between 1879 and 1881 (Levy, ed. New, 1993, p. 4).

25.] That my spirit could change with the changing skies.

27. Unship the oars] i.e. Place the oars in position to row the boat.

Ah, would what binds me could have been
30   Thus loosened at a touch!
This pain of living is too keen,
    Of loving, is too much.

[1889]

Oh, is it Love?

O IS it Love or is it Fame,
    This thing for which I sigh?
Or has it then no earthly name
    For men to call it by?

5   I know not what can ease my pains,
    Nor what it is I wish;
The passion at my heart-strings strains
    Like a tiger in a leash.

[1889]

The First Extra

A Waltz Song

O SWAY, and swing, and sway,
    And swing, and sway, and swing!
Ah me, what bliss like unto this,
    Can days and daylight bring?

5   A rose beneath your feet
    Has fallen from my head;
Its odour rises sweet,
    All crushed it lies, and dead.

O Love is like a rose,
10   Fair-hued, of fragrant breath;
A tender flow'r that lives an hour,
    And is most sweet in death.

The First Extra. *Title.*] An 'extra' is a dance additional to those on the formal dance programme at a ball. Waltzing became popular in England during the second half of the nineteenth century, although initially it was regarded as somewhat improper, as it required the partners to dance face to face in a close embrace. The waltz is in a swinging three-time imitated perfectly in Levy's verse.

O swing, and sway, and swing,
    And rise, and sink, and fall!
15   There is no bliss like unto this,
    This is the best of all.

[1889]

Philosophy

ERE all the world had grown so drear,
When I was young and you were here,
'Mid summer roses in summer weather,
What pleasant times we've had together!

5   We were not Phyllis, simple-sweet,
And Corydon; we did not meet
By brook or meadow, but among
A Philistine and flippant throng

Which much we scorned; (less rigorous
10   It had no scorn at all for us!)
How many an eve of sweet July,
Heedless of Mrs. Grundy's eye,

We've scaled the stairway's topmost height,
And sat there talking half the night;
15   And, gazing on the crowd below,
Thanked Fate and Heaven that made us so; –

To hold the pure delights of brain
Above light loves and sweet champagne.
For, you and I, we did eschew
20   The egoistic 'I' and 'you;'

And all our observations ran
On Art and Letters, Life and Man.
Proudly we sat, we two, on high,
Throned in our Objectivity;

Philosophy. 5–6. *Phyllis, Corydon*] Classic names for shepherd and shepherdess in pastoral poetry.

8. *Philistine*] originally, a warlike people in conflict with the Israelite tribes. The term was commonly used to represent the materialistic masses as opposed to the culturally enlightened few, e.g. in *Culture and Anarchy* by Matthew Arnold (1869).

12. *Mrs. Grundy*] Symbolic of rigid, conventional standards of morality and propriety. The character originated in *Speed the Plough* (1798), a comedy by Thomas Morton (?1764–1838).

25   Scarce friends, not lovers (each avers),
        But sexless, safe Philosophers.
              *   *   *   *   *   *   *

        Dear Friend, you must not deem me light
        If, as I lie and muse to-night,
        I give a smile and not a sigh
30   To thoughts of our Philosophy.

        [1889]

A Ballad of Religion and Marriage

Swept into limbo is the host
    Of heavenly angels, row on row;
The Father, Son, and Holy Ghost,
    Pale and defeated, rise and go.
5   The great Jehovah is laid low,
    Vanished his burning bush and rod –
Say, are we doomed to deeper woe?
    Shall marriage go the way of God?

    Monogamous, still at our post,
10   Reluctantly we undergo
    Domestic round of boiled and roast,

A Ballad of Religion and Marriage] In format, this is another 'ballade' (see note to 'Ballade of an Omnibus', above). This poem was not published in Levy's lifetime, no doubt because she felt it was too outspoken.

1. limbo] In Latin theology, limbo is the place of souls excluded from the full blessedness of the beatific vision, but not otherwise punished.

5. Jehovah] a form of the Hebrew Divine Name, thus signifying the Old Testament God.

6.] The burning bush refers to the shrub that burned but was not consumed on Mt Horeb when Moses heard God's call to become deliverer of his people (Exodus 3: 2); Moses is often depicted with a rod or staff, with which he struck a rock, releasing water for the thirsty Israelites (Exodus 17). Both these miracles are evidence of God's power; Moses was commonly considered a forerunner (or type) of Christ in the nineteenth century.

8.] A reference to the unprecedented level of religious questioning and doubt which appeared in the latter half of the nineteenth century. Various factors influenced this shift in attitudes, including industrialisation (which produced the realisation that people's well-being was not solely related to divine providence), Darwin and the debate about evolution, the new methods of biblical criticism (the 'Higher Criticism') which originated in nineteenth-century Germany, and the growth of feminism.

11. boiled and roast] Beef or mutton was generally served at family dinners either boiled or roasted.

Yet deem the whole proceeding slow.
Daily the secret murmurs grow;
  We are no more content to plod
15 Along the beaten paths – and so
  Marriage must go the way of God.

Soon, before all men, each shall toast
  The seven strings unto his bow,
Like beacon fires along the coast,
20   The flame of love shall glance and glow.
Nor let nor hindrance man shall know,
  From natal bath to funeral sod;
Perennial shall his pleasures flow
  When marriage goes the way of God.

25 Grant, in a million years at most,
  Folk shall be neither pairs nor odd –
Alas! we sha'n't be there to boast
  'Marriage has gone the way of God!'

Of this pamphlet 12 copies only have been printed for private
  circulation.
[1915]

---

12. slow] dull, boring.

21. let nor hindrance] Possibly an allusion to the Banns of Marriage, posted before a wedding,
which ask whether there is any 'cause, or just impediment' why the two parties should not be
married.

26. odd] The nineteenth century witnessed a growing concern, among both liberals and con-
servatives, with the plight of single women. W. R. Greg's article 'Why are Women Redund-
ant?', published in the *National Review* (1862), provided a key to the debate, advocating
emigration and vocational training as solutions. Dora Greenwell (1821–1882), herself a single
woman and poet, published an essay titled 'Our Single Women' in the *North British Review*
(Feb 1862; reprinted in *Essays*, 1866) in which she supports the expansion of opportunities
for women, as well as noting their prevalence in contemporary debate: 'If in the multitude of
counsellors there is safety, how blest must be the security of single women! Every one who
has a little spare wisdom at command, seems just now inclined to lay it out for their benefit.
As far as books go, they have become the objects of class legislation, having a literature of
their own, so abounding in hints, suggestions, and schemes for their favourable considera-
tion, that we sometimes wonder if any among the sisterhood feel at all inclined to echo Tony
Lumpkins' ungracious and unfilial rejoinder, *"I wish you would only leave my good alone"*'
(Greenwell, 1866, p. 1). Greenwell draws attention to the difficulties besetting single women
struggling for an independent and meaningful existence, writing that 'a certain eccentricity,
or at least the appearance of such, attends upon her solitary efforts . . .', thereby suggesting a
double meaning in Levy's use of 'odd' (ibid., p. 19). Cf. the title of George Gissing's novel *The
Odd Women* (1893).

BIBLIOGRAPHY

Principles of Organisation   The bibliography is in two parts. The first part is a list of references relevant to the study of nineteenth-century women's poetry generally. This includes both other anthologies of primary texts and critical commentary. Any reference dealing with more than one of the poets in this anthology will be found here. The second part of the bibliography is arranged by individual author. Within each poet's entry there is a list of primary texts (including letters) and a list of secondary sources (including biographies).

GENERAL BIBLIOGRAPHY

Aikin, Susan Hardy (1986), 'Women and the Question of Canonicity', *College English* 48: 288–301.

Allibone, Samuel Austin (1870–1), *A Critical Dictionary of English Literature and British and American Authors Living and Deceased from the Earliest Accounts to the Latter Half of the Nineteenth Century*, 3 vols, Philadelphia.

Alston, R. C. (1991), *A Checklist of Women Writers, 1801–1900: Fiction, Verse, Drama*, Boston, MA.

Anderson, Amanda (1993), *Tainted Souls and Painted Faces: The Rhetoric of Fallenness in Victorian Culture*, Ithaca and London.

Armstrong, Isobel (1972), *Victorian Scrutinies: Reviews of Poetry 1830–1870*, London.

Armstrong, Isobel (1993), *Victorian Poetry: Poetry, Poetics and Politics*, London and New York.

Armstrong, Isobel (1995), 'The Gush of the Feminine: How Can We Read Women's Poetry of the Romantic Period?', in Feldman and Kelley, eds, pp. 13–32.

Armstrong, Isobel, ed. (1992), *New Feminist Discourses: Critical Essays on Theories and Texts*, London and New York.

Armstrong, Isobel, and Virginia Blain, eds (1999), *Women's Poetry, Late Romantic to Late Victorian: Gender and Genre, 1830–1900*, Basingstoke, Hampshire, and New York.

Armstrong, Isobel, and Joseph Bristow, with Cath Sharrock, eds (1996), *Nineteenth-Century Women Poets: An Oxford Anthology*, Oxford.

Ashfield, Andrew, ed. (1995), *Romantic Women Poets, 1770–1838: An Anthology*, Manchester.

Auerbach, Nina (1986), *Romantic Imprisonment: Women and Other Glorified Outcasts*, New York.

Ball, P. M. (1976), *The Hearts Events: The Victorian Poetry of Relationships*, London.

Battersby, Christine (1989), *Gender and Genius: Towards a Feminist Aesthetics*, London.

Bax, Clifford, and Meum Stewart, comps (1949), *The Distaff Muse: An Anthology of Poetry Written by Women*, London.

Behrendt, Stephen, and Harriet Linkin, eds (1997), *Approaches to Teaching British Women Poets of the Romantic Period*, New York.

Benjamin, Marina (1991), *Science and Sensibility*, Oxford.

Bennett, Paula (1993), 'Critical Clitoridectomy: Female Sexual Imagery and Feminist Psychoanalytic Theory', *Signs: Journal of Women in Culture and Society* 18: 235–59.

Blain, Virginia (1990), ' "Thinking Back Through Our Aunts": Harriet Martineau and Tradition in Women's Writing', *Women's Cultural Review* 1(3): 223–40.

Blain, Virginia (1995), 'Letitia Elizabeth Landon, Eliza Mary Hamilton, and the Genealogy of the Victorian Poetess', *Victorian Poetry* 33(1): 31–52.

Blain, Virginia (1998), 'Anonymity and the discourse of amateurism: Caroline Bowles Southey negotiates Blackwoods 1820–1847', in B. Garlick and M. Harris, eds, *Victorian Journalism*, St Lucia, Queensland, pp. 1–18.

Blain, Virigina (1999), 'Sexual Politics of the (Victorian) Closet; *or*, No Sex Please – We're Poets', in Armstrong and Blain, eds, pp. 135–63.

Blain, Virginia, Patricia Clements, and Isobel Grundy, eds (1990), *The Feminist Companion to Literature in English: Women Writers from the Middle Ages to the Present*, New Haven, CN.

Boos, Florence (1995), 'Cauld Engle-Cheek: Working Class Women Poets in Victorian Scotland', *Victorian Poetry* 33(1): 53–71.

Boos, Florence (1996), ' "Oor Location": Victorian Women Poets and the Transition from Rural to Urban Scottish Culture', *Victorian Urban Landscapes*, eds Debra Mancoff and Dale Trela, New York, pp. 133–56.

Boos, Florence (1998), ' "We Would Know Again the Fields . . .": The Rural Poetry of Elizabeth Campbell, Jane Stevenson, and Mary Macpherson', *Tulsa Studies in Women's Literature* 17(2): 325–47.

Boos, Florence, with Lynn Miller (1989), *Bibliography of Women and Literature: Articles and Books By and About Women from 600 to 1975*, 2 vols, New York.

Breen, Jennifer, ed. (1992), *Women Romantic Poets, 1785–1832: An Anthology*, London.

Bristow, Joseph (1987), *The Victorian Poet: Poetics and Persona*, London.

Bristow, Joseph, ed. (1995), *Victorian Women Poets: Emily Brontë, Elizabeth Barrett Browning, Christina Rossetti*, Basingstoke, Hampshire, and London.

Brown, Susan (1991), 'Economical Representations: Dante Gabriel Rossetti's "Jenny", Augusta Webster's "A Castaway", and the Campaign against the Contagious Diseases Acts', *Victorian Review* 17: 78–95.

Brown, Susan (1994), 'A Victorian Sappho: Agency, Identity, and the Politics of Poetics', *English Studies in Canada* 20(2): 205–25.

Casaresco, Countess Evelyn Marinengo (1912), *The Liberation of Italy 1815–1870*, 3rd edn, London.

Castle, Terry (1993), *The Apparitional Lesbian: Female Homosexuality and Modern Culture*, New York.

Christ, Carol T. (1984), *Victorian and Modern Poetics*, Chicago and London.

Coleridge, Henry Nelson (September 1840), 'Modern English Poetesses', *Quarterly Review* 66: 374–418.

Copley, Stephen, and John Whale, eds (1992), *Beyond Romanticism: New Approaches to Texts and Contexts, 1780–1832*, New York.

Cosslet, Tess, ed. (1996), *Victorian Women Poets*, London and New York.

Curran, Stuart (1988), 'Romantic Poetry: The "I" Altered', in Mellor, ed., pp. 185–207.

Curran, Stuart, ed. (1993), *Cambridge Companion to British Romanticism*, Cambridge.

David, Deirdre (1987), *Intellectual Women and Victorian Patriarchy: Harriet Martineau, Elizabeth Barrett Browning, George Eliot*, London.

Davis, Gwenn, and Beverly A. Joyce, comps (1991), *Poetry by Women to 1900: A Bibliography of American and British Writers*, Toronto.

DeJoan, Joan (1989), *Fictions of Sappho, 1546–1937*, Chicago.

Delamont, Sara, and Lorna Duffins, eds (1978), *The Nineteenth-Century Woman: Her Cultural and Physical World*, London and New York.

Diehl, Joanne Feit (1978), ' "Come Slowly-Eden": An Exploration of Women Poets and their Muse', *Signs* 3: 572–87.

Donoghue, Emma, ed. and introd. (1997), *What Sappho Would Have Said: Four Centuries of Love Poems between Women*, London.

Easlea, Brian (1981), *Science and Sexual Oppression*, London.

Erkkila, Betsy (1992), *The Wicked Sisters: Women Poets, Literary History, and Discord*, New York and Oxford.

Faderman, Lillian (1981), *Surpassing the Love of Men: Romantic Friendship and Love between Women from the Renaissance to the Present*, London.

Fay, Elizabeth A. (1993), 'Romantic Men, Victorian Women: The Nightingale Talks Back', *Studies in Romanticism* 32(2): 211–24.

Feldman, Paula R., ed. (1997), *British Women Poets of the Romantic Era: An Anthology*, Baltimore, MD.

Feldman, Paula, and Theresa M. Kelley, eds (1995), *Romantic Women Writers: Voices and Countervoices*, Hanover and London.

Fleishman, Avrom (1985), 'Notes for a History of Victorian Poetic Genres', *Genre* 18: 363–74.

Flint, Kate (1993), *The Woman Reader 1837–1914*, Oxford.

Fredeman, William E., and Ira B. Nadel, eds (1985), *Dictionary of Literary Biography Volume 35: Victorian Poets after 1850*, Detroit.

Fuller, Margaret (1845), *Woman in the Nineteenth Century*, London.

Gilbert, Sandra M., and Susan Gubar (1979a), *The Madwoman in the Attic: The Woman Writer and the Nineteenth-Century Literary Imagination*, New Haven, CN, and London.

Gilbert, Sandra M., and Susan Gubar, eds (1979b), *Shakespeare's Sisters: Feminist Essays on Women Poets*, Bloomington and London.

Gilmour, Robin (1993), *The Victorian Period: The Intellectual and Cultural Context of English Literature, 1830–1890*, London and New York.

Greenwell, Dora (1866), *Essays*, London and New York.

Greer, Germaine (1995), *Slipshod Sybils: Recognition, Rejection and the Woman Poet*, London.

Harrison, Antony H. (1990), *Victorian Poets and Romantic Poems: Intertextuality and Ideology*, Charlottesville, VA.

Harrison, Antony H., and Beverly Taylor, eds (1992), *Gender and Discourse in Victorian Literature and Art*, DeKalb, Northern Illinois.

Helsinger, Elizabeth K., Robin Lauterbach Sheets, and William Veeder (1983), *The Woman Question: Society and Literature in Britain and America, 1837–1883*, 3 vols, New York and London.

Hickok, Kathleen (1984), *Representations of Women: Nineteenth-Century British Women's Poetry*, Westport, CT.

Hickok, Kathleen (1995), '"Intimate Egoism": Reading and Evaluating Noncanonical Poetry by Women', *Victorian Poetry* 33(1): 13–30.

Homans, Margaret (1980), *Women Writers and Poetic Identity: Dorothy Wordsworth, Emily Brontë, and Emily Dickinson*, Princeton, NJ.

Homans, Margaret (1986), *Bearing the Word: Language and Female Experience in Nineteenth-Century Women's Writing*, Chicago and London.

Houghton, Walter E. (1957), *The Victorian Frame of Mind, 1830–1870*, New Haven and London.

Hughes, Linda K., ed. (1995), *Victorian Poetry: Women Poets 1830–1894* 33(1), special issue.

Jacobus, Mary, ed. (1979), *Women Writing and Writing about Women*, London.

Jeffrey, David Lyle, ed. (1992), *A Dictionary of Biblical Tradition in English Literature*, Grand Rapids, MI.

Kaplan, Cora (1973), *Salt and Bitter and Good: Three Centuries of English and American Women Poets*, New York and London.

Kaplan, Cora (1986), *Sea Changes: Culture and Feminism*, London. Includes the important essay 'Language and Gender', pp. 69–94.

Kunitz, Stanley J., and Howard Haycraft, eds (1936), *British Authors of the Nineteenth Century*, New York.

Leighton, Angela (1992a), '"Because men made the laws": The Fallen Woman and the Woman Poet', in Armstrong, ed., pp. 342–60.

Leighton, Angela (1992b), *Victorian Women Poets: Writing Against the Heart*, New York and London.

Leighton, Angela, ed. (1996), *Victorian Women Poets: A Critical Reader*, Cambridge, MA, and Oxford.

Leighton, Angela, and Margaret Reynolds, eds (1995), *Victorian Women Poets: An Anthology*, Oxford, UK, and Cambridge, MA.

Levin, Susan (1987), 'Romantic Prose and Feminine Romanticism', *Prose Studies* 10(2): 178–95.

Linley, Margaret (1996), 'Sappho's Conversions in Felicia Hemans, Letitia Landon, and Christina Rossetti', *Prism(s): Essays in Romanticism* 4: 15–42.

Linley, Margaret (1999), 'Dying to be a Poetess: The Conundrum of Christina Rossetti', in *The Culture of Christina Rossetti*, eds M. Arseneau, A. H. Harrison, L. J. Kooistra, Ohio, pp. 285–314.

Lipking, Lawrence (1988), *Abandoned Women and the Poetic Tradition*, Chicago.

Lonsdale, Roger, ed. (1989), *Eighteenth-Century Women Poets: An Oxford Anthology*, New York.

Lootens, Tricia (1996), *Lost Saints: Silence, Gender, and Victorian Literary Canonization*, Charlottesville, VA, and London.

McGann, Jerome J. (1983), *The Romantic Ideology: A Critical Investigation*, Chicago and London.

Maynard, John (1993), *Victorian Discourses on Sexuality and Religion*, Cambridge.

Mellor, Anne K. (1993), *Romanticism and Gender*, New York and London.

Mellor, Anne K., ed. (1988), *Romanticism and Feminism*, Bloomington and Indianapolis.

Mermin, Dorothy (1986), 'The Damsel, the Knight, and the Victorian Woman Poet', *Critical Inquiry* 1: 64–80.

Mermin, Dorothy (1993), *Godiva's Ride: Women of Letters in England 1830–1880*, Bloomington and Indianapolis.

Miles, Alfred H., ed. (1891–7), *The Poets and Poetry of the Century*, 8 vols, London.

Mitchell, Sally, ed. (1988), *Victorian Britain: An Encyclopedia*, New York.

Michie, Helena (1987), *The Flesh Made Word: Female Figures and Women's Bodies*, New York and Oxford.

Moers, Ellen (1963), *Literary Women*, New York (1977).

Moir, David Macbeth (1851), *Sketches of the Poetical Literature of the Past Half-Century*, Edinburgh.

Montefiore, Jan (1987), *Feminism and Poetry: Language, Experience, and Identity in Women's Writing*, London.

Moore, Lisa (1992), '"Something More Tender Still than Friendship": Romantic Friendship in Early-Nineteenth-Century England', *Feminist Studies* 18(3): 499–520.

Morgan, Thais, ed. (1990), *Victorian Sages and Cultural Discourse: Renegotiating Gender and Power*, New Brunswick.

Nord, Deborah Epstein (1990), '"Neither Pairs Nor Odd": Female Community in Late Nineteenth Century London', *Signs* 15(2): 733–45.

Ostriker, Alicia Suskin (1986), *Stealing the Language: The Emergence of Women's Poetry in America*, Boston, MA.

Ostriker, Alicia Suskin (1993), *Feminist Revision and the Bible*, Oxford, UK, and Cambridge, MA.

Poovey, Mary (1989), *Uneven Developments: The Ideological Work of Gender in Mid-Victorian England*, London.

Postlethwaite, Diana (1988), 'Robert Chambers', in Mitchell, ed., p. 130.

Prins, Yopie (1999), *Victorian Sappho*, Princeton, NJ.

Robertson, Eric S. (1883), *English Poetesses: A Series of Critical Biographies, with Illustrative Extracts*, London.

Ross, Edmond (1988), *Affairs of the Hearth: Victorian Poetry and Domestic Narrative*, London and New York.

Ross, Marlon (1989), *The Contours of Masculine Desire: Romanticism and the Rise of Women's Poetry*, New York and Oxford.

Russ, Joanna (1983), *How To Suppress Women's Writing*, London.

Sackville-West, V. (1929), 'The Women Poets of the "Seventies"', in *The Eighteen-Seventies: Essays by Fellows of the Royal Society of Literature*, ed. Harley Granville-Barker, Cambridge, pp. 111–32.

Schlueter, Paul and June Schlueter, eds (1988), *An Encyclopedia of British Women Writers*, New York and London.

Schwartz, Joel S. (1988), 'Evolution', in Mitchell, ed., pp. 274–6.

Sharp, Elizabeth A. (1890), *Women Poets of the Victorian Era*, London and New York.

Shattock, Joanne, ed. (1993), *The Oxford Guide to British Women Writers*, Oxford and New York.

Showalter, Elaine (1991), *Sexual Anarchy: Gender and Culture at the Fin de Siècle*, London.

Spender, Dale, ed. (1992), *Living by the Pen: Early British Women Writers*, New York.

Stone, Marjorie (1994), 'Sisters in Art: Christina Rossetti and Elizabeth Barrett Browning', *Victorian Poetry* 32(3–4): 339–64.

Swanwick, Anna (1882), *Poets the Interpreters of Their Age*, London.

Swindells, Julia (1985), *Victorian Writing and Working Women: The Other Side of Silence*, Madison.

Thesing, William B., ed. (1999), *Dictionary of Literary Biography, Volume 199: Victorian Women Poets*, Detroit, Washington DC, London.

Todd, Janet, ed. (1989), *Dictionary of British Women Writers*, London.

Vicinus, Martha, ed. (1972), *Suffer and Be Still: Women in the Victorian Age*, Bloomington and London.

Vicinus, Martha, ed. (1977), *A Widening Sphere: Changing Roles of Victorian Women*, Bloomington and London.

Walker, Cheryl (1999), 'The Whip Signature: Violence, Feminism and Women Poets', in Armstrong and Blain, eds, pp. 33–49.

Weinreb, Ben, and Christopher Hibbert, eds (1983), *The London Encyclopaedia*, London.

Williams, Jane (1861), *The Literary Women of England*, London.

Wilson, Carol Shiner, and Joel Haefner, eds (1994), *Revisioning Romanticism: British Women Writers, 1776–1837*, Philadelphia.

Woolf, Virginia (1929), *A Room of One's Own*, London.

Woolf, Virginia (1979), *Women and Writing*, ed. Michèle Barrett, London.

Wu, Duncan, ed. (1997), *Romantic Women Poets: An Anthology*, Oxford and Malden, MA.

Yeo, Robert (1984), 'Scientific and Intellectual Authority in Mid-Nineteenth-Century Britain: Robert Chambers and *Vestiges of the Natural History of Creation*', *Victorian Studies* 28(1): 5–31.

INDIVIDUAL POETS

Felicia Dorothea Hemans

Texts

Hemans, F. D. (1808), *Poems*, London.

Hemans, F. D. (1812), *The Domestic Affections, and other Poems*, London.

Hemans, F. D. (1816), *The Restoration of the Works of Art to Italy: A Poem*, London.

Hemans, F. D. (1819), *Tales and Historic Scenes, in Verse*, London.

Hemans, F. D. (1820), *The Sceptic, A Poem: Stanzas to the Memory of the late King*, London.

Hemans, F. D. (1823), *The Siege of Valencia. A Dramatic Poem. The Last Constantine, with Other Poems*, London.

Hemans, F. D. (1825), *The Forest Sanctuary, and Other Poems*, London. 2nd edn 1829.

Hemans, F. D. (1828), *Records of Woman, with Other Poems*, Edinburgh.

Hemans, F. D. (1829), *The Forest Sanctuary, and Other Poems*, 2nd edn, Edinburgh.

Hemans, F. D. (1830), *Songs of the Affections, with Other Poems*, Edinburgh and London.

Hemans, F. D. (1839), *The Works of Mrs. Hemans; with a Memoir of her Life, by her Sister*, [ed. Harriett Hughes], 7 vols, Edinburgh and London.

Chorley, Henry F. (1836), *Memorials of Mrs. Hemans, with Illustrations of her Literary Character from her Private Correspondence*, 2 vols, London. 2nd edn 1837.

Commentary

Blain, Virginia (1995), '"Thou with Earth's Music Answerest to the Sky": Felicia Hemans, Mary Ann Browne, and the Myth of Poetic Sisterhood', *Women's Writing: the Elizabethan to Victorian period* 2(3): 251–70.

Clarke, Norma (1990), *Ambitious Heights: Writing, Friendship, Love – The Jewsbury Sisters, Felicia Hemans, and Jane Welsh Carlyle*, London.

Cochran, Peter (1995), 'Fatal Fluency, Fruitless Dower: The Eminently Marketable Felicia Hemans', *Times Literary Supplement* 21 July: 13a.

Feldman, Paula R. (1999), 'The Poet and the Profit: Felicia Hemans and the Literary Marketplace', in Armstrong and Blain, eds, pp. 71–101.

Fraser, Hilary (1994), '"Love's citadel unmann'd": Victorian Women's Love Poetry', in *Constructing Gender: Feminism in Literary Studies*, eds Hilary Fraser and R. S. White, with a preface by Penny Boumelha, Nedlands, WA, pp. 132–56.

Gilfillan, George (1847), 'Female Authors. No. 1 – Mrs. Hemans', *Tait's Edinburgh Magazine* NS 14: 359–63.

Haefner, Joel (1993), '(De)forming the Romantic Canon: The Case of Women Writers', *College Literature* 20(2): 44–57.

Harding, Anthony John (1995), 'Felicia Hemans and the Effacement of Woman', in Feldman and Kelley, eds, pp. 138–49.

Jewsbury, Maria Jane (1831), 'Original Papers. Literary Sketches No. 1. Felicia Hemans', *The Athenaeum* 171(5 Feb): 104–5.

Kennedy, Deborah (1997), 'Hemans, Wordsworth, and the "Literary Lady"', *Victorian Poetry* 35(3): 267–85.

Lootens, Tricia (1994), 'Hemans and Home: Victorianism, Feminine "Internal Enemies", and the Domestication of National Identity', *PMLA* 109: 238–53.

Lootens, Tricia (1999), 'Hemans and her American Heirs: Nineteenth-Century Women's Poetry and National Identity', in Armstrong and Blain, eds, pp. 243–60.

Louis, Margot K. (1998), 'Enlarging the Heart: L. E. L.'s "The Improvisatrice", Hemans's "Properzia Rossi", and Barrett Browning's *Aurora Leigh*', *Victorian Literature and Culture* 26(1): 1–17.

McGann, Jerome J. (1996), *The Poetics of Sensibility: A Revolution in Literary Style*, Oxford, pp. 174–94.

Moir, D. M. (1836), 'Biographical Memoir of the Late Mrs Hemans', in *Poetical Remains of the Late Mrs Hemans*, Edinburgh and London.

Quarterly Review (1820), 'Art. V.', review of several volumes by Hemans, *Quarterly Review* 24 (Oct).

Rossetti, W[illiam] M[ichael] (1881), 'Prefatory Notice', *The Poetical Works of Mrs. Hemans*, Philadelphia, pp. 11–24.

Rothstein, David (1999), 'Forming the Chivalric Subject: Felicia Hemans and the Cultural Uses of History, Memory, and Nostalgia', *Victorian Literature and Culture* 27(1): 49–68.

Stephenson, Glennis (1993), 'Poet Construction: Mrs Hemans, L.E.L., and the Image of the Nineteenth-Century Woman Poet', in *ReImagining Women: Representations of Women in Culture*, eds Shirley Neuman and Glennis Stephenson, Toronto, pp. 61–73.

Sweet, Nanora (1994), 'History, Imperialism, and the Aesthetics of the Beautiful: Hemans and the Post-Napoleonic Moment', in *At the Limits of Romanticism*, eds Mary A. Favret and Nicola J. Watson, Bloomington, pp. 170–84.

Trinder, Peter W. (1984), *Mrs. Hemans*, Aberystwyth.

Tucker, Herbert F. (1994), 'House Arrest: The Domestication of English Poetry in the 1820s', *New Library History* 25: 521–48.

Wolfson, Susan J. (1994), '"Domestic Affections" and "the spear of Minerva": Felicia Hemans and the Dilemma of Gender', in Wilson and Haefner (eds), pp. 128–66.

Elizabeth Barrett Browning

Texts

Barrett, Elizabeth Barrett (1820), *The Battle of Marathon*, privately printed.

Barrett, Elizabeth Barrett (1826), *An Essay on Mind, with Other Poems*, London.

Barrett, Elizabeth Barrett (1833), *Prometheus Bound: Translated from the Greek of Aeschylus, and Miscellaneous Poems*, London.

Barrett, Elizabeth Barrett (1842), 'Some Account of the Greek Christian Poets' and 'The Book of the Poets', *The Athenaeum*, London.

Barrett, Elizabeth Barrett (1844), *Poems*, 2 vols, London.

Browning, Elizabeth Barrett (1850), *Poems*, revised and selected, London.

Browning, Elizabeth Barrett (1851), *Casa Guidi Windows: A Poem*, London.

Browning, Elizabeth Barrett (1856), *Aurora Leigh*, London.

Browning, Elizabeth Barrett (1860), *Poems Before Congress*, London.

Browning, Elizabeth Barrett (1862), *Last Poems*, London.

Browning, Elizabeth Barrett (1897), *The Letters of Elizabeth Barrett Browning*, 2 vols, ed. Frederic G. Kenyon, London.

Browning, Elizabeth Barrett (1900), *The Complete Works of Elizabeth Barrett Browning*, 6 vols, eds Charlotte Porter and Helen A. Clarke, New York. Reprinted in facsimile edition, New York, 1973.

Browning, Elizabeth Barrett (1914), *Hitherto Unpublished Poems and Stories, with an Inedited Autobiography*, 2 vols, ed. H. Buxton Forman, Boston, MA.

Browning, Elizabeth Barrett (1929), *Elizabeth Barrett Browning: Letters to her Sister, 1846–1859*, ed. Leonard Huxley, London.

Browning, Elizabeth Barrett (1955), *Elizabeth Barrett Browning to Mr. Boyd: Unpublished Letters of Elizabeth Barrett and Hugh Stuart Boyd*, ed. Barbara P. McCarthy, London.

Browning, Elizabeth Barrett (1958), *Letters of the Brownings to George Barrett*, ed. Paul Landis, assisted by Ronald E. Freeman, Urbana.

Browning, Elizabeth Barrett (1969), *The Letters of Robert Browning and Elizabeth Barrett, 1845–1846*, 2 vols, ed. Elvan Kintner, Cambridge, MA.

Browning, Elizabeth Barrett (1969), *Diary by E.B.B.: The Unpublished Diary of Elizabeth Barrett Barrett, 1845–1846*, eds Philip Kelley and Ronald Hudson, Athens, OH.

Browning, Elizabeth Barrett (1973), *Elizabeth Barrett Browning's Letters to Mrs. David Ogilvy, 1849–1861*, eds Peter N. Heydon and Philip Kelley, New York.

Browning, Elizabeth Barrett (1977), *Casa Guidi Windows*, ed. Julia Markus, New York.

Browning, Elizabeth Barrett (1978), *Aurora Leigh and Other Poems*, ed. Cora Kaplan, London.

Browning, Elizabeth Barrett (1983), *The Letters of Elizabeth Barrett Browning to Mary Russell Mitford, 1836–1854*, 3 vols, eds Meredith B. Raymond and Mary Rose Sullivan, Winfield, KS.

Browning, Elizabeth Barrett, and Robert Browning (1984–), *The Brownings' Correspondence*, eds Phillip Kelley and Ronald Hudson, 14 vols to date, Winfield, KS.

Browning, Elizabeth Barrett (1989), *Robert Browning and Elizabeth Barrett: The Courtship Correspondence 1845–1846*, ed. Daniel Karlin, Oxford.

Browning, Elizabeth Barrett (1992), *Aurora Leigh*, ed. Margaret Reynolds, Athens, OH.

Browning, Elizabeth Barrett (1995), *Aurora Leigh and Other Poems*, eds John Robert Glorney Bolton and Julia Bolton Holloway, Harmondsworth.

Commentary

Byrd, Deborah (1987), 'Combating an Alien Tyranny: Elizabeth Barrett Browning's Evolution as a Feminist Poet', *Browning Institute Studies* 15: 23–41.

Cooper, Helen (1988), *Elizabeth Barrett Browning, Woman and Artist*, Chapel Hill, NC, and London.

DeLuise, Dolores, with Michael Timko (1993), 'Becoming the Poet: The Feminine Poet-Speaker in the Work of Elizabeth Barrett Browning', in *Virginal Sexuality and Textuality in Victorian Literature*, ed. Lloyd Davies, New York, pp. 87–103.

Forster, Margaret (1988), *Elizabeth Barrett Browning: A Biography*, London (1993).

Hayter, Aletha (1962), *Mrs. Browning: A Poet's Work and Its Setting*, London.

Hewlett, Dorothy (1953), *Elizabeth Barrett Browning*, London.

Leighton, Angela (1986), *Elizabeth Barrett Browning*, Sussex.

Markus, Julia (1995), *Dared and Done: The Marriage of Elizabeth Barrett and Robert Browning*, London.

Mermin, Dorothy (1986), 'Elizabeth Barrett Browning Through 1844: Becoming a Woman Poet', *Studies in English Literature 1500–1900* 26: 713–36.

Mermin, Dorothy (1989), *Elizabeth Barrett Browning: The Origins of a New Poetry*, Chicago and London.

Morlier, Margaret M. (1990), 'The Death of Pan: Elizabeth Barrett Browning and the Romantic Ego', *Browning Institute Studies* 18: 131–55.

Parry, Ann (1988), 'Sexual Exploitation and Freedom: Religion, Race and Gender in Elizabeth Barrett Browning's *The Runaway Slave at Pilgrim's Point*', *Studies in Browning and his Circle* 16: 114–26.

Raymond, Meredith B. (1979), 'E.B.B.'s Poetics 1830–1844: "The Seraph and the Earthly Piper"', *Browning Society Notes* 1(9): 5–9.

Raymond, Meredith B. (1981), 'Elizabeth Barrett Browning's Poetics 1845–1846: "The Ascending Gyre"', *Browning Society Notes* 11(2): 1–11.

Riede, David G. (1994), 'Elizabeth Barrett: The Poet as Angel', *Victorian Poetry* 32(2): 121–39.

Rosenblum, Dolores (1983), 'Face to Face: Elizabeth Barrett Browning's *Aurora Leigh* and Nineteenth-Century Poetry', *Victorian Studies* 26(3): 321–38.

Rundle, Vivienne (1986), ' "The inscription of these volumes": The Prefatory Writings of Elizabeth Barrett Browning', *Victorian Poetry* 34(2): 247–78.

Scheinberg, Cynthia (1995), 'Elizabeth Barrett Browning's Hebraic Conversions: Gender and Typology in *Aurora Leigh*', *Victorian Literature and Culture* 22: 55–72.

Simonsen, Pauline (1997), 'Elizabeth Barrett Browning's Redundant Women', *Victorian Poetry* 35(4): 509–32.

Stauffer, Andrew M. (1997), 'Elizabeth Barrett Browning's (Re)Visions of Slavery', *English Language Notes* 34(4): 29–48.

Stephenson, Glennis (1989), *Elizabeth Barrett Browning and the Poetry of Love*, Ann Arbor, MI, and London.

Stone, Marjorie (1995), *Elizabeth Barrett Browning*, Basingstoke, Hampshire.

Taplin, Gardner B. (1957), *The Life of Elizabeth Barrett Browning*, New Haven, CN.

Wegener, Frederick (1997), 'Elizabeth Barrett Browning, Italian Independence, and the "Critical Reaction" of Henry James', *Studies in English Literature, 1500–1900* 37(4): 741–61.

Woolford, John (1978), 'EBB: The Natural and the Spiritual', *Browning Society Notes* 8(1): 15–19.

Woolford, John (1995), 'Elizabeth Barrett Browning and the Wordsworthian Sublime', *Essays in Criticism* 45(1): 36–56.

Emily Jane Pfeiffer

Texts

Pfeiffer, Emily (1857), *Valisneria*, London.

Pfeiffer, Emily (1861), *Margaret; or, The Motherless*, London.

Pfeiffer, Emily (1873), *Gerard's Monument and Other Poems*, London. 2nd edn, rev. and enlarged, 1878.

Pfeiffer, Emily (1876), *Poems*, London.

Pfeiffer, Emily (1877), *Glân-Alarch, His Silence and His Song. A Poem*, London.

Pfeiffer, Emily (1879), *Quarterman's Grace and Other Poems*, London.

Pfeiffer, Emily (1880), *Sonnets and Songs*, London.

Pfeiffer, Emily (1881), *The Wynnes of Wynhavod. A Drama of Modern Life. In Four Acts and in Verse*, London.

Pfeiffer, Emily (1882), *Under the Aspens: Lyrical and Dramatic*, London.

Pfeiffer, Emily (1884), *The Rhyme of the Lady of the Rock and How it Grew*, London.

Pfeiffer, Emily (1885), *Flying Leaves from East and West*, London.

Pfeiffer, Emily (1886), *Sonnets*, rev. and enlarged edn of *Sonnets and Songs* (1880), London.

Pfeiffer, Emily (1888), *Women and Work: An Essay Treating on the Relation to Health and Physical Development of the Higher Education of Girls*, London.
Pfeiffer, Emily (1889), *Flowers of the Night*, London.

Commentary

Hickok, Kathleen (1995), '"Intimate Egoism": Reading and Evaluating Noncanonical Poetry by Women', *Victorian Poetry* 33(1): 13–30.
Hickok, Kathleen (1999), 'Why is this Woman Still Missing? Emily Pfeiffer, Victorian Poet', in Armstrong and Blain, eds, pp. 373–89.

Christina Georgina Rossetti

Texts

Rossetti, Christina (1842), *To My Mother on the Anniversary of her Birth, April 27, 1842*, privately printed, London.
Rossetti, Christina (1862), *Goblin Market and Other Poems*, Cambridge.
Rossetti, Christina (1866), *The Prince's Progress and Other Poems*, London.
Rossetti, Christina (1870), *Commonplace, and Other Short Stories*, London.
Rossetti, Christina (1872), *Sing-Song: A Nursery Rhyme Book*, London and Boston, MA.
Rossetti, Christina (1874), *Speaking Likenesses*, London.
Rossetti, Christina (1874), *Annus Domini: A Prayer for each day of the year, founded on a text of Holy Scripture*, Oxford and London.
Rossetti, Christina (1875), *Goblin Market, The Prince's Progress and Other Poems*, London.
Rossetti, Christina (1879), *Seek and Find: A Double Series of Short Studies of the Benedicite*, London.
Rossetti, Christina (1881), *A Pageant and Other Poems*, London and Boston, MA.
Rossetti, Christina (1881), *Called To Be Saints: The Minor Festivals Devotionally Studied*, London and New York.
Rossetti, Christina (1883), *Letter and Spirit: Notes on the Commandments*, London.
Rossetti, Christina (1885), *Time Flies: A Reading Diary*, London.
Rossetti, Christina (1890), *Poems: New and Enlarged Edition*, London and New York.
Rossetti, Christina (1892), *The Face of the Deep: A Devotional Commentary on the Apocalypse*, London and New York.
Rossetti, Christina (1893), *Verses: Reprinted from 'Called to be Saints', 'Time Flies' and 'The Face of the Deep'*, London and New York.
Rossetti, Christina (1896), *New Poems, Hitherto Unpublished or Uncollected*, ed. W. M. Rossetti, London and New York.
Rossetti, Christina (1897), *Maude: A Story for Girls*, introd. W. M. Rossetti, London.
Rossetti, Christina (1904), *The Poetical Works of Christina Georgina Rossetti*, ed. and with a memoir by W. M. Rossetti, London.
Rossetti, Christina (1908), *The Family Letters of Christina Georgina Rossetti*, ed. W. M. Rossetti, London.
Rossetti, Christina (1937), *Three Rossettis: Unpublished Letters to and from Dante Gabriel, Christina, William*, ed. Janet Camp Troxell, Cambridge, MA.

366

Rossetti, Christina (1963), *The Rossetti–Macmillan Letters*, ed. Lona Mosk Packer, Berkeley, CA.

Rossetti, Christina (1976), *Maude: Prose and Verse by Christina Rossetti*, ed. Rebecca W. Crump, Hamden, CT.

Rossetti, Christina (1979–90), *The Complete Poems of Christina Rossetti: A Variorum Edition*, 3 vols, ed. R. W. Crump, Baton Rouge and London.

Rossetti, Christina (1984), *Christina Rossetti: Selected Poems*, ed. C. H. Sisson, Manchester.

Rossetti, Christina, and Dinah Mulock Craik (1993), *Maude and On Sisterhoods: A Woman's Thoughts About Women*, ed. Elaine Showalter, New York.

Rossetti, Christina (1994), *Poems and Prose*, ed. Jan Marsh, London.

Rossetti, Christina (1997–), *The Letters of Christina Rossetti*, 2 vols to date, ed. Antony H. Harrison, Charlottesville, VA.

Rossetti, Christina (1998), *Selected Prose of Christina Rossetti*, eds David A. Kent and P. G. Stanwood, Basingstoke, Hampshire, and London.

Commentary

Addison, Jane (1995), 'Christina Rossetti Studies, 1974–1991: A Checklist and Synthesis', *Bulletin of Bibliography* 52(1): 73–93.

Armstrong, Isobel (1987), 'Christina Rossetti: Diary of a Feminist Reading', in *Women Reading Women's Writing*, ed. Sue Roe, Brighton, pp. 115–37.

Arseneau, Mary (1993), 'Incarnation and Interpretation: Christina Rossetti, the Oxford Movement, and *Goblin Market*', *Victorian Poetry* 31(1): 79–93.

Arseneau, M., A. H. Harrison and L. J. Kooistra (1999), *The Culture of Christina Rossetti: Female Poetics and Victorian Contexts*, Ohio.

Battiscombe, Georgina (1981), *Christina Rossetti: A Divided Life*, London.

Bell, Mackenzie (1898), *Christina Rossetti: A Biographical and Critical Study*, London.

Belsey, Andrew and Catherine Belsey (1988), 'Christina Rossetti: Sister to the Brotherhood', *Textual Practice* 2: 30–50.

Bishop, Nadean (1994), 'Sacred Frenzies: Repressed Eroticism in the Poetry of Christina Rossetti', in *Reform and Counterreform: Dialectics of the Word in Western Christianity since Luther*, ed. John C. Hawley, Berlin and New York, pp. 139–52.

Briggs, Julia (1989), 'Women Writers and Writing for Children: From Sarah Fielding to E. Nesbit', in *Children and their Books*, eds Gillian Avery and Julia Briggs, Oxford.

Bristow, Joseph (1995), ' "No Friend Like a Sister"?: Christina Rossetti's Female Kin', *Victorian Poetry* 33(2): 257–81.

Bump, Jerome (1980), 'Hopkins, Christina Rossetti, and Pre-Raphaelitism', *Victorian Newsletter* 57: 1–6.

Burlinson, Kathryn (1999), ' "All mouth and trousers": Christina Rossetti's Grotesque and Abjected Bodies', in Armstrong and Blain, eds, pp. 292–312.

Campbell, Elizabeth (1990), 'Of Mothers and Merchants: Female Economics in Christina Rossetti's "Goblin Market" ', *Victorian Studies* 33(3): 393–410.

Casey, Janet Galligani (1991), 'The Potential of Sisterhood: Christina Rossetti's *Goblin Market*', *Victorian Poetry* 29(1): 63–78.

Chapman, Alison (1997), 'Defining the Feminine Subject: D. G. Rossetti's Manuscript Revisions to Christina Rossetti's Poetry', *Victorian Poetry* 35(2): 139–56.

Chapman, Raymond (1970), *Faith and Revolt: Studies in the Literary Influence of the Oxford Movement*, London.

Cohen, Paula Marantz (1985), 'Christina Rossetti's "Goblin Market": A Paradigm for Nineteenth-Century Anorexia Nervosa', *Hartford Studies in Literature* 17(1): 1–18.

Connor, Steven (1984), '"Speaking Likenesses": Language and Repetition in Christina Rossetti's *Goblin Market*', *Victorian Poetry* 22(4): 439–48.

Crump, Rebecca W. (1976), *Christina Rossetti: A Reference Guide*, Boston, MA.

Curran, Stuart (1971), 'The Lyric Voice of Christina Rossetti', *Victorian Poetry* 9: 287–99.

D'Amico, Diane (1900), '"Choose the stairs that mount above": Christina Rossetti and the Anglican Sisterhoods', *Essays in Literature* 17(2): 204–21.

Finn, Mary E. (1992), *Writing the Incommensurable: Kierkegaard, Rossetti, and Hopkins*, University Park, PA.

Foster, Shirley (1990), 'Speaking Beyond Patriarchy', in *The Body and the Text: Hélène Cixous, Reading and Teaching*, ed. Helen Wilcox, Keith McWatters, Ann Thompson, and Linda R. Williams, New York, pp. 66–77.

Fredeman, W. E. (1965), *Pre-Raphaelitism: A Bibliocritical Study*, Cambridge, MA.

Gilroy, Amanda (1996), 'Christina Rossetti: Sisters, Brothers and the "Other Woman"', in *Beauty and The Beast: Christina Rossetti, Walter Pater, R. L. Stevenson and their Contemporaries*, eds Peter Liebregts and Wim Tigges, Amsterdam and Atlanta, GA.

Grass, Sean C. (1996), 'Nature's Perilous Variety in Rossetti's "Goblin Market"', *Nineteenth-Century Literature* 51(3): 356–76.

Gray, Janet (1993), 'The Sewing Contest: Christina Rossetti and the Other Women', *a/b: Auto/Biography Studies* 8(2): 233–57.

Gray, Janet (1999), 'Dora Greenwell', in *Dictionary of Literary Biography, Volume 199: Victorian Women Poets*, ed. William B. Thesing, Detroit, Washington, DC, London, pp. 140–8.

Griffiths, Eric (1997), 'The Disappointment of Christina G. Rossetti', *Essays in Criticism* 47: 107–42.

Harrison, Antony H. (1985), 'Christina Rossetti: The Poetic Vocation', *Texas Studies in Literature and Language* 27(3): 225–48.

Harrison, Antony H. (1988), *Christina Rossetti in Context*, Brighton.

Harrison, Antony H. (1990), 'Christina Rossetti and the Sage Discourse of Feminist High Anglicanism', in Morgan, ed., pp. 87–104.

Hassett, Constance W. (1986), 'Christina Rossetti and the Poetry of Reticence', *Philology Quarterly* 65: 495–514.

Holt, Terence (1990), '"Men sell not such in any town": Exchange in Goblin Market', *Victorian Poetry* 21(1): 51–68.

Homans, Margaret (1985), '"Syllables of Velvet": Dickinson, Rossetti and the Rhetorics of Sexuality', *Feminist Studies* 11(3): 569–93.

Hönnighausen, Gislea (1972), 'Emblematic Tendencies in the Works of Christina Rossetti', *Victorian Poetry* 10: 1–15.

Hunt, John Dixon (1968), *The Pre-Raphaelite Imagination 1848–1900*, London.

Jones, Kathleen (1991), *Learning not to be First: The Life of Christina Rossetti*, Moreton-in-the-Marsh, Gloucestershire.

Jularo, Felicita (1991), *Christina Georgina Rossetti: The True Story*, London.

Kachur, Robert M. (1997), 'Repositioning the Female Christian Reader: Christina Rossetti as Tractarian Hermeneut in *The Face of the Deep*', *Victorian Poetry* 35(2): 193–214.

Kaplan, Cora (1979), 'The Indefinite Disclosed: Christina Rossetti and Emily Dickinson', reprinted in Kaplan, 1986, pp. 95–116.

Kent, David, ed. (1987), *The Achievement of Christina Rossetti*, Ithaca, NY, and London.

Leder, Sharon, with Andrea Abbott (1987), *The Language of Exclusion: The Poetry of Emily Dickinson and Christina Rossetti*, New York.

Levy, Amy (1888), 'The Poetry of Christina Rossetti', *Woman's World* (1888): 178–80.

McGann, Jerome J. (1983), 'The Religious Poetry of Christina Rossetti', *Critical Inquiry* 10: 127–44.

Marsh, Jan (1994a), *Christina Rossetti: A Literary Biography*, London.

Marsh, Jan (1994b), 'Christina Rossetti's Vocation: The Importance of *Goblin Market*', *Victorian Poetry* 32(304): 233–48.

Marshall, Linda (1987), 'What the Dead Are Doing Underground: Hades and Heaven in the Writings of Christina Rossetti', *Victorian Newsletter* 72: 55–60.

Marshall, Linda E. (1994), ' "Transfigured to His Likeness": Sensible Transcendentalism in Christina Rossetti's "Goblin Market" ', *University of Toronto Quarterly* 63(3): 429–50.

Mayberry, Katherine J. (1989), *Christina Rossetti and the Poetry of Discovery*, Baton Rouge and London.

Mermin, Dorothy (1983), 'Heroic Sisterhood in Goblin Market', *Victorian Poetry* 21: 107–18.

Michie, Helena (1989), ' "There is No Friend Like a Sister": Sisterhood as Sexual Difference', *Journal of English Literary History* 56: 401–21.

Morril, David F. (1990), ' "Twilight is not good for maidens": Uncle Polidori and the Psychodynamics of Vampirism in Goblin Market', *Victorian Poetry* 28(1): 1–16.

O'Reilly, Shelley (1996): 'Absinthe Makes the Tart Grow Fonder: A Note on "wormwood" in Christina Rossetti's *Goblin Market*', *Victorian Poetry* 34(1): 108–14.

Packer, Lona Mosk (1963), *Christina Rossetti*, Berkeley, CA.

Palazzo, Lynda (1997), 'The Poet and the Bible: Christina Rossetti's Feminist Hermeneutics', *Victorian Newsletter* 92: 6–9.

Peterson, Linda H. (1994), 'Restoring the Book: The Typological Hermeneutics of Christina Rossetti and the PRB', *Victorian Poetry* 32(3–4): 209–31.

Proctor, Ellen A. (1895), *A Brief Memoir of Christina G. Rossetti*, London. Reprinted 1979.

Rees, Joan (1984), 'Christina Rossetti: Poet', *Critical Quarterly* 46(3): 59–72.

Ricks, Christopher (1990), 'Christina Rossetti and Commonplace Books', *Grand Street* 9(3): 190–8.

Rosenblum, Dolores (1982), 'Christina Rossetti's Religious Poetry: Watching, Looking, Keeping Vigil', *Victorian Poetry* 20: 33–50.

369

Rosenblum, Dolores (1986), *Christina Rossetti: The Poetry of Endurance*, Carbondale IL.

Rossetti, William Michael, comp. (1903), *Rossetti Papers*. Reprinted New York, 1970.

Rossetti, William Michael, ed. (1906), *Some Reminiscences of William Michael Rossetti*, 2 vols. Reprinted New York, 1970.

Sandars, Mary F. (1930), *The Life of Christina Rossetti*, London.

Sawtell, Margaret (1955), *Christina Rossetti, her Life and Religion*, London.

Shalkhauser, Marian (1956), 'The Feminine Christ', *Victorian Newsletter* 10: 19–20.

Shaw, David W. (1990), 'Meaning More Than is Said: Sources of Mystery in Christina Rossetti and Arnold', in *Victorians and Mystery: Crises of Representation*, Ithaca, NY, and London, pp. 251–75.

Shurbutt, Sylvia Bailey (1992), 'Revisionist Mythmaking in Christina Rossetti's "Goblin Market": Eve's Apple and Other Questions Revised and Reconsidered', *Victorian Newsletter* 82: 40–4.

Smulders, Sharon (1991), ' "A Form that Differences": Vocational Metaphors in the Poetry of Christina Rossetti and Gerard Manley Hopkins', *Victorian Poetry* 29(2): 161–73.

Smulders, Sharon (1992), 'Woman's Enfranchisement in Christina Rossetti's Poetry', *Texas Studies in Literature and Language* 34(4): 568–88.

Smulders, Sharon (1996), *Christina Rossetti Revisited*, New York and London.

Tennyson, G. B. (1981), *Victorian Devotional Poetry: The Tractarian Mode*, Cambridge, MA.

Thomas, Eleanor F. (1931), *Christina Georgina Rossetti*, New York.

Thomas, Frances (1992), *Christina Rossetti*, Hanley Swan, Worcestershire.

Thompson, Deborah Ann (1992), 'Anorexia as Lived Trope: Christina Rossetti's "Goblin Market" ', *Mosaic* 24(3–4): 89–106.

Waller, R. D. (1932), *The Rossetti Family 1824–1854*, Manchester.

Weintraub, Stanley (1978), *Four Rossettis*, New York.

Westcott, Right Reverend B. F. (1899), *An Appreciation of the late Christina Georgina Rossetti*, London.

Westerholm, Joel (1993), ' "I Magnify Mine Office": Christina Rossetti's Authoritative Voice in her Devotional Prose', *Victorian Newsletter* 84: 11–17.

(Julia) Augusta Webster

Texts

Webster, Augusta (1860), *Blanch Lisle and Other Poems*, Cambridge. Published under the name 'Cecil Home'.

Webster, Augusta (1864), *Lesley's Guardians*, London and Cambridge.

Webster, Augusta (1864), *Lilian Gray: A Poem*, London.

Webster, Augusta (1866), *Dramatic Studies*, London.

Webster, Augusta (1867), *A Woman Sold and Other Poems*, London and Cambridge.

Webster, Augusta (1870), *Portraits*, London.

Webster, Augusta (1872), *The Auspicious Day*, London.

Webster, Augusta (1878), *Parliamentary Franchise for Women Ratepayers*, London.

Webster, Augusta (1879), *Disguises. A Drama*, London.
Webster, Augusta (1879), *A Housewife's Opinions*, London.
Webster, Augusta (1881), *A Book of Rhyme*, London.
Webster, Augusta (1882), *In A Day. A Drama*, London.
Webster, Augusta (1884), *Daffodil and the Croäxaxicans: A Romance History*, London.
Webster, Augusta (1887), *The Sentence. A Drama*, London.
Webster, Augusta (1893), *Selections from the Verse of Augusta Webster*, London.
Webster, Augusta (1895), *Mother and Daughter. An Uncompleted Sonnet-Sequence*, introd. by W. M. Rossetti, London.

Commentary

Brown, Susan (1995), 'Determined Heroines: George Eliot, Augusta Webster, and Closet Drama by Victorian Women', *Victorian Poetry* 33(1): 89–109.
Doan, James (1981), 'The Legend of the Sunken City in Welsh and Breton Tradition', *Folklore* 92(1): 77–83.
Taylor, Tom (1865), *Ballads and Songs of Brittany*, trans. from the *Barsaz Breiz* of Vicomte Hersant de Villemarqué by Tom Taylor, London.

Adah Isaacs Menken

Text

Menken, Adah Isaacs (1868), *Infelicia*, London.

Commentary

Falk, Bernard (1934), *The Naked Lady or Storm Over Adah: a biography of Adah Isaacs Menken*, London.
Foster, Barbara M. (1993), 'Adah Isaacs Menken: An American Original', *North Dakota Quarterly* 61(4): 52–62.
Mankowitz, Wolf (1982), *Mazeppa: The Lives, Loves and Legends of Adah Isaacs Menken*, London.
Northcott, Richard (1921), *Adah Isaacs Menken*, London.

Mathilde Blind

Texts

Blind, Mathilde (1867), *Poems*, London. Published under the pseudonym 'Claude Lake'.
Blind, Mathilde (1870), *Shelley: A Lecture delivered to The Church of Progress*, London.
Blind, Mathilde (1872), *Percy Bysshe Shelley: A Biography*, London.
Blind, Mathilde (1881), *The Prophecy of Saint Oran and Other Poems*, London.
Blind, Mathilde (1883), *George Eliot*, a biography in the Eminent Women Series, London.

Blind, Mathilde (1886), *The Heather on Fire. A Tale of the Highland Clearances [In verse]*, London.

Blind, Mathilde (1886), *Madame Roland*, a biography in the Eminent Women Series, London.

Blind, Mathilde (1886), *Shelley's View of Nature Contrasted with Darwin's*, privately printed, London.

Blind, Mathilde (1889), *The Ascent of Man*, London.

Blind, Mathilde (1890), *Journal of Marie Bashkirtseff*, a translation, 2 vols, London.

Blind, Mathilde (1891), *Dramas in Miniature*, London.

Blind, Mathilde (1893), *Songs and Sonnets*, London.

Blind, Mathilde (1895), *Birds of Passage: Songs of the Orient and Occident*, London.

Blind, Mathilde (1897), *A Selection from the Poems of Mathilde Blind*, London.

Blind, Mathilde (1900), *Poetical Works*, with a memoir by Richard Garnett, ed. Arthur Symons, London.

Michael Field

Texts

Field, Michael (1889), *Long Ago*, limited to 100 copies, London. Reprinted Portland, Maine, 1897.

Field, Michael (1892), *Sight and Song*, London.

Field, Michael (1893), *Underneath the Bough: A Book of Verses*, London.

Field, Michael (1908), *Wild Honey from Various Thyme*, London.

Field, Michael (1912), *Poems of Adoration*, London and Edinburgh.

Field, Michael (1913), *Mystic Trees*, London.

Field, Michael (1914), *Dedicated: An Early Work of Michael Field*, London.

Field, Michael (1914), *Whym Chow: Flame of Love*, privately printed, London.

Field, Michael (1923), *A Selection from the Poems of Michael Field*, ed. T. Sturge Moore, London.

Field, Michael (1930), *The Wattlefold: Unpublished Poems by Michael Field*, ed. Emily C. Fortey, Oxford.

Field, Michael (1933), *Works and Days: From the Journal of Michael Field*, eds T. and D. C. Sturge Moore, London.

Commentary

Blain, Virginia (1996), 'Michael Field, the Two-headed Nightingale: Lesbian Text as Palimpsest', *Women's History Review* 5: 239–57.

Edmonds, J. M., ed. (1924), *Lyra Graeca*, London.

Fletcher, Robert P. (1999), ' "I leave a page half-writ": Narrative Discoherence in Michael Field's *Underneath the Bough*', in Armstrong and Blain, eds, pp. 164–82.

Laird, Holly (1995), 'Contradictory Legacies: Michael Field and Feminist Restoration', *Victorian Poetry* 33(1): 111–28.

Locard, Henri (1979), 'Works and Days: The Journals of "Michael Field" ', *Journal of the Eighteen Nineties Society* 10: 1–9.

Moriarty, David J. (1986), '"Michael Field" (Edith Cooper and Katherine Bradley) and Their Male Critics', in *Nineteenth-Century Women Writers of the English-Speaking World*, ed. Rhoda B. Nathan, Westport, CT, pp. 121–42.

O'Gorman, Francis (1998), 'Browning's Manuscript Revisions to Michael Field's *Long Ago* (1889)', *Browning Society Notes* 25: 38–44.

Prins, Yopie (1995), 'A Metaphorical Field: Katherine Bradley and Edith Cooper', *Victorian Poetry* 33(1): 129–48.

Prins, Yopie (1995), 'Sappho Doubled: Michael Field', *Yale Journal of Criticism* 8(1): 165–86.

Prins, Yopie (1997), 'Sappho's Afterlife in Translation', in *Re-Reading Sappho: Reception and Transmission*, ed. Ellen Greene, Berkeley, CA.

Sturgeon, Mary (1922), *Michael Field*, London. Reprinted New York, 1975.

Treby, Ivor (1998), *The Michael Field Catalogue: A Book of Lists*, London.

Vanita, Ruth (1996), *Sappho and the Virgin Mary: Same Sex Love and the English Literary Imagination*, New York.

White, Christine (1990), '"Poets and lovers evermore": Interpreting Female Love in the Poetry and Journals of Michael Field', *Textual Practice* 4(2): 197–212.

White, Chris (1992), '"Poets and lovers evermore": The Poetry and Journals of Michael Field', in *Sexual Sameness: Textual Differences in Lesbian and Gay Writing*, ed. Joseph Bristow, London.

Constance Naden

Texts

Naden, Constance (1881), *Songs and Sonnets of Springtime*, London.

Naden, Constance (1883), *What is Religion? A Vindication of Free Thought*, London.

Naden, Constance (1887), *A Modern Apostle, The Elixir of Life and Other Poems*, London.

Naden, Constance (1893), *Selection from the Philosophical and Poetical Works of Constance Naden*, comp. Emily and Edith Hughes, London.

Naden, Constance (1894), *The Complete Poetical Works of Constance Naden*, with a foreword by Robert Lewins, London.

Commentary

Hughes, W. R. (1890), *Constance Naden: A Memoir*, London.

Moore, James (1987), 'The Erotics of Evolution: Constance Naden and Hylo-Idealism', in *One Culture: Essays in Science and Literature*, ed. George Levine, Madison, pp. 225–57.

Smith, Philip E. II (1978), 'Robert Lewis, Constance Naden, and Hylo-Idealism', *Notes and Queries* 223: 303–9.

Smith, Philip E. II and Susan Harns Smith (1977), 'Constance Naden: Late Victorian Feminist Poet and Philosopher', *Victorian Poetry* 15: 367–70.

Thain, Marion (1998), 'Love's Mirror: Constance Naden and Reflections on a Feminist Poetics', *English Literature in Transition 1880–1920* 41(1): 25–41.

Rosamund Marriott Watson (Graham R. Tomson)

Texts

Watson, Rosamund Marriott (1884), *Tares*, London.
Watson, Rosamund Marriott (1889), *The Bird-Bride: A Volume of Ballads and Sonnets*, London.
Watson, Rosamund Marriott (1891), *A Summer Night, and Other Poems*, London.
Watson, Rosamund Marriott (1895), *Vespertilia*, London.
Watson, Rosamund Marriott (1904), *After Sunset*, London.
Watson, Rosamund Marriott (1912), *The Poems of Rosamund Marriott Watson*, London.

Commentary

Hughes, Linda K. (1994), ' "Fair Hymen holdeth hid a world of woes": Myth and Marriage in Poems by "Graham R. Tomson" (Rosamund Marriott Watson)', *Victorian Poetry* 32(2): 97–121.
Hughes, Linda K. (1995), 'A Fin-de-Siecle Beauty and the Beast: Configuring the Body in Works by "Graham R. Tomson" ', *Tulsa Studies in Women's Literature* 14(1): 95–121.
Hughes, Linda K. (1999), 'Feminizing Decadence: Poems by Graham R. Tomson', in *Women and British Aestheticism*, eds Talia Schaffer and Kathy Alexis Psomiades, Charlottesville and London, pp. 119–38.

Mary Coleridge

Texts

Coleridge, Mary (1893), *The Seven Sleepers of Ephesus*, London.
Coleridge, Mary (1896), *Fancy's Following*, Oxford. Published under the name 'Anodos'.
Coleridge, Mary (1897), *Fancy's Guerdon*, London. Published under the name 'Anodos'.
Coleridge, Mary (1899), *The Garland of New Poetry by Various Writers*, London.
Coleridge, Mary (1900), *Non Sequitur*, London.
Coleridge, Mary (1908), *Poems*, ed. Henry Newbolt, London.
Coleridge, Mary (1910), *Gathered Leaves from the Prose of Mary E. Coleridge*, with a memoir by Edith Sichel, London.
Coleridge, Mary (1954), *The Collected Poems of Mary E. Coleridge*, ed. Theresa Whistler, London.

Commentary

Battersby, Christine (1996), 'Her Blood and His Mirror: Mary Coleridge, Luce Irigaray, and the Female Self', in *Beyond Representation: Philosophy and Poetic Imagination*, ed. Richard Eldridge, Cambridge and New York.

Bridges, Robert (1931), 'VI: The Poems of Mary Coleridge', in *Collected Essays, Papers, &c. of Robert Bridges*, London, pp. 205–29. The essay originally appeared in the *Cornhill Magazine*, Nov 1907.

Franklin, Colin (1988), *Poets of the Daniel Press*, Cambridge.

Jackson, Vanessa Furse (1996), 'Breaking the Quiet Surface: The Shorter Poems of Mary Coleridge', *English Literature in Transition (1880–1920)* 39(1): 41–62.

[Madan, F.] (1922), *The Daniel Press: Memorials of C.H.O. Daniel, with a Bibliography of the Press, 1845–1919*, Oxford.

May Kendall

Texts

Kendall, May (1885), *That Very Mab*, with Andrew Lang, London.

Kendall, May (1887), *Dreams to Sell*, London.

Kendall, May (1889), *Such is Life*, London.

Kendall, May (1893), *White Poppies*, London.

Kendall, May (1894), *Songs from Dreamland*, London.

Kendall, May (1898), *Turkish Bonds*, London.

Kendall, May (1913), *How the Labourer Lives. A Study of the Rural Labour Problem*, with B. Seebohm Rowntree, London.

Amy Levy

Texts

Levy, Amy (1881), *Xantippe and Other Verse*, Cambridge.

Levy, Amy (1884), *A Minor Poet and Other Verse*, London.

Levy, Amy (1888), *The Romance of a Shop*, London.

Levy, Amy (1888), *Reuben Sachs: A Sketch*, London.

Levy, Amy (1889), *Miss Meredith*, London.

Levy, Amy (1889), *A London Plane-Tree and Other Verse*, London.

Levy, Amy (1915), *A Ballad of Religion and Marriage*, privately printed, London.

Levy, Amy (1993), *The Complete Novels and Selected Writings of Amy Levy, 1861–1889*, ed. Melvyn New, Gainesville, FL.

Commentary

Alderman, Geoffrey (1992), *Modern British Jewry*, London.

Beckman, Linda Hunt (1999), 'Leaving "The Tribal Duckpond": Amy Levy, Jewish Self-hatred, and Jewish Identity', *Victorian Literature and Culture* 27: 185–201.

Cheyette, Bryan (1993), *Constructions of "the Jew" in English Literature and Society*, Cambridge.

Feldman, David (1994), *Englishmen and Jews: Social Relations and Political Culture 1840–1914*, New Haven, CN.

Francis, Emma (1999), 'Amy Levy: Contradictions? – Feminism and Semitic Discourse', in Armstrong and Blain, eds, pp. 183–204.

Galchinsky, Micael (1996), *The Origin of the Modern Jewish Woman Writer: Romance and Reform in Victorian England*, Detroit.

Hunt, Linda (1994), 'Amy Levy and the "Jewish novel": Representing Jewish Life in the Victorian Period', *Studies in the Novel* 26(3): 235–53.

Lask-Abrahams, Beth-Zion (1961), 'Amy Levy and the J.C.', *Jewish Chronicle* (17 Nov).

Rochelson, Meri-Jane (1996), 'Jews, gender, and genre in late-Victorian England: Amy Levy's *Reuben Sachs*', *Women's Studies* 39(2): 173–92.

Scheinberg, Cynthia (1997), 'Canonizing the Jew: Amy Levy and the Challenge to Victorian Poetic Identity', *Victorian Studies* 39(2): 173–200.

Scheinberg, Cynthia (1997), 'Recasting "sympathy and judgement": Amy Levy, Women Poets, and the Victorian Dramatic Monologue', *Victorian Poetry* 35(2): 173–92.

INDEX OF TITLES AND FIRST LINES